AS STATE GOVERNMENT

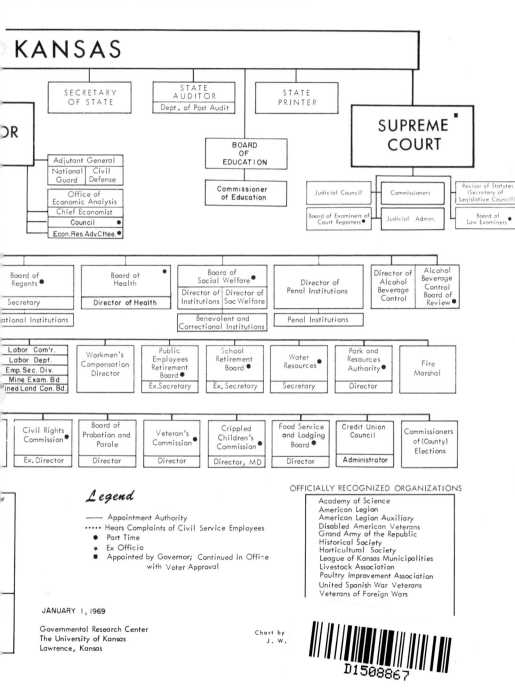

KANSAS

OR

SECRETARY OF STATE

STATE AUDITOR — Dept. of Post Audit

STATE PRINTER

SUPREME COURT

- Adjutant General
  - National Guard | Civil Defense
- Office of Economic Analysis
- Chief Economist
- Council ●
- Econ. Res. Adv. Cttee. ●

BOARD OF EDUCATION — Commissioner of Education

Judicial Council

Commissioners

Revisor of Statutes (Secretary of Legislative Council)

Board of Examiners of Court Reporters ●

Judicial Admin.

Board of Law Examiners *

Board of Regents ● — Secretary — ...ational Institutions

Board of Health ● — Director of Health

Board of Social Welfare ● — Director of Institutions | Director of Soc Welfare — Benevolent and Correctional Institutions

Director of Penal Institutions — Penal Institutions

Director of Alcohol Beverage Control

Alcohol Beverage Control Board of Review ●

Labor Com'r. | Labor Dept. | Emp. Sec. Div. | Mine Exam. Bd. | ...ined Land Con. Bd.

Workmen's Compensation Director

Public Employees Retirement Board ● — Ex. Secretary

School Retirement Board ● — Ex. Secretary

Water Resources ● — Secretary

Park and Resources Authority ● — Director

Fire Marshal

Civil Rights Commission ● — Ex. Director

Board of Probation and Parole — Director

Veteran's Commission ● — Director

Crippled Children's Commission ● — Director, MD

Food Service and Lodging Board ● — Director

Credit Union Council — Administrator

Commissioners of (County) Elections

Legend

— Appointment Authority
····· Hears Complaints of Civil Service Employees
● Part Time
✱ Ex Officio
■ Appointed by Governor; Continued in Office with Voter Approval

OFFICIALLY RECOGNIZED ORGANIZATIONS

Academy of Science
American Legion
American Legion Auxiliary
Disabled American Veterans
Grand Army of the Republic
Historical Society
Horticultural Society
League of Kansas Municipalities
Livestock Association
Poultry Improvement Association
United Spanish War Veterans
Veterans of Foreign Wars

JANUARY 1, 1969

Governmental Research Center
The University of Kansas
Lawrence, Kansas

Chart by J. W.

D1508867

The Government of Kansas

James W. Drury

The Government of Kansas

Revised Edition

The University Press of Kansas

Lawrence
Manhattan
Wichita
London

Preface

In the eight years that have elapsed since the first edition of this book, significant changes have been made in Kansas state government. Appropriate additions and revisions have been made in all chapters to reflect and report these changes.

The need which was reported for this book in 1961 is still current today. Aside from a pamphlet prepared for a somewhat different audience, there are no general books on the government of Kansas. In the days when most people believe that the "government" is something distant in Washington, D.C., there may be those who would doubt the need for such a book. Though this book does not try to convince such persons of the importance of state and local governments, perhaps it may make them a little more aware of the services and complexities of such government.

Three particular groups of people were in mind when this volume was written. Throughout the state there are a number of students interested in Kansas government. Some may be enrolled in one of our Kansas colleges, universities, or high schools, but many others are citizens who, for one reason or another, want to know how the state government operates. For this group of readers with diverse interests this book may be but the starting point for getting other information. We have included citations of general statutes and reports which in many instances will help them explore further some subject of particular interest.

In other states, as well as in Kansas, there is interest in a study of comparative state government. Those in other states need some convenient way of checking what Kansas does. For them this book, it is hoped, may be a reference tool and guide.

Thirdly, there are the teachers of government, political science, civics, or social studies in our own state. Optimistically, I would hope that such a volume might help encourage all teachers in the state to give more attention to our state and local governments. One of the reasons for relatively little teaching of the subject in the high school is the inaccessibility of information. This book may help especially the new teacher or the teacher who comes from another state to become better acquainted with Kansas government.

So many people have contributed in so many different ways to this volume that it is not practicable to identify each one and his contribution to it. In the first edition an effort was made to single out and to mention a number of those who had specially assisted in its preparation. Most of these persons are no longer associated with the Governmental Research Center at the University of Kansas and have not contributed to this edition, except in so far as they helped prepare parts of the first edition. Though all of the materials have been closely reworked and updated, I am quite mindful and appreciative of their initial assistance.

In addition to the encouragement and assistance received from some of my colleagues at the Governmental Research Center, I want to record my sincere appreciation of the efforts of a sizable number of state officials who supplied information and assistance for this volume. A special word of appreciation is due the late Dr. Ethan P. Allen, Director of the Governmental Research Center, for his encouragement and interest in both editions of this book. Mrs. Virginia Seaver of the University Press of Kansas has been most helpful in the careful, methodical, and thoughtful way in which she has edited this publication. I am thoroughly convinced that it is a substantially better volume as a result of her efforts.

Despite all of this excellent assistance I must, and do, take full responsibility for such errors of omission or commission as are to be found in the ensuing pages.   J. W. D.

January, 1969

Contents

Illustrations

Tables

The Government of Kansas

1 | *The State and Its People*

Kansas is a giant section of the Great Plains which extend through the Midwest from Texas to Saskatchewan. The very names of the states and provinces of the area give a flavor of its history, its problems, and its future—Oklahoma, Kansas, Nebraska, the Dakotas, Manitoba, and Saskatchewan. In the music of these names is to be heard the thunder of the vast herds of buffalo, the quiet beauty of the western sunset, the noise of battle, and the ceaseless rustle of wind on streams and in the open spaces. Kansas has its share of distinctive Great Plains attributes. But situated as it is, the state also possesses the characteristics of the vast intermountain empire of the Ohio, Mississippi, and Missouri rivers.

Standing in the exact center of continental United States, Kansas is a parallelogram of 411 by 208 miles, minus a small irregularity nibbled out of the northeastern corner by the Missouri River. The eastern fourth of the state with its gentle hills and valleys is more similar to western Missouri in its topographical features than to western Kansas with its flat, wind-swept areas. There are frequently substantial temperature and climatic differences between western and eastern Kansas.

Kansas was named for the Kansas River, a tributary of the Missouri River and so part of the greater Mississippi River Basin. The Kansas River represents a substantial asset, making its water available to much of the state and infrequently, as in the flood of 1951, bringing injury to those living close by. Kansas is also served by the Arkansas, Verdigris, Neosho, Marais des Cygnes, and Cimarron rivers. In the western and northern halves of the state the drainage is mostly from the west to the east, with the pattern of flow being mostly from the north to south in the southeast quarter. The more common but not unanimous view is that the name of Kansas came from the name of the river in the language of the Indians occupying the area.[1] Apparently the word was spelled in as many as 125 different ways, so that there are differences of opinion as to what the Indian word was.

The territorial act under which Kansas was organized set boundaries quite different from the state's present boundaries. As shown in the adjoining map, much of Colorado was then included in Kansas. The western boundary of the state was settled by the Wyandotte Convention at the twenty-fifth meridian west of Washington. Since the Washington meridian is on 77° 03' 02.3" west of Greenwich, the western Kansas boundary is between regular Greenwich meridians. It seems quite likely that a different boundary would have been established had the Greenwich meridian been used.[2]

Delegates from the area north of the 40th parallel attending the Wyandotte Constitutional Convention pleaded that the boundaries be drawn so as to include the Platte River. Delegates from Lawrence and Topeka were opposed to this plan, for they feared it might jeopardize the chances of having their home town become the capital of the state.

Had the efforts in 1879 to annex the Kansas City, Missouri, area been successful, Kansas would have had an area larger by approximately 60 square miles and a substantially larger population. At that time both the Kansas and Missouri legislatures approved of this change which had been proposed as early as 1855.

History

Early Spanish explorers are thought to have come as far north as Kansas in 1541 in their search for gold. Aside from a brief time almost two centuries later (1719 to 1725) when French explorers occupied parts of Kansas, the area now known as Kansas was occupied exclu-

1. Walter H. Schoewe, "Political Geographical Aspect of Territorial Kansas," *Territorial Kansas* (Lawrence: Social Science Studies, Univ. of Kansas, 1954), p. 14.
2. *Ibid.*, p. 10.

Map of Kansas Territory

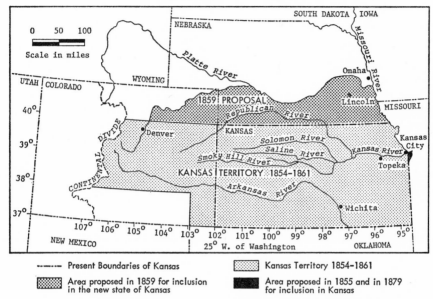

------- Present Boundaries of Kansas   ▨ Kansas Territory 1854-1861

▨ Area proposed in 1859 for inclusion in the new state of Kansas   ▨ Area proposed in 1855 and in 1879 for inclusion in Kansas

Source: Map by Walter H. Schoewe in *Territorial Kansas* (Social Science Studies, 1954).

sively by Indians. After the United States made the Louisiana Purchase in 1803, there were increasing numbers of explorations and movements across Kansas.

Congress attached the northern portion of the purchase, of which most of Kansas was part, to the Territory of Indiana. Later in 1812 it was made a part of the Missouri Territory. No special arrangements were made for administration in the area of Kansas after Missouri was admitted to the Union in 1821, and it was treated merely as part of the Indian lands.[3]

In 1830 parts of Kansas were allotted to certain Indian tribes. At about this time several federal forts were built to protect settlers in the area. Fort Leavenworth was established in 1827, Fort Scott in 1842, and Fort Riley in 1853.

In 1854 Congress passed the famous Kansas-Nebraska Act which created the Territory of Kansas and by its adoption of the principle of

3. T. M. Lillard, "Beginnings of the Kansas Judiciary," *Kansas Judicial Council Bulletin,* XXVIII (1954), parts 1 and 2, p. 3.

squatter sovereignty upset the Missouri Compromise of 1820. Under the Missouri Compromise, adopted when Missouri was admitted to the Union as a slave state, it was understood that slavery was to be forbidden in all the territory west of the Mississippi and north of 36° 30'. However, according to the Kansas-Nebraska Act the local residents of the territories were to decide whether slavery was to be allowed. This led to a conflict between the pro-slavery and anti-slavery forces in Kansas Territory, since the future of slavery in the area was to be determined by the territorial government.

Thus Kansas became the meeting ground, and in some cases the battleground, for settlers from Missouri and other southern states and those from the northern states. After four unsuccessful efforts at drafting a state constitution, as described in chapter 2, the Wyandotte Constitution was adopted in 1859, and Kansas was admitted as the thirty-fourth state on January 29, 1861.

Born amid the slavery controversy, Kansas contributed a proportionately greater number of soldiers in the Civil War than any other state in the nation. While the main battles of the War were fought elsewhere, several skirmishes occurred in Kansas.

In addition to the fighting between the whites there were troubles with the Indians until 1868, when the Indian tribes moved to Indian Territory, primarily in present-day Oklahoma.

The table on the adjoining page shows that substantial numbers of Kansas settlers came from Ohio, Missouri, and Indiana. This information becomes important, for those persons who came to Kansas brought with them the experiences and ideas which they had acquired elsewhere. For example, it is not surprising in view of the number of settlers who come from Ohio that some features of the Ohio Constitution were copied in the Kansas Constitution.

In Kansas there are still a number of areas which are proud of the influence that various parts of the U.S. had on their community. For example, Lawrence seems proud of ties with New England emigrants. In addition, there are communities where particular groups of foreign emigrants settled and concentrated sufficiently to form what at times almost amounted to little foreign enclaves.[4] An illustration of this is to

4. J. Neale Carman, "Babel in Kansas," *Your Government* (Lawrence: Governmental Research Center, Univ. of Kansas), VI (1950), 7, pp. 1-4.

TABLE 1

Population of Kansas by Place of Birth in Percentages: 1860-1910

Place of Birth	1860	1870	1880	1890	1900	1910
Total Population	107,204	364,399	996,096	1,427,096	1,470,495	1,690,949
NATIVE—U.S.						
Kansas	9.5	17.4	23.4	34.1	44.2	48.7
Illinois	8.7	9.2	10.7	9.8	7.9	6.9
Indiana	9.3	8.5	7.7	6.2	5.3	4.1
Iowa	3.5	3.6	5.6	4.6	6.2	3.8
Kentucky	6.1	4.4	3.3	2.8	2.2	1.8
Massachusetts	1.2	0.8	0.5	0.4	0.2	*
Michigan	1.1	1.4	1.3	1.0	0.7	0.7
Missouri	10.6	8.2	6.1	5.9	7.1	8.3
New York	5.9	5.1	4.4	2.8	2.0	1.4
N. Carolina	1.2	0.9	0.6	0.4	0.3	*
Ohio	10.8	10.5	9.4	8.2	6.2	4.4
Pennsylvania	6.0	5.6	5.9	4.3	3.3	2.4
Tennessee	2.4	2.0	1.6	1.3	1.0	0.9
Virginia	3.3	2.2	1.5	1.2	0.9	0.6
Wisconsin	1.3	1.1	1.5	1.0	0.8	0.7
All others	8.4	5.8	5.3	5.6	2.9	7.3
Total Native	88.2	86.7	88.9	89.6	91.4	92.0
FOREIGN-BORN						
Canada	0.9	1.5	1.3	0.8	0.6	0.4
Denmark	0.1	0.1	0.2	0.2	0.2	0.2
England	1.3	1.7	1.4	1.3	0.9	0.7
France	0.5	0.3	0.2	0.2	0.1	0.2
German States	4.0	3.7	3.2	3.6	3.1	2.8
Ireland	3.6	3.0	1.5	1.1	0.8	0.5
Norway	0.2	0.2	0.1	0.1	0.1	0.1
Russia	0.01	0.02	0.8	0.7	0.7	0.9
Scotland	0.4	0.4	0.4	0.4	0.3	0.2
Sweden	0.1	1.4	1.1	1.1	1.0	0.8
Switzerland	0.2	0.4	0.3	0.3	0.2	0.2
Wales	0.2	0.3	0.2	0.2	0.1	0.1
Not Stated		*				
All Others	0.3	0.4	0.4	0.3	0.4	1.1
Total Foreign	11.8	13.3	11.1	10.4	8.6	8.0

* .3% or less.

Source: *Census of the United States*, 1910, Vol. II; 1900, Vol. I; 1890, Vol. I; 1880,
Vol. I; 1870, Vol. 1; 1860, Vol. I.

be found in the southeast corner of Kansas, referred to for related reasons as the "Balkans."

Because of its relatively small population, Kansas cannot be regarded as one of the key states for winning a presidential nomination or election. In 1936, however, the Governor of Kansas, Alfred Landon, received the Republican nomination for President. He became the second Kansan[5] to run for this office. In 1884 Governor St. John had been the Prohibitionist party's candidate for President.

In national affairs Kansas has been famous for her contribution to two political movements—the Populist movement and prohibition. Because of the despair of farmers over their plight of abundant crops but low prices, a group of men of the Kansas Farmers' Alliance met in Topeka in 1890 to form a new political party. The party was more successful in Kansas than on the national level, but it did focus attention of the major parties on the rising agrarian discontent.

Carry Nation attracted national publicity and attention in her efforts to show how poorly the liquor laws were being enforced in Kansas. Kansas had in 1880 amended her constitution to outlaw the saloon. After more adequate enforcement of the liquor laws which was occasioned by the efforts of Carry Nation and others, the Prohibitionists could call attention in their national campaign to the success of prohibition in Kansas. Kansas continued prohibition long after it was repealed in 1933 on the national level. It was not until 1948 that the prohibition provision in the Kansas Constitution was repealed, and then only with a limitation that the "open saloon" should be forever forbidden.

Kansas has been willing to experiment politically. She was the leader in the development of the legislative council as a device for improving legislation. She was one of the leaders in the use of cash-basis budgeting as a requirement for local governmental units. The U.S. Supreme Court outlawed her efforts to find through the Kansas Industrial Court a device for settling labor-management controversies. Kansas has attracted nation-wide attention for its programs in mental health and rural health, and somewhat earlier through the campaigns

5. Dwight D. Eisenhower, who spent most of his boyhood in Abilene, Kansas, lived most of his adult life elsewhere and is therefore not included in this count.

of one of its leaders, Dr. S. J. Crumbine, for its program of public health.

The Economy

Probably the general impression of Kansas held by both its citizens and others is that Kansas is an agricultural state. Not long ago Kansas advertised herself on the automobile license tags as the "Wheat State." Kansas may rightly be proud of her share of the agricultural products of the nation. Wheat is the important crop in the western part of the state, where the large areas make possible a machine type of operation greatly different from the farming of a generation ago. Wheat may be planted on large areas in the early fall and, with adequate rain and snow, may make a productive crop with a minimum of further care until the harvest. The practices have led to the "suitcase farmers" who do not really live on the farm, and to large-scale, sometimes corporate, farming. In the eastern part of the state, corn is frequently a more important crop than wheat. In much of the central part of the state, livestock-raising is particularly important. Dodge City, in southwest Kansas, prides itself on being the "Cowboy Capital of the Nation."

While there had been a gradual growth in manufacturing activities before World War II, the aircraft industry in Wichita received a substantial impetus from that war. The spectacular growth of Wichita reflects this growth of manufacturing. Though not normally thought of as an oil-producing state, Kansas ranks sixth nationally in crude-oil production, and oil production and natural gas are important in its economy. The mineral resources include oil, gas, coal, gypsum, chalk, salt, volcanic ash, and zinc. In certain parts of the state, particularly the southeast corner, the easily available mineral resources have been exploited and now many that remain are of marginal value.

Though it is difficult to measure the importance of various parts of the economy, the accompanying tables present information which give some quantitative measures. In the 1960 census the percentage of persons employed in manufacturing was 16.6 in comparison to 12.6 ten years earlier. During this same period the percentage engaged in agriculture decreased from 23.0 to 13.3. Changes in the sources of personal income reported in the accompanying table and the growth of cities, discussed in the next section, give indications of the changes which are taking place in the economy of the state.

TABLE 2

Employed Persons by Industry Groups: Kansas, 1960

Industry Group	Number	Per cent
Agriculture	104,403	13.3
Forestry and Fisheries	83	0
Mining	14,503	1.9
Construction	48,425	6.2
Manufacturing	130,031	16.6
Railroad and Express Service	23,135	3.0
Trucking and Warehousing	12,700	1.6
Other Transportation	7,409	0.9
Communications	10,656	1.4
Utilities and Sanitary Service	13,496	1.7
Wholesale Trade	28,354	3.6
Food and Dairy Products Stores	19,933	2.5
Eating and Drinking Places	22,781	2.9
Other Retail Trade	85,119	10.9
Finance, Insurance, and Real Estate	29,767	3.8
Business Services	4,965	0.6
Repair Services	11,741	1.5
Private Households	19,491	2.5
Other Personal Services	22,734	2.9
Entertainment and Recreation Services	5,317	0.7
Educational Services: Government	41,328	5.3
Private	10,029	1.3
Welfare, Religious, and Nonprofit Membership Organizations	12,038	1.5
Hospitals	24,275	3.1
Other Professional and Related Services	19,460	2.5
Public Administration	37,111	4.7
Industry Not Reported	24,593	3.1
Total Employed	783,877	100.0

Source: U.S. Bureau of Census, *U.S. Census of Population: 1960—Kansas General and Social Economic Characteristics* (Washington, D.C.: U.S. Government Printing Offce, 1960), p. 18–188.

The People

Except for the 1940 decennial census, each Federal census has reported an increase in population. In percentages, the most rapid growth took place from 1860 to 1870, while quantitatively the greatest increase was in the following decade. The percentage of the population classified by the U.S. Bureau of the Census as urban has increased until in the 1960 census over half of the people (61.0 per cent) lived in cities. The increased use of machinery on the farm and the increased productivity of farm labor, as well as the increase of manufacturing in our urban centers, have aided the change.

The population is not evenly distributed. The dense areas of population are almost all in the eastern half. Over 84 per cent of the people live in this section.

As shown by Table 1, the percentage of foreign-born in the population has continued to drop. In the 1960 census less than 2 per cent of

TABLE 3

Personal Income in Kansas by Source: 1957 and 1967

	1957			1967		
	Millions of Dollars		Percentage of Total	Millions of Dollars		Percentage of Total
	Farm	Other		Farm	Other	
Wage and Salary Disbursements						
Farm	36		.9	34		.5
Mining		86	2.3		75	1.1
Contract Construction		138	3.6		232	3.3
Manufacturing		623	16.3		1,161	16.7
Wholesale and Retail Trade		401	10.5		741	10.6
Finance, Insurance, Real						
Estate		78	2.0		173	2.5
Transportation		222	5.8		281	4.0
Communications and Public						
Utilities		83	2.2		132	1.9
Services		184	4.8		430	6.2
Government		489	12.8		909	13.1
Other Industries		4	.1		10	.1
Other Labor Income		86	2.3		226	3.2
Proprietor's Income						
Farm	233		6.1	483		6.9
Nonfarm		451	11.8		564	8.1
Property Income		532	13.9		1,149	16.5
Transfer Payments		243	6.4		579	8.3
Less: Personal Contributions						
for Social Security		-72	1.9		-218	-3.1
Totals	(269)	(3,548)		(517)	(6,444)	
Grand Total		3,817			6,961	

Source: U.S. Department of Commerce, *Survey of Current Business*, August, 1957, p. 17, and August, 1968, p. 19.

Kansas Population Growth by Decades: Rural and Urban

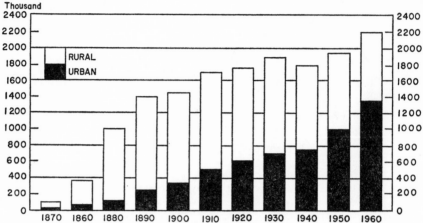

Sources: U.S. Bureau of the Census, *U.S. Census of Population: 1960, Final Report, Number of Inhabitants: Kansas*, 1961, p. 11; *idem, Advance Reports: Final Population Counts: Kansas*, November, 1960, p. 3.

the population were foreign-born whites; about 4 per cent, Negroes. Only a fraction of 1 per cent were of other races.

An interesting aspect of population, having possible political implications, is its age. The percentage of population above sixty-five years

TABLE 4
A Comparison of Selected Kansas and U.S. Statistics

Year	Subject	Kansas	U.S.
1960	Area	82,264 Sq. Mi.	3,615,211 Sq. Mi.
1960	Population per Sq. Mi.	26.6	50.5
1968	Population	2,265,170*	200,000,000 (Est.)
1960	Median Age	29.9 Years	29.5 Years
1960	Negro Population	91,445	18,871,831
1960	Foreign-born	33,268	9,738,000
1960	Per cent Urban Population	61.0%	69.9%
1960	Number of Standard Metropolitan Statistical Areas	2†	224
1960	Population in Metropolitan Areas	523,000†	116,969,000

* Figures of the State Board of Agriculture.

† This does not include Kansas City, Kansas, which is considered along with parts of Johnson County as part of the Kansas City, Missouri, metropolitan area.

old has been increasing somewhat more rapidly in Kansas than in the nation as a whole.

In 1960 only nine states had a higher percentage than Kansas of population above sixty-five years of age.[6] This characteristic seems important in relation to welfare needs, employment opportunities, and possible voter reactions.

Kansans have an average number of years of education (11.7) that is higher than the national average (10.6). With a per capita income in 1965 of $2,639, Kansas was below the national average of $2,746.

6. Research Department, Kansas Legislative Council, "Problems Pertaining to Aging" (Topeka: Publication 194, 1955), p. 3.

2 | *The State Constitution*

Kansas is today governed under the constitution which was drafted at the time of her admission into the Union in 1861. Though the state Constitution has been amended fifty-five times, it remains substantially the product of the Constitutional Convention which met at Wyandotte (now a part of Kansas City, Kansas) in July, 1859.

Constitution-Making

The politics of Kansas Territory had been boisterous and bloody. The open prairies west of the Missouri had lured not only the settler in search of land but both slaveholders and abolitionists who sought to extend or to contain the institution and practice of slavery. Railroad interests and land speculators eyed the lands between the Platte and the Arkansas as remunerative links for the east-west railroads yet to come. Personal ambitions and political strife did not stop short of open violence.

Kansas had been organized in 1854 as a territory under the terms of the Kansas-Nebraska Act. The first territorial government was controlled by pro-slavery elements.[1] Their opponents, the Free-State

1. Of substantial assistance in writing this portion of the chapter has been *The Birth of Kansas* by G. Raymond Gaeddert (Social Science Studies, Univ. of Kansas, 1940).

party, refused to recognize this government, on the grounds that its election had been made possible only by the illegal votes of a number of Missourians who had not been entitled to vote in the territory. The Free-Staters assembled in convention at Topeka in October, 1855, and drew up a constitution which included a prohibition of slavery.[2] But this document, usually referred to as the Topeka Constitution, had been drafted without authority from Congress, and the territorial governor appointed from Washington threatened to use military force to prevent its being put into operation.

The next attempt at constitution-writing was undertaken under more official though still inadequate auspices when the territorial legislature, controlled by pro-slavery men, called a convention which met at the territorial capital, Lecompton, in September, 1857. The result, the so-called Lecompton Constitution, was designed to offer fullest protection to the slaveholder. Its seventh article spelled out the inviolable "right of the owner of a slave to such slave and its increase." The Free-State party boycotted the election in December, 1857, at which this constitution was considered. Some six thousand pro-slavery votes were cast for its adoption. Meanwhile, in October the Free-Staters had won a majority in the territorial legislature and called for a second vote on the Lecompton document. This time the friends of slavery stayed home, and the constitution was voted down 10,264 to 164. A third balloting on the Lecompton Constitution, held in October, 1858, and ordered by Congress, resulted in an overwhelming rejection of the pro-slavery constitution and practically decided the outcome of the slavery question in Kansas.[3]

A third constitution had meanwhile been drafted at Leavenworth under the auspices of one faction of the Free-State party. The pro-slavery men did not participate in the referendum on this constitution. While the vote was favorable it was small, and movement for statehood under this constitution was abandoned. The Leavenworth Constitution created little interest, probably because the controversy over it had by that time reached Congress and the action of that body had paved the way for a constitutional convention which would enjoy proper stand-

2. James C. Malin, "The Topeka Statehood Movement Reconsidered: Origins," *Territorial Kansas* (Lawrence: Social Science Studies, Univ. of Kansas, 1954).

3. Gaeddert, p. 28.

ing. The same act of Congress which called for a third vote on the document proposed at Lecompton also contained specific authorization for the Territory of Kansas to form a state government under an appropriate constitution whenever the territorial population reached 93,000.

Accordingly, the Territorial Legislature, controlled by the Free-State party, called for a popular referendum on March 4, 1859, to determine whether a convention should be held. By a vote of nearly four to one the people voted for another trial of constitution-making.

The election of delegates to the Convention took place on June 7, 1859. For the first time in Kansas history, the Republican party appeared on the ballot, replacing the Free-State party. The Democratic party had for some time been active in the Territory. Fifty-two delegates were elected, thirty-five Republicans and seventeen Democrats. The apportionment of delegates had been the subject of a number of political deals in the Legislature, and the proportion of popular votes cast for each party was much closer than the number of delegates elected would indicate.

The convention assembled at Wyandotte on July 5, 1859. Most of the older factional leaders were absent; the delegates were mostly young and relatively inexperienced. They had, however, the benefit of the three previous efforts at constitution-making, and they borrowed freely from the work done at Topeka and Leavenworth.

It is interesting that the boundaries of the state became an issue in this convention. The Democrats favored pushing the northern boundary to the banks of the Platte River. While this area contained some of the richest agricultural land available, it was a Democratic stronghold. Some Republicans favored including it because of its wealth and because the added population would make it possible to meet earlier the Congressional requirement of 93,000 inhabitants before statehood for Kansas. The Republican majority, however, feared the accumulation of Democratic sentiment in the region, and the annexation move was voted down.

The location of the state capital was also a much-debated issue. Lecompton, the territorial seat of government, had never met with much approval. Indeed, it had become almost customary for the lawmakers of the territory to meet at Lecompton only long enough to adopt a resolution to adjourn to the less frugal facilities of Lawrence.

Topeka and numerous other communities vied with Lawrence for the honor of becoming the new state's capital. On the first ballot, no one site commended itself to a majority. The vote was scattered among twenty-two contenders. On the second ballot, after those cities which had received only one or two votes each were eliminated, Topeka was selected as temporary capital over Lawrence and Atchison. The selection of a permanent seat of government was left for the first state legislature. There seems to be little doubt that the choice of Topeka was the result of some extremely skillful political horse-trading.[4]

Another issue which sharply divided the Convention was what should be the basis of representation in the Legislature. According to Gaeddert, the Democrats held majorities in the older counties, while Republicans had settled more in the newer counties.[5] The Democratic members favored a House of Representatives limited to fifty members. The original draft, produced by a Republican-dominated committee, provided no limit and would have allowed the Legislature to fix the exact number. The Democrats argued for the economy of their plan, while the Republicans proclaimed their high interest in equality.

Finally the Convention compromised on a limit of one hundred. A committee of thirteen, ten Republicans and three Democrats, labored over a formula for the apportionment of legislative seats. The result was a gerrymandering scheme of representation favoring the dominant group, as was to be expected.

A noteworthy interlude in the work of the Convention was the appearance of a representative of Kansas women to plead for female suffrage. The gentlemen of the convention showed considerable hesitation but finally found properly courteous language in which to tell the ladies to go back to the kitchen.

The position of the Negro in the new state was argued extensively and with vehemence. While a section prohibiting slavery found easy acceptance, efforts to keep the Negro segregated in the schools and to prevent further Negro immigration had considerable support but not enough to carry. Significantly, however, Negroes were barred from full citizenship by the limitation of suffrage to "white" males.

4. Gaeddert, pp. 60-64.
5. *Ibid.,* p. 46.

The Wyandotte Constitution

The final product of the delegates' labors has been described as being "in keeping with the trends of the time."[6] As has often been customary, the makers of this constitution, too, followed established models. Kansas, like the other states of the Union, started in its constitution-making with general acceptance of the propositions and upon the basic precepts embodied in the Declaration of Independence and in the Constitution of the United States. The separation of powers among three branches of government, the principle of an independent judiciary, and the bicameral legislature (except for Nebraska's experiment) have been accepted by all, usually without any critical examination of their need. In addition, the constitutions of certain states have commended themselves to their sister states. At the time Kansas was involved in constitution-making, the constitutions of Ohio and Indiana in particular were regarded as models. The constitution framed at Wyandotte shows in many ways that its authors had used the Ohio Constitution of 1851 as a model. It may not be without significance that fourteen of the fifty-two delegates had been born in Ohio.

When the new Constitution was placed before the voters of Kansas it bore the signatures of only the Republican members of the Convention. The Democrats, citing the numerous instances in which their position had been disregarded, refused to sign the document. Ratification by the voters became a party issue. Pro-slavery and free-state arguments were heard once again. Each side charged the other with subservience to outside interests. But even among Democrats the urge toward statehood—which to many meant stability—had grown strong. On October 4, 1859, nearly sixteen thousand Kansans went to the polls and, by a margin of almost two to one, registered their approval of the Wyandotte Constitution.

The organization of the state government under the new Constitution could not, however, be undertaken until Congress had acted on the question of admitting Kansas to statehood; and again party divisions prevailed. Democrats were unwilling to add another Republican state to the roster just before a presidential election, and they controlled enough votes in the Senate of the United States to prevent action. It was not until January 21, 1861, when the Senators from Mississippi,

6. *Ibid*, p. 70.

Florida, and Alabama withdrew (the South Carolinians had departed two months earlier) as a prelude to the secession of their states, that enough votes could be mustered in the Senate to admit Kansas. President Buchanan signed the statehood bill on January 29, 1861, and on February 9, 1861, Charles Robinson, who had been elected first Governor under the state Constitution, proclaimed Kansas a state.

There is much argument as to what should be included in a constitution. There is, indeed, an appalling degree of discordance on the basic question of *what* a constitution is.[7] Constitution-making is a *political* process, and what eventually becomes part of a constitutional document will inevitably and primarily be determined by consideration of politics in a very realistic meaning of that word.

The setting of American politics provides the framework for all state constitutions in the United States. Separation of powers and the principle of limited rather than omnipotent government furnish the points of departure. Beyond that, there has been an increasing tendency to place in the constitutions of states provisions concerning economic or social matters, largely in order to assure for such measures (or prohibition of measures) a greater degree of immunity against change or repeal.

The Constitution of Kansas did not deviate from this trend. It embodies articles on taxation, corporations, education, etc., with some sections going into considerable detail. In this, Kansas conformed to the trends and fashions in constitution-making.

Even as amended, the Kansas Constitution is not lengthy as state constitution go. About 15,000 words long, it compares favorably with the national average of about 41,000 words.[8] Its organization is perhaps not the best possible, there being a rather extensive "catch-all" article at the end. But its ills are not so much in form or even, as a whole, in substance as in its resistance to change and the resultant protection it affords to political alignments of the past.

The Constitution consists of a Bill of Rights and fifteen articles. The Bill of Rights, organized in twenty sections, opens with an assertion of

7. For a summary of these theoretical discussions, see Francis H. Heller, *Introduction to American Constitutional Law* (New York: Harper and Brothers, 1952), pp. 1-6.

8. Computed from the table in *The Book of the States, 1968-1969* (Chicago: The Council of State Governments, 1968), p. 15.

the "equal and inalienable natural rights" of man, echoing here the words of the Declaration of Independence. In equally traditional terms, the second section proclaims that all political power rests in the people. The remaining sections list prohibitions against governmental action to protect the several rights traditionally safeguarded under the American system of government. The rights protected against federal action by the First Amendment to the U.S. Constitution are, in the fashion of the times, broken down into several sections and given more detailed enumeration. The substance and style of the entire Bill of Rights follows closely that found in the Ohio Constitution of 1851. There is only one notable deviation, in the omission of a constitutional requirement of a grand jury presentment in criminal proceedings. The proceedings of the Wyandotte Convention shed no light on the reasons for this departure from the prototype.[9]

The first three articles[10] of the Constitution proper are given over to the organization and general functioning of each of the three branches of government. These articles incorporate most of the terminology and details customarily used with respect to executive, legislative, and judicial functions in the United States and reflect political attitudes prevalent in the mid-19th century.

The executive article provides for seven officials to be elected by popular vote for two-year terms. The Governor is declared to be vested with the "supreme executive power of the state" and may require information in writing from the other officers of the executive department. Otherwise the Constitution offers no guidance for the organization of the executive branch of the government.

Article 2, on the Legislature, is marked by attention to detail, especially restrictive detail. Thus, for years the compensation payable to members was spelled out in dollars and cents—with the result that no change could be effected until the inadequacy of payment at the rate used ninety years ago became overpoweringly clear to the electorate. The entire article gives the impression of disjointedness: provisions for the holding of annual sessions and the limiting of appropriations to two

9. Gaeddert, pp. 66-67.

10. This terminology follows the general practice adopted by the constitution-writers wherein the Bill of Rights is not included among the numbered articles of the Constitution.

years are in sections placed between "schools" and "census," for instance.

The judiciary article, as was generally thought conducive to good justice in the 1850's, established a system of elective judges for all state courts. This elective feature was retained until 1958, when a new procedure was adopted for selecting Supreme Court judges. It might be noted that the Constitution initially established a minimum salary for the justices of the State Supreme Court and the district judges but that their compensation, unlike that of the lawmakers, was not fixed by the Constitution. In 1948 the Legislature was given even a freer hand to set the salary of judges.

The article on elections was very brief until three sections were added in 1914 to provide for the recall of public officers. Oddly enough, this constitutional provision for recall, though approved by the voters by a vote of 240,240 against 135,630, has remained completely dormant. The State Supreme Court has held that the system was not self-executing, and the Legislature has never seen fit to provide a procedure to implement the constitutional authorization.[11]

The succeeding articles deal, respectively, with the subjects of suffrage, education, public institutions, the militia, county and township organization, apportionment, finance and taxation, corporations, banks and currency, amendments, and finally "miscellaneous." Some of the articles are disappointingly insignificant in content. For example, the student who expects to be enlightened on the topic of county and township organization by consulting the appropriately entitled portion of the state Constitution will discover little beyond a requirement that newly created counties must have a minimum size of 432 square miles —a provision of minor significance in our day.

Amending the Constitution

The procedure established to amend the Constitution is, again, illustrative of the constitutional trends of the period of the original framing. An amendment to the state Constitution may be proposed by the vote of two-thirds of the membership of each house of the Legislature, and ratified by a majority vote of those voting at the next general election.

11. *State, ex rel.,* v. *Deck,* 106 *Kan.* 518.

The theory behind such an arrangement is that the requirement of an unusual majority in the Legislature will prevent the adoption of constitutional changes which would muzzle or suppress the minority. In practice, however, one party, the Republican party, has frequently commanded a majority in the Legislature of more than the number required. One study of the amending process in Kansas presents data which seem to show that it is not so much the two-thirds rules as the effective control by the dominant party of the legislative committee system which acts as a brake (if not a block) to the submission of more constitutional amendments.[12] The number of amendments submitted and adopted reflects the extent of flexibility in the Constitution. In 108 years of statehood, seventy-seven[13] proposals have been submitted to the voters, who have approved fifty-five of them. Whether a person considers this number large or small probably depends on whether he favors broader constitutional change than has been effected.

Actually, these changes, numerous though they may seem to some, embody little which has affected the basic nature of the political system that the Wyandotte framers envisaged. A number of amendments have become ineffective as the result of federal action. For example, the first amendment adopted authorized state banks to issue currency in denominations of one dollar or more, but within a few years state bank notes had virtually been taxed out of existence by the federal government and had been replaced by national "greenbacks."[14] Other amendments in effect cancel each other. To illustrate, the 1876 amendment relative to the terms of office of county officers was eliminated by a

---

12. In the first ninety years (through 1949) of legislative activity, 707 proposals for constitutional change were introduced in Kansas. (These included proposals for constitutional conventions.) Only fifty-eight of these were passed by the required majority and submitted to the people. Of those killed, less than 10 per cent were actually defeated by failure to obtain the necessary two-thirds majority. Fully 50 per cent met their fate at the hands of the committee to which they had been referred. These facts were taken from an unpublished research study by Joyce H. Smith in the Governmental Research Center, University of Kansas.

13. This does not include two propositions to call a constitutional convention to revise the constitution.

14. *Kansas Constitution*, Art. 13, sec. 7. The federal tax on state bank notes was upheld by the Supreme Court of the United States in *Veazie Bank* v. *Fenno,* 8 Wall. 533 (1869), and the issuance of greenbacks in *Knox* v. *Lee* (the "Legal Tender Cases"), 12 Wall. 457 (1871).

1904 amendment and, perhaps more notoriously, the prohibition amendment of 1880 was substantially modified by the voters in 1948.[15]

After 1900, constitutional changes began to reflect the increased demands for state services and, as a consequence, the increased needs for state revenue. The Legislature was given authority to levy a tax for buildings at the state educational institutions. The classification of mineral products and intangibles for tax purposes was approved by the voters, as was the taxation of motor vehicles and motor fuels. A state income tax was authorized in 1932.[16]

Two amendments became necessary in 1936 to enable the state to take part in the national government's social welfare programs. The increase of state services and the need for qualified personnel contributed to the adoption in 1940 of a civil service system for the state.[17]

Constitutional changes which affect the operation of government have been relatively few. The Wyandotte Convention, probably hoping that the Senate would develop into a council of elder statesmen, had limited the introduction of bills to the lower house. Within a few years an amendment was adopted making it possible for bills to originate in either house of the Legislature. In 1873, the legislative article was further amended to fix and limit the membership of each house. Two years later, legislative terms were changed from one to two years and the biennial cycle was set into operation which continued until 1953 when arrangements were made for annual "budget" sessions in the "off" years from the regular sessions. This continued until 1966 when annual sessions were reinstituted. The Governor was granted the item veto in 1904. Suffrage was extended in two installments so as to include all citizens regardless of race or sex.[18]

This synopsis of constitutional changes reveals that approximately one-third of the amendments pertained to the essential element of a constitution, the functioning of the governmental machinery. The remainder of the changes may properly be characterized as pertaining to matters which many students believe might better be enacted in statutes, rather than being made a part of a constitution.

15. *Kansas Constitution*, Art. 4, sec. 2; Art. 9, sec. 3; Art. 15, sec. 10.
16. *Kansas Constitution*, Art. 6, sec. 10; Art. 11, sec. 1 and 10; Art. 11, sec. 2.
17. *Kansas Constitution*, Art. 7, sec. 4 and 5; Art. 15, sec. 2.
18. *Kansas Constitution*, Art. 2, sec. 12; Art. 2, sec. 2; Art. 2, sec. 25 and 29; Art. 2, sec. 14; Art. 5, sec. 1 and 8.

TABLE 5

Amendments to Kansas Constitution by 10-Year Periods

Years	Number of Amendments Proposed	Number Ratified
1861–1870	7	5
1871–1880	8	7
1881–1890	5	2
1891–1900	2	1
1901–1910	10	6
1911–1920	8	6
1921–1930	6	3
1931–1940	7	4
1941–1950	5	5
1951–1960	11*	8
1961–1968	8	8
TOTAL	77	55

* The proposal to remove the restrictions on county sheriffs and county treasurers from serving more than two consecutive terms has been counted as a single proposal though separate votes were taken for each office.

Source: Secretary of State, *Constitution of the State of Kansas,* April, 1967, and unpublished data.

Constitutional Revision

Amending the Constitution is but one way of changing the formal content of the Constitution. The Legislature may, by a two-thirds vote of elected members, submit to the voters the question of whether a constitutional convention should be convened to revise, amend, or change the Constitution. It is generally assumed that making individual or small changes can best be done by single amendments, while broad changes or a new constitution can best be created by a convention. Sentiment for such a constitutional convention has manifested itself on numerous occasions in Kansas.

Since 1909 at least twenty-five resolutions calling for a constitutional convention have been introduced in the Legislature. Only twice, however, once in 1879 and again in 1891, were sufficient legislative majorities mustered to bring the question before the people. On the first occasion only 22,870 voted for the proposal, with 146,279 voting against it. The second time the vote was extremely close, with 118,491 voting for a convention and 118,957 voting against. But it is not precisely certain how many votes would be needed to comply with the Constitution, for it requires "a majority of all electors voting at *such* [italics added] election."[19] Because of an earlier reference this could mean a majority of those voting for members of the Legislature, but this would raise the question of whether the vote for the Representative or Senator should be used. Possibly the Legislature could establish that the total vote for Governor or Secretary of State should be used to determine the number of "all" electors. In some states not too different provisions have been interpreted as allowing merely a majority of those voting on the question to decide whether to have a constitutional convention. Given the fact that more people normally vote for candidates than for issues, this latter interpretation allows for easier revision of the Constitution. It can be hoped that the Legislature will amplify the provisions of the Constitution in any resolution calling for the question to be submitted to the voters, and that the vote will be sufficiently decisive to prevent doubts being raised.

A number of interesting questions will be raised when the Legislature and people decide to call a constitutional convention. The Constitution is silent about the number, selection, and apportionment of delegates to a convention. Can the Legislature in the call for the convention restrict the matters to be taken up by the convention? Is it the Legislature or the convention that submits the proposed changes or a new Constitution to the voters? Is this done with or without recommendations? Presumably the results of the convention's efforts would need to be ratified by a simple majority of those voting on the question; or could the convention or the Legislature impose any special restrictions on the majority required? These are matters which are not covered by the Constitution, but which will need attention when the interest in constitutional revision becomes greater.

There is currently some, but limited, interest in a constitutional convention. Periodically the subject reasserts itself. Frequently an enumeration of constitutional defects which a convention could remedy is lacking. And this lack of agreement on specific matters plays into the hands of those who are satisfied with the existing arrangements.

In December, 1957, Governor George Docking appointed a Commission on Constitutional Revision. This group was charged with

19. *Kansas Constitution*, Art. 14, sec. 2.

studying the Constitution, promoting whatever changes it saw fit, and reporting the results of its study. The twenty-two citizens who were appointed included three former Governors, two former Justices of the Kansas Supreme Court, a number of people with experience in the Legislature, three newspapermen, a housewife, and a number of educators. Though appointed by a Democratic Governor, the Commission had more Republican members than Democratic members. The nonpartisan approach which the group tried to follow is further illustrated by the fact that the Republican candidate for Governor was a Commission member.

At an early meeting of the Commission it was decided to invite the participation of the Legislative Council in its deliberations. In response, the Council appointed a committee of five to meet with the Commission. The Commission was able to persuade the Legislature to appropriate $5,000 to further its activities, and it received indirect assistance from a small grant by a foundation.

A progress report was issued by the Commission in January, 1959. Upon competent legal advice the Commission indicated that it interpreted the present amending procedures as allowing the submission to the voters of whole articles of the Constitution as single amendments. While reporting no decision yet on whether to recommend the calling of a constitutional convention, the Commission reported agreement in four separate areas which, under the interpretation suggested above, would require only four amendments, though changing a number of sections of the Constitution. The Commission recommended that home rule be granted to cities by allowing cities to pass "charter ordinances" which in certain instances would replace state statutes in regulating the local affairs of cities. In the field of taxation the Commission proposed that the Legislature's power to classify property, to exempt personal property, and to borrow be increased. With respect to the executive article, the Commission suggested that only the Governor, the Lieutenant-Governor, and the Attorney General be elected and that they be elected for four-year terms. The Commission, with a surprising amount of agreement, recommended retaining the requirement that the House have one representative from each county, but recommended having a system of mandatory reapportionment which would lead to redistribution of the Senate seats and the twenty extra seats in the

House. The Commission proposed that the salary of legislators not be set in the Constitution and that the Governor be given ten rather than three days to consider bills. Annual regular sessions were suggested, with the provision that a majority of the legislators be enabled to petition for a special session. The Legislature would be given special powers to insure the continuity of government.

These numerous recommendations serve to point to specific provisions in the Kansas Constitution which a group of public-minded citizens of the state could agree needed to be changed. The efforts and work of the Commission helped to focus attention on these constitutional inadequacies and helped to bring about some of these changes. As outlined in a later chapter, however, the substantial change in legislative apportionment arose from action by the U.S. Supreme Court. The fact that the question of legislative reapportionment has largely been solved and moved to other arenas for resolution may have a profound effect on the ability and willingness of the Kansas Legislature to submit the question of calling a constitutional convention to the voters.

Twenty-eight of the thirty-three states which were in the Union when Kansas joined have seen fit to adopt new constitutions. Some of these states have revised their constitutions more than once, and others which have since joined the Union have changed their constitutions. Today there are twelve states with constitutions older than that of Kansas.

The relative brevity of the Kansas Constitution is a factor aiding in its preservation. Only four states today have shorter constitutions. Every constitution framed after the Wyandotte meeting has been longer; some, much longer. While there are many items in the Kansas Constitution which need not have been included, its moderate length has undoubtedly contributed to its lasting power.

The test of a democratic constitution is how well it responds to the needs and wishes of the people. The Kansas record on that score is not superior nor, however, has it been dangerously deficient. One might perhaps, and fairly, say that as Kansas created her Constitution in keeping with the trends of the time, so has she developed her political structure not in the vanguard of reformers nor among the laggards but steadily, if unspectacularly, in the mainstream of the nation's course.

3 | *Popular Control of Government*

Political parties are an essential part of our governmental machinery for bringing about popular control of the government. An understanding of political parties, their processes, and their organization is thus necessary to an understanding of state government. Political parties are so important to the operation of state government that the state has established regulations governing much of the organization of parties and many of their functions.

The voters indicate their sentiments and manifest their control most clearly at elections. However, between elections party leaders seek to execute (or if out of power, to develop) programs which will attract popular approval. In addition initiative, referendum, and recall exist as devices by which groups of voters may indicate their preferences.

Political Parties in Kansas

Since the admission of Kansas to statehood, the Republican party has been the dominant party in most elections, though on occasion and for brief periods, other parties have challenged its supremacy. Over the course of years a multitude of third parties have appeared on the political scene: American Alliance, Anti-Mason, Anti-Nebraska, Workingman's Labor, Farmer-Labor, Free Soil, Liberty, Anti-Monopoly, Prohibition, Greenback, Silver, Reform, Union, Non-Partisan, Independent,

Constitutional Union, Socialist, Socialist Labor, Communist, Union Labor, Liberal Republican, National, Gold Standard, and Progressive.[1] Most of these parties tended to be based on particular issues, and disappeared with the issue. Many of them were formed as protests against the major parties.

There have actually been three parties in Kansas which might be termed major. The Republican and Democratic parties once had a strong competitor in the People's, or Populist, party. At the time that Kansas was admitted to statehood, the two "accepted" parties, the Democrats and Republicans, were split on slavery as well as on other political issues. The admittance of Kansas as a free state gave the Republican party, as the abolitionist group, an ascendancy which has never been relinquished. As has already been mentioned, the mutual distrust engendered by the slavery question resulted in the boundaries of the state being restricted at the Wyandotte Convention and in the Democratic delegates' refusing to sign the constitution adopted.

The Republican party held complete control of state politics for over a quarter of a century after the Civil War. Campaign issues usually managed to bring in the "old soldier" theme, and to cast reflection on the Democrats as the slave-and-sedition party. In 1890 a new force, the Populist party, appeared, composed of members of the Farmers' Alliance, as well as smaller third-party groups like the Greenbacks, and Union Labor. In the election of 1890 the Populists, aided somewhat by the Democrats, elected five of the seven Congressmen, won a majority in the lower house of the state Legislature, and elected one state official —the Attorney General. Aside from one election (1882) in which the Democrats had elected a Governor, this was the first time the Republicans had lost a state office. In the balloting in the state Legislature for the U.S. senatorship, Senator John J. Ingalls, a prominent Republican who had served eighteen years, was turned out by a combined Populist-Democrat vote, and a Populist was sent to Washington.

In the election of 1892, the Democrats generally supported the Populist candidates and the combined parties won the presidential electors, the majority of U.S. Representatives, all state offices, a majority in the state Senate, and a little less than half of the state House

1. W. W. Admire, *Political and Legislative Handbook for Kansas* (Topeka: G. W. Crane and Co., 1891), *passim*.

Comparison of Votes for Major Party Candidates in Kansas, 1944, 1948, 1952, and 1956

The Presidency

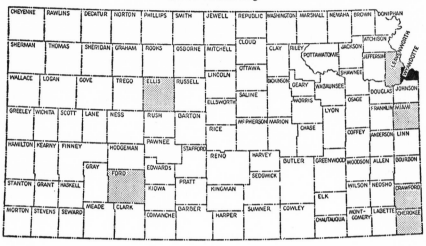

The Governorship

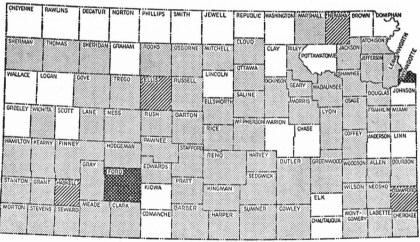

Comparison of Votes for Major Party Candidates in Kansas, 1956, 1960, 1964, and 1968

The Presidency

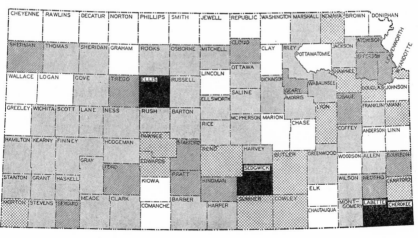

The Governorship

REPUBLICAN IN 4 ELECTIONS

REPUBLICAN IN 3 ELECTIONS

REPUBLICAN IN 2 ELECTIONS

REPUBLICAN IN 1 ELECTION

REPUBLICAN IN 0 ELECTIONS

of Representatives. It was almost a complete sweep; but without control of both houses, the party could not enact the legislation it desired. With the assistance of the Democrats, a second Republican U.S. Senator was unseated and a Democrat was sent to Washington to replace him. In 1894 an insurgent Republican party regained control of the state offices; but in 1896 the national conventions of both the Populists and the Democrats nominated William Jennings Bryan, and in Kansas the two parties fused and were largely successful in the election. In 1898 and again in 1900 the fusion of the two parties began to be tenuous, with the Populists losing strength. In both elections the Republicans made substantial headway and reasserted their supremacy. In 1901 the Republican Legislature awoke to a weakness of their opposition and passed a law which allowed no person to "accept more than one nomination for the same office" and provided that "the name of each candidate shall be printed on the ballot once and no more." This proved to be the *coup de grace* to the fusion tactics of the Democrat-Populist movement. In a short time the Populists went into the Democratic party, drifted into the Republican party, or attempted to maintain an independent party. The Populist party was never again to become a factor in state or national elections.

Since the time of the Populists, Republicans have been elected to more state offices than Democrats. On occasion the Democrats have elected a governor, owing more often than not to a defection in Republican ranks. In 1956 George Docking, a Democrat, was elected Governor after a bitter fight in the Republican primary. Two years later Governor Docking broke tradition and became the first Democrat to be elected to the governorship for two terms. At this election the Democrats won three of the six Kansas seats in the U.S. House of Representatives, the offices of State Printer, Treasurer, and Lieutenant-Governor, and increased representation in the Kansas House of Representatives. Democratic leaders were quite hopeful of future successes for their party. However, in 1960 and for the next two gubernatorial elections, the Republicans captured the governorship and state administrative offices. Despite the fact that Kansas gave her electoral votes for President to the Democratic candidate in 1964, Republicans kept control of state offices.

Robert Docking, a Democrat and the son of Governor George

Docking, was elected Governor in 1966 and 1968 to become the second Democrat to be reelected Governor. In the first of these elections his party's choice for Lieutenant-Governor was not elected. In the next chapter it is noted that more Democrats have been elected to the Legislature since the more recent legislative reapportionments. The changing urban-rural nature of the population, the growth of metropolitan areas, and the changing economic base of the state add uncertainty to its political complexion in the future.

The accompanying four maps report on the last six Presidential elections. The first pair of maps for the first four of these elections (1944 through 1956) show that Kansans have been more Republican in their voting for President than in their voting at the *same* elections for Governor. The second pair of maps for the last four Presidential elections (1956 through 1968) show an increasing number of Democratic votes and more correlation between the votes for President and Governor.

Political Party Organization

In the primary election conducted under state auspices every even-numbered year, party members elect in each precinct a party precinct committeeman and a precinct committeewoman. These precinct committeemen and committeewomen form the nucleus of local party organization. The precinct is the logical unit for the election of local active party leaders, since it is the place where the ballots are cast and counted. There is at least one precinct in each township and third-class city, and in each ward of first- and second-class cities. Any of these units may be divided into two or more precincts when it is necessary in order to accommodate the voters.

Selected by the party members, the precinct committeemen and committeewomen form themselves into party committees within their city, county, district, and state. Election (or appointment) as precinct committeeman or committeewoman is a necessary prerequisite to membership in any of the party committees. It is these various committees which do most of the party work. While most active at particular times in the election cycle, the committees formally serve two-year terms, as do the precinct committeemen and committeewomen.

All the precinct committeemen and committeewomen elected in a county comprise the county committee. For this reason the precinct committeemen and committeewomen are sometimes referred to in Kansas as county committeemen or committeewomen. The county committee normally[2] elects one of its number to be county chairman and one to be vice-chairman. Either the chairman or vice-chairman must be a woman. The county committee is a key part of political-party organization. The vigor and enthusiasm with which a county committee operates will depend upon the precinct committeemen and committeewomen. In some sections of the state there are so few members of a party, and party candidates stand so little chance of election, that the county committee is not active.

Whenever public officers are elected from districts larger than a county, separate committees are authorized. These include committees for congressional districts and state judicial and senatorial districts. The county chairman and vice-chairman of each county in the district are members of each district committee, ex officio. When the districts are composed of only one county or a part of a county, the county committee serves as the committee for the district.

Congressional district committees are organized in each of the five congressional districts in the state. These districts contain from seven to fifty-eight counties. In addition to the county chairman and vice-chairman, each county is entitled to be represented on the congressional committee by a committeeman and committeewoman for each 1,000 party votes or major fraction thereof in excess of 1,500 party votes cast in the primary at which the county committee was elected. The additional members are chosen by the respective county committees.

The state senatorial and judicial-district committees are authorized for the twenty-six multi-county senatorial districts and the twenty-four multi-county judicial districts. "Bonus" delegates may be elected to these state senatorial and judicial-district committees. These committees are not as active as the committees for congressional districts and are frequently not organized in practice, although they can be organized

---

2. In 1961 the law was changed so that it no longer requires that the county chairman be a precinct committeeman or committeewoman. The expectation is clearly that in most cases they will be, but this provision was made to provide a way to work the state political party chairman officially into the organization. Aside from the state political party chairman the political party committees are selected by a system of indirect elections within the ranks of the precinct committeemen.

at any time if it is necessary to perform an essential committee function, such as nominating a party candidate to fill a vacancy on the ticket for the November election.

The state committee of each party is composed of the chairman and vice-chairman of each of the county committees. Thus, the state committee can have as many as 210 members and is too large to act as an operating or administrative group. Consequently, this committee meets infrequently and operates principally through its officers and the State Executive Committee.

The State Executive Committee is composed of the chairman and the vice-chairman of each of the congressional district committees and the chairman of the state committee, who is ex officio chairman of the State Executive Committee. In practice, the state chairman usually is a person suggested by, or satisfactory to, the party candidate for Governor, although there have been exceptions to this practice. If the person desired by the candidate for Governor is not already a county chairman or vice-chairman, the resignation of the appropriate chairman usually is obtained, whereupon the resulting vacancy is filled by the county committee. The total membership of this executive committee cannot exceed eleven, on the basis of the present number of congressional districts.

Provision is made by law for city committees composed of precinct committeemen and committeewomen elected at the annual city primaries. This provision, however, is applicable only to mayor-council cities of over 10,000 population, since these are the only cities which hold annual partisan primaries. In 1968 there were fewer than ten cities which met these requirements. Thus these committees cannot be thought of as typical units of party organization in Kansas.

Each of the committees described previously, except the State Executive Committee, selects from its own membership a chairman and vice-chairman, who must be of opposite sex, a secretary, and a treasurer. The latter two positions may be held by the same person.

After the August primary, the several committees meet, organize, and elect officers approximately in the order in which they have been described. The organization of the state committee usually occurs at or about the time of the meeting of the party council in late August of even-numbered years.

Vacancies in the position of county precinct committeeman or committeewoman or in the membership of district and state committees are filled in the same manner as the officers originally were chosen—that is, by election within the committees' own membership. If a precinct committeeman or a committeewoman is not elected at the primary, there is no provision whereby the position may be filled. Some county chairmen, however, appoint precinct committeemen under these conditions.

Activities of the Party

Spring to August of Even-Numbered Years

During the months from spring to August of even-numbered years preparations are made for the next general election. Party leaders, frequently potential candidates themselves, talk informally with other party leaders and party members to "sound out" how much support could be gained for the candidacy of particular persons. In some cases the formal and informal party leaders encourage or "maneuver into position" possible candidates to get them to run. And by the same token, some possible candidates are discouraged from running. The county committee and chairman may likewise build up the party organization by encouraging certain persons for candidacy for precinct committeemen and committeewomen. Also, the committee may attempt to see that there will be a full and "balanced" slate for the state and local offices. Voters are encouraged to register, where registration is required, and, on occasion, to apply for change of party affiliation in order to become eligible to vote in the party primary. At this stage in the party processes it is often difficult for an observer to make a clear distinction between the activities of the party committees and of the members as individuals. In all events this activity culminates in the primary, at which the party members select the party candidates for the various offices and elect the precinct committeemen and committeewomen.

In the spring of "Presidential years," such as 1968, the county party committees are directly concerned with national politics. Kansas has no system of presidential primary. The procedure for selecting the delegates to the national conventions is substantially the same for both of the major parties. In both parties the county committees, elected twenty months before, play an important role. In the Republican party the county committees decide whether they will caucus themselves and select the persons to go to the (Congressional) district and state conventions, or whether they will call a meeting of all interested party members in the county to elect the county delegates to the district and state conventions. Only precinct committeemen and committeewomen can vote in the Democratic county meetings to elect the county delegates and alternates. Each county is entitled to a number of delegates to the district and state conventions based on the number of votes cast by the party at the last election. The Republican party uses the votes cast for the party's candidate for Secretary of State at the last general election, while the Democratic party uses the votes cast for the Democratic candidate for Governor. Both parties allow counties "bonus" delegates. District conventions elect some delegates and alternates to the national convention, and on some occasions recommend other delegates and alternates to the state convention. The state convention then generally approves the recommendations made by the district convention for delegates and alternates and elects other delegates and alternates from the state at large. The number will differ from year to year and from party to party. For example, in 1968 each of the five district conventions in the Republican party selected two delegates and two alternates, recommended another delegate and alternate, and the state convention selected five delegates and five alternates—for a total of twenty delegates and twenty alternates. In the same year the national Democratic party allowed Kansas forty delegates and thirty-eight alternates, and the state Democratic Executive Committee authorized the election of six delegates and six alternates from each district and ten delegates and eight alternates at large by the state convention. The Committee on Credentials of the national convention in both parties will, however, investigate the operations of the district conventions in determining which delegates to seat.

The Republican delegates to the national convention meet and nominate at their national convention the national committeeman and national committeewoman. The national convention formally elects those nominated, and they serve until the adjournment of the next succeeding national Republican convention. The national committee is the agency within the party which issues the call for the next convention and later hears the contests for delegate seats. The Democrats follow essentially this procedure except that the state convention, rather than the delegates, elects the national committeeman and committeewoman for Kansas.

The process of selecting delegates to the national political party convention is quite separate from the selection of the presidential electors, who are selected at the party primary. Sometimes the state conventions endorse certain party members and pay their filing fees for presidential electors as recognition for long service to the party. Occasionally candidates who are not endorsed by the state convention file and run for this office.

August to November of Even-Numbered Years

During the period from August to November in even-numbered years the committees and their members are most active, working intensively for the success of the party's candidates in the November election. This is the time of appeals to the voters by meetings, formal and informal discussions, newspaper and radio publicity and advertising, the distribution of party literature, and television appearances. While attention is centered on the major offices, voters are urged to vote for all of the party candidates. Informal committees may be organized to work for particular candidates and to help finance their campaigns, or to work among particular groups of voters. At the same time, campaign contributions are solicited from candidates, officeholders, and interested citizens. Occasionally, the party committee nominates a candidate to fill a vacancy on the ticket which has occurred after the primary.

In addition to the activities indicated above, the precinct committeemen and committeewomen and party workers encourage prospective voters to register in areas where registration is required, and to vote the "right" way. The county chairmen and committee help select the election boards and generally arrange to have "watchers" on duty at the polls to observe the balloting and the counting, to challenge voters who are not properly qualified, and to make reports to party leaders.

November of One Even-numbered Year to the Spring
of the Next Even-Numbered Year

The parties and their committees are largely inactive during the period from November of an even-numbered year till the spring of the next even-numbered year. The party in control assists in advising public officers and in recommending persons for appointment to public offices. The elected officials endeavor to maintain a close contact with the party members and particularly the party leaders. The party out of power watches for opportunities to criticize.

The Party Platform

When candidates were selected by party caucuses and conventions, such party meetings could draw up and adopt the party platform. However, when the direct primary came to be used as a method of selecting candidates, it was necessary to establish the party council, so that the candidates elected at the primary have a voice in framing the platform of their party. The party council is intended to be the general policy-making agency of each party. In practice, however, the platform is the principal business of the council and is often the only important matter brought before it.

Membership in the respective councils is determined by law. It includes the party candidates for (a) state offices, (b) U.S. Senator, (c) Representatives in Congress, (d) the state Senate, and (e) the state House of Representatives who were nominated at the preceding election. The national committeeman and committeewoman, the U.S. and state Senators of the party whose terms extend beyond the following January, and the chairman and vice-chairman of each of the party's county committee are also members of the council.

The councils of all parties meet at the state capitol following the primary election at noon on the last Friday of August, and each is called to order by the Secretary of State or a member of his staff. Each council organizes by electing a chairman, vice-chairman, and secretary from its own membership and then proceeds with the business before it. The term of office of the council is two years, and special meetings may be called for the conduct of party business during that period. Usually, however, only one meeting is held.

The law requires that the platform adopted by the party council be made public on the day following adjournment. In practice, the text usually is available almost immediately upon adoption. For some time before the council session, the subjects to be included in the platform and appropriate phraseology usually have been under consideration by party leaders, the candidate for Governor, and other interested groups. In consequence, the work of the council often consists principally of the formal adoption of a draft already prepared.

Methods of Nomination in Kansas

There are several ways by which persons may get their names on the ballot at the general election. The commonly used method is that of the direct primary, which is required for all national, state, district, county, and township offices. They are not held for city elections in cities below 5,000 and may not be held in some cities above this population if there are not more than two candidates for each vacancy.

While primaries are frequently thought of as elections *within* a political party, they are not limited to partisan elections. In nonpartisan elections they are used to reduce the field of candidates so that the successful candidates will represent a majority of those voting at the election.

To become a candidate in a primary, one must either file nomination papers, accompanied with a petition signed by a number of voters, or file a declaration of intent and pay a filing fee which varies with the office sought. In a partisan primary the one receiving the highest number of votes for each vacancy becomes the party nominee for the office, while in a nonpartisan primary the two with the highest vote for each vacancy are nominated. At the regular election, one of the persons nominated is normally elected for each vacancy.

In a partisan election a candidate may run as an independent if he files before the primary. This automatically prohibits any one of the candidates defeated at the primary from getting a "second chance" by filing as an independent for the regular election.

In the event that a party candidate, nominated at the primary, should be unable to run in the general election because of death, disqualification, or retirement, the party may name a candidate by means of a convention of the party committee for the jurisdiction concerned. For those offices or elections for which primaries are not held, nominations are made in a manner very similar to the procedures by which a candidate gets his name on the ballot for a primary election. In cities which have partisan elections but do not have primaries, nominations may be made by caucus or convention of party members. Where school elections are held at the annual meetings of the district, nominations are made from the floor.

Election Administration

Strictly speaking, registration is not a qualification for voting, but rather a means of identifying the voter, and of ascertaining that he possesses the qualifications prescribed by the state Constitution. The state Legislature has the power to require voters to establish their eligibility to vote prior to the election. As early as 1869 the state Legislature passed a registration law for persons living in cities of the first class. It was enlarged ten years later to include persons in cities of the second class.

At the present time, registration is required[3] of voters who live in all first- and second-class cities and of voters who live in Johnson, Sedgwick, Shawnee, and Wyandotte counties. Persons living outside these areas are not required to register. Where registration is required, the citizen registers with the city clerk except where there are election commissioners. Voters may register at any time during the usual office hours of the registration officer,[4] until twenty days before the election, at which time the registration books are closed and final voter lists are prepared for use at the polls.

Immediately prior to the closing of the registration books the registration officials are required to keep their offices open beyond normal office hours. Throughout the state, registration is now permanent except that a change of name or address, or failure to vote in a general election necessitates reregistration. At times in the past, periodic registration has been required in the three largest cities of the state.

Kansas statutes permit registration of persons who are under twenty-one but will attain that age before the next general election. Since the registration requirements for the general election apply also to the primary election, the Attorney General has ruled that where registration is required, persons who will be twenty-one by the general election are entitled to register and vote at the primary.

3. Registration, where required, is waived for persons in the armed services and their dependents.

4. Since 1957 certain voters have been permitted to register by mail.

The Secretary of State and county clerk or election commissioners are key officials in national, state, county, and township elections. Nominating petitions or declarations of intent to run in the August primaries are filed with these officials prior to June 20 of an election year. Candidates for offices above the county level file with the Secretary of State; candidates for county, township, or special district offices file with the county clerk or election commissioner. In the four most populous counties of the state, county election commissioners assume the election duties of the city election commissioners and the county clerks.

In addition to receiving nomination papers, the county clerk or election commissioner arranges for publishing the official notices of the election and of the candidates. He and his deputies process applications for absent-from-state and other ballots, and make up the poll books for the precinct election judges. He prepares the form of the ballot, rotating the names of the candidates in order, so that the name of each candidate will be at the top of the list for his office on approximately the same number of ballots. He has the ballots printed and distributes them to the polling places.

The clerk or election commissioner mails forms to township trustees and to the mayors of the first- and second-class cities which they pass along to the party county chairmen, who nominate judges and clerks for the elections. The trustee or mayor appoints those nominated and notifies the clerk or commissioner. It is the responsibility of the trustees and mayors to provide polling places, booths, and certain other election supplies. After the election, candidates are required to file financial statements of their campaign expenses with the clerk or commissioner. In the event that an election is contested, the clerk or commissioner serves as clerk of the election trial.

Following the election, the county commissioners officially canvass the returns from each polling place, and the county clerk or election commissioner issues a certificate of nomination or of election to the successful candidates. Later the county commissioners apportion the costs of the election among the township and cities.

In general, the Secretary of State performs the same duties for district and state offices as the county election official does for county and township offices. He receives nomination petitions, arranges the form of the state and district ballot, helps in the administration of some of

STATE OF KANSAS

GENERAL BALLOT

COUNTY AND TOWNSHIP OFFICES

List of Candidates Nominated to be voted for in the County of Douglas, November 5, 1968

To vote for a person whose name is printed on the ballot mark a cross ✕ in the square to the right of the name of the person for whom you desire to vote. To vote for a person whose name is not printed on the ballot, write his name in the blank space provided for the purpose, if any is provided, and mark a cross ✕ in the square to the right.

COUNTY OFFICES

For COUNTY CLERK	Vote for One
D. E. MATHIA, Lawrence	Republican ☐
	☐

For COUNTY TREASURER	Vote for One
BESSIE M. BENNETT, Lawrence	Republican ☐
	☐

For REGISTER OF DEEDS	Vote for One
JANICE BEEM, Eudora	Republican ☐
	☐

For COUNTY ATTORNEY	Vote for One
DANIEL A. YOUNG, Lawrence	Republican ☐
	☐

For PROBATE JUDGE	Vote for One
CHARLES C. RANKIN, Lawrence	Republican ☐
	☐

For SHERIFF	Vote for One
REX D. JOHNSON, Lawrence	Republican ☐
	☐

For CLERK OF DISTRICT COURT	Vote for One
LUCILLE E. ALLISON, Lawrence	Republican ☐
	☐

For COUNTY COMMISSIONER 3rd District	Vote for One
RAYMOND H. ICE, Lawrence	Republican ☐
	☐

CITY OF LAWRENCE

For JUSTICE OF THE PEACE	Vote for Two
CHARLES R. MURRAY, Lawrence	Republican ☐
RAY C. NEWELL, Lawrence	Republican ☐
WILLIAM J. E. COWGILL, Lawrence	Democrat ☐
	☐
	☐

the absentee voting laws, assembles election returns from each county, and acts as a member of the State Canvassing Board.

City elections are conducted at times of the year that differ from

STATE OF KANSAS

GENERAL BALLOT

NATIONAL AND STATE OFFICES

List of Candidates Nominated to be voted for in the County of Douglas, November 5, 1968

NATIONAL OFFICES

To vote for the group of electors nominated by one of the political parties place a cross ✕ in the square opposite the names of the candidates of that party for president and vice-president.

For President and Vice-President } **MUNN and FISHER** — Prohibition ☐

PRESIDENTIAL ELECTORS,
PAUL ARMSTRONG, Wichita
V. WAYNE DEVOR, Wichita
MERLE FAWLEY, Milford
GEORGE E. KLINE, McPherson
LOTTIE PRESSGROVE, Tecumseh
BEN WITT, Hutchinson
ED. WOELLHOF, Clay Center

For President and Vice-President } **NIXON and AGNEW** — Republican ☐

PRESIDENTIAL ELECTORS,
MRS. EVALINE CONWAY, Paola
DEAN EVANS, Salina
DR. EUGENE HANSON, Newton
R. W. JOSSERAND, Pratt
HENRY OTTO, Manhattan
WAYNE ROGLER, Matfield Green
EMMETT E. WILSON, Independence

For President and Vice-President } **WALLACE and GRIFFIN** — Conservative ☐

PRESIDENTIAL ELECTORS,
OSCAR N. DAVIS, Wichita
EDWARD M. GREB, Shawnee Mission
VIOLET C. HAMMONS, Wichita
DONALD L. JESSE, Topeka
KENNETH L. MYERS, Wichita
JOSEPH C. PHILLIPS, Wichita
RALPH PURVIS, Goodland

For President and Vice-President } **HUMPHREY and MUSKIE** — Democrat ☐

PRESIDENTIAL ELECTORS,
WILLIAM GRAHAM, Wichita
MRS. GEORGIA NEESE GRAY, Topeka
ROBERT D. LOUGHBOM, Kansas City
LEO MILLS, Yates Center
MRS. GRACE ROBERTS, Liberal
CHANDLER RUDICEL, Hutchinson
SAM SOSLAND, Shawnee Mission

STATE OFFICES

To vote for a person, mark a cross ✕ in the square at the right of the person's name. To vote for a person whose name is not printed on the ballot, write his name in the blank space provided for the purpose and mark a cross ✕ in the square to the right.

For UNITED STATES SENATOR — Vote for One

BOB DOLE, Russell — Republican ☐

JOSEPH FRED HYSKELL, Mound City — Prohibition ☐

WILLIAM I. ROBINSON, Wichita — Democrat ☐

For CONGRESSMAN 3rd District — Vote for One

NEWELL A. GEORGE, Kansas City — Democrat ☐

LARRY WINN, JR., Overland Park — Republican ☐

For GOVERNOR — Vote for One

ROBERT DOCKING, Arkansas City — Democrat ☐

RICK HARMAN, Shawnee Mission — Republican ☐

MARSHALL UNCAPHER, Hutchinson — Prohibition ☐

For LIEUTENANT GOVERNOR — Vote for One

JOHN J. CONARD, Greensburg — Republican ☐

JAMES H. (JIM) DeCOURSEY, JR., Mission — Democrat ☐

GLEN E. SHIELDS, McPherson — Prohibition ☐

For SECRETARY OF STATE — Vote for One

ADA HINEBAUGH, Junction City — Prohibition ☐

ELWILL M. SHANAHAN, Salina — Republican ☐

KENNETH J. STODGELL, Lawrence — Democrat ☐

For STATE AUDITOR — Vote for One

HOWARD HADIN, Leonardville — Prohibition ☐

CLAY E. HEDRICK, Newton — Republican ☐

JACK A. MYERS, Prairie Village — Democrat ☐

For STATE TREASURER — Vote for One

ALFRED BAXTER, Clay Center — Prohibition ☐

GENE LEE, Atchison — Democrat ☐

WALTER H. PEERY, Topeka — Republican ☐

For ATTORNEY GENERAL — Vote for One

KENT FRIZZELL, Wichita — Republican ☐

JERRY MUTH, Wichita — Democrat ☐

For COMMISSIONER OF INSURANCE — Vote for One

VEARL BACON, Conway — Prohibition ☐

A. CLAYTON DIAL, Kansas City — Democrat ☐

FRANK SULLIVAN, Lawrence — Republican ☐

For STATE PRINTER — Vote for One

JAMES BAYOUTH, Wichita — Democrat ☐

D. LLOYD HUYETT, Topeka — Prohibition ☐

ROBERT R. (BOB) SANDERS, Salina — Republican ☐

For STATE SENATOR 2nd District — Vote for One

RICHARD O. NELSON, Lawrence — Democrat ☐

REYNOLDS SHULTZ, Lawrence — Republican ☐

For STATE REPRESENTATIVE 40th District — Vote for One

JO ANN GRESHAM NELSON, Lawrence — Democrat ☐

MORRIS KAY, Lawrence — Republican ☐

For STATE BOARD OF EDUCATION MEMBER 3rd District — Vote for One

ARNOLD "A. R." JONES, Topeka — Republican ☐

GUY P. CROSS, Topeka — Democrat ☐

those of the national, state, district, county and township elections and normally by different officials. The city clerk is the chief administrative official for such elections. The governing body of a city acts as canvassing board for them. Members of the boards of education of school districts in first- and second-class cities are elected at city elections.

On the Kansas ballot, candidates are grouped by office rather than by party. The voter must mark his choice for each position. He is unable by a single mark to cast a vote for all the candidates of one party. The names of the candidates for each office are listed, followed by the candidate's postal address, and on the general ballot for a partisan election, by the party designation. In nonpartisan elections, the name of the candidate is the only identification which appears under the title of the office.

For each office a blank line is included for each vacancy to be filled. Thus the voter may write in and vote for a candidate of his own choice even though the name is not on the ballot.

In addition there is a prescribed form for the presentation of constitutional amendments to the electorate. On this ballot, the proposal is printed as worded by the Legislature and is preceded by the question, "Should the following be adopted?" The voter then marks his ballot to indicate *yes* or *no*.

Despite the apparent simplicity of marking a ballot, election boards frequently find a number of ballots improperly marked. As a result, sometimes the whole ballot is not counted. Occasionally such ballots may lead to election contests. The correct marking of a ballot is therefore important. Ballots must be marked in pencil[5] with a cross mark (X). The ballot must not be defaced or wrongly marked.

Voting

The original suffrage provision in the Kansas Constitution stated that the voting privilege should be extended to white male persons of twenty-one years or more who had resided in Kansas for six months and in the township or ward for thirty days and who were either citizens of the U.S. or had declared their intent to become citizens.[6] Per-

5. This does not include certain absentee ballots which may be marked with ink. (*K.S.A.*, 25-1232.)

6. *Kansas Constitution*, Art. 5, sec. 1.

sons under guardianship, those who are *non compos mentis* or insane, and those convicted of treason or felony (unless their civil rights had been restored) were specifically denied the right to vote. By an amendment in 1867 those who have been dishonorably discharged from the service of the United States, or have been guilty of defrauding the government of the United States or any state, or have been guilty of giving or receiving a bribe, were also denied the right to vote. Two other amendments to the suffrage provisions were proposed at this time: one to eliminate the word "white" from the suffrage requirements, and the other to eliminate the word "male." Both of these proposals were defeated by decisive margins. With the ratification of the Fifteenth Amendment to the U.S. Constitution (1870) the word "white" became obsolete in the Kansas suffrage provision, although it continued to appear in the state Constitution for some time.

While the plea of women for the vote had been rejected at the Wyandotte Convention, the Legislature in 1861 did allow women to vote in school district meetings.[7] Thirty-six years later the Legislature granted them the right to vote in city and school elections. In 1911 an amendment allowing equal suffrage for women was passed by a vote of 175,245 to 159,197.

Prompted by the war situation in 1917, a strong majority of the voters passed an amendment restricting suffrage to citizens of the United States. Since 1917 the Kansas suffrage laws have provided for general suffrage for all citizens over twenty-one years of age, with certain exceptions.

The people of Kansas, like those in other states, make limited use of their voting privileges. Normally about one-quarter of those eligible vote in primaries, and approximately one-half of those eligible vote in general elections in "off-Presidential years." More people vote in Presidential elections, but seldom do as many as 70 per cent of those eligible vote.

Also, the fact that there are no contests for some of the offices discourages voter interest and makes their marking of the ballot of little importance.

The percentage of participation in the contests for President and for Governor in Kansas are shown in the accompanying chart. The depres-

7. *Session Laws,* 1861, chap. 76.

TABLE 6

*Estimated Percentage of Potential Vote Cast in Kansas in Primary
and General Elections for Office of Governor: 1936-1966*

Year	Primary	General
1936	34.2%	75.1%
1938	33.4	66.5
1940	31.7	75.0
1942	21.7	43.7
1944	15.3	60.0
1946	19.8	48.3
1948	22.5	62.6
1950	27.4	50.3
1952	26.4	68.1
1954	25.7	48.2
1956	33.5	64.5
1958	23.1	54.2
1960	31.1	69.4
1962	23.1	47.3
1964	32.2	62.5
1966	22.1	50.0

Source: Hein and Sullivant, *Kansas Votes, Gubernatorial Elections, 1859-1956* (Lawrence: Governmental Research Center, Univ. of Kansas, 1958); Herman D. Lujan, *Kansas Votes, National and Statewide General Elections: 1958-1964* (Lawrence: Governmental Research Center, Univ. of Kansas, 1965); unpublished election statistics, Governmental Research Center.

sion decade, 1932 through 1940, includes the highest point since the adoption of women's suffrage—over three-fourths of those eligible. The off-year gubernatorial contests during World War II show the alarmingly low points, when less than one-half of those eligible voted. In the 1952 Presidential election the participation level rose, owing perhaps to the fact that one candidate was a native Kansan and to the extensive campaigning over the new medium of television. A study in 1952 indicated that, on the whole, political participation was higher in the rural and small counties than in the metropolitan and urban counties.[8] At that time, however, the study seemed to indicate that voter participation in the most highly populated counties was increasing, particularly in the Presidential election years.

8. Thomas Page, *Legislative Apportionment in Kansas* (Lawrence: Bureau of Government Research, Univ. of Kansas, 1952), pp. 90, 91.

Percentages of Estimated Eligible Voters Voting at General Elections
in Kansas for President and Governor, 1920-1968

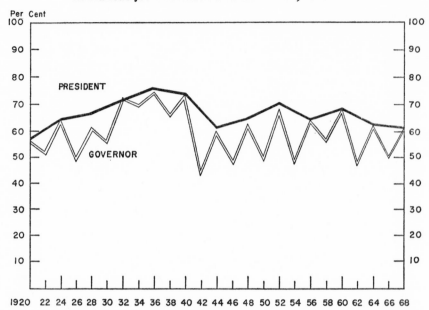

Sources: Cabe and Sullivant, *Kansas Votes: National Elections, 1859-1956* (Lawrence, Governmental Research Center, Univ. of Kansas, 1957); Hein and Sullivant, *Kansas Votes: Gubernatorial Elections, 1859-1956* (Lawrence: Governmental Research Center, Univ. of Kansas, 1958); unpublished election statistics, Governmental Research Center.

Absentee Voting

Inevitably on election day, there are eligible voters who must be absent from the ward or township in which they reside. The number of absent voters may seem so small as to be of little significance in the outcome of most elections. In close elections, however, the absentee vote may be of considerable importance.[9]

Kansas was the second state in the Union to pass absentee-voting laws. Kansas has absentee-voting laws for those voters absent from

9. For example, in 1941 the Kansas Legislative Council reported that according to a preliminary study, although absentee ballots had been less than 2 per cent of the total votes cast in Kansas, they had been a deciding factor in contests of either a state or local nature in nearly every general election during the preceding ten-year period. (Thomas L. W. Johnson, *Kansas Voter's Guide 1958* [Lawrence: Governmental Research Center, Citizen's Pamphlet Series, Univ. of Kansas], pp. 21-22.)

their homes but within the state, those absent and outside the state, those serving in the military forces, and those sick and physically disabled.

If a voter is to be absent from home on election day within the state, he may go to the polls in any precinct in the state and make an affidavit before one of the election judges that he is a qualified voter of his own precinct and is required by his occupation to be absent from his home ward. One of the election judges then administers the oath and certifies the affidavit. The ballot which he receives contains only the names of candidates for state and national office. To vote for local offices, he must fill in the names of candidates for such offices on the blank lines which are provided. The ballots are mailed to the county clerk in his home county and counted there by the canvassing board.

If the voter does not leave the state until after the absent-from-state ballots are prepared, he may go to the county clerk in his county, make application for a ballot, vote, and leave the ballot with the county clerk. If the ballots are not available before the voter leaves, he may apply before leaving and have the ballot mailed to him. If the voter is out of the state, he, or a qualified elector of his precinct acting in his behalf, may file a notarized affidavit, and the county clerk will mail the ballot and a special envelope to the voter. The voter must swear that he has not voted a federal or state war ballot; that he has personally marked the ballot, placed it in the envelope, and sealed it; and that no other person has placed any mark on the ballot.

In order to be counted, the ballot must reach the county clerk no later than 9 A.M. on the Monday before the election, for it is sent by the county clerk to the voter's home precinct, where it is counted with the other ballots.

During World War II, when many eligible voters were serving in the armed forces, the national government passed an act to facilitate voting by these persons.[10] The Kansas Legislature in 1943 enacted a law permitting Kansas citizens serving in the military forces to take advantage of the provisions of the federal law.[11] The Kansas law was

---

10. Public Law 712, 77th Congress.

11. There is a much older law (*K.S.A.*, 25-1201 ff.) governing voting of those absent from the state in volunteer military service. This law was passed to implement an 1864 constitutional amendment to allow such voting.

amended in 1953 to include times of emergency as well as war and to apply to dependents.[12]

To use this "war" ballot system, the voter mails a form post-card to the Secretary of State, who then sends the voter a "war" ballot and an oath. The ballot is returned to the Secretary of State, who sends it to the appropriate county clerk for distribution to the appropriate election precinct. This ballot is void unless it reaches the precinct by the time the polls close on election day. A person in the military service, then, may use the voting procedure prescribed in the 1943 law, or he may use the regular absent-from-state procedure. In either case, registration is waived.

In addition, those who are sick or physically disabled may apply to the county clerk for a ballot, which is handled much like the absent-from-state ballot.

Initiative, Referendum, and Recall

There is no provision in the Kansas Constitution for citizens to initiate state laws or propose amendments to the state Constitution. On the other hand, referendums are required by the Constitution in three circumstances. Proposals by two-thirds of the Legislature to amend the state Constitution are submitted to the voters for ratification. Direct approval of the voters is required if the state is to borrow for purposes other than repelling invasion, suppressing insurrection, or defending the state in time of war. Also, all banking laws must be submitted to the voters before going into force, but by judicial decision this provision has been construed to apply only to those laws concerning banks that have authority to circulate currency.[13]

Initiative, referendum, and recall were parts of a "package of reforms" introduced in the early 1900's in the U.S. for local governments. In 1909 the Kansas Legislature allowed voters in first- and second-class cities to initiate ordinances by petition. These two laws were repealed in 1927, and a new law was enacted to apply to all cities. Under this law, 25 per cent of the voters in first-class cities or 40 per cent of the voters in second- or third-class cities may propose an ordinance which the governing body must enact or submit to the voters.

12. *K.S.A.*, 25-1219.
13. *State* v. *Dietrick*, 117 *Kan.* 105.

The Legislature in 1909 and 1913 enacted recall provisions which remain in effect for first- and second-class commission (and commission-manager) cities. A recall election is held when 25 per cent of the voters petition, but an officeholder is not subject to recall during the first six months of his term of office. In recall elections the incumbent becomes a candidate along with others who submit nominating petitions. The person receiving the highest number of votes in the election is declared elected. The recall provisions have been extended to cover the boards of education in commissioner cities of the first and second class. While these recall provisions exist, apparently they are little used. There are more instances of removal by ouster proceedings than by recall.

Reflecting this reform movement, the state Constitution was amended in 1914 to allow for the recall of state and local officers, but the amendment does not prescribe the details of the recall petition. The State Supreme Court has ruled that the amendment is not self-executing.[14] Since the Legislature has not enacted implementing legislation, recall is not actually available to the voters of the state under this constitutional provision. Thus, recall is not available with respect to state, district, county, and most city offices.[15]

14. *State, ex rel.,* v. *Deck,* 106 *Kan.* 518, 522.

15. It is interesting to note that in 1953 the Legislature enacted a law allowing the recall of county officers. The law was apparently designed for one county and was made to expire January 1, 1954.

4 | The Legislature:
Composition and Organization

The legislature is one of the most important institutions by which the people seek to control their government. There are other elected officials, but it is the legislature which comes as close to representing all the people as any part of our government. Its larger size makes it possible for many and various shades of public opinion and interest to be expressed. In the nature of its operations, the legislature has special powers and relations with the people and with the other branches of government, which for some purposes make it the most important of the three branches.

The Kansas Constitution follows the typical pattern of other constitutions in the U.S. in providing for the creation of the three grand divisions of government: the legislative, the executive, and the judicial. In this separation of powers, it is presumed that the legislature will act first and pass a law which the executive will carry into effect and, should the need arise, the courts will adjudicate. The emphasis in our processes of government on written laws makes it appropriate to consider first the legislature.

Qualifications

The question of who may be a member of the state Legislature is answered in the state Constitution, which requires that members be qualified voters and residents of the county or district from which they are elected.[1] Further, the Constitution prescribes that every citizen of the United States who shall have resided in Kansas six months prior to election and in the ward or township thirty days shall be a qualified elector.[2] On the other hand, the Constitution disqualifies some from voting and thus from serving in the Legislature.[3] Members of Congress and officers of the United States are specifically prohibited from serving in the state Legislature. In the event that a state legislator is subsequently elected or appointed to any federal office, his seat is declared vacated.[4] Also specifically declared ineligible for membership are those persons convicted of embezzlement or misuse of the public funds[5] and those persons who hold state appointments or state contracts.[6]

The question has arisen whether a person can be a legislator and member of the school board or city governing body at the same time. The 1953 session of the Legislature considered but failed to pass a measure which would have permitted legislators to hold local offices.

Members must take an oath or affirmation to support the Constitution of the United States and the Constitution of Kansas and faithfully to discharge official duties. From 1949 until 1967 a loyalty oath was required of all state and local officers, including members of the state Legislature. They were required to affirm that they did not advocate, and were not members of a political party which advocated, the overthrow of the government by force. In 1967 the U.S. District Court in Kansas ruled that the Kansas statute requiring the oath violated the U.S. Constitution.[7]

While the foregoing comprise the legal restrictions on membership in the state Legislature, there is another type of restriction which may be just as significant. From 1861 until 1949 legislators received the compensation of three dollars a day originally provided for in the Constitution and a travel allowance of fifteen cents per mile for one round trip to the Capitol from their homes. Further, they were limited to a total of $150 for a regular session, and $90 for a special session.

---

1. *Kansas Constitution*, Art. 2, sec. 4.
2. *Kansas Constitution*, Art. 5, sec. 1.
3. For a further discussion of those disqualified from voting, see p. 46.
4. *Kansas Constitution*, Art. 2, sec. 5.
5. *Kansas Constitution*, Art. 2, sec. 6.
6. *K.S.A.*, 46-132.
7. 273 *F. Supp.* 178 (1967).

The effect of this policy of frugality on the personnel of the Legislature is a matter for speculation rather than for proof. One observer feels that the low salary tended to work a hardship on many would-be aspirants and to limit the number of candidates.[8] In any event, the legislators took the initiative six times[9] between the years 1900 and 1947 to amend the Constitution and increase the compensation of the members. Five times these proposals were defeated by substantial majorities. Finally in 1948 a constitutional amendment to raise the salaries and expenses of legislators was approved by the voters by almost a 100,000 majority. This amendment prescribed amounts for salaries and limits for expenses. These continued in effect until 1962 when a further amendment allowed legislators to set their salaries. Members now receive $10 per day for their services with a maximum of $900 per regular session and $300 per special session. In addition, they receive an expense allowance of $25 per day with limits of $2,250 per regular session and $750 per special session; nine cents a mile for travel performed between the legislator's home and the Capitol within a limit of not more than one round trip a week while the Legislature is in session; and a monthly incidental expense allowance for each calendar month except January, February, and March. The new rates are more in keeping with present-day price levels. The new expense allowance obviates the need for the extralegal relief previously given legislators in the form of postage allowances.[10]

Election and Apportionment

Representatives are elected for a two-year term and Senators for four years. There is no overlapping of terms in either house. Some continuity of program is assured, however, by the re-election of members, by the Legislative Council, and by the fact that a new Senate is

8. Bernard L. Barnard, "The Legislature of Kansas: An Appraisal," an unpublished Ph.D. thesis, American University, Washington, D.C., 1949.

9. In 1901, 1907, 1909, 1925, 1929, and 1947.

10. The legislators had long been voting themselves amounts up to $300 for "postage and other supplies" despite its being a widespread belief that the allowance was to offset expenses incurred in Topeka. In 1925 the Legislature voted an expense allowance to its members under such circumstances that it was declared unconstitutional (*State of Kansas, ex. rel.,* v. *Turner,* 117 *Kan.* 755). For an interesting explanation of a vote on the "postage allowance," see pp. 401-2 in the *Senate Journal 1937.*

elected only half so often as the House. Elections occur in November of the even-numbered years, and the Legislature regularly convenes on the second Tuesday of January in each year.

In the event of the death or retirement of a member, which results in a vacancy, the method of filling the seat is prescribed by law.[11] The procedure is for the county or district committee of the same political party as the former incumbent to hold a convention to name his successor and for the Governor then to appoint him to fill the unexpired term. A representative thus selected serves only for the remainder of the unexpired term. Appointments to senate vacancies occurring in the first half of the four-year term are effective only until the next general election, when a successor is elected. This system has replaced the expensive and troublesome special election for filling legislative vacancies.

Representation in the Legislature is based on a system of districts largely following county lines.[12] The historical development of this trend can be traced back to the Wyandotte Convention of 1859 at which the present Constitution was written.[13] The state Constitution originally placed a limit on the size of the Legislature, declaring that there should be no more than thirty-three Senators and a hundred Representatives.[14]

In the Wyandotte Convention an apportionment was established for a House of seventy-five members and a Senate of twenty-five. In the original apportionment only forty counties are mentioned. Twelve of the fourteen original representative districts contained two or more counties. The Legislature was authorized to determine the size of both houses within the constitutional maximum.

As people moved westward, more counties were established, and under the Constitution each one was entitled to at least one Representative. While the number of Representatives was less than the constitutional maximum, it was relatively easy to make adjustments. New

11. *K.S.A.*, 25-319 to 321.

12. For a detailed study on this subject, see Thomas Page, *Legislative Apportionment in Kansas* (Lawrence: Bureau of Government Research, Univ. of Kansas, 1952). Extensive use has been made in this section of the materials presented by Dr. Page.

13. *Kansas Constitutional Convention, Proceedings and Debates, Wyandotte July 1859* (Topeka, 1920), p. 360.

14. *Kansas Constitution*, Art 2, sec. 2 (prior to 1873 amendment).

counties were given Representatives without affecting the representation of the older counties.[15] Under an apportionment in 1871 the Legislature created ninety Representative districts in fifty-five counties, but the Legislature actually seated eight members from unnumbered districts and later granted seats to ten new counties. When the 1873 session of the Legislature was confronted with problems of whom to seat, they resolved their difficulty by seating 133 members. This action was contested, and the Supreme Court held that each house had considerable discretion in seating members. Pressure for new seats from new counties and an attorney-general's ruling that new counties were entitled to seats, led to a constitutional amendment in 1873 to set new maximum limits on both houses. The limit for the House was raised to 125 and for the Senate to forty. As might be expected, the referendum showed substantial cleavage between several sections of the state. Following this amendment in 1876 an act was passed apportioning 123 seats, and thus the Legislature was early forced into its previous practice of seating members in excess of the constitutional limit. In 1881 the House seated 137 members, but passed an apportionment bill which gave an increased proportion of Representatives to the western part of the state. The seriousness of the situation became so aggravated that in 1886 a special session was convened for reapportioning the representation. The apportionment act passed recognized eighty-eight counties. The dissatisfaction over apportionment was one of the factors leading to a referendum for a constitutional convention and also one of the factors leading to its defeat. After only minor readjustment, the House was reapportioned again in 1909. By this time all the counties had been established, and the twenty seats available for the more populous counties were distributed.

As the cities in the state grew and the state became more urbanized, the twenty seats available for distribution became more and more inadequate to make adjustments necessary for even approximating equal districts. The total result of these constitutional provisions is for representation in the House to be predominantly on a geographic basis. Because of this, there are substantial variations in population between the districts. For example, according to the 1959 Agricultural Census,

15. Thomas Page, *Legislative Apportionment in Kansas* (Lawrence: Bureau of Government Research, Univ. of Kansas, 1952), pp. 52-69.

1961 Legislative Apportionment in Kansas House of Representatives:
1960 Population

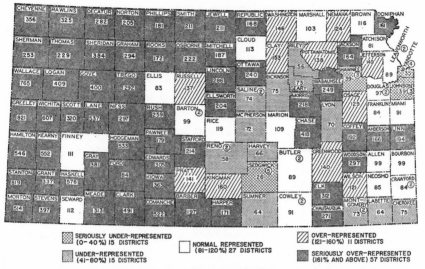

▨ SERIOUSLY UNDER-REPRESENTED (0-40%) 15 DISTRICTS	□ NORMAL REPRESENTED (81-120%) 27 DISTRICTS	▨ OVER-REPRESENTED (121-160%) 11 DISTRICTS
▨ UNDER-REPRESENTED (41-80%) 15 DISTRICTS		▨ SERIOUSLY OVER-REPRESENTED (161% AND ABOVE) 57 DISTRICTS

Based on population data of 1960 State Agricultural Census. Ninety-two counties formed single-member representative districts. The circled figures after the names of the remaining thirteen counties indicate the total number of representative districts in those counties having more than one representative. Precise population information is not available for each of these districts within a single county. While realizing that the districts within a county would not necessarily be equal, the apportionment index shown was obtained by dividing the county population by the number of districts and in turn by the representative quotient for the state.

Greeley County with 2,061 people had one Representative, while Sedgwick County with 321,503 was allowed only five Representatives. Thus if the people in Sedgwick County had been evenly divided into the five districts,[16] there would have been 64,301 people or 31 times as many as in Greeley County. To express this relationship in a different way, each person in Sedgwick County had only 1/31 as much representation in the House as a person in Greeley County. It must be noted that this condition prevailed even after the Legislature in 1959 reapportioned seven of the twenty seats which were available for legislative reapportionment. This was the first major reapportionment in fifty years. Before these changes were made even greater differences in representation prevailed. The adjoining map shows the representative districts classi-

16. Precise information on the number of people in each district is not available inasmuch as neither the Agricultural Census nor the Federal Census follows the Representative district lines.

fied into five groups, according to the number of persons in each district.[17]

Had the constitution not placed a limit on the number of seats, the demand for individual county representation could conceivably have been met by simply enlarging the House membership; or had the constitution simply allowed 125 Representatives, the state could be districted to allow for substantially equal Representative districts; but the size and geographic restrictions combined to frustrate any effort to equalize effectively the apportionment in the House of Representatives.

Like the House, the Senate is restricted in its number of members by the Constitution.[18] However, there is no restriction on the number of counties which may be included in a single senatorial district. The means are thus more readily available to the Legislature to equalize the representation in the Senate. As with the House, however, there was a marked reluctance to reapportion. There was no reapportionment from 1933 to 1947, when adjustments were made to give Johnson and Reno counties separate senatorial districts. Since then, no action was taken until 1963 despite the constitutional requirement to reapportion every five years. The 1963 reapportionment of the Kansas Senate came about largely because of a U.S. Supreme Court decision that the "equal protection of the law" clause of the U.S. Constitution required state legislatures to be apportioned on a basis of "one man, one vote." The Senate had long been apportioned more on a basis of population than had the House; but at the time of the reapportionment in 1963, the variation in districts ranged from approximately 17,058 to 321,503. On the basis of the first recent U.S. Supreme Court reapportionment decision *one* house of the Legislature had to be apportioned on the one man, one vote principle. In Kansas, attention turned first to the Senate,

17. The numbers on the adjoining maps express the percentage of representation each district has in relation to the theoretic number of Representatives to which it would be entitled according strictly to population. Thus a figure of 200 per cent reflects that the district has twice the representation to which its population would entitle it on a basis of the Representative quotient; in other words, the district has half a Representative quotient. A district with 50 per cent is said to be underrepresented because it has only half as much representation as its population would seem to entitle it to. Such a district has a population twice the Representative quotient.

18. *Kansas Constitution*, Art. 2, sec. 2.

because Senatorial districts were more equal already, many districts crossed county lines, and Senate apportionment was not restricted by the state constitutional mandate of at least one representative from every county.

The table below shows how the 1963 and 1964 Senate reapportionments changed the existing pattern. Both apportionments made for much more equally populated districts, but when the 1964 Senate reapportionment was challenged in the federal courts, it was found to violate the equal protection clause. Injunctive relief was not allowed at the time, however. Rather the Court ruled that the Senators should be allowed to serve their terms. The Court, however, retained jurisdiction and indicated that action would be taken if the Legislature did not reapportion before new Senators were elected in 1968.

The accompanying table reflects how changes in population cause a particular reapportionment to become less equitable even after only a few years. The rapidity of changes indicate how difficult, if not im-

TABLE 7

Comparison of Kansas Senate Apportionments:
1947, 1963, and 1964

	Number of Districts				
Percent of Deviation from Representative Quotient	1947 Apportionment 1962 Pop.	1963 Apportionment 1962 Pop.	1964 Apportionment		
			1963 Pop.	1965 Pop.	1967 Pop.
More than 25% over	5	0	0	0	3
20–25% over	0	0	0	2	0
15–20% over	1	0	0	1	0
10–15% over	1	4	4	3	4
5–10% over	1	7	7	6	5
0–5 % over	1	6	7	6	4
0–5 % under	0	12	11	10	7
5–10% under	2	10	6	7	10
10–15% under	3	1	5	4	5
15–20% under	1	0	0	1	2
20–25% under	1	0	0	0	0
More than 25% under	24	0	0	0	0
Total	40	40	40	40	40

Source: Data from Research Department, Kansas Legislative Council.

possible, it is to establish an apportionment which may be equal for any extended period.

In 1968 the Legislature passed two bills reapportioning the Senate, but each measure was declared invalid by the Federal District Court for Kansas. The three judges ruled that the variations between districts were too large. Under the second attempt of the Legislature, districts ranged from a high of 60,809 to a low of 52,136. Because of the pressing need for getting an apportionment to be used for conducting the 1968 election and because the Legislature had failed to pass a valid apportionment, the Court, in what it regarded as a "stop-gap" measure, devised its own plan of apportionment. The Court decreed apportionment sought to "equalize the districts populationwise as nearly as possible and at the same time recognize the integrity of county boundary lines." In explaining its redistricting the Court looked at population changes going on in the state and considered expected increases and decreases in population. Critics of the decision noted that there were wide variations between districts under the Court's own plan. In the four areas of the state with the largest concentration of population the Court recognized its inability to devise equal districts and provided for

Apportionment of Kansas Senate: U.S. District Court, March 28, 1968

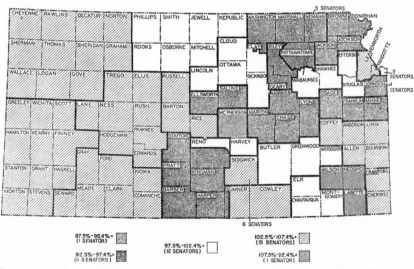

Except as noted, each district has one senator. Source: 1968 Kansas State Board of Agriculture Census and *R. M. Long et al.* v. *Robert B. Docking et al.*, 282 F. *Supp.* 256 (1968), pp. 256-260.

1966 Legislative Apportionment of Kansas House of Representatives: 1967 Population

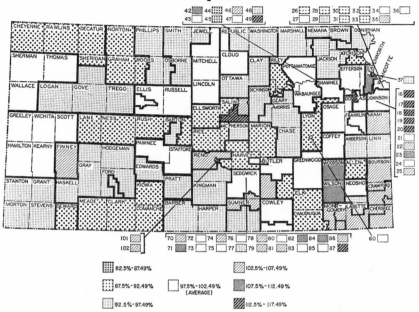

the election of six senators from Sedgwick County, four from Johnson County, three from Wyandotte County, and three from Shawnee County augmented by Wabaunsee County.

Later U.S. Supreme Court decisions established that it was not enough for *one* house of the state legislature to be apportioned on a basis of population. *Both* houses had to be so apportioned. In effect this meant that the State constitutional provision for at least one representative from each county was ruled to be in violation of the U.S. Constitution. After a court case in Kansas and a limited delay, the Legislature in special session in 1966 reapportioned the House of Representatives. While there were charges that district lines were drawn to help incumbents, and particularly incumbents of the majority party, it is significant that the Legislators were able to agree on a plan. A large number of changes were brought about by this reapportionment. Wichita was assigned essentially eighteen seats; Topeka, eight; Kansas City eleven; and Johnson County, ten.

The accompanying map shows the extent to which the 1966 House reapportionment conforms to the one man, one vote principle. As with the Senate, changes in population may be expected to further alter the extent to which the House apportionment meets this test.

Changes in population provoke problems in apportioning the Legislature. Precisely how much deviation in population between the districts will be allowed by the U.S. Supreme Court is not yet known. It is clear, however, that if legislative districts do not follow county lines (as many Senate and House districts do not) there *can* be greater equality between the districts. The U.S. Supreme Court has suggested that when county lines are not followed, the Court will expect and *require* even greater equality of population between the districts.

The problem of reapportionment is a continuous and recurring one. The gross inequalities of representation of so many decades have been eliminated. Though the Legislature acted on reapportionment under considerable pressure from the courts, the fact that it acted is significant. The thorny problem of reapportionment was for a time considered to be one that the Legislature could not (or would not) handle. Illustrative of this attitude was the recommendation of the Governor's Commission on Constitutional Revision for the creation of administrative machinery to handle administratively the legislatively sensitive problem of reapportionment.

The manner in which the Legislature responded to the demand for reapportionment indicates some hope that the Legislature itself may be able to agree on the adjustments needed in the future to keep the apportionment current—adjustments which appear minor in comparison to those made in 1963 and in 1966. Agreement on reapportionment may, however, be more difficult should changes occur in the relative political strength of the two major parties.

Most importantly, the question arises as to what is likely to be the effect of the reapportionment on public policy. Before, when urban areas were so significantly underrepresented, there was concern, with some evidence, that distribution of the sales tax residue and liquor revenues and welfare and highway financing were decided on the basis of an urban-rural split, with the urban areas being slighted. One careful observer concluded, however, even before the major reapportionment, that his "analysis does not support a conclusion of sharp and irrepressible conflicts between rural residents and city dwellers as such."[19]

19. Page, p. 148.

A more recent study on the integration of the new legislators from metropolitan districts reports that while significant changes were made in the leadership in the Legislature in 1967, the new legislators from metropolitan areas did not have the percentage of important committee chairmanships and vice-chairmanships to which their numbers would seem to entitle them. It may be expected that it will take several sessions of the Legislature for the new representatives from metropolitan districts to develop seniority and legislative acceptance of their efforts to exercise leadership in the Legislature. It may be that the districts in metropolitan areas will be politically less stable, and the resulting turnover may affect the leadership potential of the legislators from these areas.

Background of Members

Since the earliest years the Legislature has been largely composed of members with agricultural or legal backgrounds. As shown by the accompanying table, merchants and bankers are the groups supplying the next largest numbers of legislators.

Many members of both houses are "first-termers." In the twelve years ending with 1966, the Senate lost approximately 57 per cent of its members at the end of each term, while the losses in the House averaged about 40 per cent each two year term. Most of the losses in both houses were "voluntary," at least in the sense that they were not occasioned by a defeat in the primary or in the general election. One study found that the legislators credited insufficient compensation, lack of appreciation, and lack of interest with being responsible for most voluntary departures.[20]

At one time, a practice existed in a number of two- and three-county senatorial districts which contributed to the high rate of retirement. Custom dictated that the Senator yield to a man from another county in the district, so that the other county could have its turn in having a Senator. This practice of rotating office between counties appeared to work with reasonable regularity in some districts.[21] However, with the major reapportionments of the Senate of the last several

20. Barnard, p. 42.
21. Page, p. 125.

TABLE 8

Occupational Classification of Kansas Legislators by Per Cent:
1951-1965 and 1967

Occupation Class	1951-1965			1967		
	% House	% Senate	% Total	% House	% Senate	% Total
Agriculture	42.1	17.8	36.2	24.0	25.0	24.2
Law	18.0	43.4	24.2	24.0	45.0	29.1
Merchant	12.0	11.9	12.0	22.4	7.5	18.8
Banking	2.4	5.0	3.0	4.0	0	3.0
Miscellaneous	16.5	10.3	14.9	20.0	10.0	17.6
Real Estate and Insurance	3.2	8.4	4.5	1.6	10.0	3.6
Medicine	1.1	1.6	1.2	1.6	0	1.2
Printing and Publishing	4.7	1.6	3.9	2.4	2.5	2.4

Sources: Unpublished data, University of Kansas Governmental Research Center.

years, it is difficult to see that this practice has been operating in recent years.

A tabulation of experience reported by legislators showed Senators with an average of 12.9 years of governmental experience and Representatives with 9.7 years of such experience.[22]

Political Party Affiliation of Members

Kansas is predominantly a one-party state. Only once since 1900 have the Republicans not had a majority in both houses of the Legislature. Normally the Republican party has a wide majority in both. In recents years when there have been such large majorities, factionalism and splits have developed within the Republican party. Issues do arise in the Legislature where differences within the party are marked. Occasionally the controlling majority may have to be more concerned about mustering votes in their own party than about the Democratic opposition.

22. The tabulation was made from information appearing in the December, 1967, issue of the *Kansas Government Journal.* An earlier summary in the December, 1954, *Kansas Government Journal* reported that Senators in 1955 averaged 22.4 years, and Representatives 15.2 years, of government exeprience. The difference between the 1967 and 1954 data is probably explained by differences as to what was considered governmental experience.

TABLE 9
Political Affiliations of Kansas Legislators: 1901-1967

Year	House Republican	Senate Republican
1901*	66%	83%
1903*	78	82
1905	86	92
1907	77	92
1909	69	88
1911	56	88
1913	41	48
1915	53	48
1917	69	78
1919	88	75
1921	90	95
1923	76	95
1925	72	80
1927	73	80
1929*	81	93
1931	60	93
1933	52	58
1935	60	65
1937	60	63
1939	86	62
1941	78	88
1943	90	90
1945	96	97
1947	86	98
1949	76	85
1951	84	85
1953	84	88
1955	71	88
1957	66	80
1959	55	80
1961	65	80
1963	71	80
1965	65	68
1967	62	68

 * In 1901, 1903, and 1929 there were appreciable numbers of Representatives of third parties. Since 1929 there have been no third-party members in the House or Senate.
Sources: Barnard (as cited for Table 7), p. 30; House and Senate Journals.

Regular, Budget, and Special Sessions

From 1861 until 1875 the Legislature met annually as required by the Wyandotte Constitution. In this later year a constitutional amendment was adopted which provided for sessions in alternate years beginning in 1877. The sessions are held in the Capitol and begin on the second Tuesday in January.

From 1955 through 1966, budget sessions were held in even-numbered years, alternating with the regular sessions. The constitutional amendment authorizing such sessions limited them to the consideration of only "the governor's budget report, appropriation bills for the succeeding fiscal year, revenue bills therefor, and such bills, resolutions, or motions as may be necessary to provide for the expenses and conduct of the budget session." Annual approval of the budget, such as was in fact arranged for by this amendment, was thought necessary to allow adequate time for the careful consideration of appropriations. With annual consideration of the budget, estimates need to be made

Organization of Kansas Senate: 1968

twenty to twenty-two months in advance, and appropriations need to be made for about fifteen months in the future. In 1966 the voters approved a change in the Constitution to allow for "regular sessions" of the Legislature each year; but in "off years" (i.e., even-numbered calendar years) the session is limited to sixty days, except that the Legislature may by a two-thirds vote extend it.

A special session of the Legislature can be called at the discretion of the Governor, and in such a case, his proclamation outlines the reasons for the special session. Normally he will recommend certain action. Reasons for calling special sessions have usually been urgent.[23] Since 1900 there have been fourteen special sessions of the Legislature.[24]

While the Governor assigns the reasons for the call, the Legislature is not confined to the subjects listed. Once convened, the Legislature may take under consideration any matters which it so desires, bound only by the normal constitutional regulations governing legislative acts.

Organization

The formal organization of the Legislature begins with its convening at the beginning of each session. The Secretary of State presides over the House until it is organized. Senators meet, with the Lieutenant-Governor calling them to order.

The first item on the agenda for both houses is the receipt of the certificates of election of the members, and the administration of the oath of office. According to the Constitution,[25] each house is the judge of the elections, returns, and qualifications of its own membership.

Following the certification of the members, the majority party in the Senate holds a caucus to determine who shall be named President pro-tem. In addition, certain salaried employees are also selected at this caucus. Nonmembers are appointed Sergeant-at-Arms, Chaplain, and Postmaster. Similarly, the majority party of the House caucuses to name a Speaker and a Speaker pro-tem from its ranks and to appoint a Clerk, a Sergeant-at-Arms, a Doorkeeper, and a Postmaster from

23. For a sample proclamation calling the Legislature into special session, see *Laws of Kansas, 1966.*

24. Special sessions occurred in 1903, 1908, 1919, 1920, 1923, 1928, 1930, 1933, 1934, 1936, 1938, 1958, 1964, and 1966.

25. *Kansas Constitution,* Art. 2, sec. 8.

Organization of Kansas House of Representatives: 1968

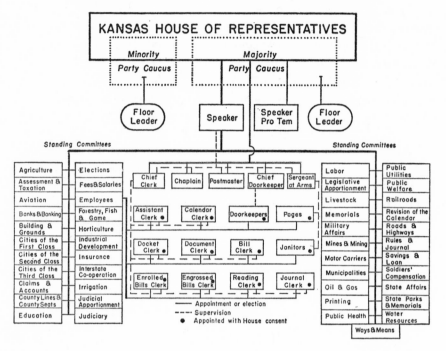

outside the House membership. The minority party of each chamber caucuses and chooses its floor leaders.

Having thus organized for business and having notified the other house of this fact, each body adopts its own rules for the conduct of business and guide to parliamentary procedure. Seats are assigned, and telephone service is provided. The house then passes memorial resolutions honoring those former members who have died since the close of the previous session.

Having disposed of the first essentials of organization, the two houses then meet in a joint session in the House chamber to hear the Governor's opening message. At the start of a regular session of the Legislature, this will consist usually of a restatement of the party's campaign promises plus special recommendations of the Governor. The speech also acts as a "state of the state" address to call the legislators' attention to the problems facing the state.

Committee Structure

After the joint meeting to hear the Governor's message at the beginning of a session, both houses meet separately to assign members to the various permanent committees, of which the presiding officer appoints the chairmen and members. Certain basic considerations usually guide the naming of these committees. For instance, each of the state's congressional districts normally receives representation on each committee.[26] Normally members with previous experience are selected as chairmen. The majority party assumes control over the committees by having its members elected to the chairmanships and by seeing that it has a substantial majority in all. The table below shows how closely the membership on committees has approximated the proportion of each party in each house.

The number of standing committees has varied considerably as shown in the adjoining table. In 1955 the Senate added a committee on water resources, in 1957 a committee on committees, and in 1961 a committee on interstate cooperation. In the Senate in 1967 the number of persons assigned to each committee ranged from five to twenty, with only the judiciary committee having twenty members—the judiciary committee automatically includes all Senators admitted to practice law in Kansas. There was a total of 289 committee assignments, with the result that on the average each senator was a member of seven committees. However, the small number of "veteran" members are frequently assigned to a great number of the more important committees,[27] and the volume of work for them becomes extreme. One observer of the Kansas Legislature estimates that some Senators, if they were actually able to attend all meetings of all committees to which they are named, would consider as committee members over 300 bills in a regular session.[28]

In practice, members apportion the time they spend in committee meetings, choosing on the basis of importance and expediency. Less important committees find it difficult to schedule meetings which the committee members can attend.

26. Barnard, p. 55.
27. Barnard, p. 64.
28. Barnard, p. 61.

TABLE 10

Committee Membership in the Kansas Legislature by Political Party: 1951-1967

	Republican		Democrat	
	% in the Chamber	% on Committees	% in the Chamber	% on Committees
Senate				
1957	80.0	81.7	20.0	18.3
1959	80.0	71.8	20.0	28.7
1961	80.0	83.2	20.0	16.8
1963	80.0	82.1	20.0	17.9
1965	67.5	70.6	32.5	29.4
1967	67.5	70.1	32.5	29.9
House				
1957	66.4	66.8	33.6	33.2
1959	55.2	56.0	44.8	44.0
1961	65.6	66.3	34.4	33.7
1963	71.2	71.0	28.8	29.0
1965	64.8	68.2	35.2	31.8
1967	62.4	62.8	37.6	37.2

Source: *Senate* and *House Journals.*

TABLE 11

Number of Standing Committees in the Kansas Legislature in Selected Years

Year	Senate	House
1901	32	50
1911	39	54
1913	28	53
1915	42	55
1939	46	38
1949	29	43
1955	30	43
1957	31	43
1959	31	43
1961	32	45
1963	32	45
1965	32	45
1967	32	45

Source: 1901-1939, Barnard, p. 56; 1949-1967, *Senate* and *House Journals.*

In the House the committee system is less demanding. That body, in the last four sessions, has had forty-five committees; but since it possesses three times as many members, the demand on individual members is likely to be less. Committees in the House tend to be larger than in the Senate. House committees ranged in size from three to twenty-three members in 1967. In that year there were 547 committee assignments, with an average of somewhat over four per representative. As in the Senate, there is a tendency to appoint the veteran members on several of the most important committees.[29]

In both houses the lawyers, as a professional group, are given more committee chairmanships than their numerical strength would justify.[30] An analysis of the membership on the more important committees reveals, particularly in the Senate, that there is substantial overlapping of membership. This makes it more difficult to schedule committee meetings, but it also points to the method by which the legislative leaders control the important actions of the Legislature.

The work of individual committees assumes even more importance in the legislative process in Kansas than in many bicameral states. By custom, some of the companion committees of the House and Senate divide jurisdiction between themselves.[31] For example, the House Committee on Fees and Salaries makes recommendations on *county* salaries, while the Senate Fees and Salaries Committee makes recommendations on *state* administrative salaries. The House Education Committee concerns itself with primary-school problems, while its Senate counterpart works with high schools. Similar divisions are customarily followed between the House and Senate Ways and Means committees.[32] In practice, the appropriate committee considers a proposal or makes a recommendation which is generally accepted by its own chamber, the committee of the second house, and the second house. Serious wrangles between the two houses develop when a house or a committee concerns itself with matters which "belong" to the other house.

29. Barnard, p. 65.
30. Barnard, p. 72.
31. For a fuller discussion of this interesting custom see Page, *op. cit.*, pp. 132-33.
32. In Kansas the Ways and Means committees consider appropriations, as well as taxation bills.

Select and Special Committees

In addition to the standing committees which examine proposed legislation, there are other types of committees whose work is essential to the legislative process. Both houses have calendar committees which meet to assign the places on the legislative calendar to bills as they near the voting stage. This committee generally determines whether legislation will come to a vote, and is thus a key committee.

Whenever the two houses of the legislature fail to agree on the specific provisions of a bill, a conference committee composed of members from each house is named. These committees arbitrate the matter and attempt to find a compromise agreeable to both houses. In the 1967 regular legislative session there were sixty-five conference committees appointed. This number, while typical of more recent sessions, is significantly larger than the average of twenty-five reported for the sessions from 1901 to 1947.[33]

33. Barnard, pp. 78, 79.

5 | The Legislature: Powers and Procedure

By the Constitution the legislative power of the state is vested in the Kansas Legislature, no distinction being drawn between the House of Representatives and the Senate with respect to the initiation or consideration of bills. Each occupies an equal position in the law-making process.

Powers of the Legislature

Unlike the national government, the state government is one of reserved or residual powers. Powers not delegated to the federal government remain with the state or with the people. The State Supreme Court has held that the state government does not have inherent powers.[1] By the last section of the bill of rights to the Kansas Constitution, "All powers not herein delegated remain with the people."[2]

The State Supreme Court has said that the clause in the Constitution giving legislative power to the House of Representatives and to the Senate is a substantial grant of power. In an early case, the court indicated that in defining the proper subjects of this legislative power the court could be guided by what was held to be a proper exercise of legislative power in other states. On this assumption the court held, for

1. *Leavenworth County* v. *Miller,* 7 *Kan.* 298.
2. *Kansas Constitution,* Bill of Rights § 20.

73

example, that the Legislature could enact a law authorizing counties to issue bonds to encourage railroads.[3]

In addition to this general grant there are included in the Kansas Constitution a number of provisions granting definite powers to the state government. It is primarily through legislative action that the powers of the state government are implemented. In this category are the constitutional grants to:

Provide for intellectual, educational, vocational and scientific improvements by establishing and maintaining public schools, educational institutions and related activities. (Art. 6, sec. 1.)

Provide by law for unemployment compensation and contributory old-age benefits and may tax employers and employees therefor. (Art. 7, sec. 5.)

Provide for organizing, equipping and disciplining the militia. (Art. 8, sec. 2.)

Provide for a uniform and equal rate of assessment and taxation. (Art. 11, sec. 1.)

Adopt, construct, reconstruct and maintain a state system of highways.[4] (Art. 11, sec. 9.)

Encourage the purchase, improvements and ownership of agricultural lands and the occupancy and cultivation thereof. (Art. 15, sec. 11.)

Regulate, license and tax the manufacture and sale of intoxicating liquors, and may regulate the possession and transportation of intoxicating liquors. (Art. 15, sec. 10.)

Provide by general law, applicable to all cities, for the incorporation of cities and the methods by which city boundaries may be altered, cities may be merged or consolidated and cities may be dissolved. (Art. 12, sec. 5.)

Participate financially in such [welfare] aid and supervise and control the administration thereof. (Art. 7, sec. 4.)

Moreover, the legislature is given a number of specific powers which are incidental to the operation of the state government. These include:

3. *Leavenworth County* v. *Miller*, 7 *Kan.* 314.

4. It is interesting to note that the power of the state to engage in its two biggest functions today—highways and social welfare—comes from constitutional amendments.

Each house shall establish its own rules; and shall be judge of the elections, returns and qualifications of its own members. (Art. 2, sec. 8.)

The legislature may confer upon tribunals transacting the county business of the several counties, such powers of local legislation and administration as it shall deem expedient. (Art. 2, sec. 21.)

The governor and all other officers under this constitution shall be subject to impeachment for any misdemeanor in office. (Art. 2, sec. 27.)

The tenure of any office not herein provided for may be declared by law. (Art. 15, sec. 2.)

The legislature may make provisions for a merit system. (Art. 15, sec. 2.)

Perhaps the largest grant of power which the state has is one not mentioned in the Constitution. The state has the police power—the power to protect the public health, public safety, public convenience, and public morals, to prevent fraud, and to suppress public nuisances. Technically this power is reserved to the people, but the people act through their representatives.[5] On this basis the Legislature may act as instructed by the voters, and the real limits of the legislators' powers are to be found not from grants of power so much as from the restrictions in the Constitution.

The federal Constitution contains various restrictions of the powers of Kansas state government,[6] but more important for our purposes are the restrictions within our own state Constitution. The Bill of Rights to the Kansas Constitution states the rights of the people to free speech, habeas corpus, freedom from self-incrimination, and other commonly held personal freedoms.[7] The Bill of Rights serves to limit action by the state and agencies thereof.

There are also several important limitations in the Constitution on

5. *Manning* v. *Davis,* 166 *Kan.* 281.

6. For an analysis of these restrictions which are applicable to all the states, see *American State Government* by W. Brooke Graves, p. 31.

7. In the Kansas Constitution there is no "due process of law" clause. The passage most similar to this clause, which appears in many state constitutions, is found in paragraph 18 of the Bill of Rights. It reads, "All persons, for injuries suffered in person, reputation, or property, shall have remedy by due course of law...."

the financial operation of the state. Among those relating to legislative action are:

No tax shall be levied except in pursuance of a law, which shall distinctly state the object of the same; to which object only such tax shall be applied. (Art. 11, sec. 5.)

No direct ad valorem tax shall be laid on real or personal property for such [unemployment compensation and old-age benefits] purposes. (Art. 7, sec. 5.)

The state may contract public debts; but such debts shall never, in the aggregate, exceed one million dollars, except as hereinafter provided. (Art. 11, sec. 6.)

No debt shall be contracted by the state except as herein provided, unless the proposed law for creating such debt shall first be submitted to direct vote of the electors of the state at some general election. (Art. 11, sec. 7.)

The state shall never be a party in carrying on any work of internal improvement except . . . a state system of highways . . . flood control works and works for the conservation or development of water resources. (Art. 11, sec. 9.)

In the matter of legislative procedure, there are constitutional prohibitions against the passage of special legislation when laws of a general nature and uniform application can be employed.[8] Corporations may not be created except under general acts.[9] Both municipalities and private corporations come under this general prohibition against special legislation. As another limit on procedure, bills must be read by sections on final passage,[10] and no bill may contain more than one subject.[11] No appropriation bill may be made for a longer term than two years.[12]

---

8. Kansas Constitution, Art. 2, sec. 17. This provision was interpreted by the courts as allowing the Legislature itself to choose when a general law could be made applicable. In 1906 an amendment to the Constitution made the courts the judge as to whether a general law could be made applicable.

9. *Kansas Constitution*, Art. 12, sec. 1.

10. *Ibid.*, Art. 2, sec. 15.

11. *Ibid.*, Art. 2, sec. 16.

12. *Ibid.*, Art. 2, sec. 24.

Steps in the Enactment of a Law: 1968

The HOUSE of REPRESENTATIVES | THE SENATE | ADMIN. OFFICIALS

The HOUSE of REPRESENTATIVES: INTRODUCING MEMBER | Staff of The Chief Clerk of the House — CHIEF CLERK | READING CLERK | OTHER CLERKS | SPEAKER of the HOUSE | HOUSE STANDING COMMITTEE | COMMITTEE of the Whole House

THE SENATE: THE SENATE | SECRETARY of the SENATE | PRESIDENT of the SENATE

ADMIN. OFFICIALS: STATE PRINTER | SECRETARY of STATE | THE GOVERNOR

Introduction of Bill

First Reading

Record of First Reading

Printing of Bill

Second Reading

Record of Second Reading

Reference to Standing Committee

Consideration by Standing Comm.

Reading of Report of Standing Comm.

Record of Report of Standing Comm.

Consideration by Committee of the Whole

Reading of Report of Committee of the Whole

Record of Report of Committee of the Whole

Third Reading Roll Call and Vote

Record of Third Reading and Vote

Certification

Procedure followed Similar to that in House

Certification

Reading of Message from Senate

Record of Bill's Return from Senate

Signature of Chief Clerk of House

Signature Speaker of the House

Printing of Bill on Parchment

Preparation of Correct Copy for Enrollment

Signature of Secretary of Senate

Signature of President of Senate

Signature of The Governor

Enacting a Law

Passage of a bill in the Kansas Legislature follows a comparatively simple and normal pattern,[13] as shown by the chart on page 77.

Introduction of a Bill

Any member or group of members, including a committee, may propose a bill. Either house may originate a bill on any subject, and there is no restriction on the number of bills that a member may introduce. While there is no constitutional or statutory limit on the time for the introduction of bills, each house usually determines by resolution near the beginning of each session a date after which only bills proposed by committees will be considered. By the same type of legislative custom all bills pertaining to appropriations are introduced by the committees on Ways and Means in the two houses.[14]

First Reading

To introduce a bill, a member merely hands his written proposal to the reading clerk who reads the title of the bill, assigns it a number, and records it. The clerk's reading of the title constitutes the first legal reading of the bill. The numbered document is now dispatched to the state printer's office, where normally 1,200 copies of the bill are printed. This number is sufficient to supply the legislators, the various reference services, and interested citizens.

Second Reading

When the printed copies of the bill are returned (normally the next day), the second reading occurs. This also is by title, except on rare occasions when there is a demand for full reading. The bill is then referred to a standing committee, a select committee, or the Committee of the Whole. In this second reading, there are variations from time to

13. For a complete and detailed description, see Frederic H. Guild, *Legislative Procedure in Kansas* (Lawrence: Governmental Research Center, Univ. of Kansas, 1956).

14. As a matter of division of labor, the House and Senate Ways and Means committees divide the appropriations work. Each committee has hearings for certain state agencies; its counterpart in the other house hears the others. The committee and the other house are expected to accept the recommendations for "their agencies."

time. Rules may be suspended so that there is no time lapse between the first and second readings. Occasionally there may be debate on the proposal, but in most cases the bill is simply referred to one of the committees.

In ordinary operation, the sponsor of the bill will make known to the presiding officer of the particular house which committee he wishes to consider the proposal. Normally, the Speaker of the House or the President of the Senate then assigns the bill to that committee for study. The assignment by the chair may be, but rarely is, overridden by action on the floor.

Action by Committee

When a bill has been sent to a select or standing committee for examination, the committee may choose to hold public or private hearings and to invite interested parties to testify. On the basis of its hearings and deliberations the committee makes a report to the full chamber. The report of the committee is that the bill be passed, that the bill be amended and passed as amended, that the bill be not passed, or that the bill be referred to another committee.

The final vote on committee approval is in closed or executive session.[15] However, a minority of the committee may file its own report when it disagrees with the majority on the disposition of the bill.

In an effort to prevent the committees from "killing" bills by merely not making reports, the rules of both houses require committees to report on each bill. Despite this rule, many bills sent to committees are never reported back for action. This is particularly true towards the close of the session.

Normally, bills which are introduced by committees are assigned directly to the Committee of the Whole and thus bypass consideration by a standing or joint committee. Exceptionally, under a suspension of the rules, other bills may be sent directly to the Committee of the Whole from second reading.

Action by the Committee of the Whole

With a favorable report of the standing or select committee, or the proposal of a bill by a committee, or by the house memberships' over-

15. Frederic H. Guild, *Legislative Procedure in Kansas* (Lawrence: Governmental Research Center, Univ. of Kansas, 1956), p. 21.

ruling of an unfavorable report, a bill goes before the Committee of the Whole. This body is simply the entire membership of a single house acting as a general committee. The Speaker of the House or the President of the Senate relinquishes the chair, and the body goes into committee session. Then all bills under general orders (those bills noted above) are read and debated section by section before the house, meeting as a Committee of the Whole. Amendments to each section are considered, with the amendments proposed by a committee receiving priority. The Committee of the Whole may recommend that the bill be passed, passed with amendments, or rejected, or it may set the bill aside for more deliberation.

On most occasions the majority committee report will be accepted, and the fate of the bill will depend largely upon the recommendation of the select or standing committee. Occasionally, however, a member will successfully move that a bill be placed on general orders for action of the Committee of the Whole despite the unfavorable report of a standing committee. Another method of overriding a committee report is to move the substitution of a minority report for that of the majority. Should two-thirds of the membership of the body concur, such action will be taken.

Action by the First House

The Committee of the Whole then reports its action to the house. If the committee reports favorably and the house accepts the report, the bill is sent to the Secretary of State for engrossment prior to third reading. Engrossment consists of making a new corrected, typed copy of the bill, containing all amendments and checked for grammatical and typographical accuracy.

When the engrossed bill is returned to the house of origin, the bill is placed on third reading, and must be read in full. This final reading is normally a formality, for in most cases the approval of the Committee of the Whole is tantamount to passage. Occasionally, there are departures from the constitutional requirements. For example, bills may be hurried through on third reading, only the first line of each section being read aloud. Any member may demand a full reading of any bill, and sometimes in the House several bills may be read aloud simultaneously. With the completion of the third reading, amendments may be proposed, but this is a very rare occurrence. A roll call vote is taken on each measure, though several bills may be grouped together for "bulk voting." At this stage the outcome of the bill has been largely determined, and the roll-call vote is normally routine. If, however, the bill is amended, it is returned to the Secretary of State for reengrossment.

Each member is required under the rules of each house to vote on each bill, and is given the opportunity of explaining his vote at the time the roll is called. Members are seldom actually required to vote. However, if a bill seems to be failing because an insufficient number of members are present, a "call of the house" may be held. This consists of locking the chamber doors and keeping members in while the Sergeant-at-Arms and his assistants go through the building to find absentees. After passing the first house, the bill is then sent to the other house for its consideration.

Action by the Second House

The processes outlined above are repeated in the second house. If the bill is passed in exactly the same form as by the first house, it is sent to the Governor for his consideration. Should the bill be rejected by the second chamber, the bill dies and does not become a law. If the bill is amended and passed, then it is returned to the first house for concurrence on the amendments. Should the first house not concur, a conference committee with members of both houses is appointed to meet and to "iron out" the differences. Generally the houses will accept the report of the conference committee, but should agreement not be possible, additional conference committees may be appointed. If the houses cannot agree and become deadlocked, the bill dies.

The last days of a session are generally very busy, usually with somewhat over half of the total number of laws being passed in the second chamber in the last three working days. The number of actions taken is even larger if the adoptions of conference committee reports are included, as perhaps they should be, since they indicate final legislative decisions. The leadership in both chambers has sought to reduce the last minute rush; but such typically occurs.

Action by the Governor

Upon securing the agreement of both houses, the bill is reengrossed if it has been amended, and then enrolled—that is, printed on parchment by the State Printer and signed by the officers of both houses. The bill is then transmitted to the Governor, who may sign it and make it a law. If he wishes, the Governor may hold it for three legislative days without action and let it become a law without his signature, or he may veto it.

To veto a bill, the Governor writes a formal veto message and returns it to the House of Representatives, regardless of the house in which it originated. The Governor may veto individual items in an appropriation bill. Should the Governor veto a bill, a two-thirds majority of those elected in each house is necessary to override his objections. Such instances are rare indeed.[16]

Theoretically, the Governor may employ a pocket veto by holding a bill without signature for three days after the Legislature adjourns. In practice, however, the Legislature generally continues in session three days after the passage of its last bill so that the Governor may not use his "pocket veto."[17]

The Calendar

Each house publishes a daily calendar to show the status of proposed bills and to set forth the order of business for the day. There is a standing committee in each house which revises the calendar and designates the time for consideration of particular bills. These committees become particularly important towards the end of the session, when they can change the order of consideration of bills and thus determine which bills will get to the floor and which will die on the calendar. Since a two-thirds vote of the house's membership is necessary to change the calendar, the calendar committee is important in the legislative process.

Publishing the Law

According to the Constitution the Legislature may determine the time when a law is to become effective. The Legislature may direct that

16. For further information on the use of the veto, see p. 106.
17. Exceptionally, for example, the Governor exercised the pocket veto over four bills in the 1958 budget session.

a law shall be effective from the date of its publication in the official state paper, but normally laws are made effective upon their appearance in the *Session Laws,* a bound volume prepared by the Secretary of State which contains indexed copies of all laws passed during the session.

The *Session Laws* are compiled in the *General Statutes,* which contains a systematized collection of all laws of a general nature in force at the time of printing. The first general collection of laws of the Territory of Kansas is composed of those adopted by the first legislative assembly at the Shawnee Manual Labor School in 1855, which are usually known as the Bogus Statutes. At the time of the adoption of those laws, the pro-slavery party was in control of the Legislature. The Free-State party questioned the legality of the election of a large number of the legislators on the ground that they had been elected by nonresidents who came into the Territory merely for the purpose of voting. The Free-State party denied the validity of laws passed at this and other meetings of the territorial Legislature which were dominated by the pro-slavery elements. When in 1859 the Free-State party had a majority in the territorial Legislature, a board of commissioners was selected to prepare an entire code of laws, upon all subjects of general legislation pertaining to the interests of the Territory. The board reported a code of laws to this same session of the Legislature, which adopted the code and repealed the *Laws of 1855.*

After the close of the regular session of the state Legislature in 1862, the general laws then in force were compiled by a joint committee of

TABLE 12

Legislative Source of Laws by Chamber, Regular Sessions: 1959-1967

	1959	1961	1963	1965	1967
Total Number of House Bills	512	489	463	604	651
House Bills Becoming Laws	224	243	224	309	286
Percentage of House Bills Becoming Laws	43.8%	49.7%	48.4%	51.2%	43.9%
Total Number of Senate Bills	346	408	449	415	462
Senate Bills Becoming Laws	189	227	276	220	204
Percentage of Senate Bills Becoming Laws	54.6%	55.6%	61.5%	53.0%	44.2%

Source: *House* and *Senate Journals,* 1959-1967.

the two houses and subsequently were published in a volume known as the *Compiled Laws of 1862.*

In 1867 the Legislature authorized the Governor to appoint three commissioners to revise and codify the civil and criminal codes of procedure and all state laws of a general nature. The commissioners reported to the next session of the Legislature, which adopted their recommendations. This compilation was entitled the *General Statutes of 1868.* Subsequently in 1876, 1889, 1897, 1899, 1901, 1905, 1909, 1915, 1923, 1935, 1949, and 1963 the statutes have been revised and compiled.[18] The title of the 1963 compilation was changed to *Kansas Statutes Annotated.* The compilation in 1923 was more extensive and was prepared by a legislatively authorized committee and then adopted by the Legislature. Under different auspices and under slightly different titles other compilations were made in 1879 and 1885.

In order to provide for continuous revision of the statutes, the Legislature in 1929 created the office of "revisor"[19] of statutes. Immediately after the close of each regular session, he is required by law to compile, edit, annotate, and index the laws of a permanent nature passed by the Legislature and to add them to the general statutes of the state by means of supplements which are printed each two years. Since 1965 these supplements have been published in the form of inserts to the 1963 revision of the statutes.

Legislative Aids

Faced with such a multitude of proposals, bills, and resolutions, the Legislature would almost surely be overwhelmed were it not for the aids which it has established. Foremost among these is the Legislative Council. With at least forty-four states now having such a council, Kansas can be proud of having been the first state to have one. Established by law in 1933 "to prepare a legislative program in the form of bills or otherwise, as in its opinion the welfare of the state may require, to be presented at the next session of the legislature," the Council is a deliberative and investigative body composed of ten Senators appointed by the Lieutenant-Governor and fifteen Representatives appointed by

18. A more extensive list of both official and public collections of the laws is to be found at the end of the supplements to the general statutes.

19. The revisor (so spelled) is apparently more than a reviser.

the Speaker of the House. Appointments made by these two officers are subject to majority approval of the respective houses. The Lieutenant-Governor is chairman of the Council; the Speaker of the House becomes vice-chairman; and the Revisor of Statutes acts as secretary.

The Council is bipartisan, with each party having membership in proportion generally to its membership in each house of the Legislature. During the first decade of the existence of the Council, no party was allowed to have more than two-thirds of the seats in the Council.[20] Practically, this meant that the Democrats in some years got a larger number of seats than their numbers in the Legislature would justify. During some of this time not enough Democrats were elected to allow this requirement to be satisfied. This provision for a maximum on the majority party was dropped in 1943.[21] In 1967-68, with a membership of 32 per cent of the Senate and 38 per cent of the House, Democrats were given 29 per cent of the seats on the Council.

Organization of Kansas Legislative Council: 1968

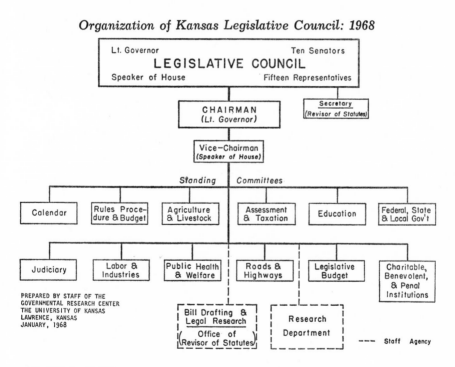

20. *K.S.A.,* 46-301.
21. *Session Laws,* 1943, chap. 192.

Between legislative sessions the Legislative Council meets quarterly to consider those matters referred to it by the Legislature and "proposals" by any member of the Legislature.

Much of the Council work is done by the Council committees listed in the organization chart shown on this page. The committees hold hearings at the regular quarterly meetings and at other times between Council meetings upon approval by the Council. The committees make reports to the Council, which in turn makes recommendations to the Legislature.

In addition to these occasional preliminary bulletins, the Council publishes a full report of its findings and recommendations a month before the beginning of each regular legislative session.

The Legislative Council has developed a research staff, responsible for the gathering and compilation of facts and materials. The research staff has demonstrated its usefulness and has earned the respect of the Legislature.[22] The availability of the factual reports prepared by the research staff has aided the Council and the Legislature in their consideration of legislation.

Over the years the Council has helped the Legislature resolve many difficult issues. Frequently the Legislature will refer to the Council matters upon which it has been unable to agree. Despite the controversial aspects of some of the Council proposals, a large percentage of its recommendations are enacted into law.[23] If the Council can agree upon a recommendation, the Legislature can probably agree upon the same compromise. This is particularly true because the Council members are normally the veterans of several legislative sessions and tend to be the leaders of the Legislature.

During the course of its existence the "little legislature," as the Council has come to be known, has assumed a very important role in providing leadership for the Legislature and in maintaining continuity of legislative program. This role of the Council is being subjected to study and redefinition and possible change in the next several years

22. Bernard L. Barnard, "The Legislature in Kansas, An Appraisal" (Unpublished Ph.D. thesis: Washington, D.C., American University, 1949), pp. 199-201.

23. For a discussion of the Council and its operation, see Cape and Bay, *An Analysis of the Kansas Legislative Council and Its Research Department* (Lawrence: Governmental Research Center, Univ. of Kansas, 1963).

because of the annual sessions of the Legislature. With each house now having at least two sessions, it may be that some of the more important committees may hold meetings between sessions, develop their own staffs, and perform functions not too dissimilar to those of the Council.

The staff of the Research Department of the Legislative Council is available for the use of members and committees throughout the legislative session and performs much the same function for the whole Legislature during the sessions as it does throughout the rest of the biennium for the Council.

There are several other devices designed to assist the state lawmakers. Perhaps the most important of these is the office of the Revisor of Statutes, which maintains a confidential bill-drafting service for members of the Legislature. Working under the direction of the legislator, the office writes the bill in proper form, checking it for accuracy and for its relations to existing statutes.

The state library provides both a general and a specialized reference service for the use of legislators. In addition to the standard legal and statutory references, the library maintains an index of all bills submitted in the Legislature since 1909, and during the session it publishes an index of the bills introduced. In addition the library prepares the "Kansas Bill Locator" which shows the actions taken on the various bills.

Either house (or both houses acting together) may ask the Attorney General to submit a legal opinion with regard to legislation under consideration. Private members may also informally request and receive legal advice from him. In helping a legislator draft a bill, the Revisor of Statutes often works together informally with the Attorney General to get an opinion on the legality of a statute while it is yet in the drafting stage.

The Governor in the Law-Making Process

In addition to the veto powers described earlier, the Governor plays an important role in the law-making process. Prior to the opening of each biennial session of the Legislature, each administrative agency of the state is required to submit a report to the Governor accompanied by an enumeration of proposed statutory changes and recommended legislation. These proposals are then grouped into the Governor's "state of the state" message or sent as separate proposals to the Legislature. Moreover, the Governor submits to the Legislature a budget which has been prepared and analyzed by the Department of Administration.

In practice the Governor plays a substantial role, both in the presentation of suggested legislation and in the actual passage of bills. Over the years the existence of one-party domination has meant that the Governor, as the titular party head, can exert great influence on legislative proposals. While the veto is sparingly used, it is most often sustained. The Governor can exert considerable pressure on the Legislature by means of his position within the party. Members frequently come to be considered as "administration men" or "anti-administration men."

When the Governor and the Legislature have been of different political parties, as was true in 1967, the Governor has been able, particularly in conjunction with the more than one-third Democratic members of the house, to exert substantial influence on legislation.

Other Sources of Legislation

Another distinct source of legislative proposals is the State Commission on Interstate Co-operation, which concerns itself with proposals concerning uniform laws or reciprocal agreements, or with laws designed to facilitate relations between the state and federal government. Through its memberships in the Council of State Government and in the Commission on Uniform State Laws, the Kansas Legislature considers proposed model uniform acts. As of November, 1967, Kansas had enacted twenty laws proposed by the National Conference of Commissions on Uniform State Laws.[24]

While these are the several formally constituted channels of receiving legislative proposals, a great number of enactments stem from suggestions made by nongovernmental lobby groups and by local officials. Though no accurate figures are available on the basis for the opinions of legislators, one observer estimated that about one-third of all legislation comes from the lobbyists and local administrators, another third

24. Council of State Government, *Book of the States 1968-69* (Chicago, 1968), pp. 87-94.

from state administrative agencies through the biennial report system, and the final third from the legislators.[25]

Lobbying

No discussion of the modern legislative practice would be complete without the mention of lobbies and lobbying. Since 1909 Kansas has had a law requiring the registration of legislative agents and counsels. Though legislative agents and counsels are differentiated in the statute, the distinction is not entirely clear. A legislative counsel appears in behalf of a group and has the privilege of arguing before committees and of examining witnesses called before the committees. The legislative agent is employed or retained to influence legislation and does not have these privileges. Neither is supposed to be on the floor of the Legislature during a business session. Under Kansas law, the lobbyist is under no obligation to disclose the amount, source, or use of its funds.

In both the 1963 and 1965 sessions of the Legislature there were 400 or more agents or counsels registered with the Secretary of State. In the latter session a law was passed requiring that agents and counsels in the future pay a small fee and be issued an identification badge to be worn when they appeared in the Capitol. In 1967 and 1968 there were somewhat fewer lobbyists registered. A review of 215 registrations in 1968 showed that eighteen lobbyists were associated with insurance companies, fourteen with public utilities, thirteen with labor, and eleven with public health. Five or more agents or counsels were registered as having special interests in agriculture, beverages, credit unions, education, oil and gas, and transportation. In some cases sufficient information was not available to meaningfully classify the lobbyist. The problem of controlling lobbying is a difficult one, since, with the high turnover rates among legislators, the lobbyists often have more experience and more acquaintance with the legislators and the legislative processes and problems than does the average Senator or Representative.

The Legislature in 1967 passed a law requiring the public disclosure of any substantial financial interest of the Governor, Lieutenant Governor, and members of the Legislature in any business directly or in-

25. Barnard, p. 131.

directly affected by any bill or resolution.[26] The term "substantial interest" was defined to include a holding of five per cent or more of a business. The Governor and the legislators were permitted to make a general disclosure of all the businesses in which they had a substantial interest and thus not be involved in the sometimes difficult question of just what businesses were affected by bills or resolutions of the Legislature. Other provisions of the law extended to elected or appointed officers and employees of the state where there might be conflicts of interest.

Improvements in Legislative Procedure

The committee system of the Kansas Legislature needs serious study in order to find methods to make better use of the abilities of all legislators, and to relieve the pressure on a few. The number of standing committees could be profitably reduced, and membership on remaining committees could be enlarged to the benefit of the legislators and the public. More of an attempt could be made to minimize duplication of membership among the most vital, time-consuming committees.

Among the questions of procedure, the full reading of bills prior to roll call could be dispensed with, so that a great deal of time would be saved, particularly in the crowded hours toward the end of the session. The bill is discussed in full in the Committee of the Whole, and modern printing facilities obviate the necessity of further oral reading. In present practice, this final reading is largely meaningless, and the total effect is merely to consume precious time. A new system of mechanical voting was authorized by the 1955 Legislature, and the physical act of voting has been much speeded up.

The limitations which the Legislature had when it was meeting in "budget sessions" had raised some questions and problems—questions which the recent constitutional amendment for annual sessions obviates. Annual sessions give the Legislature more time to consider budget matters and also other more general subjects. With annual sessions, some of the standing committees may want to have meetings between sessions and may move to developing their own staffs and ways of collecting information and making decisions. The future role of the Council and its relationship to the standing committees of the Legisla-

26. *Sessions Laws,* 1967, chap. 464; K.S.A., 75, 4301.

ture, as well as the more extended participation of the full membership of the Legislature will likely modify previous procedures and affect the operation of the Legislature. The newly more frequent meetings may well lead to an enlarged role of the Legislature in Kansas government.

In many respects, however, the Kansas Legislature has shown a willingness to experiment with legislative procedures. The Legislative Council, its research bureau, the Revisor of Statutes, and the State Library and indexing service are evidences of this willingness.

6 | The Governor

A recurring problem of democratic government is how much power should be given the chief executive. Efficiency of operation seems to require that the executive should have the sole responsibility and the accompanying power to administer the laws. Yet the possibility of misused power suggests that executive control should be scattered among many officials. The evolution of the position of governor in the American system of state government reflects various attempts to solve this perplexing problem.

Because of their experience with colonial governors, who in eleven of thirteen colonies were the appointees of the disliked British monarch, the framers of early state constitutions showed a distinct mistrust of the executive. Consequently they made the executive subordinate to the legislature. In most cases the governor was given neither a veto power over legislation nor the authority to call or to dissolve the legislature. He possessed but limited power of appointment and removal. Other officers in the executive branch were appointed by and were responsible to the legislature. Only in New York and in the New England states was he elected by the people; in the other states the legislature appointed him.

During the nineteenth century the American governor gradually gained more power. Election by the people became the general way of selecting the governor. His term of office was extended from one to two years, and in some states to four years. The legislature came to have less control over appointment of executive officers, but this did not automatically mean that the governor gained power, for more and more executive officers were elected. The idea seemed to be that democratic government was more secure if governmental power was divided among several executive officials and boards and the legislatures.

It was at this stage of development that the Wyandotte Convention met in 1859 and drew up the Kansas Constitution. By this document the Kansas Governor was but one of six elected executive officers. And in 1865, after the Legislature had held four annual sessions and had established the statutory framework of government, the Governor had power to appoint only the officers of the militia and members of six part-time boards, but no full-time administrators. Gradually the Governor has obtained more appointive power. He now appoints the administrative heads of a number of the more important state agencies. There are, however, six executive officers who are elected, and several others who are appointed by the Supreme Court.

Since the days of early statehood the Governor's pardoning power has not been changed much, and, on the whole, his constitutional and statutory duties concerning the Legislature have remained constant, except for the addition of the item veto in 1904. Informal leadership of the Legislature and political leadership of the state are very important avenues of augmenting the Governor's powers, but are so intangible that they escape measurement. It seems safe to conclude that the powers and the general prestige of the office of governor has increased since Kansas became a state in 1861.

The Man

The Kansas Constitution states that "no member of Congress, or officer of the state, or of the United States, shall hold the office of governor." But other than that, the state Constitution and statutes are void of qualifications for the governorship. The Lecompton Constitution of 1857 specified that the Governor be thirty years of age, a citizen of the United States for twenty years, and a resident of the state for five years. But when the Wyandotte Constitution was written, no such requirements were included.

However, informal qualifications seem to exist as far as the voters are concerned. Does the candidate have a pleasing personality? Is he tactful? Is he a good speaker? Of what organizations is he a member? Is he married and does he have a family? Is he intelligent without being an "ivory-tower intellectual"? Is he known to be honest, temperate, witty, and just plain "human"? What is his occupation? Is he a "God-fearing" man and a member of some church? Has he had military service? Is he a long-time resident of the state? Has he had experience in public affairs? A candidate does not have to satisfy all of these informal requirements, yet he will meet a considerable number of them. These are the kinds of requirements that party leaders look for in the candidate they will support at the primary.

An examination of the backgrounds of the thirty-five men elected Governor reveals that nineteen of the group were in their forties when elected.[1] Twenty-one of those elected have had experience in the state Legislature, with a large number having had either experience in state administrative offices or in local government. It was not until 1914 that a native Kansan was elected Governor; no one who was born south of the state's southern border or farther west than Ford County in Kansas has been elected Governor. Twelve of the thirty-five men who have been elected Governor were lawyers, while six were newspapermen. Five of the Governors have been bankers, and four farmers or stockmen. Six of the men elected Governor since 1900 have been Democrats. Not all Governors have publicly announced their religious preferences, but of those announcing, all have identified with Protestant sects. Early Governors were not active joiners, but later incumbents have belonged to a number of associations. All but one had experience in public affairs at the time of the election. The nature of this experience is shown in Table 13. All but one were married, and this one had an unmarried sister who made her home with him and served as hostess at the executive mansion.

These summaries tell a little of the personalities of the Governors, and suggest some of the "practical" requirements for Kansas Governors.

1. The source of most of the information in this paragraph is an article by Professor James E. Titus in *The Western Political Quarterly*, Volume XVII, No. 2, entitled "Kansas Governors: A Resume of Political Leadership." I have brought his article up to date by adding information on the last two Governors—Governors William Avery and Robert Docking.

The Office

In Kansas the Governor is elected at the general election which is held on the Tuesday following the first Monday of November in each even-numbered year. In this election, the candidate receiving the highest number of votes is declared the winner, even if this number is not a majority of votes cast. In case of a tie vote the two houses of the Legislature, in joint ballot, are authorized to decide the outcome of the election, but this has never happened.

The Governor's term of office begins on the second Monday of January following his election and runs for two years. Although there is no limitation on the number of terms which one person might serve, no Governor has served more than two terms. Up to 1967, of the thirty-five Governors, eighteen were elected for two terms; nine of the last twelve Republicans elected were re-elected.

In 1861 the Legislature, in its first session, set the salary of the Governor at $2,000. This amount was increased to $3,000 in 1872, to $5,000 in 1903, to $8,000 in 1945, to $10,000 in 1949, and to $15,000 in 1953. The 1967 Legislature raised it to $20,000, the current salary. In addition to his salary, the Governor is furnished residence at the Executive Mansion at state expense and is provided with an official hospitality account and a contingency fund.

According to the Kansas Constitution, the governor (like all other constitutional officers) is subject to "impeachment for any misdemeanor in office." The House of Representatives draws up articles of impeachment and appoints a board of managers to present the articles to the Senate. Concurrence of two-thirds of all Senators is necessary for conviction. Impeachment proceedings have been instituted only once. Such action was taken against the first governor, Charles Robinson, but the Senate failed to convict him.

Should a vacancy in the office of governor come about by death, impeachment, or resignation, the Lieutenant Governor acts as Governor until the term expires. This situation has occurred three times in Kansas history: Nehemiah Green became Governor in 1868 when Samuel J. Crawford resigned the governorship two months before his term expired to command the Nineteenth Regiment; Frank Hagaman took over from Frank Carlson for nearly two months in 1950 when the latter was elected to fill an unexpired term as United States Senator;

TABLE 13

Governors of Kansas—1859-1968: Years of Experience in Public Office Prior to Being Elected Governor

Governor*	Local Government	State Government			National Government			Total
		Adm.	Leg.	Judicial	Adm.	Leg.	Judicial	
1. Robinson (R) 1861-63			1					1
2. Carney (R) 1863-65			2					2
3. Crawford (R) 1865-68			1					1
4. Harvey (R) 1869-73			5					5
5. Osborn (R) 1873-77		2	3		3			8
6. Anthony (R) 1877-79		3			3			6
7. St. John (R) 1879-83			4					4
8. Glick (D) 1883-85	4		14					18
9. Martin (R) 1885-89	12		1					13
10. Humphrey (R) 1889-93		4	6					10
11. Lewelling (P) 1893-95								0
12. Morrill (R) 1895-97	6		10			8		24
13. Leedy (P) 1897-99			4					4
14. Stanley (R) 1899-1903	7		2					9
15. Bailey (R) 1903-5		4	2			2		8
16. Hock (R) 1905-9			4					4
17. Stubbs (R) 1909-13			6					6
18. Hodges (D) 1913-15			8					8
19. Capper (R) 1915-19								0
20. Allen (R) 1919-23		5						5
21. Davis (D) 1923-25	7		12					19
22. Paulen (R) 1925-29	4	2	4					10
23. Reed (R) 1929-31		3		1				4
24. Woodring (D) 1931-33								0
25. Landon (R) 1933-37								0
26. Huxman (D) 1937-39	6	1						7
27. Ratner (R) 1939-43	4		6					10
28. Schoeppel (R) 1943-47	10	3						13
29. Carlson (R) 1947-50		4				12		16
30. Arn (R) 1951-55		2		1				3
31. Hall (R) 1955-57	2	4						6
32. Docking, G. (D) 1957-61								0
33. Anderson (R) 1961-65	6	4	4					14
34. Avery (R) 1965-67			4			8		12
35. Docking, R. (D) 1967-	3							3
Totals	71	41	103	2	6	30	0	253

TABLE 13 (concluded)

Type of Experience	Number of Governors
Local Government	12
State Legislative	21
State Administrative	13
State Judicial	2
National Administrative	2
National Congress	4
National Judicial	0

* This table includes only those elected to the governorship, and thus does not list Green (Nov. 4, 1868, to Jan. 11, 1869), Hagaman (Nov. 28, 1950, to Jan. 8, 1951), and McCuish (Jan. 3-14, 1957), who served as Governors for short periods of time.

Source: James E. Titus, "Kansas Governors; A Resume of Political Leadership," *The Western Political Quarterly*, Vol. XVII, No. 2 (June, 1964), p. 364; and additional information for the last two Governors.

and Fred Hall resigned and accepted an appointment by his successor, John McCuish, to the Kansas Supreme Court.

Without the assistance of a personal staff the Governor would be unable to perform his various legal and extra-legal duties. By statute the Governor is authorized to appoint a private secretary, a pardon attorney, and other employees as he may deem necessary and within available appropriations. Not being strictly determined by statute, the organization of the Governor's office varies somewhat under different Governors. Frequently there are important staff assistants to the Governor who are officially on the payrolls of other agencies. In 1967, for example, the personnel of the Governor's office included an executive assistant, an urban affairs specialist, an education specialist, a press secretary, a research assistant, a pardon attorney, a technical assistant, a personal secretary, three typists, and one receptionist-typist. The executive assistant to the Governor is responsible for the coordination of office and liaison work with the state and national parties. He acts as the general administrator for those matters which cannot be handled directly by the Governor. The urban affairs specialist acts as the Governor's adviser on urban and community problems throughout the state. He works closely with federal officials who are concerned with problems of this type, including persons in the Department of Housing and Urban Development and the Office of Emergency Planning. The education specialist functions in a somewhat similar capacity for matters concerned with education. In his role as educational adviser, he is often called upon to meet with various education groups, such as the Kansas Teachers Association. Because of the rapid growth in federal programs which require the personal attention of the Governor, especially in the areas of health, education, and welfare, there has been created a need on the part of the office of the Governor to have full-time personnel to handle these numerous matters.

The press secretary arranges all news conferences and prepares press releases for the Governor. Although a large part of the press secretary's time is devoted to public relations, he is responsible for keeping the Governor informed as to what is happening on the state and national scene. This task involves the daily reading of from eighteen to twenty different newspapers. He reads and analyzes the papers and makes his report to the Governor. The research assistant lends assistance to the entire staff in matters that require research. Much of his work has been directed by education and urban affairs specialists, since their work requires a great deal of research.

As a result of the passage of the Economic Opportunity Act of 1964, the Office of Technical Assistance was created and is tangential to the office of the Governor. This office is composed of a coordinator, program developer, field representative, office manager, and secretary. He acts as the Governor's adviser on health, welfare, and civil rights as well as directing the economic opportunity functions of the Technical Assistance Office.

The internal organization of the office of the Governor depends largely on the Governor himself and is not institutionalized. The size of the office staff and the appropriations needed to support the office become on occasion the subject of partisan attack.

Executive Powers

The Kansas Constitution states that "the supreme executive power of the state shall be vested in a governor, who shall see that the laws are faithfully executed." The precise meaning of "the supreme executive power of the state" is not spelled out in the Constitution; nor is it precisely defined in any one statute. Instead, the powers and duties of the chief executive are scattered throughout the statute book. Even these do not tell exactly what the Governor does, for much of his influence and leadership in state administration comes from his position as nominal head of his political party. Thus, to know the executive powers of the Governor one must understand both the statutory and the extra-legal powers which he exercises.

The Kansas Governor has general supervision over the many administrative agencies which are headed by boards or officers whom he appoints. Excluded from this category, however, are important departments which are headed by elected officers. These include the State Treasurer, the Attorney General and the Kansas Bureau of Investigation, the State Printer, the Secretary of State, the Commissioner of Insurance and the Insurance Department, and the State Auditor. A few other administrative agencies come under the direction of the Supreme Court. But since most administrative officers and boards are appointed by the Governor, they do consult with him on matters of policy and furnish him with information concerning the operation of their agency. Nevertheless the Governor, with his small staff and the many demands on his time, is frequently unable to provide any but the most general and limited supervision over the many administrative agencies shown on the chart in the end sheets of this book. The result is many semi-independent agencies operating with limited supervision by the chief executive and only casual coordination.

Appointment and Removal Power

A considerable amount of control which the Governor has over the state administrative organization is from his power of appointment. The extent of this power is shown in Table 14. About one-half of those appointed serve four-year terms; this means that in his first term a governor has under him many administrators whom he did not appoint. Eighty-six appointments, about one-fourth of the total, require consent of the Senate. During the last three sessions of the Legislature the Governor has submitted to the Senate for confirmation an average of forty names a year.

Even in the case where he may make an appointment without senatorial consent the chief executive is limited somewhat in his appointing power. In some instances the statutes provide qualifications of citizenship, residence, and professional competence. Some appointments are limited as to the political affiliation of the appointees: the nine members of the Board of Regents must be selected "from among

TABLE 14

Number of Appointees, Term and Method of Appointment

	Method of Selection		
	Appointment by Governor	Appointment by Governor with Advice and Consent of Senate	Total
Length of Term			
Two years	37	1	38
Three years	66	15	81
Four years	88	69	157
Pleasure of Gov.	31	1	32
Other	15*	0	15
Total	237	86	323

* Includes five members of the Supreme Court Nominating Commission, who are appointed for six-year terms, and seven Supreme Court justices appointed by the Governor from among those nominated by the Nominating Commission.
Source: *K.S.A.*

the members of the two political parties casting the highest and second highest number of votes respectively for secretary of state at the last preceding general election," and no more than five shall be members of the same party. Another type of limitation is that on the place of residence of the appointee: in six boards there must be one member from each congressional district, and in two other boards there must be one member from each of six districts set up by statute. Even without this restriction there is a tendency for gubernatorial appointments to be fairly evenly distributed among the congressional districts; this tendency represents one of the informal requirements which the Governor must meet as he makes appointments. These informal requirements, such as availability, are not too easy to specify, yet they can be brought out partially by the following questions which a governor must ask: Are all sections of the state represented in appointive offices? To whom do I owe a favor for working for me in the last election? Is there any "faction" of the party that needs a share of appointments?

Not only does the Governor have 321 appointments to make, but he also may make appointments to fill vacancies in any state or county office, and in the supreme or district courts, vacancies in city courts, and vacancies in the position of United States Senator. Persons appointed to fill such vacancies hold office until the next general election.

The Kansas chief executive may remove only about one-fifth of the state officers whom he appoints; this includes fifty-one individuals in sixteen offices or agencies. Reasons for removal vary with the office. In some cases it is "for cause"; in other instances it is "for neglect of duty, incompetency, or improper conduct." For some removals, but not all, a hearing must be held. In addition, eleven appointees hold office "at the pleasure of the governor"; this, of course, means that the chief executive may dismiss such an appointee at any time. Any gubernatorial appointee committing an unlawful act may also be removed from office before the expiration of his term by legal action commenced by the state Attorney General.

Financial Control

The Governor exercises general supervision and control over the spending of state administrative agencies by deciding what of the agency requests to include in his recommendations to the Legislature. The budget director, who is appointed under civil service, reviews the agency requests for appropriations and makes recommendations to the executive director of the Department of Administration. The executive director is appointed by and serves at the pleasure of the Governor. Some agencies do not feel bound by the Governor's budget recommendations and may try to get more money from the Legislature than the Governor recommends. However, most agencies will be content with the amount the Governor recommends and will consider that recommendation as being of assistance to them in getting the money from the Legislature. There are special arrangements for allowing a newly elected governor to become familiar with the budget requests even before he takes office.

The Governor is chairman of the State Finance Council, which may advise in the preparation of the budget, but the Governor has the responsibility for submitting a budget to the Legislature. Practically, however, the Governor must consider the important role the members of the Finance Council are likely to play in determining the legislative outcome of his budget requests. To this extent the Finance Council operates to weaken the control of the Governor over budget preparation. Moreover, it approves rules and regulations of the Department of Administration and can hear and decide appeals by any state agency from decisions of the executive director of the Department of Administration.

The Governor can veto all or any item of an appropriation bill, though this action is not often taken. Once funds are appropriated by the Legislature, the Governor has limited control. If, in the opinion of the executive director and budget director, the statutorily prescribed conditions are met, the Finance Council may establish a system of allotments. Under this system the agency's appropriations would be divided into monthly, quarterly, semiannual, or annual allotments and could be spent only in the amounts allotted. The allotment system has been required of only one small agency.

Law Enforcement, Executive Clemency, and the National Guard

The Governor helps enforce the laws by extraditing criminals and by the offering of rewards. The power of extradition is derived in part from the United States Constitution, which says: "A person charged in any state with treason, felony or other crime, who shall flee from justice, and be found in another state, shall on demand of the executive authority of the state from which he fled, be delivered up to be removed to the state having jurisdiction of the crime." This authorization of extradition is implemented by the Kansas Uniform Criminal Extradition Act of 1937,[2] which superseded earlier laws dating back to territorial statutes. Under this act the Kansas Governor is given the duty of having "arrested and delivered up to the executive authority of any other state of the United States any person charged in that state with treason, felony, or other crime, who has fled from justice and is found in this state." In a like manner the Governor, upon request of the prosecuting attorney involved, is empowered to requisition from the executive authority of any other state the return of a fugitive from this state. In doing so he issues a warrant to some agent, commanding him to receive the fugitive and convey him to the proper officer of the county in which the crime was committed.

Offering of rewards is a second way in which the Governor aids law-enforcement. The statutes on rewards are ambiguous. One statute permits him to offer a reward not exceeding five hundred dollars for apprehension and delivery of any escaped criminal "charged with a

2. K.S.A., 62-727 to 757.

capital offense, or with a felony." A second statute allows him to offer a reward up to three hundred dollars for apprehension and delivery of an escapee "charged with or convicted of a felony."

The Governor is authorized to employ special attorneys with the powers of assistant attorneys general to make investigations to insure that the criminal laws of the state are enforced. Instead of employing his own attorneys, the Governor may request the Attorney General to prosecute in all criminal or civil matters relating to his office.

According to the state Constitution, "the pardoning power shall be vested in the governor, under regulations and restrictions prescribed by law." The Legislature has enacted some regulations and restrictions upon the Governor's pardoning power. He may pardon,[3] or commute the sentence of any person convicted for any offense against a state law, provided that he notify the trial judge and prosecuting attorney of the county in which the conviction was had, and provided that he give thirty days' notice in the official county paper. Upon granting a pardon, or commutation, he must certify his action to the clerk of the district court in which the conviction was had.

In 1957 the Legislature, in one of its several penal reform measures, provided for the creation of the State Board of Probation and Parole to consider automatically the paroling of those imprisoned at our three penal institutions, the Penitentiary, Reformatory, or Women's Farm. Two years later the Attorney General initiated court action to question the power of the Governor to grant paroles. Previously Governors had granted paroles as an appropriate exercise of their power to pardon. The district court ruled that the Governor could not grant paroles in view of the new broader statute concerning the powers of the parole board. Before the case was appealed, a new Governor took office (interestingly, the new Governor was the previous Attorney General who had begun the action), and the practice of granting paroles was discontinued. This did not affect the constitutional power of the Governor to grant pardons.

Pardons must be in writing and attested by the Great Seal of the state. Statutory restrictions on commutations exist and vary with the

---

3. A pardon is a complete release from the legal penalties for an offense; a parole is a conditional and revocable release from an unexpired sentence; and a commutation is a reduction of a sentence or penalty.

penalty. A sentence of capital punishment may be reduced to life imprisonment or to a term of not less than ten years at hard labor, while any sentence for imprisonment, with or without hard labor, may be shortened. A fine may be reduced. To each regular session of the Legislature the Governor must communicate a list of all persons pardoned in the preceding year. In the two-year period from January 1, 1966, to January 1, 1968, the Governor issued 42 pardons or commutations of sentences.

The Kansas Constitution provides for a militia which, in general, includes all able-bodied male citizens between the ages of twenty-one and forty-five years. But in 1885, after the Civil War and skirmishes with Indians were over and the need for an active militia had passed, the Legislature established two classes in the militia, the Kansas National Guard and the Kansas Reserve Militia. Only the former functions today. Under the Constitution, the Governor is commander-in-chief and appoints the Adjutant General as chief-of-staff, who administers the National Guard.

The National Guard has an annual encampment, and all members, both enlisted men and officers, are required to attend. The Governor, as commander-in-chief, has the power to order the National Guard into active service "in cases of breaches of the peace, tumult, riot, or resistance to process in this state, or imminent danger thereof." Any sheriff or mayor may request the commander-in-chief to call out the guard.

Other Duties

Interstate agreements. As chief executive, the Kansas Governor represents his state in the adoption of interstate agreements. Such compacts cover three areas in particular: rivers (for an equitable distribution of water for use in the Republican River basin and in the Arkansas River basin and for automatic change of the state boundary line as the Missouri River changes its course), oil and gas conservation, and interstate crime control. The nature of these agreements is discussed in greater detail in the chapter on intergovernmental relations. Also, the Governor represents the state in all other official business with other states.

Proclamations. Normally, when a third-class city attains a population of over 2,000 inhabitants, the Governor declares by public proclamation such city to be a second-class city; similarly, when a second-class city attains a population of over 15,000 inhabitants, he declares by public proclamation such city to be a first-class city.[4] By statute he is "authorized and directed" to issue annual proclamations calling for the display of the flag on and the observance of the following days: Arbor Day, the last Friday in March; Mother's Day, the second Sunday in May; Flag Day, June 14; and General Pulaski's Memorial Day, October 11. Occasionally a law is passed which permits him to issue an executive order in the form of a proclamation. He did this in 1946 to dissolve the state Council of Defense, in 1950 to reestablish it, and in 1949 to declare that the tax and licensing provisions of the Liquor Control Act were in effect. Beyond these required proclamations the Kansas chief executive issues frequent proclamations to designate a certain day, week, or month as a special occasion. Examples of this are Newspaperboy Day, Music Week, and Dairy Month. Over a period of years, proclamations were issued at the rate of about forty-five a year.

Ex Officio Duties. Not only does the Governor have sole responsibility for distinct portions of the state administration, but also, through serving ex officio on boards, he shares responsibility for other portions with other state executive officers. He is an ex officio member of six boards: (1) State Finance Council; (2) State Highway Patrol Pension Board, which controls the Highway Patrol pension fund; (3) State Board of Canvassers, which canvasses the results of state general elections and in case of a tie vote for any state officer, except Governor or Lieutenant Governor, determines by lot which of two candidates shall be elected; (4) Executive Council, which has charge of the care and management of the Statehouse and grounds, and designates the official state paper; (5) Kansas Commission of Interstate Cooperation, which works for cooperation with other states; and (6) Kansas Armory Board, which obtains and equips sites for armory purposes. The functions of some of these boards are presented in greater detail in other chapters.

Miscellaneous. The Governor has various miscellaneous powers because of his position as chief executive. He is authorized to transact all state business with the national government. Any rule promulgated by the Port of Entry Board may be appealed to the Governor by the

4. In 1953 the Legislature allowed cities to stay in their class even if they exceeded the minimum population for the next class.

Highway Commission, or its vehicle department, the Corporation Commission, or the director of revenue; and the governor's decision is final.

Legislative Powers

An organizational chart of Kansas state government suggests that there is a strict separation of power between the chief executive and the Legislature. However this is not so, for the Governor has certain legislative duties which stem from the Constitution and the statutes, and in addition he offers the Legislature political leadership in matters of policy formulation. These duties have been discussed in previous chapters.

The number of bills frequently submitted to the Governor in the last several "working" days limits the consideration which can be given to each bill. On occasion, the State Printer gets so far behind that the Governor has had "to stop his clock" in order to have an opportunity merely to receive the engrossed bills. With over half of the bills being submitted during the last few days, this problem of the end-of-the-session rush is quite serious.

No matter what action the Governor takes, he must keep a record of the number and title of every act and joint resolution presented to him for his approval; this record shows the date of receipt and the date of approval or the date of return with objection to the Legislature. All acts and joint resolutions which become laws, including those becoming laws without the signature of the Governor, are required to be deposited by him in the office of the Secretary of State without delay.

As a rule the Governor vetoes few bills. In the five regular legislative sessions ending in 1955, when the Governor and the majority of the Legislature were of the same political party, the Governor vetoed sixteen bills and none of the vetoes was overriden. In two regular sessions, a budget and a special session (1955-1959) Governor George Docking, a Democrat, vetoed thirty-six bills passed by a Republican-dominated legislature. Only one became law despite his veto. The use of the veto for the last seventeen years is shown in Table 15 below.

The use made of the veto power does not tell the full story. The Governor can send word to the Senate or the House of Representatives that he will veto a bill if it is passed; this action can be just as effective in killing a bill as the actual veto. This threat of veto is related to the

TABLE 15

Use of Veto by Governor During Legislative Sessions, 1951-1968

Sessions	Veto General Law	Veto Local Law	Number Laws with Items Vetoed	Total	Number of Laws Enacted
1951	2	0	1	3	527
1953	1	0	1	2	478
1955	3	1	0	4	445
1956 (Budget)	0	0	1	1	63
1957	11	0	1	12	542
1958 (Budget)	6*	0	0	6	67
1958 (Special)	2	0	0	2	37
1959	13	1	2	16	415
1961	4	0	1	5	473
1962 (Budget)	0	0	0	0	47
1963	6	0	0	6	516
1964 (Budget)	0	0	1	1	45
1964 (Special)	0	0	0	0	7
1965	3	0	0	3	564
1966 (Budget)	0	0	0	0	47
1966 (Special)	0	0	0	0	17
1967	19	0	3	22	519
1968	14	4	1	19	412

* Includes 4 pocket vetoes.
Source: *Session Laws.*

whole question of the Governor's political and nonstatutory leadership of the Legislature.

Extralegal Powers

The Governor has not only constitutional and statutory powers, but also certain powers and duties arising extralegally. Perhaps these powers better explain the place of the Governor in Kansas than do his legal powers; yet it is very difficult to enumerate just what these powers are. Probably the main source of the Governor's extralegal powers is his position as nominal head of his political party.

Political Leadership

As was the case with his extralegal powers over state administration, the Governor's political leadership of the Legislature stems from his position as titular head of his political party. Much of his influence arises from the fact that the Legislature ordinarily elects as its leaders men who are friendly to the Governor and his legislative program. During some sessions when the Governor and the legislative majority are of the same party, the Governor has held daily conferences with the Speaker of the House, the House majority floor leader, the president of the Senate (Lieutenant Governor), and the president pro tem of the Senate. Sometimes the state chairman of the party has met with them. This group, with the Governor acting as chairman, may make the "party" decisions on such matters as what bills to push and what bills to kill. Although decisions of this group are not recorded and documented, probably the vast majority of its decisions are accepted by most of the members of the majority party of the Legislature.

Acting on his own, the Governor has certain other means of leadership. A Representative brings a proposed bill to him to ask whether or not it should be introduced. In debate, when a Senator asks of another Senator, "Does your amendment come from the second floor?" he inquires whether the amendment might have been suggested by the Governor, whose office is on the second floor of the Statehouse. Delegations call on the Governor to gain his support for some piece of legislation; citizens write him about various bills. The chief executive has no vote in the Legislature, but persons interested in particular legislation recognize his position of leadership. Newspapers recognize this position, too, for editorially they praise him for his leadership or condemn him for lack of it. Even though the state Constitution provides that "the legislative power of this state shall be vested in a House of Representatives and Senate," as things actually operate, the Governor holds a key spot in the legislative process considerably beyond that assigned him under the formal constitutional division of powers.

Administrative officers, usually having received their appointments from the Governor, consult him on matters of policy; yet he cannot legally force them to do so. Even though the Governor does not, in most cases, have the power to remove, he exercises considerably more administrative supervision than one would think by merely reading the statutes. He can use political pressure to supervise other elected executive officers.

Another source of the Governor's nonstatutory power is the prestige which his office holds in the eyes of the people of the state. School children, and adults, too, visiting the Statehouse want to see the Governor, or at least to go into his office. He is invited to speak at conventions, celebrations, commencements, and the like; he has to turn down most invitations, but even so he may be away from his office two or three days a week in the spring when commencements and conventions are especially frequent. When people want something done by the state government they often write him, whether concerning a parole for a relative, a job with the state, a son wanting to enter the state medical school, or some other such subject. In a real sense, in the minds of the people, the Governor is the head of the state government.

7 | *Administrative Organization*

While the Constitution establishes the broad outlines for the government of Kansas, it leaves largely to the Legislature the responsibility for organizing the various branches of state government. The management and direction of the administrative branch is a task shared by many. As new functions have been assumed by the state, new offices and agencies have been established. The establishment of new agencies and the extension of the work of others have resulted in overlapping, duplication, and complicated relationships among various agencies and departments. It is to these broad considerations of organization that this chapter is devoted.

The Present Organization

An analysis of the present administrative organization of the state reveals a large number of separate agencies, most of them headed by a board or commission, and a group of independently elected officials charged with administrative functions. The chart on the end sheets of this book shows these numerous agencies, with the list on the following page indicating the origin and method of selection of the governing body of each agency. A number of these agencies have subordinate divisions which by some definition could be listed separately, adding further to the list. This would be particularly true of the educational

TABLE 16

Agencies of Kansas State Government by Function, Origin, Year of Establishment, and Method of Selection: 1968[a]

Office or Agency	Origin	Year Estab.	E	G	GS	Ex	Other
I. *General Government*							
Administration, Director, Department of	New Agency	1953	1				
Attorney General	Constitution	1861	1				
Auditor, State	Constitution	1861	1				
Canvassers, Board of	Constitution	1861				5	
Capitol Area Planning Commission	New Agency	1965		5		3	1
Civil Rights Commission	New Agency	1953		5			
Civil Service Board	Reconstituted Agency	1953			3		
Court Reporters, Board of Examiners of	New Agency	1941					5[e]
Economic Analysis, Council for	New Agency	1963		2		1	
Economic Analysis, Director, Office of	New Agency	1963		1			
Economic Development Commission	Reconstituted Agency	1963		9			
Election Commissioners (County)	Reconstituted Agency	1947		4[d]			
Executive Council	New Agency	1879			6		
Finance Council, State	New Agency	1953			6		
Governor	Constitution	1861	1				
Interstate Cooperation Commission	New Agency	1941			15		
Judges' Retirement Board	New Agency	1953		2	3		
Judicial Administrator	New Agency	1965				1	
Judicial Council	New Agency	1927			2		7[e]
Legislative Council	New Agency	1933			2		25[f]
Legislature	Constitution	1861	165				
Lieutenant Governor	Constitution	1861	1				
Motor Vehicle Reciprocity Commission	New Agency	1951			7		
Municipal Accounting Board	New Agency	1938		6	1		
Printer, State	Constitution	1904	1				
Property Valuation, Director, Dept. of	Reconstituted Agency	1957		1			
Records Board	New Agency	1945			3		

TABLE 16 (continued)

Office or Agency	Origin	Year Estab.	E	G	GS	Ex	Other
Revenue, Director, Dept. of	Reconstituted Agency	1957		1			
Revisor of Statutes	New Office	1929					1
Secretary of State	Constitution	1861	1				
State Purchases, Committee on	New Agency	1953		1	2		
Supreme Court	Reconstituted Agency	1861					7
Supreme Court Commissioner	New Agency	1963					2
Supreme Court Nominating Commission	New Agency	1959		5			6
Surety Bonds Committee	New Agency	1965				3	
Tax Appeals, Board of	Reconstituted Agency	1957			3		
Treasurer, State	Constitution	1861	1				
Treasury Examiners, Board of	Reconstituted Agency	1933				3	
Veterans Commission	New Agency	1953			3		
II. Protection to Persons and Property							
Abstractors Bd. of Examiners ..	New Agency	1941		3			
Accountancy, State Board of	New Agency	1951		5			
Adjutant General	Statute	1861			1		
Alcoholic Bev. Con., Bd. of Review	New Agency	1949		3			
Alcoholic Bev. Con., Director ..	New Office	1949		1			
Architects, Reg. and Ex. Bd. for	New Agency	1949		5			
Armory Board	Repl. Ks. Armory Bd.	1947		6	3		
Athletic Commission	New Agency	1925			3		
Bank Commissioner	Reconstituted Office	1947			1		
Banking Board	Reconstituted Agency	1961		9			
Basic Science Examiners, Board of	Reconstituted Agency	1957		5			
Brand Commissioner	Reconstituted Agency	1947		1			
Charter Board	New Agency	1898			3		
Coal Mine Examiners, Board of	Repl. Bd. Mining Ex.	1955					3g
Consumer Credit Commissioner	New Agency	1955		1			
Corporation Commission	Consolidating Agency	1933		3			
Credit Union Council	New Agency	1968		7			
Engineering Examiners, Board of	Reconstituted Agency	1947		5			
Fire Marshal	Reconstituted Office	1939		1			
Food Service and Lodging Bd.	Reconstituted Agency	1965		6			

TABLE 16 (continued)

Office or Agency	Origin	Year Estab.	E	G	GS	Ex	Other
Hearing Aid Dispensers, Bd. of Ex. of	New Agency	1968		5			
Highway Patrol, Superintendent of	New Office	1937		1			
Insurance, Commissioner of	New Office	1927	1				
Investigation, Director, Bureau of	New Office	1939					1[h]
Judge Advocate General	Statute	1921					1[i]
Labor Commissioner	Reconstituted Office	1949			1		
Landscape Architects, Bd. for Reg. & Ex.	New Agency	1968		3			
Law Examiners, Board of	New Agency	1903					5[e]
Livestock Sanitary Commissioner	Reconstituted Office	1905		1			
Military Board	New Agency	1901		2		2	3
Real Estate Commission	Reconstituted Agency	1954		5			
Safety Council	New Agency	1939				12	
Savings and Loan Board	Repl. Bldg. and Ln. Bd.	1943		5			
Savings and Loan Commissioner	Repl. Bldg. & Ln. Com.	1943		1			
Veterinary Examiners, Board of	Reconstituted Agency	1959		5			
Workmen's Compensation Dir.	Reconstituted Agency	1961		1			
III. *Highway and Transportation*							
Highway Commission	Reconstituted Agency	1927		6			
Port of Entry Board	New Agency	1933				3	
Turnpike Authority	New Agency	1953		2		3	
IV. *Natural Resources*							
Agriculture, Board of	Reconstituted Agency	1917					12[j]
Forestry, Fish and Game Com.	Repl. F.F. & G. Com.	1961			5		
Grain Adv. Commission	New Agency	1953			5		
Grain Inspector	Reconstituted Office	1907			1		
Horticultural Society	New Agency	1869					
Livestock Association	New Agency	1943					
Livestock Commission	New Agency	1943		6	1		
Mined Land Conservation & Recl. Bd.	New Agency	1968				1	10
Nuclear Energy Advisory Council	New Agency	1963		11			
Park and Resources Authority	New Agency	1955		5	4		

TABLE 16 (continued)

Office or Agency	Origin	Year Estab.	Method of Selection[†]				
			E	G	GS	Ex	Other
Poultry Improvement Association, Kansas	New Agency	1949					x[k]
Soil Conservation Committee	Reconstituted Agency	1951				2	7[l]
Water Resources Board	New Agency	1955			7		
Wheat Commission, Kansas	New Agency	1957		7			
V. Health							
Barber Examiners, Board of	Reconstituted Agency	1939		3			
Cosmotologists, Board of Reg. for	Reconstituted Agency	1961		3			
Dental Board	Reconstituted Agency	1943		3			
Embalming, Board of	New Agency	1907		3			
Healing Arts, State Board of	Reconstituted Agency	1957			11		
Health, Board of	Reconstituted Agency	1951			10		
Mental Retardation, Council on	New Agency	1968					12
Nurse Registration, Board of	Reconstituted Agency	1949		5			
Optometry Examiners, Board of	Reconstituted Agency	1923		3			
Pharmacy, Board of	Reconstituted Agency	1953		5			
Physical Therapists, State Exam. Com. for	New Agency	1963		3			2[m]
Podiatry, Boards of Examiners	New Agency	1927		1		1	1[m]
Psychologists, State Bd. of Exam. of	New Agency	1967		7			
Recreation, Joint Council on	New Agency	1965		7	8		
VI. Correction							
Penal Institutions, State Director of	Reconstituted Agency	1957			1		
Probation and Parole, State Board of	New Agency	1957			3		
VII. Education							
Academy of Science	New Agency	1868					
Antiquities Commission	New Agency	1967			5		
Cultural Arts Commission	New Agency	1965		12			
Education, Board of	Constitution	1966	10				1
Education, Commissioner of	Constitution	1966					
Higher Education Facilities Commission	New Agency	1965		5			
Historical Society	New Agency	1879					
Librarian, State	Reconstituted Office	1963				1	

TABLE 16 (concluded)

Office or Agency	Origin	Year Estab.	E	G	GS	Ex	Other
Library Advisory Com., State	Reconstituted Agency	1963		6	1		
Regents, Board of	New Agency	1925			9		
Research Foundation	New Agency	1963		6	6		
School Fund Commissioners, Board of	New Agency	1879			3		
VIII. Public Welfare							
Alcoholism, Commission on	New Agency	1953		5			
Co-ordination Council for the Blind	New Agency	1957					8
Crippled Children Commission	New Agency	1931		5			
Social Welfare, Board of	New Agency	1939			3		
IX. Miscellaneous							
American Legion[k]	New Agency	1919					
American Legion Auxiliary[k]	New Agency	1920					
Disabled American Veterans[k]	New Agency	1953					
Fair Managers, Board of	Reconstituted Agency	1953				13[n]	
Grand Army of the Republic[k]	New Agency	1882					
Highway Patrol Pension Board	New Agency	1947				2	1[o]
League of Kansas Municipalities[k]	Revised Agency	1953					
Pension Bd., Bureau of Investigation	New Agency	1951				2	1
Public Employees Retirement Board	New Agency	1961		7			
School Retirement Board	New Agency	1941		4	2		
United Spanish War Veterans[k]	New Agency	1915					
Veterans of Foreign Wars[k]	New Agency	1953					

a This table differs substantially from the table on p. 00, based on the McKay-Hallman study. Primarily the difference in number is explained by the fact that the previous study listed certain semi-autonomous institutions separately.

b E=Elected; G=Appointed by Governor; GS=Appointed by Governor with consent of the Senate; Ex=Ex officio.

c Appointed by the Supreme Court.

d A commissioner is appointed for each county over 130,000 population.

e Appointed by Chief Justice of the Supreme Court.

f Ten Senators by the president of the Senate; fifteen Representatives by the Speaker of the House.

g Appointed by the Labor Commissioner.

h Appointed by the Attorney General.

(Continued on p. 116.)

and welfare institutions. An effort has been made to classify the agencies according to functions. However, the assignment of particular functions is in some instances open to question.

In addition to the large number of full-time and part-time boards and commissions, the Legislature has shown a desire to use the device of ex officio boards. These have added even further to the number of separate agencies with administrative responsibilities.

With significant exceptions, the general pattern has been to have state agencies presided over by boards or commissions. Normally the board or commission is appointed by the Governor. In turn it appoints a secretary or executive director to supervise the day-to-day operation of the agency in conformance with the policies which it determines. There are wide differences within the state organization as to how this system actually operates. The interest, time, and experience of the Governor, the area of operations, the immediate past history of the agency board personnel, and the apparent interest of the public in the function are all factors which will influence how much attention the Governor will give the agency and its governing body. Similarly, the board members may, for a wide variety of reasons including many of the above, be active or they may just let the secretary have a free hand in running the agency. The experience, knowledge, philosophy, and popularity of the board secretary or director will greatly affect the way the agency is administered and operated. The organization chart in the front of this book on the printed end sheets shows only the several general formal patterns of relationships between the Governor, board, and secretary. No attempt is made to show the many different patterns of relationships which grow out of the widely differing operating conditions and personal interrelationships.

---

i Appointed by the Adjutant General.

j Agricultural delegates elect the Board.

k Officially recognized agency.

l One appointed by U.S. Sec'y of Agric.; one, by Kansas State Bd. of Agric.; five elected by Soil Conserv. Dist. Supervisors.

m Bd. of Med. Reg. and Exam. selects.

n Bd. of Agric. and the Sec'y of the Bd.

o Elected by members of the Highway Patrol.

Sources: *K.S.A.*

Though the number of agencies headed by boards and commissions have increased more rapidly than those headed by single administrators, there has been an increase in the number of single-headed agencies. The increase in such agencies is shown in the table below.

In addition to the elected administrative officials, whose offices are discussed below, there are a limited number of agencies headed by a single executive. The Department of Administration and the Adjutant General are staff agencies so organized, while the Labor Department and the office of Alcoholic Beverage Control are illustrative of the line departments with single heads.

Elected State Officials

The elected state officials are part of the administrative organization of the state and are shown in the previous chart and included in the tables. These officials—the Attorney General, Secretary of State, State Printer, Commissioner of Insurance, Auditor, and Treasurer—are engaged in administrative functions not unlike the work performed in other agencies in state government. They are elected by the voters and are directly responsible to them. This fact gives them a special status

TABLE 17

Number of State Administrative Agencies for Selected Years:
By Type of Organization

| | | Boards and Commissions* | | | |
| | | Chiefly or | Appointed | | |
Year	Single Administrator	Exclusively Ex Officio	Part-Time	Full-Time	Total
1865	10	5	6	0	21
1885	19	8	8	1	36
1905	24	12	18	1	55
1925	21	14	22	4	61
1950	27	20	45	3	95
1968*	30	21	59	2	112

* The Board of Education is not included in this tabulation since it is elected. The data for 1968 was computed on a basis somewhat different from that of the McKay-Hallman study.

Source: McKay and Hallman, *State Governmental Organization in Kansas* (Lawrence: Bureau of Governmental Research, Univ. of Kansas, 1950), p. 15; *K.S.A.*

and degree of independence of the Governor not generally characteristic of other state administrators.

Functions of most of these state administrative executive officials are discussed in other appropriate chapters, but a few have such general administrative responsibilities that their functions will be discussed here.

The Attorney General

"Next to the Governor of the state, the Attorney General is probably the officer with the greatest power and authority of any officer under our constitution."[1] This arises from the multiplicity of his duties at a state and local level.

The Attorney General represents the state in all cases which come before the State Supreme Court and may be required by the Governor or the Legislature to prosecute or defend the state in the courts of various other states or in the federal courts. He is required to advise and to assist all other state officers in all civil matters. In a number of agencies there are assistant attorneys general who do legal work for these departments. For example, in the act creating the Department of Administration, the Attorney General was authorized to appoint an assistant attorney general who is the attorney for the department and who receives such compensation as is fixed by the attorney general with the approval of the executive director of the Department of Administration. In addition to this the Attorney General is required to render advice and assistance to all of the 105 county attorneys and may be asked to give opinions interpreting various provisions of the statutes.

The Attorney General is an important law-enforcement official. While the director of the Alcoholic Beverage Control Board is primarily charged with the enforcement of the provisions of the Alcoholic Beverage Control Act, the county attorneys and the Attorney General are given duties in connection with the enforcement of this act. In the event of any failure or alleged failure by a county attorney to enforce criminal laws locally, including the alcoholic beverage control law, the Attorney General may on his own action supersede the county attorney in the enforcement of such laws.

---

1. Harold R. Fatzer, "The Attorney General," *Your Government* (Lawrence: Governmental Research Center, Univ. of Kansas), V (1949), 1, p. 4.

The Attorney General is also charged with the prosecution of all ouster suits against public officials alleged to be guilty of not properly performing the duties of their office. He represents the Governor of the state in all procedures for the extradition of fugitives from justice. The Attorney General exercises supervision over the Kansas Bureau of Investigation.

Whenever a resident of Kansas dies without a will and without any known heirs, the Attorney General is required to represent the state of Kansas in the procedures before the probate court, in order to conserve the estate for the benefit of the state permanent school fund. The Attorney General is also required to pass on the validity of all municipal bonds issued in the state of Kansas and upon the validity of all surety bonds required of various state officers and employees.

In addition to these other duties, the Attorney General is also a member of the State Executive Council, the State School Fund Commission, the State Charter Board, the State Printing Commission, the State Board of Canvassers, the Arkansas River Compact Commission, the State Records Board, and the Missouri Boundary Commission for the State of Kansas.

In addition to the assistants with responsibilities for specific departments, there are several assistants employed within the immediate office of the Attorney General. Effective in January, 1969, the Attorney General will receive a salary of $17,500 a year for his services to the state.

The Secretary of State

The Secretary of State has been described as the chief housekeeper of state government.[2] He is custodian of various important state papers and performs numerous ministerial tasks which are important for the successful administration of the affairs of the state. He is responsible for publishing the *Kansas Directory; Election Statistics; Legislative Directory; Directory of County Officers of Kansas; Kansas Facts; Summary of Kansas Primary Election Laws; Trademarks and Service Marks;* and *Constitution of the State of Kansas with Amendments.* In addition the Secretary of State receives from state agencies their bi-

2. Vern H. Schneider, "The Secretary of the State," *Your Government* (Lawrence: Governmental Research Center, Univ. of Kansas), IV (1948), 7, p. 4.

ennial reports and is charged with publishing a consolidated biennial report. These consolidated reports contain much information about the operations of the agencies, their goals, and their problems.

Particularly important is the function of the Secretary of State as an administrator of election laws. He receives the filings of various candidates and notifies the county clerks of these filings for district, state, and national offices. He receives the abstract of the votes cast for such offices in each of the counties. As a member of the State Board of Canvassers, he takes part in the counting of the election returns from the various counties and declares the successful persons elected. He transmits to each house of the Legislature a list of the members officially elected.

Legislative counsels and agents register with the Secretary of State. He is the custodian of all enrolled bills and resolutions. When the Legislature adjourns, the Secretary of State supervises the publication of session laws and joint resolutions and distributes copies of the laws to the officials entitled to receive copies.

The Secretary of State is a member of the Executive Council, the Charter Board, and the State Printing Commission. The term of this office is only two years, like the term of the other elected state officials. Since 1933, only four persons have held this office. The Secretary of State receives $12,650 per year for his services.

State Printer

In only one other state (Nevada) is the State Printer elected. As an elected state official, in Kansas, the State Printer is responsible for doing all of the printing for the state. This includes all official reports, forms, statute books, catalogues, and various publications requested by the several state departments, boards, and commissions. Under certain circumstances, the printing of state agencies may be done by private printers on contract or by state agencies with duplicating facilities. The salary of the State Printer, beginning in January, 1969, is set at $12,650 per annum.

Lieutenant Governor

Though the Lieutenant Governor's duties are primarily legislative, he does have some limited executive duties. In Kansas, the Lieutenant Governor is chairman of the Committee on Interstate Co-operation and is a member of the Finance Council in addition to being the presiding officer of the Senate and chairman of the Legislative Council. The chief importance of the office comes from the fact that the Lieutenant Governor may become Governor of the state, as has happened in Kansas on three occasions. Contrary to the practice of some other states, the Supreme Court of Kansas has held that the mere absence of the Governor from the state does not entitle the Lieutenant Governor to act as Governor. The Lieutenant Governor, as the President of the Senate, becomes Governor in the case of the death, impeachment, resignation, removal, or other disability of the Governor. In case of the Lieutenant Governor's becoming Governor and then vacating the office, the President pro tem of the Senate assumes the office of Governor. Should the President pro tem of the Senate not be able to serve, the Speaker of the House of Representatives serves as Governor. The matter of the continuity of government was the subject of a constitutional amendment approved by the voters in 1960. The amendment became the basis of legislative action in 1961 when the Secretary of State, the Attorney General, the Chancellor of the University, and the President of Kansas State University were designated in that order as successors to the office of Governor in addition to those named above. Beginning in 1969 the Lieutenant Governor receives $8,000 a year plus $25 a calendar day for each regular or special session within specified maximums.

Problems of State Administrative Organization

Many of the present problems of state arise from the growth of state government during the century of its existence. The accompanying chart shows the relatively simple outline of administrative agencies in 1865. One appreciates the substantial growth of state agencies when he compares this chart with the earlier one.

The accompanying table shows the growth of agencies from 26 in 1865 to 142 in 1950. Were a tabulation made of the present number of agencies on the basis used in the table, the number would be in excess of 150. The classification of agencies by major function at various intervals suggests the changing nature of state government. It has changed from one primarily regulatory in nature to one which furnishes a positive program of service to the people.

The number of separate agencies alone presents problems of coordination. The organization chart tends to oversimplify complicated relationships which exist among the Governor, the boards or commissions, their executive secretaries, the Legislature, and affected interest groups. The administrative structure largely just grew over the century, with limited attention to any general pattern or design. The various parts of Kansas state government have mostly existed as semi-independent agencies, operating with limited knowledge of the operation and functions of the other agencies.

This type of organization fitted nicely into the pattern of state government. The new agencies were normally created as the result of some need, which a portion of the citizens of the state had been able to persuade the Legislature actually existed. The special groups were anxious to help to see that "their" agency functioned properly and were anxious to have persons sympathetic to their views in charge of the administration. To the extent that such agencies could be kept free

TABLE 18

Number of Offices, Agencies, Departments, Ex Officio Boards, and Institutions* in Kansas by Functional Groups for Selected Years

	1865	1885	1905	1925	1950
I. General Government	11	17	22	20	35
II. Protection to Persons and Property	4	7	13	10	26
III. Highways and Transportation	0	0	0	2	2
IV. Natural Resources	1	7	12	16	17
V. Health	0	0	5	10	11
VI. Hospitals and Institutions for the Handicapped	0	5	6	8	9
VII. Correction	1	2	5	6	6
VIII. Education	7	8	15	17	14
IX. Public Welfare	0	1	4	5	7
X. Miscellaneous	2	2	1	7	15
TOTAL	26	49	83	101	142

* The number used in the McKay and Hallman study cited in the table included the major institutions as separate agencies. In the list of agencies appearing earlier and in the organization chart such institutions are not shown separate from the agency of which they are a part.

Source: McKay and Hallman, *State Governmental Organization in Kansas, 1865-1950* (Lawrence: Bureau of Government Research, Univ. of Kansas, 1950), p. 14.

ORGANIZATION OF KANSAS STATE GOVERNMENT
January 1, 1865

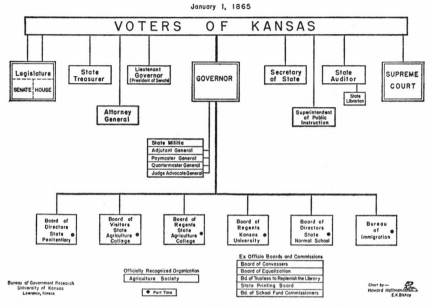

of gubernatorial control, the special groups had little to fear from even an unsympathetic governor. In a large measure these agencies had their own special funds and, for the most part, their own personnel and special support.

The use of boards and commissions was adapted to this type of organization. Boards and commissions seemed desirable as a means of representing various parts of the state and various interest groups. It was assumed that the wisdom of three or five commissioners would be greater than that of a single administrator. In a board type of organization, each of the two political parties could be given some representation. With this system it was possible to have a kind of "check" within each agency. Such a type of organization was consistent and was further encouraged by the general distrust of the executive which may be traced back to colonial times.

The use of this type of organization was further encouraged by efforts to compartmentalize state government and to have nonpartisan administration of certain segments of the state's operations. For example, the professional social-welfare worker and the professional educator and, in a large measure, the citizens supporting each of these functions will want the administration of the program to be isolated from partisan politics. If these principles are valid for these areas, can they not with equal validity be extended to others? Thus it is that the pressures are strong for state government to be little more than a collection of semi-independent agencies.

This type of organization was more tolerable when the functions of state government were few and relatively simple. As, however, more and more services to the people of the state have come to be expected and the state government has assumed many regulatory activities, this type of organization has presented more problems and difficulties.

Within the state there are two channels through which greater coordination can be achieved—the Governor and the Legislature. Yet significant problems develop when either of these channels is tried.

In many ways the Governor, as the chief executive of the state, is the most likely avenue through which the agencies can be integrated. It is he who normally appoints the members of the boards and commissions. Yet as we have seen in chapter 6, the Governor is somewhat limited in his removal power, and since many of the board members serve longer than the Governor's two-year term, often not until the Governor's second term will he have appointed a majority of the members of the various boards and commissions. With respect to the elected state officials, the Governor does not have even these powers to use in coordinating their activities.

Further, the Governor is limited in the extent to which he can coordinate and direct the activities of the state agencies by the many demands on his time and energies and by the two-year term, with its accompanying limit on his experience and need for political "fence-mending." Frequently the Governor is limited by his own political philosophy, for he may believe that the executive is but one of three coordinate branches of government and should have a limited leadership role.

The Legislature, by its control over the finances of agencies, can also do much coordination and supervision. Through the device of earmarking special funds, the Legislature has sought to simplify its problem and actually to encourage the agencies in their sense of autonomy. The committee organization of the Legislature frequently makes it more difficult for the Legislature to be the coordinating device. The special interests that support particular agencies are active in the Legislature and serve to make legislative efforts at coordination more difficult.

The administrative reorganization of 1953 was an interesting effort to enhance the coordinating powers of both the Governor and the Legislature. The difficulties of the current efforts at administrative organization can be understood only if this history of the independence of agencies is understood.

State Administrative Reorganizations

There have been two broad moves for administrative reorganization of state government in the last fifty years. Though there were earlier efforts at state reorganization in Ohio and New York, in 1917 Illinois led the way with a major state reorganization. These and the subsequent wave of state reorganizations emphasized the integration of various state departments and agencies and a reduction in their number. The goal was to reorganize the agencies on a functional basis, each of the major functions of state government being assigned to one department. As a further feature of this reorganization, each of these departments was to be headed by a single executive appointed by the Governor. A number of states were affected by these ideas of administrative reorganization. Kansas was little affected by them, except possibly in the gradual increase in the number of agencies placed under the supervision of single individuals instead of boards or commissions.

In the next thirty years there were numerous instances of minor administrative reorganizations in Kansas, some of which, according to one study, were due to political changes in the office of Governor and efforts to gain quicker control over the appointments which the Governor makes.[3]

In March, 1950, in response to the nation-wide publicity and popularity which had been generated by the Commission on Reorganization of the Executive Branch of the U.S. government, headed by former President Hoover, Governor Carlson appointed the Commission on

---

3. Edwin O. Stene, "Planning and Politics of State Reorganization in Kansas," *Southwestern Social Science Quarterly*, XX (1939), No. 2, pp. 150-64.

State Administration Organization. The Commission, popularly known as the "Little Hoover Commission," held a number of meetings and was assisted by numerous agencies, but was without substantial funds and staff. The Commission hurried its deliberations in order to make a report to the 1951 Legislature.

The Kansas Little Hoover Commission was guided largely by the principles of administrative reorganization which had been largely accepted by other states in the reorganization of state government.[4]

Despite the existence in Kansas of numerous exceptions to the broad principles of organization it accepted, the Commission made a limited number of recommendations. It made specific recommendations for the consolidation of the Joint Merit System Council and the Civil Service Department. The Commission's effectiveness was influenced by the time limit imposed by its desire to have a report ready for the 1951 Legislature and by the lack of appropriations. It had been unable to make a comprehensive survey, and recommended to the Legislature that a study group be appointed with adequate appropriations. This last recommendation was not adopted.

The most important contribution of the Commission was the stimulus for a broad change in the financial structure of the state. Though the subject had been studied several times, the attention of the Commission to the coordination of staff services led to the establishment of the Department of Administration. The changes finally incorporated into the new financial organization also led to a change of auditing procedures and a post audit of expenditures independent of the executive. These changes in financial procedures will be discussed in a later chapter.

When the Legislature received the report of the Little Hoover Commission concerning a Department of Administration, the Governor did not feel the time was appropriate for establishing such a department. A compromise was effected by which a Division of Administration was created within the office of governor, and instructed to work toward the establishment of a uniform system of financial accounts and to aid in preparing the way for a central Department of Administration. The division cooperated with a Legislative Council committee in study-

4. Governor's Commission on State Administrative Organization, *Report on Kansas State Administrative Organization*, 1950, p. 16.

ing and drafting legislation for its creation, and in 1953 the Legislature finally created it.

Thus Kansas became one of the states which sought to effect administrative reorganization through a Department of Administration. This plan assumed that the Governor would be able to control and coordinate the numerous state agencies by the judicious supervision, auditing, and inspection of a central department. By controlling budget estimates and by continuous management audits, preaudit of financial transactions, centralized purchasing, and the recruitment, supervision, and direction of civil service personnel, the Governor, through his appointed Director of Administration, would presumably be able to direct the whole operation of the state government.

As part of the compromise worked out in the administrative reorganization, a legislatively oriented council was created to approve the rules and regulations of the Department of Administration. Though the power of the Governor to coordinate the activities of state agencies was strengthened by the creation of this Department, a check was put upon his powers in the form of the Finance Council, which was composed of the Governor, the Lieutenant Governor, the President pro tem of the Senate, the Speaker of the House, and the chairmen of the Senate and the House Ways and Means committees. Containing four members of the Legislature, the Finance Council represents a curious blending of legislative and administrative powers in a state where the legislative, executive, and judicial powers have constitutionally been separated. The constitutionality of the Finance Council has been challenged in the State Supreme Court and has been upheld.[5]

At the start, however, the new administrative organization was beset with political difficulties which prevented the plan from working as its framers had intended. Shortly after the plan went into operation, a split developed in the Republican party which made it difficult for the Governor, though a Republican, to work with the other members of the Finance Council. Governor Hall was succeeded by Governor George Docking, who, as a Democrat, found it better to continue the practice established by Governor Hall of calling infrequent meetings of the Finance Council. On one occasion two years elapsed between such meetings. This legislative-executive rivalry was further indicated

5. *State of Kansas, ex rel.,* v. *Fadely,* 180 *Kan.* 653.

in 1959 by a bill calling for quarterly meetings of the Council. Passed by the Republicans in the Legislature, the bill was vetoed by the Governor, who was thus able to forestall meetings of the Finance Council and possibly actions which he did not favor.

The appointment in 1957 of the Special Legislative Committee on Economy and Efficiency, with funds to employ a special staff and with instructions to make a report to the 1959 Legislature, was another indication of legislative concern in administration. While officially appointed essentially to obtain information for legislative action, many of its recommendations on administration did not require statutory action. The operation of the committee over a two-year period of hearings and investigations made of it a kind of "watchdog" committee, scrutinizing the operation of the administrative branch under the official control of a Governor of a party different from that of the majority of the Legislature. The appointment of Democrats to this committee may have made it a bipartisan effort for good government, rather than a partisan effort to discredit the administration. In any event, it does reflect executive-legislative rivalry in the field of administration.

The effect of the administrative reorganization of 1953 has been to give the Governor a means of coordinating the agencies of state government. Further strengthening of the office of governor is possible through the imposition of an official[6] system of quarterly allotments and through the development of closer gubernatorial control over agency operations. It may be that this control can come only through reducing the number of agencies and using more single-executive agencies, in order to reduce the job of governor to more manageable proportions. Any forecasts of the likelihood of further strengthening of the Governor's control of administration must consider legislative-executive rivalry, the long and strong pressures for agency autonomy, and the broad question of its desirability in the context of democratic control of the government.

---

6. In chapter 8 the system of encumbrance authorization and the circumstances under which a system of allotment can be required are outlined.

8 | *Financial Administration*

The fiscal operations of the state government include budgeting, accounting, purchasing, treasury operations, control of state printing, and auditing. The administration of these fiscal operations can be used to control and coordinate the activities of the state departments and agencies. For a number of years these fiscal functions were divided among the Legislature and six elected or appointed officers. The functions and the responsibility for them were substantially changed by the act creating the Department of Administration.

The creation of this Department reflected a move to give both the Governor and the Legislature greater control over financial matters. The Governor is given power to appoint the Executive Director of the Department of Administration, who holds office at the pleasure of the Governor. The directors of the six subordinate divisions of the department are appointed within the classified civil service by the Executive Director with the approval of the Governor. Through these subordinates it is expected that the Governor would be able to exert substantial control over the operation of the numerous state agencies. Kansas, like other states using this type of state administrative organization, recognizes the importance of money in the accomplishment of the state services and activities. Through the control of the purse strings it is expected that central direction will be given to all state operations. The major divisions of the Department reflect the main

129

avenues through which such control is expected to be exercised: a budget division, an accounts and reports division, a purchasing division, an administrative services division, an architectural services division, and a personnel division.[1]

The Budget Division

The chief work of the Budget Division is the annual preparation of estimates of expenditures and revenues for the Governor. The budget is itself a thick document containing many figures and much information about the state's operations. It is also much more, in that it is one of the few places in which all of the activities and programs for state services are presented. In the decisions which the budget recommendations reflect, state activities are balanced one against another in their claims for state support. Since the revenues of the state are limited, the agencies are competitive in their requests for support. Money recommended for one agency is not available for others. While the Governor's decision as to how much he will recommend is personal, the job of the Budget Division is to collect, analyze, and present information which will enable the Governor to make sound decisions.

The budget process begins when, on or before September 1 of each year, the Budget Director distributes budget forms to each spending agency. The agencies fill in the amounts which they want to request for their operations during the next fiscal year. Agencies are being asked to estimate amounts that they will begin to spend ten months later (July 1 of the following year) and will not end spending until twenty-two months later (June 30 of the year after next). Having to estimate expenses and revenues so far ahead is one of the troublesome aspects of budget preparation. Price levels and demands for service may substantially change so as to make the budget estimate out-of-date.

The law requires that the forms be prepared so as to show the actual expenditures for at least the last preceding completed fiscal year, the estimated expenditures for the current fiscal year, and the requested

1. Reflecting the current trend in the field of public management to view personnel as a staff function, the 1953 administrative reorganization law transferred the personnel from a semi-independent Civil Service Commission to the Department of Administration. The functions and the powers of the Personnel Director and the Personnel Division are discussed in the chapter on personnel.

expenditures for the next fiscal year. The Budget Director may also require that the estimated expenditures be classified by fund, agency, function and character of activity, and object of expenditures. The Budget Director may further require that the revenue estimates show the basis upon which the estimates were made and factors involved in making these estimates. He may also request work programs and such supplemental and supporting data as may be required in preparing the budget.

These forms must be completed and returned to the Budget Director not later than the first day of October. These various requests are then reviewed by the Budget Director and his staff. A tentative budget is determined, and, no later than the tenth of November, the Budget Director notifies each state agency of any revisions of its request. The agencies then have ten days in which to ask the Executive Director of the Department of Administration for a hearing on their budget requests.

The Finance Council, whose composition and organization has been described earlier, may advise in the preparation of the state budget. Members of the Council, customarily the chairmen of the Ways and Means committees, are appointed by the Council to represent it in the budget hearings. The hearings are held during the first half of December. On the basis of the hearings, the Governor, or the Budget Director acting for the Governor, makes a decision; the final estimates are consolidated, and the budget is prepared for formal submission to the Legislature as the Governor's recommended budget. However, if it is an election year and a new Governor has been elected, the Budget Director is required by law to report the budget estimates to the incoming Governor as soon as they shall be made known, and shall make available to him all information, staff, and facilities of the Department relating to the budget. The incoming Governor or his representative is entitled to attend all the hearings on the tentative budget. After the incoming Governor has had an opportunity to review, amend, or approve the tentative budget, it is known as the "governor's budget report." It is to be presented to the Legislature within three weeks after the convening of the regular legislative session.

According to law, the budget as submitted to the Legislature must consist of three parts.

Part I shall consist of a budget message by such governor, including his recommendations with reference to the fiscal policy of the state government for the ensuing budget period describing the important features of the budget plan. . . . The general budget summary may be supported by explanatory schedules or statements classifying the expenditures contained therein by state agencies, objectives and funds and the income by state agencies, funds, sources and types. The general budget summary shall include all special or fee funds as well as the state general fund. . . .

Part II shall embrace the detailed budget estimates both of expenditures and revenues, showing the requests of the state agencies, if any, and the incoming governor's recommendations thereon. It shall also include statements of the bonded indebtedness of the state, showing the actual amount of the debt service for the last completed fiscal year, and the estimated amount for the current fiscal year and for the next budget period, the debt authorized and unissued, and the condition of the sinking funds.

Part III shall consist of a draft of a legislative measure or measures reflecting the incoming governor's budget.[2]

Up to this point the preparation of the budget has been chiefly the work of the executive branch and more particularly the Governor and his staff. The two exceptions to this are the power (and duty) of the Finance Council to advise and consult in the preparation of the budget, and in the inclusion of legislators in the budget hearings requested by the agency heads. Formally, the Governor has the power to recommend to the Legislature whatever amounts he and his staff think desirable, but, realistically, the Governor must consider the reactions of the legislators who are members of the Finance Council and who are likely to play important roles in the legislative consideration of his budget.

When presented to the Legislature, Ways and Means committees of the House and Senate can start their review and consideration. This involves deliberation, hearings, and further justification, and, frequently, further requests by state agencies. A representative of the Department of Administration is assigned to assist the Ways and Means committees of the Legislature in its hearings. As described earlier, the appropriation work is divided between these committees. Each committee considers the requests of the particular agencies which by

2. K.S.A., 75-3721.

custom have been allotted to it, and gives only perfunctory consideration to the requests of other agencies.

The text of appropriation bills as proposed in the Governor's budget becomes a basis on which the committees draw up their bills. In general, appropriation bills are treated like other measures before the Legislature. The Governor, however, does have an item veto with respect to such measures. Being laws of limited duration, they are not included in the General Statutes, but are printed in the Session Laws.

Though the appropriation bills of the major state agencies are frequently not passed until the closing days of the session, the time limit on the Legislature is such that the measures are passed and approved before the new fiscal year begins.

The Budget Division of the Department of Administration has certain duties in the execution of the budget. To provide a degree of flexibility in the appropriation legislation, any state agency may submit a request to the Budget Director for authority to transfer a part of its fund from one item to another item. If this is approved by the Budget Director, the Finance Council then considers the request. If it in turn approves, the amount is transferred from one line item on the appropriation to another line item and is reported to the Accounts and Reports Division.

The law creating the Budget Division emphasizes the continuous responsibility of this division to keep in touch with the operations of various state agencies. Budgeting cannot appropriately be regarded as a once-a-year event. The Budget Division is directed to "analyze the quantity and quality of services rendered by each agency and the needs for such services and for any new services." Further, it is expected by the statutes to provide management analysis service to all state agencies.

The 1953 law also permits the use of a system of allotments. Under such a system, the amounts appropriated by the Legislature would be divided into sums which the agencies could spend only during the time for which they were allotted. Allotments aim to prevent an agency from spending too much during the first months of the fiscal year and then perhaps having to ask for supplemental appropriations during the last of the fiscal year. Under an allotment system, an appropriation is only an authority to spend which may be further controlled. In Kansas, such an allotment system becomes effective only upon the advice of the Budget Director and the Executive Director and then under rules approved by the Finance Council. However, if it appears that the resources of the general fund or any special revenue fund are likely to be insufficient to cover the appropriations made against such funds, the Executive Director, on the advice of the Budget Director, is required by law to inaugurate allotments. This is to insure that the expenditures for any particular fiscal year will not exceed the available resources from that fund for that year. Any allotment decisions made by the Executive Director may be appealed to the Finance Council. While a system of allotments may be a useful device for budget execution, it has not been generally used.

Accounts and Reports Division

The Accounts and Reports Division under the Controller is directed to formulate and maintain a system of central accounts. The Controller designs, revises, and directs the use of accounting records and fiscal procedures and prescribes the uniform classification of receipts and expenditures for all state agencies. The system is designed to provide records showing at all times by funds, accounts, and other pertinent classifications the amounts appropriated, the estimated revenues, actual revenues or receipts, the amounts available for expenditure, the total expenditures, the unliquidated obligations, actual balances on hand, and the unencumbered balances of allotments or appropriations for each state agency. A separate account is established for each line item of appropriation measures; and before obligations may be incurred, the appropriate state agency requests that the amounts needed be set aside for purchases or spending during the period covered. This step seeks to prevent overspending in the first part of the fiscal year and is in addition to the preauditing described below.

The Controller is charged with the preauditing of all claims, bills, or accounts, or demands arising from contracts made by the state. This refers to the examination of every receipt, account, bill, claim, or demand for funds in the state treasury arising from activities carried on by state agencies. In this connection the Controller is directed to ascertain that each obligation has been incurred in accordance with law and appropriate rules and regulations and that the amount is correct and unpaid. Before any payment is made on any account, the Controller must approve of such payment. He must satisfy himself that the bill or claim on state funds was ordered by an act of the Legislature or was contracted by a duly authorized agent of the state in pursuance of the state law. Having determined that the amounts are legally due the claimants, the Controller issues warrants which are countersigned by the Treasurer. He sends the Treasurer a duplicate copy of his record of all warrants.

On the other hand, the Treasurer is directed to send to the Controller copies of all receipts and documents showing money received by the state treasury. The Controller examines and audits such receipts.

At least once a month and annually the Controller prepares a report showing the fiscal condition of each fund; and on or before the fifteenth of November of each year, the Controller reports on the financial transactions of the preceding fiscal year. He receives requests for information on the fiscal condition of any state agency and is directed "to deal co-operatively" with such an agency. He compiles data as necessary for the budget and as may be requested by the Executive Director.

The Controller designs and directs the use of various inventory records to show all fixed and movable property of the state. His records are based upon physical inventories verified by inspection.

Purchasing Division

The Purchasing Division is responsible for centralized purchasing in the state. This includes purchasing, renting, or otherwise providing supplies, materials, equipment, or contractual services for all state agencies. The Purchasing Director has the power to authorize any state agency to purchase directly certain specified supplies, materials, equipment, or contractual services under prescribed conditions and procedures. The Division may maintain storerooms, fix standards of quality and quantity, and develop specifications and consult with the several state agencies who use the supplies. The Division may require state agencies to report the stocks, supplies, and materials on hand and prescribe the manner of inspecting all supplies and materials.

In general, all purchases are made after competitive bids from the lowest responsible bidder. The Director of Purchases determines who that bidder is. In all cases in which there are two equal bids and one is by an out-of-state bidder, the law requires that preference shall be given to the bidder from within the state. The Director of Purchases may reject any or all bids and may call for a new letting of bids for a particular purchase. Specifically excluded from the controls of the Purchasing Division are those contracts for the construction, improvement, reconstruction, and maintenance of the state highway system and the acquisition of rights-of-way for state highway purposes. These purchases are made by the State Highway Commission under different laws.

New Divisions of the Department of Administration

The Legislature in 1965 provided for the creation of two additional divisions in the Department of Administration. The State Architect, which office had been independent for sixty years, was integrated into the Department of Administration. Since the creation of the Department of Administration in 1953 the State Architect had been associated with the Department in various ways. In addition to making plans, specifications, and estimates necessary for the construction and repair of state buildings, supervising construction of all state buildings, and inspecting construction material, the new Division is responsible for the care, management, and control of the Statehouse, the State Office Building, the Kansas Technical Institute properties, the office building at 801 Harrison Street, the Memorial Hall, the Governor's Mansion, and all other buildings and grounds in Shawnee County now or hereafter owned by the State, for which custody has not otherwise been assigned by law.

An administrative services division has been authorized by law, but activation of the Division is awaiting the assignment by the Legislature of more central service responsibilities. Meanwhile the Accounts and Reports Division operates a central mail service section; the Budget Division a surplus property section; and the Personnel Division a central duplicating service section.

The Legislature in Financial Administration

The legislative branch takes part in the financial administration of the state in several ways. Some of its leaders act ex officio as the Finance Council, which approves or disapproves the rules and regulations of the Department of Administration. The Council may provide for independent investigations of state agencies within the limits of available appropriations.

By unanimous vote the Finance Council may authorize expenditures from the state emergency fund. Such money may be used only to preserve the public health and protect persons and property from extraordinary conditions arising after the regular appropriations have been made; to make absolutely necessary repairs or temporary replacements of any state building or equipment which has been destroyed or damaged by sabotage, fire, flood, wind, tornado, or act of God; or, in limited circumstances, to supplement funds already appropriated.

Part of the legislative interest in the creation of the Department of Administration stemmed from a desire for more complete and prompt fiscal information. The Accounts and Reports Division with its mechanized accounting system is in a position to help the legislators obtain such information. The arrangements which were made for the Finance Council to advise on the budget give these legislative leaders an opportunity for advance information on budgetary matters.

Through the Legislative Council other legislative leaders are sometimes more closely involved with financial and other administrative questions. This is particularly true of the various committees of the Council which meet quarterly or more often and frequently have conferences and meetings with administrative officials.

The timing of the legislative sessions fits well into the spending process. Since the Legislature now has annual meetings, it can adjourn, knowing that it will reconvene before the end of the year for which it is appropriating money.

The system of special funds which has been used in Kansas has further increased the Legislature's role in financial administration. The fiscal reorganization of 1953 was imposed upon a complicated system of special-fund financing which has long been in effect. Before 1953 Kansas had been described as a state with an executive budget, but the budget that the Governor presented concerned only the general fund, which represented about one-sixth of the total revenues of the state. The remainder of the revenue was to be found in over 200 special funds. Since that time the revenue credited to the general fund has come to be a larger part of the total revenue of the state. In 1967 slightly over

40 per cent of the total state revenues was received into the general fund. One of the major developments in this trend occurred in 1965, when the retail sales tax fund was combined with the general revenue fund.

Under this type of financing, the Legislature had earmarked the revenues from particular sources for spending for particular purposes. Whenever a new function of state government had been started, ideally there had been new revenues for financing it or its financing could be tied into some already existing source of revenue. It was hoped that thus dividing the problem of financing and budgeting would simplify it. A system of financing could be established which would last for a number of years. Demands for new or increased services and changes in the revenues upset these financing arrangements and made it necessary for the Legislature to turn its attention to financing the particular area of state government where trouble had developed. Over the years the system did allow for stabilized taxes and charges, and in some respects it simplified the problem of finance.

Moreover, it has come to be recognized that some revenues are properly to be used only for accomplishing particular functions. It is commonly accepted, for example, that gasoline taxes and automobile license fees should be used only to construct and maintain the highways. The Constitution requires that these funds be used only for these purposes. Similarly, most people would accept the idea that money collected as fees for the care of patients in state hospitals should be used only for maintaining such hospitals. There are other revenues which would likewise be considered as special funds, dedicated to particular purposes.

A similar example of this type of financing is to be found in licensing boards. When particular professional groups have come to the Legislature and asked that professional licensing boards be established, the Legislature has provided that there should be levied against those being licensed an amount adequate to cover the expenses of the licensing board. For example, the funds which are collected for licensing barbers are used in the administration of the barbering code. These and like revenues are not regarded as a part of the general revenues of the state. Presumably the functions are being carried on to further the general welfare of the state, but they are financed by the particular groups concerned. Typically, the licensing boards indicate to the Legislature the expected expenditures for the next fiscal year and the Legislature appropriates from the boards' funds the money needed. Normally surpluses were carried forward. In this framework of operations it is not surprising that the various interest groups came to regard the special funds as "their own funds." Generally the Legislature interfered little with the agencies' spending of their own money.

In continuing this fund approach to finances when the sales tax was enacted, the Legislature established the sales tax fund to which the receipts from the new tax were to be credited. The tax was enacted to help finance social welfare and school aid and to reduce the general property tax. In keeping with these purposes, the 1937 Legislature provided for the appropriation of various amounts from the sales-tax fund for social-welfare purposes and for school aid. Any amount remaining in the fund—and it was expected that there would be a residue —was to be distributed among the local units of government to reduce the property tax. Succeeding sessions of the Legislature have provided for different divisions of the sales-tax fund, leaving a different amount of "sales-tax residue" for distribution to the local units of government. As the sales tax became more and more productive, the "residue" increased. The Legislature in 1947 put a limit of $12,500,000 on the amount to be distributed to the local units of government for the reduction in their property-tax rate. This limit has since been maintained in the distributions of the sales-tax revenues authorized by succeeding legislatures. On occasion before 1965, when the sales-tax fund was combined with the general fund, some of the revenues from the sales tax were transferred to the general fund from which appropriations were made for various state functions. Since 1965 the distribution has been made through the local ad valorem tax reduction fund.

Because of the understanding when the sales tax was enacted, some have claimed that such transfers to the general fund were inappropriate and "improper." Some advocates of school aid, for example, claim that money would have been available earlier for high-school aid if the sales-tax fund had not been "robbed." If gasoline taxes are "dedicated" for the highways, why they argue, cannot sales-tax revenues be earmarked for the purposes which were originally the basis for enactment of the sales tax?

Still another problem arises from the system of financing by special funds as illustrated by the sales-tax residue. Since 1947 the Legislature has allowed local units of government to receive $12,500,000. Although the channel for distributing the "sales tax residue" has varied, the local units and indeed the taxpayers have become accustomed to the distribution of this amount. While there is no doubt as to the legal authority of the Kansas Legislature to change this amount, or to discontinue making the distribution as one governor urged, certainly many practical problems would be raised for the local units and perhaps even the legislators themselves, if they were to reduce substantially the amounts for this distribution.

The existence of the various special funds has served to increase the total amount of money-on-hand needed to operate the state government. When balances are divided among so many special funds, larger total balances are necessary to insure continuous operation, since tax collections may be delayed or not synchronized with the needs for expenditures.

The existence of these various special funds, therefore, and the practices which have developed concerning them have served both to simplify the financial problems of the various legislatures and to make them more difficult. Particularly has it become more difficult for the Legislature to get a total picture of the operations of Kansas state government. Pressure on the Legislature for more revenues has caused the Legislature to search for all available funds. Existing balances in the various special funds have been "recaptured" to an extent not regularly done before. One of the results of the better reporting and better budgeting procedures adopted in 1953 has been a reduction in the independence of the various special fee funds. For example, in 1957 when the office of the Director of Revenue was reorganized, the Legislature discontinued the special operating fund for the Revenue Department.

The Kansas Legislature has numerous other ways of exerting substantial influence on finance administration. While the details of the appropriation acts vary from agency to agency, the Legislature normally specifies various purposes for appropriations. Some items, particularly those for the Legislature's own operation, are very specific. Most of the larger agencies have their appropriations divided between salaries and wages, other operating expenses, and items for even relatively small capital improvements and repairs. Some appropriations are divided by statute among the divisions of a department or board. The use of detailed appropriations makes it necessary to have more separate appropriation accounts and makes it desirable to have the greater flexibility between items that arises from the legal authority of the Finance Council to allow transfers from one item to another within the same appropriation.

The Legislature's control over expenditures is not affected by review of the estimates by the Budget Division, for the Legislature may raise or lower the Governor's request as desired. So, in addition to the legislative representation in the budget hearings, the Legislature, particularly through its committees, can work over the budget as it desires and in effect remake the budget. In this connection it should be mentioned that in some cases individual agencies do not feel bound to support the Governor's budget. Rather these officials may try to persuade the Legislature to restore cuts which the Governor or his staff has made.

The Legislature further controls the procedure and framework by which the budget is prepared and executed. For example, it was an act of the Legislature which established and gave powers to the Budget Division. In still a different way the Legislature controls the general level of the budget by determining the revenues which the state government will have. Moreover, the Legislature receives reports from the Auditor on the postaudits and can take such action as seems necessary to correct any irregularities. The Legislature can also appoint study committees to examine the work of the executive department.

State Treasurer

While other state agencies collect most state revenues, the Treasurer acts as custodian of all state money. All fees and taxes collected by state departments and agencies must be deposited in the state treasury. The departments and agencies which receive small amounts of revenue make their deposits monthly, while the larger revenue-receiving departments make their deposits daily or weekly. The Treasurer makes receipts in duplicate, one copy of the receipt being sent to the Controller, who examines and audits the receipts.

The state Treasurer is responsible for the safekeeping of all state money deposited in various banks which are designated as state depositories by the Board of Treasury Examiners. This board consists of the Bank Commissioner, the Executive Director of the Department of Administration, and the state Auditor, and meets in the office of the state Treasurer the first Monday of July in odd-numbered years. There are various statutory restrictions limiting the Board of Treasury Examiners in the selection of depositories and in the allotment of money to each. It is the duty of the Board of Examiners to examine at least once a month without previous notice the books, vouchers, accounts, and records of the state Treasurer and to compare his books, vouchers, accounts, and records with those of the state Auditor.

After the Controller has prepared and signed warrants to pay the claims against the state, the Treasurer verifies that there are adequate funds to pay the warrants and then signs them.

All bonds of the state and all of its instrumentalities including cities and counties are registered with the state Treasurer. As fiscal agent for the state, the Treasurer receives money and pays both interest and principal to the bondholders. The Treasurer serves as an ex officio member of the State Executive Council, the School Retirement Board, the Highway Patrol Pension Board, the Kansas Bureau of Investigation Pension Board, the Kansas Judges' Retirement Board, the Kansas Official Court Reporters' Retirement Board, and the Board of Canvassers. Sixteen different persons have served as state Treasurer since 1900. Beginning in 1969 the salary of the Treasurer is $12,650.

State Auditor

The Constitution provides for an elected state Auditor without specifying his duties. For a number of years, the state Auditor audited the proposed expenditures before payment was made. In the financial reorganization of 1953 this function was assigned to the Controller, and the state Auditor was made responsible for the postaudit. Now he audits the claims and payments after the money has actually changed hands.

The 1953 financial reorganization law provided for the creation of a Department of Postaudit and a Director of Postaudits who acts under the supervision of the state Auditor. The Director of Postaudits makes a complete examination and verification of all accounts, books, records, inventories, vouchers, receipts, funds, securities, and assets and other evidence of financial transactions of all state agencies at least once a year, and oftener if deemed necessary, or as may be directed by the Legislature or the Governor. The Director of Postaudits may examine the accounts of the Treasurer of the state and the Controller of the Department of Administration.

The Department of Postaudit prepares the budget forms for local units of government and receives and files certified copies of such budgets. The audits which are required of certain local units of government are filed in this department. If the audit of local books by the private auditors reveals discrepancies, the Department of Postaudit brings these discrepancies to the attention of the local governing board.

The Auditor, in the discharge of his duties, may require state agencies to preserve and to make available such records and accounts and documents as are necessary. Whenever any audit or examination or investigation by the auditor reveals any malfeasance, misfeasance, or nonfeasance on the part of any officer or employee of the state, a written report is prepared by the Auditor. The report is filed with the Governor, the Attorney General, the state agency concerned, the secretary of the State Finance Council, and the secretary of the Legislative Council. The Attorney General is directed to institute civil proceedings to recover such funds and to begin ouster proceedings or criminal proceedings against the person concerned. In addition to such unusual reports, the Auditor makes such reports as he deems desirable to the Legislative Council and to the Legislature.

The state Auditor is ex officio Register of the state land office. In this capacity he issues titles in the name of the state for the sale of lands owned by the state and preserves records of documents dealing with state lands.

The Auditor is also ex officio a member of the Executive Council, the Board of Treasury Examiners, and the State Board of Canvassers. In addition, the Auditor records all bonds issued by a city, township, school district, or other municipality. Beginning in 1969, he receives a salary of $12,650 a year.

9 | *Revenue System*

The revenue structure of the state is complex and largely the product of unplanned growth. As the functions and services of government have been expanded to meet the changing technological, social, and economic needs of the people, new revenues have been added by turning to new sources of revenue or to raising existing tax rates. The system of special funds long used in Kansas has served to focus attention on those portions of state activities which were needing more money. This system of financing encouraged the piecemeal approach to revenues.

State grants and sharing of taxes with local governmental units and the receipt by the state of federal grants have further complicated the revenue system of the state. In one sense there is but one source of revenue to the governments of Kansas—the people. While in this chapter most emphasis will be placed on the revenues to state government, it is desirable to keep in mind the total revenue pattern rather than to compartmentalize it. Particularly is this true because of the substantial fiscal interdependence and relationships of the various governmental units.

The accompanying table shows the various sources of revenue for the operation of Kansas state government and the relative importance of each.

TABLE 19

Sources of Operating Revenue, State of Kansas, by Amount and Percentage: Fiscal Year 1968

	Amount*	Per cent
TAXES		
Property Taxes (ad valorem)		
Tangible	$ 7,969,921	1.2
Intangible	2,346	0
Motor Carrier	1,147,071	.2
	$ 9,119,339	(1.4)
Income and Inheritance Taxes		
Income—Corporations	18,369,531	2.9
Income—Individuals	76,969,116	12.0
Income—Financial Institutions	1,811,501	.3
Inheritance	7,501,454	1.2
	$104,651,603	(16.3)
Sales, Use, Ownership, and Other Excise Taxes		
Sales Tax	$108,362,319	16.9
Consumer's Compensating Tax	6,712,782	1.0
Retailer's Compensating Tax	10,536,943	1.6
Cigarette	17,532,069	2.7
Motor Fuels	62,173,306	9.7
Cereal Malt Beverage	2,242,239	.3
Liquor Enforcement	2,406,757	.4
Alcoholic Liquor	4,174,352	.6
Motor Vehicle Registrations	29,074,420	4.5
Corporation Capital Stock	821,797	.1
Wheat	427,845	.1
Motor Boat Registrations	61,551	0
	$244,526,394	(38.0)
Gross Receipts Taxes		
Car Companies and Owners	288,222	0
Express Companies	5,166	0
Insurance Companies		
Insurance Premiums (Foreign)	8,700,391	1.4
Insurance Premiums (Firemen's Relief)	500,884	.1
Insurance Premiums (State Fire Marshal)	227,734	0
Other	888	0
	$ 9,723,289	(1.5)

* Since cents were dropped from all of these figures, the columns do not add exactly to the totals shown.

TABLE 19 (continued)

Payroll Taxes

Employment Security Contributions	$ 16,345,495	2.5
TOTAL TAXES	$384,366,123	(59.8)

SERVICE CHARGES

Charges for Inspections, Supervisions, Examinations, and Audits	$ 3,009,316	.5
Charges for Technical and Skilled Services Other Than Inspectional	1,994,416	.3
Charges for Services in Connection with Corporate Insurance and Other Organizations	372,919	.1
Charges for Clerical Service, Issuance of Certificates and Copies in Agency Offices	708,950	.1
Charges for Education and Libraries	21,654,049	3.4
Charges for Care and Hospitalization of Persons	14,005,702	2.2
Charges for Admissions	324,602	.1
Charges for State Office Building Telephone	405,478	.1
Other Service Charges	1,876,797	.3
	$ 44,352,233	(6.9)

LICENSES

Occupational Permits, Registrations, and Licenses (business)

To Render Personal Services	624,631	.1
To Engage in Businesses	1,458,021	.2
Motor Carrier Businesses	1,093,337	.2
Special Vehicle Permits	102,608	0
Other	8,568	0

Nonoccupational Permits, Registrations, and Licenses (nonbusiness)

To Hunt, Fish, or Trap	2,056,011	.3
To Operate Motor Vehicles	1,949,408	.3
Other	238,355	0
	$ 7,530,944	(1.2)

SALE OF COMMODITIES

Manufactured Products (including printing)	$ 4,605,122	.7
State Printed Matter and Publications	581,840	.1
Farm, Garden, and Orchard Crops, Dairy Products, Processed or Produced	566,237	.1
Livestock and Poultry	584,145	.1
Salvage, Scrap, Obsolete and Condemned Materials	37,256	0

TABLE 19 (concluded)

Usable Condemned Equipment	428,515	.1
Sale of Meals and Processed Foods	4,482,356	.7
Other Sundry Articles and Commodities	1,381,153	.2
	$ 12,666,626	(2.0)
INTERDEPARTMENTAL SALES		
College and University Clearing Account	$ 4,490,662	.7
TOTAL AGENCY EARNINGS	$ 69,040,465	(10.7)
REVENUE FROM THE USE OF MONEY AND PROPERTY		
Interest, Dividends, Premiums, and Discount		
Interest on Deposits	$ 7,046,749	1.1
Interest and Dividends from Investments	4,974,245	.8
Other	60,270	0
	$ 12,081,265	(1.9)
Rents and Royalties		
Unimproved Land	$ 62,735	0
Real Estate Buildings	273,281	0
Halls and Rooms in State Buildings	7,899,379	1.2
Oil, Gas, Mineral, and Sand Royalties	258,250	0
Other Rents	467,358	.1
	$ 8,961,005	(1.4)
TOTAL REVENUE FROM THE USE OF MONEY AND PROPERTY	$ 21,042,271	(3.3)
GIFTS, DONATIONS, AND FEDERAL GRANTS		
Federal Grants		
Highways and Bridges	$ 38,733,662	6.0
Public Health	11,884,159	1.8
Assistance and Relief	47,241,219	7.4
Employment Security Administration	4,692,047	.7
Education and Research	39,841,646	6.2
Other Purposes	12,914,743	2.0
	$155,307,478	(24.2)
All Other Grants, Gifts, Donations, and Contributions	$ 12,778,158	2.0
TOTAL GIFTS, DONATIONS, AND FEDERAL GRANTS	$168,085,636	(26.2)
OTHER REVENUE		
Other Revenue	$ 185,845	0
TOTAL OPERATING REVENUE	$642,720,342	

Source: Department of Administration, *Financial Report for Period July 1, 1967, to June 30, 1968*, pp. 20-21.

Property Taxes

Of the taxes included in the present system, the oldest historically is the property tax. Taxes are levied upon real estate, personal property —both tangible and intangible—and public-service corporation property. While the total amounts being raised from the property tax have increased over the years because of the use made by local governments, the state government has been relying less and less on this source for revenue. The accompanying table shows the marked decline in the percentage of revenue coming from the property tax despite the general increase in the actual amounts collected.

A number of factors account for this nation-wide decline in the relative importance of the property tax for state revenue. The states, including Kansas, have had difficulty in providing for equal assessment of property throughout the state. As long as comparable property is assessed at different points in the state at different amounts, a state property tax is unequal. Also, the states have found other tax sources which they can use much more easily and feasibly than can local units of government. The effect has been for the states to turn to those other taxes and to leave the property taxes more for the local units.

The state of Kansas, however, makes several property-tax levies. Special levies have been authorized for buildings at the educational and eleemosynary institutions. Though the Legislature on its own authority could have made such levies, these levies were authorized in constitutional amendments. Through this device, a referendum was actually held on whether to have such levies. The amendments did not set the amount of the levies, but left this to the Legislature. The Legislature now provides for a three-fourths mill levy for the Kansas Educational Building Fund, one-fourth mill levy for the State School Dormitory Fund, and one-half mill levy for the Kansas Charitable Institutions and Mental Hospitals Building Fund. In addition to these levies, in the past, variable levies have been made for repaying the bonds issued to pay soldiers of World War I a bonus and for the general fund of the state. Until 1956 the Commission of Revenue and Taxation was directed to estimate the condition of the state general fund and to make whatever levy was necessary to meet the demands on the fund. At this

TABLE 20

Receipts by Kansas State Government from the Property Tax by
Amount and Per Cent of Total Operating Revenue for Selected Years

Year	Amount	Per cent
1880	$ 843,575	54.84
1890	1,404,417	48.02
1900	1,715,731	45.14
1910	2,622,408	43.27
1920	4,720,681	52.55
1930	6,097,926	18.54
1940	6,127,247	10.96
1950	12,044,681	6.68
1960	7,948,894	2.22
1965	10,552,121	2.27
1966	9,071,519	1.57
1967	8,614,198	1.41
1968	9,119,340	1.42

Sources: James T. McDonald, *State Finance: Revenues of the State of Kansas,
1915-1953* (Lawrence: Governmental Research Center, Univ. of Kansas,
1955), p. 32; Auditor Reports, State of Kansas (Topeka: State Printer);
Department of Administration, *Financial Report for Period July 1, 1959,
to June 30, 1960*, pp. 18-19; *idem, Financial Report for Period July 1,
1965, to June 30, 1966*, pp. 22-23; *idem, Financial Report for Period July 1,
1967, to June 30, 1968*, pp. 20-21.

time the procedure was revised, and levies may be made only upon
specific authorization of the Legislature. With the soldiers' bonus re-
paid and the general sentiment against the state's making a levy for the
general fund, the percentage of state revenue from this source may
decline even further.

Over the years a popular reaction to the taxing of household effects
has developed. This grew out of the difficulty of locating and viewing
such personal effects and the problem of having assessments uniform
even within the same assessing district. Some citizens resented an
assessor personally coming into their homes each year to view their
household effects, including such personal items as rings, watches,
cameras, and silver table service. Moreover, in many counties auto-

mobiles had come to be an important part of all of the personal property assessed. In 1964 the constitution was amended to exempt from taxation household property that was not used in the production of income.

In addition to the levies on real and personal tangible property, there is a tax on intangible property. Until 1924, such property was taxed at the same rate as tangible property. Since intangible property is relatively easy for the owner to hide, it had long been thought that much intangible property was avoiding taxation. Also, the intangibles which were declared were assessed at a higher per cent of value than the real property. In an effort to get more of such property declared and in fairness to those who do declare the property, it was decided to tax intangibles at a lower rate. Until 1959 intangible property was taxed uniformly throughout the state at the rate of five mills ($.005) per dollar. The 1958 session of the Legislature authorized the taxpayer to choose between paying a five-mill tax on his intangibles or 3 per cent of the income from such intangibles. The taxpayer has to furnish information on his intangibles and their earnings at the time he files his state income tax rather than at the time his personal property is assessed. Requiring the reporting of intangibles with the reporting of income has increased the accuracy of both.

Property-tax administration has gone through many changes since Kansas became a state. With the creation of a state tax commission in 1907 and its subsequent development into the present State Department of Property Valuation, the state has assumed responsibility for general supervision of local assessing. Although townships, cities, school districts, and special districts have their own budgets and levy property taxes separately, the county is the primary unit which assesses property. The other subdivisions use the assessments made by the county. The county clerk is ex officio county assessor, except in nine of the larger counties of the state, where county assessors are elected or appointed. The county assessor is responsible for assigning a value to the real property and personal property used in producing income. He may appoint deputies to assist him as may be necessary. The state Department of Property Valuation assesses the property of utilities and informs the county assessor of the equalized value of the utilities within the county.

While the State Commission on Revenue and Taxation and its suc-

Ratio of Assessed Valuation to Sales Price: Real Property, 1967

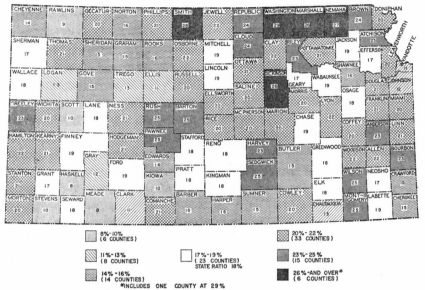

Source: *Report of Real Estate Assessment Ratio Study for the Calendar Year 1967* (State of Kansas, Property Valuation Department, 1968).

cessor in this connection, the Board of Tax Appeals, has broad authority to equalize the assessments set by local assessors and to order reassessments from county to county, there are wide variations in assessment levels. The differences are apparent in the map showing the results of the sales-ratio study. Since 1949, the Legislature has required that annual studies be made of the relation between the assessed valuations and the sale price of those pieces of real property which change ownership each year. This relationship, referred to as the assessment ratio, is different from county to county, and frequently there are substantial differences within the same county. Since the property tax is used more locally, it is more important for equality of taxation that there be as little difference within the county and local units as possible. Some local officials have long doubted the accuracy of the assessment ratio study; there are many problems in making such a state-wide study.[1]

1. "Can you Count on the Kansas Assessment Ratio Study?", *Kansas Government Journal*, April 1958, pp. 200-2.

Despite these doubts, the study has done much to focus attention on the problem of unequal assessment.

This inequality of assessment is a long-standing problem. In 1953 the Legislature provided for the appointment of the Kansas Citizens' Commission on Assessment Equalization. The Commission was given an appropriation enabling it to have a staff, which helped organize local-study commissions in almost every county in the state. The local commissions made recommendations to the state commission, which in turn made recommendations to the Legislature. These were far-reaching and included recommendations for appointing the local assessor in counties above 15,000, for local advisory assessment committees, for the use of more scientific methods of appraisal, for assessing as of 1 January rather than 1 March, for an expanded county board of equalization, and for the exemption of household goods and personal effects from taxation.[2] The commission also recommended the reorganization of the Commission of Revenue and Taxation, making changes not unlike those made in 1957 when the Property Valuation Department was created. However, the study commission did urge that the Department be given more powers to supervise local assessments than it was given by the law. The Commission proposed a system whereby the assessments levels throughout the state would all be raised to 50 per cent of the actual value. In rejecting the recommendations of the Commission for more equalized assessments through mandatory state action, the Legislature chose to continue the system of trying by persuasion, education, and information to bring about more uniform assessments. The Legislature has shown some willingness to use the sales ratio study as a basis for distributing state aid. Counties may be encouraged to raise their assessment levels if more state money is distributed on the basis of assessed valuations. The Legislature would probably want to accompany any broad changes of assessment levels with changes of the mill-rate limits, which it imposes on the taxing powers of local governing units.

While not enacted immediately, a number of the recommendations of the 1955 Commission have been adopted. An assessment manual was published in 1963. This manual is a substantial step in encouraging the

2. Kansas Citizens' Commission on Assessment Equalization, *Report* (Topeka, 1954).

more scientific assessment of the property in the state. In 1963 the Legislature amended the law and introduced a new term, requiring assessors to assess all property at 30 per cent of its "justifiable" value. By 1968 all counties had had or were in the process of having a reappraisal to bring their assessments into conformity with this requirement. In 1968 the Legislature specifically required the state Department of Property Valuation to publish a list of those counties which were assessing as required by the state law and those which were not. After considering an appeal made by a county which was not complying, the Department was to issue orders for adjusting the valuations to the average assessments in the area. Counties may now require their assessors to attend assessing schools and may join with other counties in employing a full-time assessor. Refinements have been introduced to improve the assessment-ratio study.

Changes in assessment levels and procedures come slowly. Apparently fear and uncertainty of what changes might mean to the individual taxpayer lead him to tolerate the present system with its inequities. The individual taxpayer may appeal his assessment to the County Board of Equalization (the County Board of Commissioners ex officio) and ultimately, if he desires, to the Board of Tax Appeals. In the fiscal year ending June 30, 1968, the Board heard 1,137 grievances, 85 protests, and was in the process of hearing 639 appeals from taxpayers. With 105 assessors and a number of deputy assessors and assistants, the Property Valuation Department and the Board of Tax Appeals have a most difficult job of trying to get uniform and equal assessment throughout the state.

A further assessment function performed by the State Department of Property Valuation is that of assessing all public-service corporations doing interstate or intercounty business in the state. These corporations may file appeals of their assessment with the State Board of Tax Appeals.

Income and Inheritance Taxes

The Kansas inheritance tax, established in 1909, is imposed on all property which passes by will or by laws regulating the succession of property in absence of wills or by deed, grant, or gift in contemplation of death. The tax is levied on nonresidents as well as residents. Property which changes hands under a bona fide purchase is exempt from the inheritance tax, as is property which is transferred to a governmental unit or agency for a use that would be exempt from the property tax.

The rate of taxation and the amount of exemption vary with the nearness of the relationship of the grantee to the grantor. Three classes of grantees are established: Class A—the surviving husband or wife, lineal ancestors, lineal descendants, adopted children, lineal descendants of adopted children, and the spouse of a son or daughter of the deceased; Class B—brother or sister of the deceased; Class C—all others. An inheritance exemption of from $15,000 to $75,000 is allowed Class A survivors, the latter amount being for surviving spouse only; $5,000 for Class B; and none for Class C. If the value after exemptions is less than $200, no tax will be imposed. The rate of tax varies by class and by the amount of the inheritance: in Class A, 1 per cent to 5 per cent; in Class B, 3 per cent to 12½ per cent; in Class C, 10 per cent to 15 per cent. There is a further provision that the total amount of the tax must equal 80 per cent of the federal estate tax. If it does not, an additional tax is imposed, equal to the difference between the total of the state taxes and 80 per cent of the federal tax.

The taxes imposed by this act are payable to the county treasurer in the county in which probate is made. The Director of Revenue determines the amount of the tax, and certifies the amount to the probate court. Upon receipt of the tax money, the county treasurer retains 5 per cent of the amount for the county general funds. The remainder is submitted to the Director of Revenue each quarter on the first days of January, April, July, and October. Amounts received by the state Treasurer from this tax are credited to the state general revenue fund. Appeals on the tax are heard by the State Board of Tax Appeals.

Though it was necessary to amend the state Constitution in order to tax incomes, Kansas instituted such a tax in 1933. Certain exemptions and deductions are allowed before the tax is levied annually at the following rates upon the net income of every resident and upon the net income of every nonresident which is derived from sources within the state:

Amounts of Income	Per Cent of Tax
$ 0 - $2000	2
$2000 - $3000	3½
$3000 - $5000	4
$5000 - $7000	5
over $7000	6½

A tax is imposed upon the income derived by estates from any kind of property held in trust. Individuals carrying on business partnerships are liable for income tax only as individuals. Corporations annually pay a tax of 4½ per cent of the entire net income derived from property located in and business transacted within the state during the taxable year.

Civic, charitable, fraternal, and cooperative organizations are exempt from this tax. Individual taxpayers are allowed a $600 exemption for themselves and an additional $600 exemption for their spouses and each dependent. Returns are made to the office of the Director of Revenue on or before the fifteenth of April. The amounts collected are credited to the state general revenue fund.

A withholding-tax plan became effective January 1, 1966. Appropriate amounts are withheld by employers and are forwarded to the Department of Revenue. Later in the same year the voters approved a constitutional amendment allowing for uniformity between the federal and state income tax laws. The Legislature is authorized by this amendment not only to adopt by reference the income-tax laws of the United States as they exist, but also as they may be enacted by Congress. The amounts collected from inheritance and income taxes have increased in recent years and now account for almost one-fifth of the total state revenue.

General Sales and Excise Taxes

In recent years the general sales tax and the excise taxes, of which there are several, have been the biggest sources of state revenue. A general sales tax of 3 per cent is levied upon the gross receipts received from the retail sale of tangible personal property within the state; from telephone or telegraph services, excepting interstate services; from the sale or furnishing of gas, water, electricity, and heat; from the sale of meals or drinks from places where they are regularly sold; from the sale of admissions to any place of amusement, entertainment, or recreation, excepting to state or county district fairs and to educational, religious, or charitable activities; from the operation of coin-operated amusement devices; and from renting rooms by hotels and motels.

The tax is paid by the consumer to the retailer. It is the duty of each retailer to collect the full amount of the tax, and it is unlawful for him to assume or absorb the tax. On or before the twentieth of each calendar month, every retailer must make a return to the Director of Revenue. All revenues collected or received from these taxes are deposited each week with the state Treasurer, who credits them to the retail sales tax fund.

The sales tax was enacted essentially as a depression measure, particularly to pay for the large social-welfare program which was established on a state-wide basis at that time. Also, the money from the sales tax was to be used for school aid and for distribution to local units of government to reduce the property tax. The rate of the tax was 2 per cent from 1937 to 1958, and 2½ per cent from 1958 until 1965 when it was changed to the present 3 per cent. For the first two years tokens were used to collect the tax. Since that time, when approved by the Director of Revenue, agreements with retailers are authorized to facilitate tax collections. A scale of collecting sales tax has been established. In certain types of business where sales of particular amounts are frequent, the scale may result in excess collection, but the scale is expected to average out for collections at the rate of 3 per cent. The sales tax has been a very productive source of revenue for the state, increasing manifold over the thirty-two years of its use.

A compensating-use tax is levied on the articles purchased in other states which are shipped or returned to Kansas. Technically this is a 3 per cent tax imposed on the privilege of using, storing, or consuming articles of tangible personal property. The Director of Revenue collects the tax.

A cigarette tax, established in 1927, is levied upon all cigarettes sold, distributed, or given away in the state, at the rate of eight cents a package. The Director of Revenue is charged with its administration. He prepares stamps to be affixed to each package of cigarettes and sells these stamps to wholesale dealers in amounts of $400. The stamps are sold at a discount of 3¾ per cent from face value to cover the costs to the wholesaler of putting the stamps on the cigarette packages. Funds arising from the sale of such stamps are turned over daily to the state Treasurer.

Seventy-five per cent of the proceeds from the sale of cigarette stamps is deposited to the state general fund; 25 per cent is set aside and distributed to the treasurers of the 105 counties once each three months on a population basis. Within the county the treasurer places one-half of the amount received in the county general fund and distributes the other half among the cities of the county in proportion to their population.

An excise tax on cereal malt beverages was added in 1937. This tax is assessed against the wholesaler, though arrangements may be made for breweries to pay the tax and to affix the tax insignia to the container. Wholesalers and distributors are required to post a bond to insure full compliance with the act. Retailers are required to affix stamps on the containers within twenty-four hours after the receipt of any beverage upon which the tax has not been paid. The rate is ten cents per gallon. The money collected from this tax is credited to the general revenue fund.

The repeal of the prohibition amendment to the state Constitution in 1948 led to an alcoholic beverage control act and a tax on alcoholic beverages in 1949. The rate of tax varies with the beverage. The tax is paid to the Director of Alcoholic Beverage Control and is credited to the general fund.

For the purpose of providing revenue which may be used by counties and cities in the enforcement of the liquor control act, an additional tax of 4 per cent on the gross sales of the various retail stores is collected from the consumer and reported by the retailer. The Sales Tax Division of the Department of Revenue collects it. One-fifth of the amount collected is credited to the general fund, and the remainder to the county and city alcoholic liquor control enforcement fund. On the fifteenth of March, June, September, and December of each year, the state Treasurer apportions this latter fund to the counties, 50 per cent on the basis of population and 50 per cent on the basis of each county's equalized tangible assessed valuation for the preceding year. Within the county, the county treasurer credits the county general fund with 50 per cent of the amount distributed by the state, and 50 per cent is divided among the various cities of the county on the basis of population, regardless of whether they allow the sale of alcoholic beverages.

The five preceding excise taxes are important sources of revenue to the government in Kansas, accounting for almost two-fifths of the total operating revenues of the state government. Some of these taxes have been assigned to sponsor particular functions. In part they have been used as sources of state aid to local government or to share with local governments for specific purposes, such as welfare, school aid, liquor enforcement, and reduction of the property tax.

Highway-Use Taxes

Under the original Constitution of Kansas, the state government was prohibited from being a party in carrying on any work of internal improvement.[3] The coming of the automobile made this provision unduly restrictive, because it prevented the state from engaging in the important task of highway-building. As early as 1913 Governor Hodges recommended that a constitutional amendment be submitted that would make an exception of highways and bridges.[4] Each succeeding governor remarked on the inadequacy of the county plans and benefit district plans for equipping the state with a highway system until 1928, when the Legislature submitted a constitutional amendment to the voters. The amendment was adopted by a four-to-one vote in November, 1928. One of the sections to the amendment permitted the state to engage in highway construction, but provided that no property tax could be levied nor any bonds issued by the state for such highways. Another section gave the state power to levy special taxes upon motor vehicles and motor-vehicle fuels for highway purposes.[5]

To support the highway program, money is raised from the (1) motor-vehicle fuel tax, (2) operators' and chauffeurs' licenses, (3) manufacturers' or dealers' licenses, and (4) motor-vehicle registration.

Motor-Vehicle Fuel Tax

When this tax was first enacted in 1925, gasoline was taxed at two cents a gallon. The rate was increased a cent in 1929, 1944, and 1949 so

3. *Kansas Constitution,* Art. 11, sec. 9.
4. *Senate Journal,* 1913, pp. 20–22.
5. *Kansas Constitution,* Art. 11, secs. 9 and 10.

that the current rate is five cents a gallon. The tax is collected by the Director of Revenue. Two per cent of the amounts collected is credited to the general fund, and of the remainder, 80 per cent is assigned to the highway fund and 20 per cent to the special county road and city street fund.

While different formulas have been used from time to time in the distribution of the special county road and city street fund, in 1955 the Legislature provided for an initial distribution of $2,500,000 to cities on the basis of population and $4,000,000 to counties on the basis of the secondary road mileage in each county. Any amounts remaining in the fund after this distribution are divided equally between cities and counties on the same basis as used in the initial distribution. The amounts given to the cities must be used for streets and highways, and those given to counties are used to match secondary federal-aid-fund grants.

Operators' and Chauffeurs' Licenses

Since 1931, motor-vehicle operators and chauffeurs have been required to have licenses. The licenses are issued by the Motor Vehicle Department only after the applicant has established his competence as an operator or chauffeur. The fee varies with type of application, but is nominal. Fifty per cent of the fees received from motor-vehicle operators and 25 per cent of the fees from chauffeurs' licenses are credited to the state safety fund, which is distributed to provide funds for drivers' training courses in the schools in Kansas. The remainder of these fees is credited to the state highway fund.

Motor-Vehicle Registration

While the fees for motor-vehicle registrations have varied, the present rates, as established by the 1955 session of the Legislature, are as shown in the accompanying table. In 1968 over $29,000,000 was collected from this source.

For a number of years Kansas imposed a ton-mile tax on motor carriers, but in 1955 this tax was repealed. In its place the registration charges on trucks were raised. Higher rates are established for trucks which travel over 6,000 miles.

Arrangements are made for manufacturers and dealers to receive special dealer's license plates. They receive three plates for a $30 fee

TABLE 21
Schedule of Fees for Motor-Vehicle Registration

Type of Vehicle	Rate
Motorcycles	$ 5.00
Trucks and Truck Tractors	8.50 to $1,050.00, depending on weight and use.
Other Motor Vehicles	10.00 to $20.00, depending on weight.
Trailers	5.00 to $20.00, depending on weight.
Electrically propelled vehicles	5.00
Buses	15.00 to $60.00, depending on capacity.

Source: K.S.A., 8-143.

and may acquire other sets of plates for $10 each. The amounts collected from this source, as well as the registration fees on individual automobiles, are collected by the county treasurer, who retains a small fee and sends the bulk of the amount to be credited to the highway fund.

Privilege Taxes, Licenses, and Fees

In 1871 a law was enacted which required every out-of-state insurance company doing business in the state to pay a tax of 2 per cent of its gross premiums. All insurance companies have to pay certain admission and annual fees for the privilege of doing business in the state. These collections go into a special fund and are used primarily to maintain the office of the Commissioner of Insurance. In addition, since 1939 each fire insurance company has had to pay a levy of not more than 0.75 per cent of its gross cash receipts to the state Insurance Commissioner. The amount thus collected is deposited to the credit of a special fund for the maintenance of the department of the state Fire Marshal. These fees from insurance companies are primarily for regulation and do not provide the state with any sizable portion of its revenues.

In addition to the fees and licenses on insurance companies, there has been a corporation franchise tax since 1866. All domestic corporations which have received their charters at least six months prior to December 31 of any year must make a report to the Secretary of State, showing the condition of the corporation at the close of business on the

31st day of December preceding. The report must be made on or before March 31 and must contain, among other facts, the name; location of principal office; names of the officers; date of annual election of officers; amount of authorized capital stock and the par value of each share; amount of capital authorized, issued, and paid up; nature and kind of business and place or places of business; a statement of assets and liabilities; a list of stockholders and post-office address of each; and changes in these particulars since filing of the last annual report. The annual rates for out-of-state and domestic corporation franchise taxes vary according to the amount of paid-up capital stock as shown in the adjoining table. These annual fees are credited to the general fund.

Licenses are also required for such occupations as selling cigarettes. While the rates have varied, the present schedule provides for $25 for wholesale dealers and distributors, $10 for manufacturer's salesmen licenses, and $6 for retail dealers and for each vending machine. All fees are collected by the Director of Revenue, paid to the state Treasurer, and credited to the general fund of the state on the first day of each calendar year.

While the cities and counties are authorized to issue licenses for retailing cereal malt beverages, wholesalers and distributors for such beverages are licensed by the Director of Revenue. The fee for these licenses is $300 and must be paid annually as long as the license is re-

TABLE 22

Kansas Annual Corporation Franchise Tax

Corporations with Paid-up Capital Stock	Annual Tax
$ 0 to $ 10,000	$ 10
10,000 to 25,000	25
25,000 to 50,000	50
50,000 to 100,000	100
100,000 to 250,000	125
250,000 to 500,000	250
500,000 to 1,000,000	500
1,000,000 to 2,000,000	1,000
2,000,000 to 3,000,000	1,500
3,000,000 to 5,000,000	2,000
5,000,000 or more	2,500

Source: K.S.A., 17-702.

newed. A separate license for wholesalers is required for each establishment operated. All license fees collected by the Director of Revenue are paid into the state treasury, and the state treasury credits them to the general fund of the state.

Though much oil and gas are produced in Kansas and the question of a severance tax had been raised from time to time, it was not until 1957 that Kansas had a severance tax. As the demand for more revenues became more acute, there developed more interest for this type of tax. Supporters of school aid saw in the severance tax a possible way to get more money for schools. The question was further complicated by the claim of oil producers that they were paying what amounted to a severance tax in the form of property taxes. Local governments, getting most of their revenues from the property tax, feared that a state severance tax might affect their revenues. In any event, in 1956 the Legislature enacted a 1 per cent gross-receipts severance tax, but the law, when tested in the courts, was found to be unconstitutional because of a technical feature.[6] When the Legislature met again it was unable to agree on a severance-tax law.

In addition to these major license and privilege taxes, fees are charged when licenses are issued by the examining boards. Typically, 20 per cent of the fees collected by these agencies are credited to the general fund, and the remainder to special funds from which the Legislature appropriates money for the boards to use in their operations.

Other Taxes

The unemployment compensation tax is assessed against the employer to provide payment to the employees when they are out of work. In a sense the unemployment tax does not constitute a revenue to the state, since the state government merely acts as a custodian for the funds thus acquired and must use the money to pay benefits to the unemployed who come under the terms of unemployment compensation law. This tax is discussed further in chapter 19.

A tax of 4 per cent of the gross receipts is imposed on express companies operating in Kansas. Express companies must make and file with the director of property valuation taxation a statement containing

6. *State, ex rel.*, v. *Kirchner,* 182 *Kan.* 437.

information which is used to determine "the gross receipts" of each company. The Property Valuation Department collects the tax, and receipts are credited to the state general fund. This tax was established at a somewhat lower rate in 1907.

Another tax of limited importance is the excise sales tax of 3 per cent for the privilege of selling, licensing, or disposing of the rights to perform musical and dramatic-musical compositions. This tax was established in 1939 and is paid annually to the Treasurer on or before March 15, on the gross receipts of the preceding calendar year.

A grain tax is levied against every grain dealer and producer. The tax is levied in lieu of all general property taxes and is one-half mill per bushel upon all grain handled or produced. Thus it is a tax for the privilege of engaging in the business of producing or dealing in grain. Every dealer is required to register with the county clerk of the county in which he proposes to do business. At the time and place of making a personal-property return to the local assessor, every dealer and producer must furnish a statement of bushels of grain handled or harvested by him during the preceding calendar year. The county clerk then computes taxes against each dealer and producer and includes the amount of the tax on his personal-property statement. The money collected from this tax is credited to the county general fund. The tax on grain dealers has been one-half mill per bushel since this tax was first established in 1941. Since 1945 the tax has been levied only on the grain of those producers harvesting over 1,000 bushels of grain.

Agency Earnings

About 10 per cent of the revenues of the state come from charges so clearly identified with particular agencies that they are classified as agency earnings. Somewhat over half of these earnings are derived from charges which state agencies make for their services. In most instances these charges are not designed to cover all of the actual cost of the services. Tuition paid by students at the state institutions of higher learning and charges made to the families of patients at the mental hospitals are illustrative of these types of collections.

Included in this same general classification are the revenues from various types of licenses and permits. In general, these licenses and permits are issued for purposes of regulating the business or operation being conducted rather than for the purpose of raising revenue. Incidental to the state's operations, a number of salable commodities are produced and income from their sale is credited to this source of revenue.

Federal Grants-in-Aid

Financial aid received by Kansas from the national government plays an important part in state finance. Kansas received its first monetary grant-in-aid in 1890, in the form of a payment to Kansas State College for instruction in agriculture, English, and science. Other minor grants were started in the first quarter of the twentieth century, and in the late twenties federal funds for highways began to be made to the Kansas state government. After 1935 several different grants-in-aid were commenced for social-welfare and health purposes. The amount of federal aid received has increased greatly during the last two decades as shown in the adjoining table.

TABLE 23
Federal Aid to Kansas: Selected Fiscal Years

Year	Amount of Grant	Total Operating Revenue	Per Cent Federal Aid of Total State Receipts
1915	$ 116,348	$ 5,260,011	2.21
1925	303,617	14,732,716	2.06
1935	8,030,792	35,877,301	22.38
1945	7,789,419	74,311,983	10.48
1950	37,587,230	180,303,212	20.84
1955	43,219,546	230,215,216	18.77
1960	94,136,295	358,613,713	26.25
1965	116,115,802	464,884,492	24.98
1966	136,797,350	577,389,657	23.69
1967	140,005,257	612,138,541	22.87
1968	155,307,478	642,720,342	24.16

Sources: Hein and McDonald, *Federal Grants-in-Aid in Kansas,* Special Report #50, Governmental Research Center, Univ. of Kansas, 1953, p. 17; James T. McDonald, *State Finances, Revenue of the State of Kansas 1915-1953,* p. 37; Department of Administration, *Financial Report for Period July 1, 1954, to June 30, 1955,* p. 15; *Financial Report for Period July 1, 1959, to June 30, 1960,* p. 19; *Financial Report for Period July 1, 1965, to June 30, 1966,* p. 23; *Financial Report for Period July 1, 1967, to June 30, 1968,* p. 21.

Kansas now receives more than thirty regular grants-in-aid from the national government, and the total amount of money received for 1968 amounted to over $155,000,000. About 30 per cent of the amount was for assistance and relief, 26 per cent for education and research, 25 per cent for highways and bridges, 8 per cent for public health, 3 per cent for employment-security administration, and the remainder for other functions. The federal funds are divided among the various states on one or more of six bases: (1) population, (2) special need, (3) amount spent by the state, (4) financial need, (5) area, and (6) uniform amount per state.

Administration of the Kansas Tax System

During the time when the property tax was almost the sole source of revenue for state and local governments in Kansas, there was no state administrative organization to provide for its assessment and collection. The county clerk was responsible for assessing, and the county treasurer for collecting, property taxes. The county treasurer was required to pay the state Treasurer the amount due the state.

Though there were early criticisms of the property assessment, few attempts were made to improve the assessment system. In 1869 a law was enacted for the central assessment of railroad property by a board of assessors, to be composed of assessors elected from each Congressional district. Three years later a special study commission was appointed, but its recommendations were not adopted. The Central Board of Assessors was reconstituted in 1876 and made to consist of the Lieutenant Governor, Attorney General, Secretary of State, and state Treasurer, serving ex officio. In addition to its duties of assessing all the railroad property in the state, this ex officio board was directed to assess the property of intercounty telephone and telegraph corporations.

The principle of centralizing responsibility for the operation of this system was not carried further until 1907, when the State Tax Commission was created. This Commission consisted of three members appointed by the Governor for overlapping terms of four years. The Tax Commission was given broad powers of supervising the assessment system, prescribing uniform systems of auditing and accounting, requiring reports, summoning witnesses, and recommending legislation in accordance with its findings. Of considerable importance was its power to require the reconvening of the county board of equalization to act in accordance with the findings of the commission. As a board of equalization, the Tax Commission was also given the power to equalize assessments among all counties and minor subdivisions of the state.

At the beginning of the twentieth century the changing functions and increases in costs of government made mandatory a broadening of the tax base, and between 1907 and 1930 many new taxes were added. Among these were motor-vehicle registration fees, motor-fuels taxes, motor-carrier ton-mile taxes, cigarette stamps and licenses, motor-manufacturer and -dealer licenses, and the inheritance taxes. The Commission was given the responsibility for administration and collection of these taxes.

Other taxes were collected by various offices until 1933, when an attempt was made to consolidate some of the tax-collection functions. The Department of Inspection and Registration was created to replace the offices of state Oil Inspector, state Fire Marshal, and state Hotel Commissioner. The Department was assigned responsibility for licensing cigarette dealers and collecting cigarette taxes. Several years later it was given similar responsibilities for the cereal malt beverage tax. Thus the major tax-collecting functions were divided between the Department of Inspections and Registration and the Tax Commission.

In 1939 the Legislature created the State Commission of Revenue and Taxation, and the powers of the old Tax Commission relating to the income tax, the sale and compensating-use taxes, and the inheritance tax were transferred to the new Commission. The actual responsibility for administering these tax laws was vested in a Director of Revenue, who was to be under the supervision of the Commission. The Department of Inspections and Registrations was abolished and its tax-collecting functions were transferred to the new Commission. Tax collections were not fully centralized, however, for the new Department was given no responsibility for collecting the corporation-franchise tax, the motor-vehicle registration tax, or the ton-mileage tax.

In studying administrative organization in 1950, the "Little Hoover Commission" noted that the organization of the Commission of Revenue and Taxation was confusing. The three-man full-time Commission was in charge of the Department and, at the same time, the Director of Revenue had the statutory duty of administering the Commission's tax-collecting functions. The law "makes his work subject to the supervision of the commission, which means that major administrative decisions must wait until the commission can spare the time from this other work and can convene to confer with the director."[7] Since the time that the Commission can devote to administration is limited, decisions are therefore delayed, and "the present arrangement is scarcely conducive to prompt effective administration."[8] The Governor's Commission felt that the Commission of Revenue and Taxation should be "divorced from the solely administrative functions now vested in the Director of Revenue and should confine its attention to the exacting work in the quasi-legislative and quasi-judicial field, which is voluminous enough to demand all of its time."[9]

The Legislature heeded these and other criticisms and in 1957 abolished the Commission of Revenue and Taxation. At that time the functions previously performed by this Commission were transferred to the Department of Revenue, the Department of Property Valuation, and the Board of Tax Appeals. The Director of Revenue, who is appointed by the Governor, supervises the collection of the inheritance tax, cigarette tax, income tax, motor-fuel taxes, sales tax, and cereal malt beverages tax. In addition to his duties of supervising these divisions, the Director of Revenue is a member of the Port of Entry Board. The Department of Property Valuation is responsible for administering the laws relating to the general property tax, assessing public-service corporations, assessing private car-lines and motor carriers, and supervising the laws relating to mortgage registration.

The Board of Tax Appeals is concerned primarily with appeals from rulings of the Director of Revenue and the Director of Property Valuation, emergency warrant and emergency levy applications from the subdivisions of the state, tax-grievance appeals, exemption-of-property appeals, and equalization and review of appeals from taxpayers on their property assessments.

At the time of this reorganization, the Legislature discontinued the practice of allowing the tax-collecting agency a share of the taxes it

7. Commission on State Administrative Organization, *A Report to the Governor of Kansas* (Topeka: 1950), p. 5.

8. *Ibid.*, p. 5.

9. *Ibid.*, p. 5.

collected. Previously the common pattern was for a percentage of the taxes collected to be credited to a special revenue collection fund which was used to finance the operations of the collecting agency. Now the taxes collected are credited to the appropriate fund, and the operating expenses of the agencies are paid from the general fund. This represents an interesting step away from the use of special funds.

Several principles may be observed in the legislative approach to tax administration. The property tax has been influenced by the desire to keep the control of the system on a local basis. Once established, the principle of central supervision of the property-tax system has not been abandoned, though some groups still want local officials to retain a large degree of local authority in the administration of the general property tax. The Legislature has shown a willingness to add new kinds of taxes. Coincident with the expansion of government activities and a corresponding increase in governmental expenses, a search for new bases of tax measurement added many new taxes to the statutes. The inability to secure equitable property assessment and the realization that taxes based solely upon property as a measure of ability to pay were not necessarily equitable led the Legislature to turn to other sources of revenue. The Legislature has sought to consolidate the collection of state taxes in a single agency.

Balancing Revenues and Expenditures

Following World War II when many state services and programs had been curtailed, the accumulated surpluses enabled the state to spend more than it received. It was not until 1958 that the Legislature had either to provide more revenues or curtail state services. Because of the constitutional restrictions, the Legislature could not consider borrowing. In view of previous experimentation with the severance tax, the Legislature turned to an increase in the sales, income, and inheritance taxes and to the extension of the sales tax to hotel and motel rooms to raise the needed revenue.

As more and more services have come to be expected of the state government and as inflation has decreased the purchasing power of the dollar collected, the state has had to find more revenues. Only with difficulty have revenues been kept current with the increased expenditures. Major changes in state programs, such as increased state aid to schools, have had to be related to tax changes. In the view of some, one of the best ways to insure frugality in government is to keep revenues low.

Tax increases are never popular, yet the recent past suggests that expenditures are likely to increase more rapidly than revenues within the existing revenue structure. Pleas for increased state aid to schools and other local units of government, for new and better highways, and for services will have to be reconciled with the willingness of the people to support the state and its operation.

10 | *Personnel Administration*

In 1915 Kansas became the ninth state to adopt a general civil service system.[1] However, after five years of operation the law was allowed to remain completely inoperative for two decades.[2] The Legislature resorted to the simple expedient of making no appropriation to the civil service agency, and vacancies on the commission were not filled. Since the original state Constitution prescribed a maximum tenure of four years for all officers of the state, the political leaders had a convenient excuse for the removal of employees who had received appointments under the system.

The constitutional provision on tenure was considered by some an obstacle to an effective merit system. Consequently, when pressures again impelled legislative consideration of a personnel program in the late 1930's, the constitutional uncertainty provided the means for securing a direct expression of popular sentiment. In 1939 the Legislature approved the submission to the voters of a proposed constitutional amendment which would partially repeal the four-year tenure proviso and authorize the enactment of a merit-system law. The amendment

1. *Session Laws,* 1915, chap. 156.
2. William H. Cape and Edwin O. Stene, *State Civil Service in Kansas* (Lawrence: Governmental Research Center, Univ. of Kansas, 1954), pp. 5-12. Much of the information for this chapter comes from this study.

was adopted by the voters in the regular election of 1940 by almost a two-to-one majority.

With a popular mandate clearly before it, the Legislature passed a new civil service law in 1941.[3] The act provided for a three member, unpaid Civil Service Board, which appointed a professional director. The Director was given civil service tenure and had authority to appoint the subordinate personnel of the Department. The Board served as the policy-determining and appellate body of the Department. It adopted and modified, as deemed necessary, a set of civil service rules and regulations and a compensation schedule for the classified service and for the "classified-exempt" service.[4] As an appellate body, the Board reviewed decisions of the Director and disciplinary action of appointing officers when employees were charged with the violation of the civil service law. On its own motion or at the request of the Governor or others, the Board was directed to make investigations concerning the enforcement of the act.

The Director of Civil Service, who was responsible for the day-to-day activities of the Department, served also as the secretary and technical adviser to the Board. He directed the preparation of examinations, the rating of candidates for state employment, and the maintenance of eligible lists. In 1953, as a part of the fiscal reorganization which has already been discussed,[5] the organization for personnel administration in the state was revised.

Personnel Division

In the early stages of the plans for setting up the Department of Administration, there was no thought of including the personnel function within the new Department.[6] However, as finally approved, the bill made personnel one of the four divisions of the Department of Administration. The inclusion of personnel was opposed by a few per-

3. *K.S.A.*, 75-2925.

4. The "classified-exempt" service included approximately 237 positions in which duties were comparable to those of the classified service positions, but which were otherwise outside of the civil service jurisdiction. *K.S.A.*, 75-2935.

5. See chapter 7, pp. 126-27.

6. Peter Bart and Milton Cummings, Jr., "The Transfer of the Kansas State Civil Service Department" (University, Alabama: Univ. of Alabama Press, Inter-University Case Program, 1956).

sons who feared that this change would mean the abandonment of the civil service concept.

Essentially, the Civil Service Department was transferred to the Department of Administration and became the Personnel Division of the Department. Major responsibility for policy-determination was assigned to the State Finance Council, all six members of which are elected officials. The Finance Council has final authority to adopt and amend civil service rules and regulations, to approve additions to and changes in the classification system, and to approve any changes in the salary schedule. It also has authority to make investigations concerning the enforcement or effect of the civil service law.

The three-man Civil Service Board, whose members are appointed on a bipartisan basis by the Governor for overlapping four-year terms, retains the function of hearing appeals from classified employees on dismissals, suspensions, or other disciplinary action taken by their administrative superiors, and on decisions of the Personnel Director and the Executive Director regarding the admission of candidates to examinations or the placement of their names on eligible lists. The Board also appoints a committee to examine candidates for Personnel Director whenever a vacancy occurs in that office. The Executive Director of the Department of Administration, with the approval of the Governor, appoints the Personnel Director from among the three highest candidates certified by the examining committee.[7]

Members of the Civil Service Board are subject to removal by the Governor for malfeasance or neglect of duty, and after due notice and hearing. In that connection, question has arisen as to whether the Board can act only in response to complaints or whether its members are obligated to take action when they have information of illegal political pressures on employees. Members of the Board had assumed that formal complaint was a necessary prerequisite to action. In 1955 the Governor removed two of the Board members on charges that they were negligent, for they had taken no steps against known cases where classified employees were directed to engage in political campaigns. Even if the board members were negligent for failing to act against known violators, it is not clear how extensively they should engage in investigations on their own initiative to detect cases of violation. Since

7. *K.S.A.*, 75-2929 and 75-3703.

the Board does not hold regular meetings, it is not clear how individual members are to discharge their responsibilities.

Within the Department of Administration the Personnel Director is responsible to the Executive Director and may be removed by him for cause, subject to appeal to the Civil Service Board. Internally the Personnel Division is organized around its four principal areas of activity: namely, classification, recruitment and examination, transactions and certification, and office services. In addition to these four sections, there is a small research section which works closely with the Director of the Division. Clerical employees are for the most part employed in the transactions and certifications unit, while a majority of the professional technicians are in the recruitment and examinations unit. Pending the activation of the administrative services division of the Department of Administration, the Personnel Director is responsible for the operation of the central duplicating services section.

Classification of Positions

When the Civil Service Department came into being in 1941, its first major task was the classification of positions under its jurisdiction. By contract arrangement, the Public Administration Service of Chicago was engaged to prepare the initial classifications. Virtually all positions within jurisdiction of the civil service agency were classified. Minimum desirable qualifications were prescribed and salary ranges assigned to the several classes of positions. On September 16, 1942, the classification plan was formally adopted, and almost 6,000 positions were grouped into eight major occupational services.[8] These groups were further subdivided into 297 classes of positions.

Since the initial installation, the maintenance and revision of the classification plan have become the direct responsibility of the personnel staff. New classes are established from time to time, the specifications of existing classes are revised, classes are sometimes consolidated and a few have been abolished. The classification section is engaged continually in reviewing the duties and responsibilities assigned to posi-

8. The groups were (1) administrative and clerical, (2) construction and trade, (3) health and welfare, (4) custodial and maintenance, (5) law enforcement, (6) education, (7) agriculture and conservation, and (8) engineering and related trades. Cape and Stene, pp. 45-56.

tions in the state service. Most of the specific studies are undertaken at the request of the state agencies concerned, although the personnel agency may review classifications on its own initiative. All new classes and all transfers of positions from one class to another must be approved by the Finance Council. Since reclassifications call for financial adjustments, the director of the Budget Division must be consulted before proposals are submitted to the Council.

The Finance Council assigns or reassigns classes of positions to salary ranges.[9] The inflationary times and the comparatively low pay scale in state employment have resulted in the Division receiving many requests for reclassifying particular positions to higher-ranking classes. With a limited staff, the Division has been hard pressed to resist the pressures for "upgrading" jobs.

In addition to the normal maintenance and revision of the classification plan, the personnel agency has been called upon to classify two groups of positions that were not within its original jurisdiction. The civil service law of 1941 had excluded from the jurisdiction of the Civil Service Department those positions which had been placed under a "joint merit system" in order to qualify for federal grants-in-aid. At that time the Legislature sought to avoid any federal supervision of the state civil service system. Ten years later, however, the joint merit system agency was abolished, and its responsibilities transferred to the Civil Service Department.[10] This change meant the addition of approximately 200 new classes of positions to the state system.

The other expansion involved the "classified-exempt service." The original civil service law exempted from the classified service a number of clerical and junior supervisory positions in the elective offices. For these exempt positions the salaries had been fixed by law. But during the postwar inflation, the salaries fixed by statute lagged behind those of the classified service, and legislative determination of salaries was found to be excessively cumbersome. For purposes of salary adjustment, therefore, the Civil Service Board was assigned responsibility in 1949 to classify these positions, which in other regards are exempt from

9. The Legislative Committee on Economy and Efficiency recommended that the Personnel Division, not the Finance Council, should approve the creation and abolition of job classifications.

10. *Session Laws,* 1951, chap. 451.

civil service.[11] In 1953 all of the classification functions were transferred to the Department of Administration. As of January, 1968, in the classified service there were approximately 20,000 positions which were assigned to over 810 classes, while an additional 237 positions fell into the "classified-exempt service." There were approximately 7,500 employees in the unclassified service. The faculties at the various state educational institutions accounted for about four-fifths of the unclassified service.

Wage Administration

Throughout the history of the Civil Service Department and its successor, the Division of Personnel, the general salary trends have been upward. The responsibility to prepare and revise salary schedules to meet prevailing labor costs was initially assigned to the Civil Service Department. That responsibility subjected the Department to criticism from operating agencies. Those that had funds to meet rising costs demanded more freedom to increase salaries; while the agencies and institutions with limited funds complained that they were forced to increase salaries unnecessarily.

Before the civil service law was in effect, salaries were prescribed either by the Legislature or by the operating agencies. The outstanding feature of the pay plan was its lack of uniformity. When the classification of positions was installed in 1941, for example, it was found that the monthly salaries for positions classified as Clerk-typist I ranged from $55 to $190.

The original classification plan provided a degree of uniformity of salaries in the classified service, and laid the groundwork for a system of salary-classification for positions in the unclassified service. The present system is based upon a series of pay ranges. The ranges, or grades, are numbered from sixteen through fifty-three, and steps are designated by letters A through H. Each class of positions is assigned to a range, and compensation rates may be changed only by assigning a class to a higher or lower range. New employees may start at step A in the pay range for their particular classification, but agencies are authorized to start employees at steps B or C in order to attract competent recruits. Most agencies in 1968 were beginning most of their employees

11. *K.S.A.*, 75-2935a.

at the C step. The difference between each range is 5 per cent, and within each range there are seven steps allowing 5 per cent increases between each step.

Since the salary pattern was first adopted in 1943 there have been numerous changes, both in the amounts assigned to the ranges and in the ranges to which particular classes of positions are assigned. New salary ranges have occasionally been added to the top of the scale with fifty-three being the highest range in 1968. No positions are assigned to any of the lowest fifteen ranges, so that in effect thirty-eight ranges are used. In 1968 beginning salaries varied from $242 to $1341 a month, the maximum under the classified service being step H in range 53 at $1,886 a month.

In the past the Finance Council has made only a few cost-of-living adjustments or general changes in the amounts assigned to the salary ranges. Instead the Council has resorted to the expedient of assigning particular classes of positions to higher ranges. The problem of this approach is that the responsibility and difficulty of these positions have not changed relative to the other classes that have not been reassigned. Thus inequities and injustices develop through this type of piecemeal approach and further piecemeal action becomes necessary. For these and other reasons the Legislative Committee on Economy and Efficiency recommended that this practice be discontinued and a general salary survey be made. Such a salary survey has not been made.

Recruitment and Selection

The Kansas civil service law is based upon the traditional assumption that there is available at all times a surplus of employable persons to fill government jobs. A system of competitive and "practical" examinations is prescribed, and the personnel agency is directed to maintain eligible lists from which names may be drawn when employing agencies request the certification of qualified candidates. Under the "rule of three" the personnel agency certifies the three top names on an eligible list for each vacancy. Even the relaxation of the rule of three has failed to overcome the tendency of eligible lists to become out-of-date.

The traditional civil service selection procedures tend to be inadequate for effective recruitment and selection in times of full employment. Normally the announcement of an examination date sets a closing date for applications, probably a month or more after the announcement is published. After the closing date there is an interval of two or more weeks before the examination is held; and the examination is followed by an interval necessary for the computation of grades and the preparation of eligible lists. Such a recruitment process is not adapted to a full-employment economy in which job-seekers can find with relative ease jobs that in most cases they consider more desirable than government employment. A delay of two months or more between announcement and the certification of names to appointing authorities frequently means that a large proportion of the applicants are no longer available when appointments are offered.

Various attempts have been made to adapt the recruitment and examination system to actual conditions. For example, the law makes provision for temporary or provisional appointments when appropriate eligible lists are exhausted, but it limits the period for which these appointments can be made, and restricts the reappointment of temporary employees. The underlying assumption is that new eligible lists will be sufficient to replace all temporary employees. This is not in accord with experience. The personnel agency is frequently fortunate if it has applicants to fill new vacancies, and is not prepared to insist that operating agencies replace provisional employees. The most effective way of reducing the number of temporary employees is to persuade the incumbents to take examinations in order to secure permanent status. Where the employing agencies cooperate in this process, the examinations become largely a device for the post-validation of eligibility.

To speed up the recruitment and selection process, the Division uses consolidated announcements wherein the vacancies in several related classes are listed, and has adopted the practice of giving examinations at frequent intervals or when applicants come to the personnel office. Thus some examinations are continuously open and interested applicants can be examined, rated, and certified with dispatch. For an area as large as the state, however, continuous examinations can be used effectively only if examinations are available at various points in the state. Thus far the authority to examine and rate applicants has not generally been delegated to operating agencies.

The formal recruitment and selection process is relatively simple. Announcements of opportunities are printed in circular form and distributed to employment agencies, to newspapers, schools, colleges and other public places, and to business firms or individuals that might be in a position to bring the information to the attention of interested persons.

The application form serves as a basis of identifying the candidate when he appears for his examination and also is used to measure initially his qualifications. Normally a written examination, or a performance examination is given where the number of applicants and the nature of the work make such performance tests practicable. Written examinations are given the most weight for those classes that include large numbers of positions, such as those in the clerical and accounting classifications. Assembled examinations are usually dispensed with for positions in the executive and professional classes. Written tests are not normally required of those applying for positions as laborers. The oral interview is also used in the evaluation of applicants and in the selection of executive and professional personnel.

The final grade of an applicant is a weighted combination of the ratings on training and experience, the written examination, and the oral interview. The usual practice is to reduce the relative weight of the written examination as the importance of the positions concerned increases, until, for positions of major importance, the ratings are often based entirely on the applicant's training and experience and the interview.

The civil service law designated a grade of "70" as passing. But modern examination systems do not lend themselves readily to grading on the basis of percentages, and so the passing score is in fact decided upon before the official score is computed. The lowest score decided upon as satisfactory in light of the demands of the positions and available applicants may be translated into a grade of 70, and other scores are computed accordingly. Veterans' preference points are awarded, where appropriate, after the official score has been computed. War veterans are given ten extra points on their grades, and disabled veterans are given fifteen points. However, a veteran must pass an examination in order to receive preference points.[12]

After the grades have been determined and veterans' preference points added, the names of successful applicants for each classification are placed on an *eligible list* in order of score. In case of a tie score,

12. K.S.A., 75-2955.

however, a veteran is always listed ahead of a nonveteran. The eligible lists are used as the basis for certifying applicants when names are requested by appointing authorities.

Certification and Appointment

When a vacancy occurs in the state service, the appointing official initiates the selection process by submitting a requisition to the Personnel Division. If an appropriate eligible list is available, the Personnel Division certifies names in accordance with the rule of three, as modified by the law and as provided in the rules of the Department of Administration. The Director of the Personnel Division is authorized, with the approval of the Executive Director of the Department of Administration, to certify more than three names when it is "in the best interest of economy and efficiency."[13] When no eligibles are available, the operating agency is authorized to make a provisional appointment. Theoretically, the provisional appointment can be continued only until eligibles are available from the next examination for the particular classification, but the eligible lists are seldom adequate to fill new vacancies, with the result that a provisional appointment is normally continued unless the incumbent qualifies through the examination process.

In the years of civil service in Kansas the recruiting conditions have never been what, in past years, were considered normal. First wartime shortages of personnel and then the post-World War II full-employment economy have served to make the job of recruitment more difficult. Low wages and the low prestige of state employment have led, in many cases, to poorly qualified employees, a condition which in turn leads to lower prestige of employment and little inclination to raise wages. For much of this period, approximately 22 per cent of the state classified service were serving in a provisional status. At the urging of the Legislative Committee on Economy and Efficiency, the Personnel Division made substantial progress in reducing the number of those provisionally employed. In January, 1968, slightly under 5 per cent of the classified positions were held by provisional employees.

Provisional employees provoke many problems. In this type of employment, violations of the civil service concept are most likely to

13. *K.S.A.*, 75-2943.

occur.[14] Serving in a provisional status creates uncertainty of employment for both the employee and the employing officials. If the employee is not continued in employment, the agency and the state lose the time and money spent in training the employee and in his becoming adjusted to the organization.

Provisional appointees are advised to take examinations at their earliest opportunities, but even so the Personnel Division has not had sufficiently long eligible lists to insist upon the replacement of those who did not take examinations when offered. As a result the examinations, while serving to exclude unqualified candidates, do not fulfill the theoretical goal of insuring the selection of the best qualified applicants.

Civil service employees are subject to probationary appointments, usually for six months. On or before the end of the probationary period, the appointing official is required to certify to the Personnel Director that the appointment has been terminated or that the employee's performance is satisfactory and that he should be retained. In special cases requests may be made for extension of the probationary term. An employee is not entitled to compensation beyond the probationary period unless the Personnel Director has received notice of appointment on permanent status or a request for an extension of the probationary appointment.[15]

Positions above the beginning level are normally filled by promotion. An employee may be advanced to a higher classification through any one of three methods: namely, (1) by taking the regular examination for the higher-class position, (2) by taking a departmental promotional examination, or (3) by taking a state-wide promotional examination. For promotional examinations within one department, the practice is to give unassembled noncompetitive examinations and to question the applicants mostly on matters pertaining to duties of the department. Promotional examinations, both competitive and noncompetitive, are given at the request of the departments. Test scores are combined with efficiency ratings and length of service to determine the ratings on promotional examinations.

14. Legislative Committee on Economy and Efficiency, *Report*, II (1959), 15.
15. William H. Cape and Edwin O. Stene, *State Civil Service in Kansas* (Lawrence: Governmental Research Center, Univ. of Kansas, 1954), p. 84.

Conditions of Employment

Hours of work for full-time employees are determined by the appointing authorities of the several state agencies. Each agency, however, is required to report its time schedule to the Director of Administration. Most agencies now operate on a forty-hour week, though in the past there have been differences in the work week.

The establishment of a merit system was followed by a definite policy regarding vacations and sick leaves. Classified employees with less than ten years of service earn annual leave at the rate of one day a month. Those with ten or more but less than fifteen years earn one and one-quarter days a month, while those with fifteen or more years of service earn one and one-half days a month. The amount of annual leave that may be accumulated varies from eighteen to twenty-four days, depending on the length of service of the employee. Hourly employees also earn annual leave. Sick leave is earned at the rate of one day for each month of service and may accumulate without limit.

Leave without pay may be granted by appointing authorities for a maximum of one year. Military leaves are effective for the period of service in the armed forces.

The civil service law directed the personnel agency to establish standards of performance "and a system of service ratings."[16] A system of service ratings was installed in 1947 and revised in 1963, but relatively little has been done toward the establishment of performance standards. The rating system provides for an "adjective rating" (excellent, very good, satisfactory, fair, unsatisfactory) of at least twelve items or characteristics of an employee's performance. Supervisory personnel are rated on additional items. Each employee is rated by his immediate superior, and space is provided for the employee's signature as evidence that the rating has been made known to him. Ratings of "excellent" and "unsatisfactory" are supported by the citation of specific evidence.

There is evidence that the ratings are not taken too seriously by supervising officials. A substantial majority of the employees are rated as excellent or very good. Low ratings create unpleasant working-relationships and handicap the agency in making salary adjustments or getting positions reclassified.

16. *K.S.A.*, 75-2943.

One of the controversial issues of government employment is the participation of employees in political or other organizations that seek to influence government policy. Kansas law does not restrict the political activities of civil service employees, although it prohibits the solicitation of money or political service from employees by administrative or supervisory officials. In 1955 the Governor dismissed two members of the Civil Service Board for neglect in the enforcement of this rule.[17] Employee participation in the preceding primary campaign was well known; but coercion would have been difficult to prove, especially when no complaints were filed by any employees. The Governor's dismissals were not challenged, since the law gives him wide discretion. If the opposing candidate had been nominated, probably no disciplinary action would have occurred. In short, the experience illustrates the difficulty of enforcing restrictions on coercion or solicitations of employees who are free to engage in political activities if they so choose.

Labor-union activities have been looked upon with less favor than political activities, despite the absence of legal restrictions on unionization. In 1943 an effort to organize state employees was short-lived, when the Governor issued a public statement opposing the union and labeling the organization as a pressure group on the Legislature.[18] Members of highly organized skilled crafts, especially the employees in the state printing plant, belong to craft unions, and a few employees belong to the American Federation of State, County, and Municipal Employees. While the state makes no contracts with the unions, at one time the power of some of the craft groups was recognized indirectly, through provision that workers in certain skilled trades should be paid at the "prevailing rate." In the last several years, most of the employees paid on this basis have been converted to a monthly basis and are paid under the schedule of salary ranges. There are some indications that the attitude toward public-employee unions is changing and that the unions are going to become more active.

From 1949 until 1967 all officers and employees of the state, counties, cities, or other municipalities, and teachers in public and private schools

17. This action occurred at a time when the Board was about to hear a case involving the dismissal by the Governor of the state Purchasing Director. The Governor removed the Board members at least in part because he feared his dismissal of the Purchasing Director would otherwise not receive an unprejudiced hearing.

18. *Topeka Daily Capital*, Aug. 14, 15, 22, and 23, 1943.

and colleges were required to sign an oath that they did not advocate and were not members of a political party which advocated the overthrow of the government by force. In 1967 a three-man U.S. district court declared this oath law unconstitutional. In 1968 the Legislature enacted a new loyalty oath law,[19] which required a simple affirmation to support the U.S. and Kansas constitutions and to discharge faithfully the duties of the office.

Layoffs arising out of reduction of force or reinstatement of personnel on military leave are determined on the basis of a formula that takes into account seniority and service ratings. Employees who are laid off are entitled to priority when an appointing authority requests certification. Because of the large turnover in state service, the lay-off rules have been applied in only a few instances.

Separations

For a wide variety of reasons, state employment has a large turnover. One report set the average time that an employee served in the classified service at two and a half years.[20] In a number of classes of positions the turnover was considerably higher. Turnover is costly from the agency point of view as well as from that of the Personnel Division. Turnover means more vacancies; more examinations to prepare, give, and rate; more eligible lists; and more transactions to handle. For the employing agency it means most often a break in service, with other employees having to be shifted around to absorb temporarily some of the work of the employee who has left. When a new employee becomes available there is the orientation and training period while the new employee is adjusting to the job, and production is not likely to be up to the normal level. One estimate put this cost of training at $800,000 a year.

Undoubtedly the relatively low wages paid state employees contribute to turnover and point to the need for a general wage survey. The Legislative Committee on Economy and Efficiency noted that opportunity for promotion, working conditions, security, location of the job, and the demands of private employment were also factors. All of

19. *1968 Session Laws of Kansas*, chap. 106.
20. Legislative Committee on Economy and Efficiency, *op. cit.*, 12, 13.

these considerations suggest the need for making state employment more attractive and for the development of a state career service.

A career service should provide for an orderly way for separating those employees who have reached the age when they are no longer fully efficient.

In 1961 the Legislature established the Kansas Public Employees Retirement System to provide retirement benefits for most state employees. Each participating employee contributes 4 per cent of his salary, and the employing agency contributes a rate which has varied between 5.35 and 4.0 per cent. Currently the employing agency contributes 4 per cent of the wages paid for retirement benefits and 0.5 per cent for a group insurance program. Retirement benefits are set at 1 per cent for each year of credited participating service, based on the employee's final average salary. For those employed before the system became effective, benefits are based on 1 per cent for each year of service. This is in addition to the Federal Old Age and Survivors' Insurance Program, which covers all state employees and the employees of many local governments.

Separate systems were continued for employees of the state Highway Patrol, the Kansas Bureau of Investigation, district judges, district court reporters, and school employees. Nonteaching employees of the Board of Regents were included in the new system, while teaching employees were put under the nation-wide Teachers Insurance and Annuity Association program.

The new state system allowed local units of government to participate, and a substantial number of them have seen fit to do so. As of January 1, 1968, there were 119 cities, 105 county social-welfare boards, 80 counties, 39 libraries, 13 agricultural extension councils, 10 townships, and 46 other units of local government, including recreation commissions, cemetery districts, soil-conservation districts, drainage districts, urban-renewal agencies, hospitals, joint boards of health, and others.

Most employees who leave state employment do so voluntarily. Any employee may be dismissed at any time for cause. If such dismissed employee has served his probational period and thus has gained "permanent" status, he is entitled to a hearing before the Civil Service Board. If the Board finds that there was insufficient cause or that he was dismissed for political, religious, or racial reasons, the employee is reinstated and paid his salary for the time since he worked. On the other hand if, as is more often the case, the Board finds the dismissal for reasonable cause, the employee's service is officially ended. Similar appeals are allowed permanent employees in instances of suspensions and demotions. Persons who have been provisionally appointed or who are serving their probational period are not entitled to such appeals. They are merely entitled to a statement of the charges and can ask only for administrative appeals within the agency. The formal appeal procedure requires that the aggrieved employee has first appealed to the appointing authority and that he is dissatisfied with the decision of the appointing authority.

The number of such dismissals is not an accurate measure of how effective the supervisors are in weeding out the unsatisfactory employees. Nor is it a measure of how effective the examining procedure is in selecting only qualified employees. Actually, dismissal occurs only in the most unusual cases. If the employee is not suitable, he may be reassigned or, in some cases, the supervisor will encourage him to resign. In public employment it is important, and sometimes difficult, for the reviewing authority to hear the cases in such a way that the employee will feel that he is being treated fairly and the supervisor will feel that he and his work are not on trial.

Unsolved Problems

Some of the problems of administering the personnel system of the state have already been described. However, one major criticism often directed at civil-service laws and procedures is that they do not in fact establish a merit system. Sometimes the charge is made that the system is manipulated and controlled for purposes of political patronage. At other times the rigid enforcement of rules and policies is said to obstruct, rather than to facilitate, the appointment and advancement of well-qualified personnel.

If a few cases prove the point, both of these charges could doubtless be substantiated. Political influence certainly has not been eliminated. The rule of three permits a limited consideration of political acceptability, and appointing officials sometimes make a practice of inquiring into applicants' political status. Pressures on applicants to withdraw from consideration may open the way for favored appointments. Oral interview ratings may at times be influenced by known attitudes of prominent politicians; and certainly the experience that politically selected provisional employees obtain on the job helps them qualify later in the examination. On the other hand, residence requirements, specific training and experience requirements, and the failure of possible candidates to make applications when examinations were announced may prevent approval of applicants whom the appointing officials consider more competent than any of the eligible list. Position classifications have sometimes restricted the freedom of action desired by operating agencies, and doubtless there have been times when personnel officials have disagreed with the responsible officials regarding the proper course of action. Promotions are largely within the control of appointing officials so long as prescribed routines are followed and the appointees are reasonably well qualified. Incidents might be cited in support of either the charge of political favoritism or that of inflexible bureaucracy.

But perfection is not to be expected. On the one hand, social pressures cannot be disregarded completely; and on the other hand, regulations that have merit as general policy may result in unwise or unfortunate decisions in specific instances. The question is not whether politics has been eliminated, nor is it a matter of whether the best candidate has been appointed in every instance. Rather it is, Has either politics or bureaucratic red tape obstructed the operation of the intended merit system to such degree as to justify serious consideration of a return to the earlier spoils system?

The answer to that question seems to be clearly in the negative. A few administrative officials probably feel that they could select capable personnel without the restrictive features of a central personnel system; but even if that is true, their disadvantages are more than offset by gains in other areas where the spoils system was so strong that administrators and supervisors had little control over their own employees. A before-and-after comparison is impossible, especially because of the fact that the civil service system of Kansas came into being at the very time when the whole nation experienced a rapid shift from a large labor surplus to a widespread shortage of labor. There is, however, some evidence of three important differences. First, the obviously incompetent candidate is eliminated with relative ease; that was not the case under the spoils system. Secondly, considering the changed labor market, the average department or agency head has more freedom of selection under the civil service system than he had under the spoils system, when candidates were "certified" to him by county chairmen or state party headquarters. And thirdly, the employee who has been selected through civil service procedures and is assured of a degree of security so long as he performs his duties satisfactorily, feels a greater loyalty and responsibility to his administrative superior than did the employee who owed his appointment to a local county chairman or some other political leader. There may still be employees who feel these outside obligations, but certainly they are the exception rather than the rule.

It is not easy to find the correct balance for a public personnel office between the policing type of operation necessary for maintaining a civil service merit system and the service type of operation desirable for an auxiliary management staff agency. The Personnel Division was urged by the Legislative Committee on Economy and Efficiency to emphasize the service, rather than regulatory, side of its operations. Presumably one of the basic reasons for including the personnel function in the Department of Administration was to promote the use of personnel as a management tool.

Critics note the increase in the number of state employees—an increase which has been greater proportionately than the increase in the population. In any organization the size of the state government there is need for continuous attention to the management and supervision of the operations at all levels. There are many ways open to the Personnel Division for furthering the improvement of management and supervision. The Division has established the Advisory Personnel Council consisting of the personnel officers of the major state agencies. Through such contacts and closer awareness of operating problems, many of the detailed personnel operations can be delegated and performed at levels closer to the operating level. Thus, the Personnel Division may be freed for training, more recruitment, more test validation, and other activities which would further enhance the effectiveness of state employees.

11 | The Courts

The judicial system of Kansas follows a pattern familiar to many American states. It is characterized by a hierarchy of tribunals, a proliferation of local courts established to make justice widely available, and the popular election of judges.

The history of courts in the area began in territorial days.[1] The first judicial officers appointed in the Territory were apparently justices of the peace named by Governor Reeder late in 1854. President Pierce appointed three judges to serve as the territorial Supreme Court. These three judges may have held court as district judges earlier, but there are no records. In any case it is certain that they did not convene as a court of last resort for the Territory until July 30, 1855, when Governor Reeder and the territorial Legislature had become embroiled in a bitter feud. The Governor had called the territorial Legislature to meet at Pawnee (now a part of the Fort Riley military reservation). The legislators met at Pawnee but decided on their own to move the place of their meeting to the Shawnee Mission, in what is now Johnson County. Governor Reeder maintained that the Legislature was without power to adjourn to a different meeting place and refused to sign the acts adopted at Shawnee Mission. The Legislature then requested the Su-

1. T. M. Lillard, "Beginnings of the Kansas Judiciary," *Kansas Judicial Council Bulletin,* 28th Annual Report (1954), p. 3.

preme Court to convene and rule upon the validity of the session at the location chosen by the assembly.

The court specially took the question under advisement, not as a court, but as individual judges. Chief Justice Samuel Lecompte and Associate Justice Rush Elmore recorded their view that the assembly was legal and its enactments valid. Relying on this informal opinion, the Legislature proceeded to enact a general body of laws to govern the Territory. The third judge, Saunders W. Johnston, wrote a brief statement arguing that the members of the court had no right to render opinions except in regularly presented cases. It should be noted that Lecompte and Elmore were Southerners, and Johnston a Northerner, and that the composition of the Legislature was such as to make it known to Free-Staters as the "Bogus Legislature."[2]

The territorial court, so inauspiciously inaugurated, functioned until it was replaced by state courts in 1861. The first State Supreme Court session was held on October 28, 1861, with Chief Justice Thomas Ewing, Jr., and Associate Justices Samuel A. Kingman and Lawrence D. Bailey on the bench.[3]

The state Constitution under which Kansas was admitted to the Union vested judicial power in ". . . a Supreme Court, district courts, probate courts, justices of the peace, and such other courts, inferior to the Supreme Court, as may be provided by law;. . . ."[4] It is to these courts that we now turn our attention.

The Supreme Court

Originally, the Supreme Court consisted of a chief justice and two associate justices, elected for overlapping six-year terms. In 1900 a constitutional amendment changed the composition of the court to seven justices, with the senior justice in terms of service holding the position of chief justice.[5]

The Legislature has established a minimum age of thirty and four years of legal practice as qualifications for election.[6] There are neither constitutional nor statutory provisions relating to the disqualification of

2. *Ibid.*, pp. 4-6.
3. *Ibid.*, p. 8.
4. *Kansas Constitution*, Art. 3, sec. 1.
5. *Kansas Constitution*, Art. 3, sec. 2.
6. *K.S.A.*, 20-105; *Session Laws*, 1915, chap. 208, as amended by *Session Laws*, 1917, chap. 153.

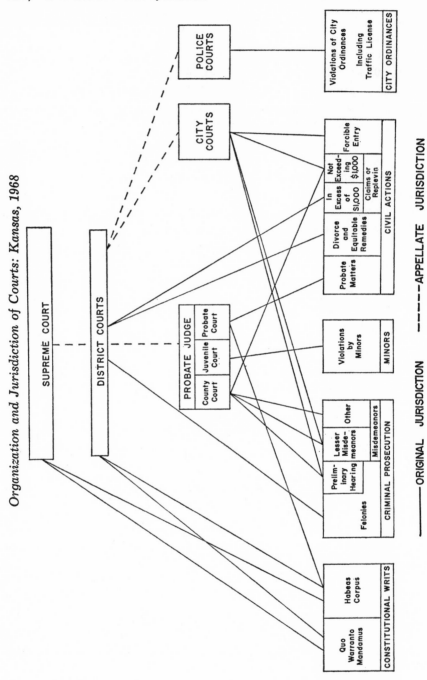

Organization and Jurisdiction of Courts: Kansas, 1968

justices or to the selection of a substitute for a justice who may have disqualified himself.[7] The compensation of members of the Supreme Court is now set at $21,500 per annum, except for the Chief Justice, who receives $22,500.[8]

The Constitution requires the Supreme Court to hold one term each year in Topeka. By statute, the first Tuesdays in January and July are fixed for its convening.[9] The Supreme Court has both original and appellate jurisdiction. The former includes the three extraordinary remedies of quo warranto, mandamus, and habeas corpus. The appellate jurisdiction is subject to legislative provision which has, since the beginning of the state government, allowed all customary forms and processes by which lower-court judgments may be reviewed.

The work of the Kansas Supreme Court has been described by three men who were members of that body: Justices Hugo T. Wedell, Robert T. Price, and Edward F. Arn, in articles written by them for the *Kansas Judicial Council Bulletin*.[10] In contrast to the practice observed in the Supreme Court of the United States, cases are assigned to individual justices in the Kansas Supreme Court before they have been taken up in conference. After the arguments have been heard, the justices meet in the office of the Chief Justice and then, following a system of rotation based on seniority, justices are assigned the job of writing opinions for the cases heard that day. The justice assigned to prepare the opinion may find himself dissenting from his own opinion. Justice Price observed that when he was placed in that position, "it did seem a bit awkward."[11] However, he generally endorsed the system of the absolute rotation of justices in the assignment of opinions.

The justices ordinarily hear oral arguments for one week each month. On the Wednesday of the following week the conference at which the cases are discussed begins and normally lasts through Saturday. The remaining two weeks of the month are given over to the writing of opinions. In the conferences of the justices, the junior justice presents "his" cases first and so on according to seniority. In voting, the

7. *Aetra* v. *Travis,* 124 Kan. 350, 354; *Barber County* v. *Bank,* 123 Kan. 10, 14.

8. *K.S.A.,* 75-3120d.

9. *K.S.A.,* 20-102.

10. July, 1942; April, 1950; and December, 1951.

11. "Off the Record," *Kansas Judicial Council Bulletin* (Topeka: Kansas Judicial Council), XXIV (1950), 5.

most junior justice votes first, except that the justice whose case is being voted on is the last to announce his vote. This procedure differs markedly from that followed by the Supreme Court of the United States.

Opinions are required to be in writing, and the justice delivering the opinion must file with the clerk the syllabus to be published in the official reports.[12]

Quantitatively, the work of the court over the last thirty years is presented in the accompanying total. Approximately one-third of the cases filed are dismissed, the remainder being decided after full argument on the merits of the case.

Though the Judicial Council had earlier recommended changing the method for selecting justices of the Supreme Court, the Legislature in 1957 submitted a proposed constitutional change to the voters to allow for the nonpartisan selection of judges. The proposal, which was approved, was patterned after a system used in Missouri. The Governor now appoints persons to fill vacancies on the Supreme Court from lists of three persons nominated by a Supreme Court Nominating Commission. The Commission consists of a chairman selected by the Kansas Bar Association and two members from each congressional district. One of these members must be a lawyer selected by the members of the bar association residing in that district, while the other, a lay member, is appointed by the Governor. The members of the Commission are for-

TABLE 24

Cases Disposed of by Kansas Supreme Court:

1928, 1938, 1948, 1958, 1968

Fiscal Year	Cases Appealed		Original Jurisdiction	Total
	Civil	Criminal		
1928	529	101	46	676
1938	388	41	32	461
1948	244	23	93	360
1958	388	23	17	428
1968	201	77	41	319

Source: "Summary of the Work of the Supreme Court," *Kansas Judicial Council Bulletin*, XLII (1968), pp. 6-10.

12. K.S.A., 20-111.

bidden to hold either appointive or elective public office or any official position in a political party. Members of the Commission are themselves ineligible for nomination to the Supreme Court during the period of their membership on the Commission and for six months thereafter.

After the Governor appoints a person from among those nominated, this person serves as justice for at least a one-year period. At the first general election following the judge's completing one year of service, the name of the new justice is submitted on a nonpartisan ballot with voters merely being asked to indicate whether the justice should be continued in office. The justice does not "run for election" in the traditional sense, but instead stands on the record of his service. If the vote favors his continuing in office, the justice serves for six years, at the end of which time a similar referendum is held. There is no limit on the number of terms a justice may serve. If the voters decide against continuing the justice in office, a vacancy is created and the process starts over again.

The Supreme Court justices thus selected are prohibited from making contributions to, or holding offices in, political parties and from taking part in political campaigns.

Critics of the scheme claim the system will not eliminate politics from the courts, that it gives too much power to a select group of lawyers, and that the plan for popular rejection works to eliminate only the most glaringly unsatisfactory judges. The proponents of the system hail it as a happy compromise, keeping up both the best characteristics of the method of appointing judges and an element of popular control.

In 1965 the Legislature enacted the Judicial Department Reform Act which allowed the grouping of judicial districts to divide the state into six judicial departments. Each of the six justices is assigned to a department, and supervises the work of the district courts in his department. The Office of Judicial Administrator was established to assist in this work. Information is maintained in the Administrator's office on the case load in each district court. District judges are assigned to hear cases in other districts in order to equalize the dockets of the district courts and to facilitate the hearing and deciding of the cases. Judicial conferences are held at least once each year allowing the justice to assemble all the district judges in "his" department to consider the business of the department.

District Courts

The Constitution originally established five districts, with one judge to be elected in each district for a four-year term.[13] As new counties were organized, they were attached to existing districts. In 1867 the Legislature created, by the required two-thirds majority, four additional districts and has added other districts from time to time.

Keeping districts of appropriate size for the effective operation of the district courts has long been a problem. A major redistricting took place in 1895, when the state was divided into twenty-nine judicial districts. Changes were made from time to time, generally merely by detaching a county and forming a new district, until in 1968 there were thirty-eight districts. After consideration at several earlier sessions, the Legislature in 1968 redistricted the state for judicial purposes and constituted twenty-nine districts.

Today there are twenty-nine districts, as shown on the accompanying map. Eighteen districts range in size from three to seven counties; three districts have but two counties; and eight districts consist of only

Judicial Districts and Departments: Kansas, January, 1969

Judicial departments are shown in various patterns and are identified with large numbers (1-6); judicial districts have smaller numerals, and where there is more than one division, the "subnumbers" indicate the number of divisions. For example, Pratt County is in the fifth judicial department, the nineteenth district, which has three divisions.

13. This provision formed Article 3, section 5, of the original constitution and was eliminated in 1958 when this article was amended.

one county. Almost half (fourteen) of the districts have but one judge. Districts which have more than one judge are said to have divisions, which frequently consist of specified parts of the district. In these instances, if the district is composed of more than one county, the judge is required to be a resident of the division but is elected by the voters of the entire district. In the more populated counties which form separate districts, there are divisions with a judge for each division. The judges are elected at large by the voters of the district and have their cases assigned by the administrative judge. An example of such a district is the eighteenth judicial district (Sedgwick County), which has seven divisions.

Further, in 1968, to help keep more uniform work loads and to expedite the work in district courts, the Legislature required that district courts examine their caseloads once a month in single-county districts and once every three months in multi-county districts. In each district having more than one division the Supreme Court appoints one of the judges as administrative judge, and he has general control over the assignment of cases within the district. In four of the more populous judicial districts the Supreme Court was authorized to increase or reduce the number of divisions as needed.

The district court in Kansas is the general trial court, with broad civil and criminal jurisdiction. Civil actions of divorce and claims involving any amount of money may be begun in it. Prosecutions of both felonies and misdemeanors may also be heard. The district court acts as appellate court for the probate and county courts, justice-of-the-peace courts, city courts, and police courts. The table on page 196 shows the types and nature of the cases handled by district courts.

The typical arrangement in Kansas is for the district judge to ride his circuit, visiting the county-seat towns in his district and holding court when he is in them. To help the judge, and incidentally the lawyers and people having business with the court, a clerk of the court is elected in each county. This official handles the records and serves as a local representative for the district judge.

District judges are elected for four-year terms on a partisan ballot, some being elected at each general election. However, the principle of rotation has not been applied to this office. While in earlier years the trend was not so pronounced, the elections of district judges have fre-

TABLE 25

Types of Cases Handled by Kansas District Courts for Year Ending June 30, 1968

CIVIL CASES

Divorce	10,937
Other Domestic Relations	2,775
Auto Negligence	2,007
Other Tort	844
Actions Concerning Sentencing	102
Foreclosures	1,051
Real Property	1,857
Contractual	4,205
Injunction, Mandamus, Quo Warranto	251
Other	1,428
TOTAL	25,457

CRIMINAL CASES

Felonies	
Against Person	819
Against Property	1,659
Other	398
Misdemeanors	
Driving while Intoxicated	185
Other Traffic	154
Other	135
Appeals from Lower Courts	
Driving while Intoxicated	402
Other Traffic	461
Other	432
TOTAL	4,645
GRAND TOTAL:	30,102

Source: "Summary of District Courts," *Kansas Judicial Council Bulletin*, XLII (1968), 32 and 40.

quently been without contest in either the primary or the general election.[14]

14. Research Department, Kansas Legislative Council, *Selection of Judges* (Topeka: Publication No. 211, 1956), p. 19.

Probate and County Courts

In each county in Kansas there is a probate court which has responsibility for probating or proving wills, settling estates, guardianship proceedings, control of the property of infants, and committing the insane to hospitals. In addition, the probate judge acts ex officio as judge of the juvenile court. In this capacity the judge hears criminal prosecution against girls under the age of eighteen and boys under the age of sixteen. A few of the larger counties with more juvenile problems allow their probate judges to appoint special officials to help them in investigating the cases which come before them.

In order to have courts more available for trying certain types of cases, a large and increasing number of counties have established county courts. The county commissioners may by statute create such a court. Most simply, this means that when the county commissioners have so decided, the probate judge, in addition to his other duty, serves as judge of the county court. Under these conditions the judge can hear cases involving certain misdemeanors and civil cases involving claims for $1,000 or less.

County courts have been assigned jurisdiction over cases previously decided by justices of the peace and are now required to exist in all counties in which there is not a city court, a court of common pleas, or a magistrate court with county-wide jurisdiction. The judges are

TABLE 26

Growth of County Courts: Selected Years

Date	Total Cumulative
1923	3
1928	15
1933	24
1938	34
1943	42
1948	54
1953	54
1958	72
1963	76
1968	93

Source: *Kansas Judicial Council Bulletins, 1924-1968.*

TABLE 27
Work of County Courts: Year Ending June 30, 1968

Type of Case	Number
Civil	4,503
Criminal	63,668
Total	68,171

Source: *Kansas Judicial Council Bulletin,* XLII (1968), 55, 58.

elected for two-year terms, as are most county officers. Their salaries
are fixed by statute and vary according to the population of the county.

Justices of the Peace

When the Constitution was written and for a number of years after-
wards, the township justice of the peace was a more important official
than he is today. Under the Constitution two justices of the peace are
to be elected in each township and the Legislature is authorized to increase the number as needed. The Legislature has used this authorization to allow for the election of two justices of the peace from all
cities of the first and second class and from cities of the third class with
a population over 1,000 which have, by a special procedure, separated
themselves from the township in which they are located.

To a large measure the office of justice of the peace has fallen into
disuse and seems to be atrophying. It is probably impossible to find the
exact number of offices which are now filled. In most elections no candidate files for the office, and in only a few are there any contests.[15]
Since a justice continues in office until his successor has qualified, many
offices which now are vacant for practical purposes may not be legally
vacant.

The jurisdiction of justices of the peace has long been quite limited.[16] In 1965 it was further restricted in counties where there is a
county court or a city court, a court of common pleas, or a magistrate

15. One study made in 1954 suggested that the number of offices filled was between 5 and 17 per cent of the number authorized. (James W. Drury, *Township
Government in Kansas* [Lawrence: Governmental Research Center, Univ. of Kansas, 1954], p. 27.)

16. Ruth Y. Wetmore, *The Justice of the Peace in Kansas* (Lawrence: Governmental Research Center, Univ. of Kansas, 1960).

court with county-wide jurisdiction.[17] In these counties the justices of the peace have no civil or criminal jurisdiction except in civil cases where the amount claimed does not exceed one dollar. By establishing county courts in those counties where the justices of the peace still had this limited jurisdiction, the Legislature in 1967 for all practical purposes abolished this office.[18]

City Courts

In 1897 the Legislature, perhaps recognizing the problems in the justice-of-the-peace courts, created a city court for Kansas City. Two years later city courts were authorized for Atchison, Coffeyville, Leavenworth, Topeka, and Wichita, by name. These courts were in general given jurisdiction comparable to that of the justice of the peace, except that they were given a somewhat larger jurisdiction in civil matters. Generally these statutes remain in effect and govern the operation of the courts in these cities. The Wichita court has come to be known as the Court of Common Pleas. In this court and the city court of Kansas City, there are now three and two divisions respectively. In 1948 a magistrate court, with jurisdiction comparable to the city court, was established for Johnson County. In 1923 and in 1939 more general acts were passed allowing the governing bodies of certain cities to establish city courts. Governing bodies in cities in excess of 9,000 population are authorized to establish city courts whenever there is a need for such courts under one or the other of these more general laws. Under these laws, city courts have been established in Chanute, Independence, Pittsburg, Arkansas City, Salina, Hutchinson, and Winfield.

City courts were given originally much the same jurisdiction as the justice-of-the-peace courts. They could hear civil actions for the recovery of money or personal property only when the sum involved did not exceed $300 and for trespass on real estate only when damages did not exceed $100. They generally have jurisdiction only in cases of misdemeanors in which the fine could not exceed $500 and the imprisonment could not exceed one year.

In addition to handling those cases which a justice of the peace was then allowed to hear, the city courts were given a somewhat expanded

17. *K.S.A.*, 61-101.
18. *K.S.A.*, 20-302a.

TABLE 28

Work of City Courts: Year Ending June 30, 1968

Type of Case	Number
Civil	21,460
Criminal	40,251
Total	61,711

Source: *Kansas Judicial Council Bulletin,* XLII (1968), 59, 60.

civil jurisdiction. Though the exact jurisdiction differs from court to court, most courts are allowed to hear civil actions involving claims of up to $1,000. The trend seems to be for the Legislature further to expand the city courts' jurisdiction. The accompanying table reports on the nature of cases considered by them.

The judges of the city courts must be lawyers. In some instances their salaries, which are set by statute, are paid from city funds and in other instances from county funds. Some of the judges are elected at city elections; others, at general elections. Typically the courts have clerks and marshals, some of these officials being elected and others being appointed.

The city courts should not be confused with the municipal courts described below.[19]

Municipal Courts

All cities are authorized to establish municipal courts. Their jurisdiction extends only to violations of city ordinances. When in the course of hearing such violations it appears that state criminal laws have been violated, the cases are to be transferred to justice-of-the-peace or county courts. By far the most common violations with which police courts are concerned are traffic violations. The judges in most cities of the second and third classes are elected; in cities of the first class and in mayor-council-manager cities of the second and third class they are appointed. These judges receive no regular salary, but instead depend on costs assessed against the persons tried. In 1968 there were reported to be 467 judges of municipal courts.

---

19. Normally the city courts and municipal courts are separate and distinct courts, except that in city courts created under K.S.A., 20, 142a, the judge of the city court may also serve as judge of the municipal court.

Small Debtors' Courts

As a special type of local court, the Legislature in 1913 authorized boards of county commissioners or the mayor and council or the commission of a city to establish small debtors' courts. When such a court is established, "a reputable resident citizen of approved integrity who is sympathetically inclined to consider the situation of the poor, friendless, and misfortunate"[20] is to be appointed as judge. Before the judge may entertain a suit, the plaintiff must show to the satisfaction of the court that his financial resources are so restricted that he cannot employ a lawyer or use other courts. The jurisdiction of such courts is limited to small debts and accounts not exceeding $20, in cases where the defendant resides within the city or county in which the court has jurisdiction. No information is available as to how many such courts were established; it appears that none are now operative.

The Work of the Courts

The broad outlines of the work of the various types of courts in Kansas has been indicated in paragraphs above describing the jurisdiction of the several courts. The courts provide forums for deciding controversies between individuals arising from damages sustained by an injured party or from breaking of contracts. They also decide cases in which it is alleged that a person has violated a criminal law. When these criminal laws are broken there is a public prosecutor, most often in Kansas the county attorney, to represent the state and bring action against the alleged offender.

The accompanying chart portrays the many steps involved in a criminal prosecution. These steps are typical of those followed in most states, with the possible exception that indictment by information is used much more commonly than indictment by grand jury. Grand juries are required to be summoned by district courts upon presentation of a petition, with from 100 to 700 signatures, depending on the size of the county.[21]

Another important function of the courts is to act as protectors of the people's liberties, guaranteed by the state Constitution. A review

20. *K.S.A.*, 20-1302.
21. *K.S.A.*, 62-901.

of the numerous annotations of the bill of rights to the Kansas Constitution suggests this role of the courts. A review of the cases, and indeed a constitutional history of the several provisions, would be necessary to assay the full contribution of the courts in this field.[22]

The Judicial Council

As a move to coordinate and to improve judicial procedures and work, the Judicial Council was established in 1927. It is composed of a Supreme Court justice, two judges from different district courts, four lawyers, and the chairmen of the House and Senate Judiciary committees. Except the last, all are appointed by the Chief Justice of the Supreme Court for four-year terms. The Council is an advisory group, with power to make recommendations concerning the work of the judiciary. The Council collects and publishes data on the work load of the courts and, from time to time, has made and supported suggestions which have improved their operation.

One of the most far-reaching proposals which the Council has made concerns the reorganization of the whole court system of the state. This plan calls for a unified system, in which there would be but one court in the whole state. There would, of course, be many divisions of the court to allow easier access. Such a general plan for states has long been recommended by the American Bar Association. With but one court it would be easier to administer the work of its various divisions, allowing judges to be given more specialized assignments and to be moved, as need arises, to equalize the work. The details of this plan have been developed and incorporated into a proposal which has been recommended by the Judicial Council to replace the present judicial provision of the Constitution. To date, this recommendation of the Council has not been enacted.

The Council has been much more successful in its recommendations concerning changes in the procedures in the district courts. Council action facilitated the development and adoption of the probate court. Council studies in the areas of fresh pursuit and interstate extradition,

22. A further analysis of this subject is available in an unpublished M.A. thesis of the University of Kansas entitled "Civil Rights and Liberties in Kansas: A Summary of Legislative and Judicial Action in the Fields of Equal Rights, Religious Liberty, and Liberty of Speech and Press," by Phillip E. Jones.

Steps in Criminal Prosecution: Kansas, 1968

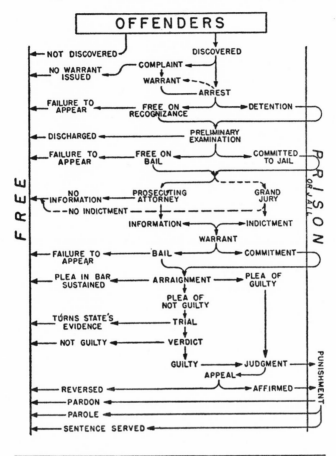

Adapted from a chart by Francis H. Heller

divorce pleadings, and uniform court records have led to improvements in judicial procedures.

Problems

Parts of this chapter have suggested areas of dissatisfaction with the court system in Kansas. The change in the method of selecting Supreme Court justices revealed dissatisfaction with partisan elections as a method of selecting them. Broadly, the same charges made against the old method of electing justices would apply with equal pertinence to the present methods used for electing district, probate, and city court judges. Experience gained in selecting our Supreme Court justices may lead to willingness to extend this or a similar plan to other judges.

The dissatisfaction with the old methods of electing justices reflects at least some doubt about the quality of our judges. The move to replace justice-of-the-peace courts as seen in the establishment of city and county courts shows a desire to require more full-time judges, with presumably more legal training. The law passed by the Legislature in 1951 requiring that probate judges in counties of a certain size be lawyers reflects this same concern. The passing of the justice-of-the-peace courts also suggests that there is less need today for the large number of local courts originally provided for in the Constitution.

Increased attention to the administration of justice has been clearly shown in the development of the office of Judicial Administrator and the responsibility assigned to the several justices in organization of the state into judicial departments. These developments have been significant in equalizing the work of the district courts and may be ways of accomplishing many of the same goals that would be accomplished by a unified court system for the state.

12 | Law Enforcement and Correction

Law enforcement in Kansas has changed markedly since the middle of the nineteenth century when statehood was achieved. In 1861 the methods for enforcement were very rudimentary. Primary responsibility for the protection of property, preservation of order, and guarantee of civil rights rested with the elected county sheriff and two constables in each township. For further assistance, the sheriff could appoint deputies and call out the militia in his county.[1] Formal prosecutions were handled by the elected county attorney, but most reported law violations were taken before a justice-of-the-peace court and the arresting officer or complaining party assumed the responsibility to present the case against the defendant. In many instances these public officials did not devote full time to their work. The state government assumed little responsibility for the enforcement of law. Other than the Governor, who could call out the state militia, no state agency had the authority to employ peace officers.

After 1880, and particularly in the first two decades of the 1900's, the reliance on local law-enforcement officers began to decline. The reasons for this change are familiar to all students of sociology. County boundary lines began to divide people into governmental units. The increase in population, mobility of the people, growth of commerce and

1. *Session Laws*, 1861, chap. 49. Every able-bodied male citizen between the ages of twenty-one and forty-five years was required to serve as a militiaman.

industry, and increased interdependence compelled greater uniformity of enforcement. Secondly, some of the new laws and administrative regulations required more constant inspection of products or persons if the full value of the prohibitions was to be realized. This constant surveillance could be better achieved by the creation of special state agencies instead of by relying on local law-enforcement officers. A few of the new duties assumed by the state are illustrated by the new agencies created from 1870 to 1920: Board of Agriculture, 1872; State Sealer of Weights and Measures, 1877; Board of Health, 1885; Silk Commissioner, 1889; State Sugar Inspector, 1889; Board of Telephone and Telegraph Assessors, 1897; State Factory Inspector, 1898; State Fish Warden and Deputies, 1899; State Board of Medical Registrations and Examinations, 1901; Livestock Sanitary Commissioner, 1905; Dairy Commissioner, 1907; Entomological Commission, 1907; State Board of Embalming, 1907; Livestock Registry Board, 1909; State Apiarist, 1911; Office of Fire Marshal, 1913; Kansas State Board of Review, 1917.

The names even of some of these agencies suggest activities which many persons would not associate with law enforcement. Law enforcement means more than policing to protect persons and property, solving crimes, and apprehending criminals. Today policing and regulatory functions of government are blended with service functions. The police officer who is directing traffic at an intersection is performing both a regulatory and a service function.

Although, in the legal sense, full police powers were not given to all of the state agencies or to those created in later years, they did have the authority to inspect premises, products, or persons to determine compliance with the law. The culmination of this trend toward centralization of the police function occurred in the middle and later 1930's with the creation of the State Highway Patrol and the Kansas Bureau of Investigation, and in 1949 with the creation of the Alcoholic Beverage Commission.

State Law-Enforcement Agencies

The Governor

The Governor, as the chief executive officer of the state, is ultimately charged with the enforcement of all laws. In the words of the Constitution of Kansas, "The supreme executive power of the state shall be vested in a governor, who shall see that the laws are faithfully executed."[2]

What methods he was to employ to carry out this mandate are not detailed. Presumably, though, the Governor may employ special investigators to ascertain if a law has been violated, and he can file a complaint against any offender in the proper court.

In extreme situations where there is a "forcible obstruction to the execution of laws or reasonable apprehension of it," he may call out the state militia.[3] The concept of a militia has, however, changed greatly since the early statehood days. Today the Governor has authority to appoint an adjutant general, who is the commanding officer of the National Guard for the state of Kansas. The maintenance of the guard, composed of able-bodied men who volunteer for service, is a joint federal-state program. It can be called to duty by the Governor to help in various types of emergencies. Probably most frequently the Guard is called out at the request of local law-enforcement authorities to help them in cases of natural disaster. This work may involve some law-enforcement activities, but will also include many types of services. In times of national emergency, whole units of the National Guard may be called into national service, becoming part of the Army of the United States.

The Guard is financed by both the national and state governments. By serving in it, men may fulfill their national obligation for military service.

Helpful as the Guard is for various types of emergency, to use it for the day-to-day activities of law enforcement is not practicable. Consequently, the Governor is compelled to rely on other agencies created by the Constitution and the Legislature to assist him in the execution of laws.

Attorney General

While much of the work of the Attorney General is discussed elsewhere, the office should be mentioned as important in law enforcement. He must prosecute for the state all cases which the Governor and Legislature require. He consults and advises all county attorneys on matters

2. *Kansas Constitution,* Art. 1, sec. 3.
3. *Kansas Constitution,* Art. 8, and *K.S.A.,* 48-203, 48-238.

pertaining to their official duties. This consultation is primarily in the form of writing attorney general's opinions to clarify statutes and lend the moral support of his office. Occasionally, of course, he may take an active part in suspected violation at the local level. In addition, the Legislature has specifically required him to enforce some eighty-four laws, such as those affecting monopolies, unfair trade discriminations, oil prorations, gambling, intoxicating beverages, advertising, future trading, and grain inspection.

While it is the duty of the Attorney General to enforce many laws, his immediate staff is composed of lawyers, who as assistant attorneys general prosecute violators in court. In the office there are three authorized investigators who have the police powers of other peace officers, but major investigatory activities are handled by the Kansas Bureau of Investigation.

Kansas Bureau of Investigation

Established in 1939 within the office of the Attorney General, the Kansas Bureau of Investigation (popularly known as the KBI) has a legislative mandate to investigate any matter which the Attorney General may request.[4] In practice, however, the Bureau has not operated precisely in this manner. The Kansas Bureau of Investigation is known better, and is promoted by the agents, as a service agency for local law-enforcement officials. In this capacity, the Bureau investigates all major felonies if requested to do so by local officers. In those parts of the state where the population is sparse and there are insufficient and inadequately trained local officers, as a matter of course the KBI investigates nearly all felonies. Such a service cannot be given to all municipalities and counties, because the personnel of the bureau is restricted by law to twenty-five agents. But probably more significant than the limited personnel is the fact that the KBI has deliberately fostered a concept that it is *not* a state police force and that it intervenes in local matters only when requested to do so.

As a part of its investigative activities, the KBI maintains a fingerprint file and other identification records which are available to local officers. All agents of the Bureau are excluded from the civil service,

4. *K.S.A.*, 75-711, 712.

but electoral changes in the office of the Attorney General have seldom resulted in personnel changes.

Kansas State Highway Patrol

Quite distinct from the KBI is the Highway Patrol, which was established in 1937. Its major activities are limited by statute to enforcement of the laws on motor-vehicle inspections, vehicle licenses, drivers' licenses, and the patrolling of the highways in the interest of safety.[5] All troopers are, however, given the full powers of local peace officers and are permitted to assist local officials in the apprehension of fugitives.

The organization of the Highway Patrol is unusual in several respects. The Superintendent is appointed directly by the Governor and serves at his pleasure. If the Superintendent is promoted from the ranks and his services as Superintendent are later terminated, he then assumes a rank not lower than the one he previously held. All troopers are employed for four-year terms under a modified civil service system, and all officers must have served in the ranks for five years before being promoted. Despite the fact that the Superintendent serves at the will of the Governor and all other members serve on four-year appointments, they are forbidden to participate in political campaigns. No trooper may be dismissed except for cause and after a hearing.

The law provides that the state must be divided into districts to which troopers are assigned, and it also sets out in detail the total number of troopers as well as the number of command officers in each grade. In 1955 the Highway Patrol was authorized to police the Kansas turnpike on a contractual arrangement with the Kansas Turnpike Authority. The Legislature authorizes the number of officers the Patrol may employ. In recent years increases have been allowed with the current maximum being 250.

In the less populated counties the Patrol plays a very important role, for the troopers are the only police officers to patrol the state highways. Since most of the sheriffs do not have enough deputies to cover their entire county, they restrict their activities to county roads. In this respect, the Highway Patrol acts as a supplement to local law enforcement. Participation in raids, publication of a weekly bulletin which

5. *K.S.A.*, 74-20a02.

contains a list of stolen property, automobiles, and wanted persons, and maintenance of a state-wide radio network to assist local peace officers have extended the Patrol's functions more into the criminal areas than was the original intent of the law.

Alcoholic Beverage Commission

Even more specialized than the Highway Patrol is the Alcoholic Beverage Commission, established in 1949 to regulate the sale of intoxicating liquors.[6] An integral part of the organization of the ABC is the enforcement branch, with special agents, who have the authority of peace officers, to enforce the liquor laws and administrative rules promulgated under them. These officers concern themselves almost exclusively with the illegal sale of liquor, and in this capacity are viewed as a supplemental law-enforcement agency by local officials. Particularly are their services appreciated by the smaller police departments that do not have trained investigators who know how to gather the proper evidence to assure conviction. The ABC in turn depends upon the local officers to relay to it the names of licensees suspected of violating the laws.

The ABC is administered by a Director appointed by and serving at the pleasure of the Governor. All agents are employed by the Director according to regular civil service procedure.

State Fire Marshal

The state Fire Marshal, who is an appointee of the Governor for a four-year term,[7] is primarily concerned with inspections of public buildings in the interest of fire protection. However, he is also a law-enforcement officer, for by statute, he must investigate all fires suspected to be of incendiary origin. While neither the Marshal nor his deputies have the general authority of a peace officer, they do have the power to subpoena records and witnesses, and they can enter any building in which there has been fire at any time in the day or night to investigate the cause of the fire.[8] His staff of four investigators is viewed by local officers in much the same light as that of the ABC. They are specialists in the detection of arson and as such are a supplement to the

6. *K.S.A.*, 41-101 to 41-2708.
7. *K.S.A.*, 75-1510.
8. *K.S.A.*, 31-203, 204.

body of local officers. The activities of the Fire Marshal are financed by a special statutorily dedicated tax on fire-insurance premiums. The office of Fire Marshal has been criticized frequently because of alleged political partisanship in recruiting employees. In 1933 it was abolished in favor of a new state Department of Inspection and Registration, only to be reestablished in 1939. The Legislative Committee on Economy and Efficiency recommended in 1957 that the duties of the Marshal be transferred to other agencies—and that the office of Fire Marshal be abolished. This recommendation was not followed.

Fish and Game Wardens

Following the practice in many other states, Kansas has a separate Commission responsible for enforcing the fish and game laws.[9] Employees of the Commission are called game protectors and may be either full-time or non-salaried people who have evidenced an interest in fish and game protection and have received a commission. There is no distinction in the general police power of the two groups, and both have the authority to make arrests with or without a warrant if the state game laws are violated. In 1968 the normal complement of full-time commissioned protectors was fifty-three. Many protectors serve as federal game protectors and also deputy sheriffs in the counties in which they serve. The organization and activities of the Forestry, Fish and Game Commission in the conserving of wildlife are discussed elsewhere.

Director of Revenue

The Director of Revenue collects most of the state taxes. As the collector, he is empowered to employ deputies having the full power of peace officers to assist in the enforcement of the tax on motor-vehicle fuels and the transportation of oil and liquid fuels.[10] These inspectors, eleven in number, are appointed under civil service. An additional sixty-two persons are engaged as inspectors and collectors to enforce other tax laws (sales and use, income, and cigarette).[11]

These inspectors also enforce the laws on taxation of commercial

9. *K.S.A.*, 32-155.
10. *K.S.A.*, 55-515.
11. Inspectors engaged in the enforcement of other taxes do not have the power of peace officers.

vehicles entering the state and using the highways. When these latter laws are the object of enforcement, the inspectors act for the Port of Entry Board, which is composed of the Director of Revenue, Director of Highways, and Chairman of the Corporation Commission.

Other Agencies

The Legislature has conferred on many other agencies the responsibility to enforce specialized laws. Most of these agencies merely investigate and report their findings to the local sheriff and county attorney or the Attorney General. Some of them have the right to inspect records and premises and to subpoena records and witnesses to a hearing. In this category fall such agencies as the Corporation Commission, the Insurance Department, the State Board of Health, the State Board of Agriculture, and the Banking Board.

Local Enforcement Agencies

In terms of the number of police officers, investigations, and arrests, the major work of law enforcement is done by local officers who enforce state as well as local laws. Primarily, these local officers are the sheriff and county attorney elected in each county and the policemen appointed in each city. Theoretically, there is some assistance from the two elected constables in each township, but few constables are elected and fewer still ever are interested enough to qualify for the office. Outside the corporate limits of cities, firemen have the powers of police officers when they are engaged in fighting fires.[12] The best available information shows 1,684 *full-time*[13] municipal law-enforcement officers. This does not include county sheriffs and their deputies, marshals in small cities, nightwatchmen who may be appointed as deputy marshals, and other such officials.

Neither statutory authority nor a large number of police officers at the local level guarantees that laws will be enforced. Other factors and conditions frequently cause less than ideal enforcement. First, there is no clear definition of jurisdictional responsibility between the city and county police officers. City police officers are required by law to enforce

12. K.S.A., 80-1506.
13. An unpublished survey of police officers by the Governmental Research Center, Univ. of Kansas, in April, 1968.

state law. In larger cities this is a necessity because no sheriff force in the state is sufficiently large to provide adequate service to both urban and rural areas. From this lack of clear jurisdictional responsibility, friction frequently develops. The sheriff usually wants to be consulted on all violations occurring within the city, since the voters there are his constituents too, just as are the rural voters. On the other hand, if the city policemen are more experienced than the sheriff or his deputies, they may be reluctant to risk the solution of a case by revealing information to the county officers or to share credit for solving a case. However, the city can never completely ignore the sheriff, because the prosecution and detention of prisoners for state offenses is exclusively a county function.

A second major problem for local law-enforcement departments is personnel. Employment as a policeman frequently is an interim job to be kept only until a better job can be located, and in many instances it is supplemented with other employment. A survey of the qualifications of local policemen suggests that the average policeman is between thirty and thirty-five years of age, almost graduated from high school, has been employed as an officer for between five and ten years, and had received no police training before his appointment.[14] A turnover of 20 per cent a year within a department is not exceptional. Sheriffs and their deputies are not too different from the man described above, but since 1964 the Constitution no longer limits sheriffs to two consecutive two-year terms. Perhaps the change in the Constitution and the practices growing out of it will lead to longer tenure for sheriffs and deputies alike.

Another major change in this connection was the establishment of the Kansas Law Enforcement Training Center. Since 1951 the Legislature has, by a line item in appropriations to the University of Kansas, provided a modest amount to sponsor an annual training school for peace officers (a term used so as to include both policemen and sheriffs). Gradually the item was increased to allow a limited regional training program. In 1968 the Legislature took the first steps toward establishing near Hutchinson, in part of a deactivated naval airstation, an academy to train state and local law-enforcement officers. As a part

14. Not all departments were as poorly manned as these averages indicate. Some of them employed top-grade men and provided a great deal of training.

of the University of Kansas this agency is to offer training courses in law enforcement, with a basic course of 120 hours of instruction in law enforcement. After July 1, 1969, all persons who are appointed as law-enforcement officers must have completed the basic course or do so within a year. The training center is planned to be self-supporting, with fees paid by the agency or unit employing the law-enforcement official. It is anticipated that this training center and the training done under its auspices will usher in a new era of law enforcement in Kansas.

The training center is viewed as a significant step toward greater professionalization of police work in the state. However, more free movement of men and officers between departments, with less attention to seniority in particular departments, would facilitate further professionalization. Increasingly, agencies are recruiting outside their own departments for the job of chief, but this practice may be expected to expand and be extended to others on the force. The inclusion of local officials, including law-enforcement officials, under the state retirement system may be expected to encourage mobility of peace officers at least within the state.

Related to personnel is the problem of financial support. Low budgets, which result in low salaries and little equipment, are common. It is not unusual for officers to furnish their own uniforms, sidearms, and ammunition; and in some cities and counties the officers use their own cars, for which they are paid mileage. In order to supplement his salary, the average policeman may work at another job while off duty. Very few departments have sufficient equipment to conduct more than the most elementary investigations. The lack of financial support is also seen in the fact that the departments are understaffed, which makes a 48-hour week not uncommon, precludes payment for overtime, and forces officers to testify in court on their own time.

Finally, there is the traditional attitude toward the police which reduces the effectiveness of law enforcement at the local level. There is concern that the police not have "too much" power. This has led to a multiplicity of law-enforcement agencies, unwillingness to have a state police force, and sometimes restrictions on them such as the former constitutional restriction limiting persons to two consecutive terms as sheriff. Moreover, urban living has resulted in many of us not wanting to get into other people's problems (and quarrels), with the result that observers or bystanders frequently do not report to the police or help in ways that would tend to improve law enforcement.

These problems by themselves might not be considered too serious, except that concomitantly violations of the law are increasing. This increase stems from a larger and more mobile population, a greater number of laws, and a generally more complex society. Many violations now require the services of a specialist to detect and prosecute, and involve the expenditure of large sums of money. There are several solutions to these problems: greater local financial support; consolidation of city and county forces and expansion of training; and also expansion of state activities in this field.

Some, but limited, progress has been made in Kansas toward the solution of these problems. Efforts to professionalize local employment and raise the requirements for personnel help to make citizens and governing bodies more willing to pay higher wages to law-enforcement officials. Local budgets have increased, and doubtless, in some cases, the law-enforcement departments have improved their position.

The new state Peace Officer Training Center holds much promise for improved law enforcement.

Correction

Those whom the law-enforcement officials apprehend and the courts find guilty of breaking the law may be sentenced to one of the five correctional institutions of the state. There is some confusion and difference of opinion as to the proper philosophy, and from one individual case to another there may be further differences as to just what purpose is expected to be accomplished by confining the offender. Society is protected from his acts while he is incarcerated, and the offender is punished by not being allowed his freedom. Yet more constructively, we have gradually come to realize that most of those who are confined in an institution will be released and will become a part of society again. Whether they will then conform to the laws and restraints which our society imposes depends in no small part upon what kind of treatment they receive while at the institution. The more progressive view of the work of these correctional institutions is that they should be rehabilitative and educational in nature rather than merely custodial. It is because of these considerations that in recent years attention has been directed toward improving and modernizing our correctional institutions.

The state penitentiary at Lansing, which has over two-thirds of all those persons now confined by the state, is the oldest institution in Kansas[15] and was provided for in the state Constitution of 1859. Started in 1864 and interrupted by the Civil War, the original structure was completed in October, 1867. From 1861 to 1935 a total of seventeen different commissions were appointed to inquire into the management of the penitentiary. Since 1935 the Legislative Council and its committees have considered numerous aspects of the penitentiary's operations.[16] The Council made broad inquiries into the penal system in 1955 and 1956, which resulted in a series of substantial recommendations to the 1957 Legislature.[17] Most of these recommendations have been adopted.

Many of the specific recommendations concerned the physical plant of the penitentiary and were made a part of a scheduled ten-year program of physical improvements. Additionally, and probably of even greater importance, were the recommendations for a revised administration of the penal system for the establishment of a modern system of classification and orientation of prisoners, for an expanded educational program, for a broader and more workable system of prison industries, for larger payments to prisoners upon separation, and for a more adequate parole system.

The legislature has experimented over the years with various types of administrative organization for supervising the penal institutions. In an effort to provide for the employment of trained and experienced personnel at the institutions, the Legislature in 1957 created the office of Director of Penal Institutions, who was made responsible for administering the three penal institutions. The law established minimum qualifications for the Director, which require that he be at least thirty-

15. Theodore Heim, "The Administration and Organization of the Kansas State Penitentiary," an unpublished M.A. thesis, Univ. of Kansas, Lawrence, Kansas, 1960.

16. Kansas Legislative Council, *The Prison Labor Problem in Kansas* (Topeka: 1938); *A Program for Kansas Prisons* (Topeka: 1938); *The Physical Properties of the Charitable and Penal Institutions of the State* (Topeka: 1946).

17. Kansas Legislative Council, *The Penal and Correctional Institutions of the State* (Topeka: 1956).

five years of age and have at least five years of experience as an executive officer in the administration of a federal or state penal or correctional institution. Subsequent legislation made the minimum requirements more flexible. The Governor, who appoints the Director subject to Senate confirmation, may remove the Director before the end of his four-year term for disability, inefficiency, neglect of duty, or malfeasance in office; but the Director is entitled to a hearing. The Director appoints the Warden of the penitentiary and exercises approval over the appointment of the key officers and employees appointed by the Warden. The goal is to establish a nonpolitical experienced administration for the penal system. Related administrative recommendations included an in-service training program and higher pay for the guards.

As a part of the effort to strengthen the rehabilitation aspects of the institutional program, the Legislature in 1961 established the Kansas State Reception and Diagnostic Center at Topeka. The primary function of the new agency is the evaluating of all male felony offenders sentenced for one year or more. The inmates at the Center are examined and interviewed and observed intensively as a part of the evaluation process. Judges may consider the evaluation of those convicted and, on occasion, may put some of those convicted directly on court-supervised probation. This depends on the prescribed statutory minimum and maximum sentences and how much time the person convicted has already been in jail before his actual sentencing. The aim is to find and apply to the individual offender the particular program which is most likely to assure his maximum rehabilitation. Steps have been taken to expand the general and vocational education programs at the penal institutions.

Broad changes in the operations of the prison industries were suggested by the Council and approved by the Legislature. Prison authorities agree that it is extremely important for the proper operation of a prison that inmates be kept busy. Yet products made with prison labor may be sold at prices below those of products made outside prisons. This has occasioned opposition to the indiscriminate sale of such products. State agencies were required in 1957 to purchase prison-made goods, and political subdivisions were authorized to buy such products. Prison officials were given broader authority in deciding what products should be manufactured and were enabled to implement their decisions through a revolving fund to purchase needed equipment.

The system for handling paroles was revised in 1961, and a new Board of Probation and Parole was established. The Board consists of three full-time members appointed by the Governor with the advice and consent of the Senate. The Director of Parole and Probation is appointed by the Board and is under civil service. The Director appoints parole officers, who supervise those whom the Board finds eligible for parole. The system provides for more adequate supervision of the parolees and those who are placed on probation by the courts without being sentenced to the penitentiary, reformatory, or industrial farm. To insure the maximum likelihood of success in rehabilitating the parolee, the parole must come at the proper time and with the proper arrangements being made.[18]

In the fiscal year ending June 30, 1968, the Board released 700 prisoners on parole and 241 conditionally. These figures do not include one pardon and eight commutations of sentence that the Governor granted in the 1967 calendar year.[19] Since 1957 the Governor has been able to pardon or commute sentences only after the Probation and Parole Board has made a report on the case or has had thirty days in which to make a report.[20]

The State Industrial Reformatory at Hutchinson and the State Industrial Farm for Women at Lansing have many of the same problems which have been discussed above with respect to the penitentiary. Young men between the ages of sixteen and twenty-five may be sentenced upon their first conviction to either the penitentiary or the reformatory. Under specified conditions the Director of Penal Institutions may transfer inmates from the penitentiary to the reformatory and from the reformatory to the penitentiary. Women over the age of eighteen who have been convicted of any offense against the criminal laws of the state which is punishable by imprisonment of more than thirty days are sentenced to the Industrial Farm for Women.

18. This would preclude the kind of arrangements made in the past, when there was a recorded case of a parolee being released from prison with so little money that he was forced to steal food and money to maintain himself until he received his first pay check.
19. For more information on the pardoning power of the Governor, see p. 103.
20. *K.S.A.*, 62-2216.

An important innovation in the state correctional program began in June, 1961, when the first honor camp was established. Since that time the honor-camp program has been expanded, and there are two permanent camps and one mobile one with a total capacity of 136 inmates. While it assists in relieving the over-crowded conditions of the reformatory and the penitentiary, the program gives inmates who can qualify an opportunity to serve the time in more constructive work and in a more desirable atmosphere than the prison.

The state is also building a 240-man minimum-security facility adjacent to the Reception and Diagnostic Center in Topeka. The Kansas Correctional Treatment Center is planned for youthful, nonviolent first offenders. The state does not have a facility for this type of offender except for the honor camps. The emphasis in the new facility will be on vocational education. It is not for the acutely disturbed or those committed to criminality. The construction of the facility is being financed in part with federal funds, and appropriations from the prison-industries funds and from general revenues.

In keeping with some of the more current developments in other states, the Director of Penal Institutions has recommended statutory authority for work release. Several states have experimented with such programs to help prepare the prisoner for his adjustment to society.

In addition to three correctional institutions under the director of penal institutions there is the Industrial School for Boys, near Topeka, and the Industrial School for Girls, near Beloit. These two institutions are for delinquent children, who, in the terms of the law, are boys less than sixteen or girls less than eighteen years of age, who have committed an act which, if committed by an older person, would be a felony or who have been adjudged "miscreant" three or more times.[21] Such persons are committed to the schools by a juvenile court and under law are to remain there until twenty-one years of age unless discharged sooner as reformed, or paroled. In practice, few boys remain at the boys' school beyond the age of seventeen, for after six months' good conduct after release from the institution the boys will be accepted for military service. The girls stay at the girls' school for an average of about twenty-four months. Courts of record and probate courts can also commit to the girls' school girls under eighteen years of age when

21. *K.S.A.*, 38-802.

liable for imprisonment or when they are found to be "incorrigible." In recognition of the somewhat different types of cases handled, the boys' and girls' schools are administered as a part of the division of institutional management of the Board of Social Welfare. It is possible for the Board of Social Welfare, through a complaint in the district court, to transfer a boy from the Industrial School to the reformatory, though they are separately administered. Also, inmates at the reformatory and at the penitentiary may be transferred to the State Hospital for treatment or custody.

The accompanying table gives an indication of the size of operation of these three correctional institutions. Over $6,600,000 was appropriated for the 1969 fiscal year for them from the general funds. Additional amounts were available from special funds.

Much improvement has been made in modernizing our correctional institutions. Wide-sweeping changes were made in the laws in 1957. These gave promise of greater progress in achieving a goal of rehabilitating as many of the offenders as possible, but such a program presents many problems of operation and a challenge to those charged with its administration.

TABLE 29
Average Daily Population of Kansas Correctional Institutions for Selected Years

Fiscal Year	Penitentiary	Industrial Farm for Women*	Reformatory†
1920	718	89	350
1930	1798	164	957
1940	1778	77	615
1950	1399	53	425
1955	1594	62	417
1960	1643	53	567
1965	1727	98	896
1968	1458	64	656

* Established in 1918
† Opened in 1895
Sources: Kansas Legislative Council, *Special Report and Recommendations on the Penal and Correctional Institutions of the State* (Topeka, 1956), pp. 18, 62, 75, 105, 125; Theodore Heim, "The Administration and Organization of the Kansas State Penitentiary" (unpublished M.A. thesis, Univ. of Kansas, 1960), p. 17; and unpublished data from the Office of the Director, Penal Institutions.

13 | Public Education

The organic act of 1854 which created the Territory of Kansas made no mention of education, but the settlers, pro-slave and free-state alike, joined to promote the establishment of free common schools. All three of the constitutions under which Kansas sought, unsuccessfully, to become a state provided for the creation of common-school districts, though they differed concerning the method and extent of state supervision. In 1855 the territorial Legislature provided for the formation of school townships with three trustees and an examiner as the governing body. No central organization was established at this time. Two years later the Legislature made the board of county commissioners the head of the local school districts. Further changes in 1858 provided for the election of territorial and county superintendents of schools.

The Wyandotte Constitution under which Kansas became a state provided that "the legislature shall encourage the promotion of intellectual, moral, scientific and agricultural improvements, by establishing a uniform system of common schools, and schools of a higher grade, embracing normal, preparatory, collegiate and university departments." Further sections called for the election of state and county superintendents of public instruction and the raising and apportionment of school funds. In the Act admitting Kansas into the Union in 1861, sections 16 and 36 of each township were set aside for schools, and seventy-two sections of land were granted for the support of a state university.

Today local school districts and the state are responsible for carrying out educational functions in Kansas. The state establishes general standards by legislation and by administrative regulation and supervision through the State Department of Public Instruction. Subject to these limitations, the local school districts have considerable freedom in formulating educational policy and determining administrative practices.

Local School Districts

School districts are the key units in the elementary and secondary educational system of Kansas. Although the state plays a much more active role in shaping public-school policy today than was true even twenty years ago, the districts retain considerable autonomy. Subject to state levy limits on taxation and to certain requirements for state financial aid, the districts determine the financial support given their schools. They employ and dismiss teachers, subject to general state laws. The instructional program is determined primarily on the local level, within the general framework that state-adopted textbooks and state curriculum requirements must be followed.

The state Legislature originally established two types of school districts—common-school districts and city-school districts. This system was adequate as long as the public schools offered only limited elementary education. These districts were usually of insufficient size to support high schools, which began to assume popularity toward the end of the nineteenth century. New types of districts were established for the purpose of supporting high schools only. Over the years the Legislature has authorized a variety of different types of local school organizations.

Consolidation of School Districts

School districts in Kansas were organized initially when the greater part of the population lived on farms and transportation was extremely limited. As a result, school districts generally followed the lines of small-community groupings. The district pattern that resulted was criticized early in the state's history. In the late 1860's the state Superintendent of Public Instruction expressed concern that many districts were too small to provide an adequate property-tax base for supporting schools. Once established, however, the school-district boundaries settled into a rigid pattern which resisted change despite the changing character of the state.

Little was accomplished in the way of district reorganization, although most state superintendents have encouraged either voluntary or legislative consolidation and reorganization. There were no statutory provisions for disorganizing depopulated districts until 1893 and 1899.[1] The number of school districts, including the city districts, reached its peak in 1896, when there were 9,284 districts. The decline in enrollment in small rural schools began as early as 1908. The number of students in one-teacher schools dropped from 187,893 in 1908 to about 15,551 in 1958-59.[2]

The contrast between the established school-district pattern and that needed for an efficient educational system became increasingly evident in the 1930's. The shift of population to the towns and cities left many rural districts practically depopulated. Improved transportation not only made school transportation over greater distances feasible, but also shifted community centers to the towns in many cases. The financial difficulties of the Great Depression also emphasized the inequalities of the property-tax base in a system of small districts. Finally, many people questioned the value of the education made available in districts with such limited finances and so few pupils.

The rapid increase in closed schools dramatically presented the need for district reorganization. Before 1930, with over 8,000 elementary-school districts, frequently about 250 schools were closed each year. By 1939 there were more than 1,000 closed schools and by 1945 more than 2,200.[3] In 1945 the state Legislature enacted a plan for mandatory reorganization of common-school districts by county committees. The state Supreme Court declared the law unconstitutional in 1947, but the Legislature validated the reorganizations that had been completed. Despite the strong opposition to the reorganization act, the number of

1. F. H. Guild, "Reorganization of School Districts in Kansas," in Howard A. Dawson, Floyd W. Reeves, and others, *Your School District* (Washington, D.C.: Department of Rural Education, National Education Association of the United States, 1948), p. 181.
2. Kansas Educational Survey, *Bulletin,* No. 6, March-April, 1959, p. 5.
3. Guild, pp. 182-84.

districts had been reduced from 8,113 to 5,438 in the two years—a reduction of 2,675.

Since 1947 reorganization has continued on the local level at a more rapid pace. Under a 1951 law, all common-school districts which fail to maintain a school for three consecutive years must be disorganized.[4] In 1958-1959 there were 2,427 districts operating elementary schools. There were in that year 1,007 one-teacher districts, in marked contrast to the 7,270 one-teacher districts in 1945.

The organization of high-school districts posed special problems. There have never been proportionately as many high schools closed as elementary schools. In 1958-59, 30 of the 341 rural high-school districts were closed. However, the number of high schools with low enrollments was large. In the school year 1958-59, over 40 per cent (228) of the 564 operating high schools had an enrollment of 60 or less. An additional 202 schools had 150 or fewer students. Many districts faced difficulties in raising sufficient revenue from their assessed valuation for financing high schools. One result was a tendency for districts to compete for territory not in a high-school district. Also, some cities reorganized their high schools as rural high-school districts in order to expand their property-tax base. Although this solved the immediate financial distress, educational administrators viewed this step unfavorably, for it increased the number of overlapping districts and separated the control of elementary and secondary schools.[5]

The Legislature passed another school-district reorganization law in 1963. Careful attention was given to avoid the constitutional questions of the previous law. The new law provided for all territory of the state to be in school districts that offered full programs of instruction from grades one through twelve with authority to operate kindergartens and, under certain conditions, junior colleges. The State Department of Public Instruction was in the center of county-reorganization plans and was called upon to perform many duties which had previously been done by the county superintendents. Though contested in a number of cases, the 1963 unification law has been upheld by court decisions.

Very dramatic progress has been made under the unification law in

4. *K.S.A.*, 72-831.
5. John Jacobs, "Educational Problems in Kansas," *Kansas Government Journal,* XLIII (March, 1956), 148.

simplifying the different kinds of school districts and in reducing the number of districts as shown in the accompanying table.

Unified school districts operate as governmental units with an

TABLE 30

Number and Types of School Districts in Kansas:
1963 and 1968

1963 Type	Number
Cities of the First Class	13
Cities of the Second Class	84
Unified	5
Common School, Elementary and High	146
Common School, Elementary Only	753
Common School, Grades 1-9	2
Common School, One Teacher	330
County Board of Education	1
Fort Leavenworth Board	1
Johnson County Special	11
Sedgwick County Special	8
Rural High School, Regular	267
Rural High School, Russell Plan	12
Rural High School, Grades 7-12	3
Sedgwick County Special High School	1
Community High School	20
Closed Common School Districts	169
Closed Rural High School Districts	14
Total	1,840

1968 Type	Number
Unified Under Acts of 1963 and 1965	308
Unified Under Special Legislation	2
Nonunified Districts: Rural High Schools	2
Second Class City District	1
Common School Districts	17
Total	330

Source: Adel F. Throckmorton, *Kansas Educational Progress: 1858-1967* (State Department of Public Instruction, 1967), p. 108, and unpublished data from the State Department of Public Instruction.

elected six-member governing board. The board has final authority in determining school policy and in controlling the use of school property. The board discharges its responsibilities by appointing a superintendent who makes recommendations to it.

Board members are elected for four-year staggered terms on a non-partisan ballot. While originally in the unification plan districts with cities of over 10,000 population were required to elect board members from the district at large, now all districts have a choice of using any of three election plans for their board members. These three plans are: (1) election of all board members at large; (2) dividing the unified district into three subdistricts," in each of which two candidates are selected in the primary, with all voters of the district then voting on the six candidates; and (3) dividing the district into six subdistricts, with the voters in each subdistrict nominating and electing the board member from their subdistrict. Most districts use the "three-district plan," with nomination from each of the three districts and election at large. The board may by resolution move to change to another plan of election, but the question must be submitted to the voters in the district. An individual elector may submit a plan to the state Board of Education, which if approved must then become the basis of a petition and ultimately a referendum in the district.

School boards no longer conduct their own elections; the county clerk or county election officer is now responsible for school elections.

Thus in the last few years much change has occurred in the local pattern for carrying out the education function. The goal of unification has been largely achieved. School-district reorganization does not in itself close individual schools. Indeed, one of the conditions of the 1963 school unification law was that no separate "attendance center" (school) would be closed without the consent of the patrons in that attendance area. The local unified boards will over the years make the necessary adjustment of attendance areas in their districts.

School Finances

School financing has long been a problem in Kansas. The ad valorem taxes levied by the district on real and personal property located within the district are the most important single source of school revenue. While there are wide variations in districts, considering all districts in the state, about 42 per cent of the operating revenues for schools comes from the district ad valorem property tax as shown by the table on page 228. Since the assessed valuations of school districts vary widely, there are wide differences in the ability of the districts to finance their schools. The wealthier districts are able to support schools with comparatively low tax rates, while the poorer districts have difficulties in raising sufficient funds to support adequate schools. The wide differences in assessment levels further complicate the problem. Tax-levy limits are established by the Legislature and restrict the amounts that districts may raise. School construction costs are financed almost entirely from local ad valorem taxes except for the districts which receive federal assistance because of expanded enrollments caused by federal activities in the area.

Local districts also levy an ad valorem tax to support community junior colleges and area vocational schools. They also receive part of the intangible property tax. A state-wide levy of five mills is made on intangible property (or taxpayers may choose to pay a percentage of the income from their intangible property). The school district receives one-fourth of the intangible tax collected in the district.

Counties make levies and pay money to the school districts within their boundaries. Part of the general state plan for financing schools calls for the counties to levy an ad valorem property tax for the County Foundation Fund. Each county is required to make a levy to raise the amount which the Commissioner of Education computes according to state law and certifies to the county clerk. The amount which each county is required to raise is the amount which a 10 mill tax would have raised had the county real property been assessed at the same level as the overall statewide assessment ratio. Thus the effect is that the mill rate is higher than 10 mills if the county assessment level is below the state average and is lower than 10 mills if the county assessment level is higher than the state average. Within the county, the County Foundation Fund is distributed to the individual school districts located wholly within the county on the basis of the number of certified employees in the district. For districts in more than one county the distribution is based on the per-pupil share and per-certified-employee teaching in home-county buildings.

Additionally, districts receive funds from the county-school fund

TABLE 31

Sources of School Operating Revenue, Kansas: 1967-1968

Sources	Amount	Per cent
Local		
Local Ad Valorem Taxes	$132,859,274	41.6
Area Vocational-Technical	1,993,106	.6
Local Ad Valorem Taxes—Community Junior Colleges	3,317,298	1.0
Intangible Tax	1,125,016	.4
Total	(139,294,694)	(43.6)
County		
County Foundation Fund	47,904,182	15.0
County School Funds (Fines and forfeitures)	1,425,000*	.5
County Out-district Tuition—Junior Colleges	1,688,736*	(.5)
Total	(51,017,918)	(16.0)
State		
State School Foundation Fund	88,758,391*	27.8
Local Ad Valorem Tax Reduction (Sales Tax Residue) **	7,072,576*	2.2
State Annual School Fund	1,524,328	.5
State Junior College Aid Fund	768,200*	.2
State Junior College Matching Fund	640,166*	.2
State Safety Fund	671,873	.2
State Special Education	2,085,000*	.7
State Vocational Education	380,734*	.1
State Area Vocational-Technical	1,307,003*	.4
State Manpower Developing Training	50,130*	0
Total	(103,258,401)	(32.3)
Federal		
Federal Elementary and Secondary Act, Titles I and II	11,558,000*	3.6
Federal Elementary and Secondary Act, Title III	2,213,590*	.7
Federal Area Technical	2,326,685*	.7
Federal Vocational Education	873,780*	.3
Federal Manpower Development Training Act	1,061,159*	.3
Public Law 874 Maintenance and Operation	6,500,000*	2.0
National Defense Education Act, Titles III and V	1,034,000*	.3
Work Study Program	114,534*	0
Adult Basic Education	232,402*	.1
Total	(25,914,150)	(8.1)
GRAND TOTAL	$319,485,163	100.0

** Includes junior colleges but not municipal universities.
Source: Unpublished data, Office of State Superintendent of Public Instruction.
* Estimated

and from other districts for tuition for junior college students attending in that district. Money from fines and forfeitures, the sale of stray animals, the sale of confiscated liquor, and limited other minor sources is placed in the County-School Fund. The Fund is apportioned among the schools according to an annual school census of persons between the ages of five and twenty-one.

Until recent years, the state provided only a small proportion of school revenue. Historically, the major type of aid was the state Annual School Fund established by the state Constitution.[6] In accordance with national policy of the time, the state received grants of public lands for the support of public schools on admission to statehood. Proceeds from the sale of these lands and from minor sources, such as unclaimed estates, are deposited in a trust fund known as the state Perpetual School Fund.[7] The state Annual School Fund is made up of the income from the investment of the state Perpetual School Fund, annual fees charged out-of-state insurance companies, motor-carrier taxes, and a portion of the money paid the state by the national government from mineral leases. The Annual School Fund is distributed to the common-school and city-school districts according to an annual school census of all persons between the ages of five and twenty-one.[8] The fund provides only a negligible portion of total school revenues.

Today the major part of state aid to local school districts comes from the state School Foundation Fund. The Fund was established in 1963, and payment began in 1965-66. In a sense the state Foundation Fund replaces the state Elementary-School Finance Fund and the state High-School Finance Fund. Though the present distribution formula differs from previous ones, the various programs have been built upon the state guaranteeing to each district a specific amount of support. Assuming a satisfactory pupil-teacher ratio, the present school foundation plan bases the state guarantee on the number of credit hours of the teachers and the number of years of teaching experience of the teachers. The amount the state contributes to the local districts is the state guar-

6. The subject was included in Article 6, section 4, of the original Constitution. It was replaced by an amendment in 1966.
7. Now the state Perpetual School Fund is provided for in Article 6, section 7c, of the amended Constitution.
8. *K.S.A.*, 27-118, 40-252, 72-2301, 72-2303a, 79-6a04.

antee less (1) the district's share of the state Annual School Fund, the intangible tax, and the County School Fund; (2) one-fourth of the federal payments to the district under Public Law 874; and (3) an amount calculated to measure the county's ability to support the schools.

The county's ability is expressed in terms of dollars per certified employee but is based on (1) the per cent of the valuation of the property in the county (as adjusted by the state sale ratio study) to the total state valuation and (2) the per cent of total individual income in the county to the total state income. The county with a high valuation and/or high personal incomes has "higher ability," and thus higher deductions, which mean in turn less state aid. Less state aid tends to mean a higher ad valorem property tax by the individual district.

More important than the complicated mechanics of the system is an understanding of the thinking and philosophy behind the foundation plan. The state guarantee is predicated on the salary of a journeyman teacher being a given amount each year (in 1967-68, $7600). The guarantee of the district depends on how many hours of college training and how many years of experience the teachers have up to a maximum of 210 credit hours and 15 years experience per teacher. Based on this "criteria of quality" the district is encouraged to employ as highly qualified teachers as it can, for the district's guarantee goes up for each credit hour and each year of experience of the teacher—i.e., to the maximum of 210 credit hours and fifteen years of experience. All the deductions, it will be noted, are from amounts which come from "outside" the school district—at least these deductions are not dependent upon the willingness or ability of the individual district to raise money within its district from the property tax.

In order to insure that local districts did in fact reduce the amount raised from the ad valorem property tax when increased state aid became available, local school districts were restricted to spending for operations only 104 per cent of the per-pupil expenditures of the preceding year. The School Budget Review Board has been established to review requests for exceptions to this limit and to allow increases above 104 per cent of the previous year's per-pupil expenditures.

School districts, as well as all other local units of government, receive money from the distribution of the sales-tax residue. Within

the county, the fund is apportioned among local governing units according to the general-property taxes levied. Its purpose is to shift the
incidence of taxation from the property tax, and it must be used to
reduce the property tax. Consequently, it does not augment the total
resources for school revenue.

State funds are also distributed to some schools for encouraging
special programs. The oldest of these is the vocational educational program which has been sponsored since 1917 by the state, in cooperation
with the national government. High schools offering vocational training
programs approved by the State Board of Education are eligible for
state and federal grants.[9] Two programs for special education are oper-
ative in the state. The first, established in 1951, authorizes state grants
to schools offering special classes for mentally retarded children and
special instruction for home-bound and hospitalized children. The
second, which began in 1953, grants state funds to schools offering
other types of special education such as special training for mentally
retarded children and for home-bound children. Schools approved by
the division of special education of the State Department of Public
Instruction receive grants for these purposes.[10]

Schools are receiving more and more assistance from the national
government. The total amount (somewhat over 8 per cent in 1967-
68) can no longer be considered minor, though some individual districts
may not take part in the individual programs identified in Table 31 and
thus do not receive federal funds. Many high schools receive national
funds through the vocational training programs described above. Two
types of special assistance are given to a few schools whose enrollments
have been affected by federal activities, such as military installations,
defense industries, federal schools or other federally owned property.
The payments are viewed as contributions in lieu of taxes on federal
property. First, schools with a certain percentage of their students
coming from families who live or work on federal property receive assistance for operation and maintenance of the schools. Second, a few
schools are eligible for federal grants to aid in school construction.
Although usually not classified as a part of school revenue, many

9. *K.S.A.,* 72-4304.
10. *K.S.A.,* 72-5344 to 5367.

schools in the state receive federal money and commodities under the school lunch program.

The County Superintendent of Public Instruction

From the date of establishing the state Constitution until 1969 the office of County Superintendent of Public Instruction existed as an important local office for coordinating the activities of the local school districts and boards. As the number of school districts became smaller and more of the districts had full-time qualified superintendents with professional training, the work and importance of the office decreased. In 1966, when the voters adopted a broad new amendment restructuring the whole educational system of the state, the office of County Superintendent of Public Instruction was in effect disestablished by forbidding the election of such official. The State Commissioner of Education will take over many of the functions previously performed by this local official.

State Department of Public Instruction

The major responsibility for supervising the public educational system now lies with the newly elected State Board of Education. The original Constitution established the position of State Superintendent of Public Instruction.[11] In 1873 the state Legislature added a State Board of Education, which, until the beginning of this century, was concerned primarily with the certification of some of the teachers in the state. The State Department of Public Instruction had limited authority because of the wide acceptance of the desirability of keeping control of education at the local level. At times the Department was influential in initiating and promoting educational reforms, but this depended upon the State Superintendent and on special historical circumstances.

A legislative reorganization of the Department in 1915 enhanced its importance. The addition of four school supervisors enabled it to maintain regular contact with local school systems for the first time. However, educational circles still expressed dissatisfaction with its limited effectiveness. In 1945 the Legislature again reorganized the Department. Since then, increased appropriations and additional statutory

11. *Kansas Constitution*, Art. 1, sec. 1.

authority have assisted the Department in taking a more active part in shaping a state educational program.

1945-1969

The Department was under the direction of the elected State Superintendent of Public Instruction and an appointive State Board of Education. Despite the fact that the office of State Superintendent was elective, only five men held the office in the last thirty years.

The Governor appointed the seven members of the State Board of Education for three-year overlapping terms. No person engaged in educational work was eligible for appointment. One member was appointed from each of the congressional districts of the state, with the remaining two members being appointed from the state at large. The members had to be affiliated with one of the two major political parties, but no more than four could belong to the same party. Further, no more than three could reside in school districts governed by boards of education of first- and second-class cities.

The Legislature had divided responsibility between the State Superintendent and the Board. Generally, the Superintendent was the responsible head of the department, and the Board was a compromise between a policy-forming and an advisory board. The Superintendent was empowered to formulate policy and regulations governing the fields of teacher certification, college accreditation, elementary- and high-school accreditation, curriculum, and special education. The regulations took effect only on approval by the Board, which had the statutory authority either to approve or to reject the proposals. The Board was empowered neither to propose policy nor to amend the proposals of the Superintendent, although it might do so informally. The Board had greater authority in textbook adoptions, since it could establish policies and adopt textbooks on its own initiative as well as consider proposals of the State Superintendent. The Board was authorized to act only in an advisory capacity in fields other than those mentioned.[12]

The State Superintendent had exclusive control over the department budget. The Superintendent submitted the requests directly to the Budget Division of the Department of Administration. Subject to civil service regulations, the Superintendent also had exclusive control

12. *K.S.A.,* 72-109, 72-115, 72-125, 72-5336.

over the employment, direction, and dismissal of most departmental personnel. In a few cases, Board approval of appointments was required.[13]

The statutory division and definition of authority of the State Superintendent and the Board proved to be no guarantee that harmonious relations would prevail. The independent selection of the Superintendent and the Board did not facilitate cooperation. Disagreement over textbook policies and adoptions, for example, led to differences in recent years.

There were differing views as to the most appropriate methods for selecting the Superintendent and the Board. Educational groups usually favored a constitutional amendment permitting an appointive State Board of Education to select the Superintendent, and some questioned whether appointment by the Governor would be the best means of insuring board members of high quality.

1969-Future

The Legislature proposed, and the voters approved, in 1966, a constitutional amendment to restructure the office of Superintendent. An entirely different philosophy of administration was incorporated in the constitutional amendment. Powers and responsibility were vested in an elected ten-man State Board of Education. Each new board member is elected from a special district created for this purpose, consisting of four contiguous senatorial districts. A special problem was posed in the election of the first Board, because the 1968 apportionment of senators was declared unconstitutional. An opinion of the Attorney General was issued which approved of the use of the senatorial apportionment established by the 1968 Legislature, even though it had been declared unconstitutional for purposes of electing state senators.

Amid much difference of opinion on the point, the Legislature finally decided to have the State Board elected on a partisan basis. The State Board is assigned by the Constitution "general supervision of public schools, educational institutions and all the educational interests of the state" except for those functions alloted to the Board of Regents. The State Board of Education appoints the Commissioner of Education who serves at the pleasure of the State Board. As the new organization goes

13. *K.S.A.*, 72-5335.

into effect in the state, the office of State Superintendent of Public Instruction consists of three major sub-sections—Division of Accreditation and Certification, Division of Instructional Services, and Division of Administrative Services.

The Department of Public Instruction establishes the requirements for teachers and certifies as qualified those applicants meeting these requirements. For purposes of teacher-training, it also accredits the colleges of the state—the state institutions of higher learning, private and religious colleges, and junior colleges. Preliminary work in framing standards for certification and college accreditation is performed by the Advisory Council on Teacher Education, a quasi-public body organized by the Department. It is composed of representatives from accredited colleges and various educational associations.

The elementary and high schools of the state are accredited and classified by the Department of Public Instruction. Standards for these purposes cover such areas as enrollment, teacher preparation, physical plant, equipment, curriculum, and community and school attitudes. The classifications are reviewed annually from the findings of reports and field visits.

The Department of Public Instruction establishes the curriculum requirements for both the elementary and high schools. This includes the adoption, subject to statutory requirements, of the required and optional subjects a school may offer, the sequence of subjects, and the credit allowed. The Department also prepares and publishes curricular guides for teachers, which are printed by the state and sold to school districts. The Department staff also assists local schools in curricular reorganization, student guidance, and testing and evaluation.

Kansas statutes have required elementary and high schools to use textbooks adopted by the former State Board of Education.[14] The new Board of Education, i.e. the Board first elected in 1968, was charged with adopting guidelines or rules for textbooks.[15] Textbook advisory committees were appointed by the Board (and presumably will be continued).[16] Composed mostly of educators, these committees are established to provide professional advice to the Board, which may

14. *K.S.A.*, 72-4151.
15. *1968 Session Laws of Kansas,* chap. 658.
16. *K.S.A.*, 72-4148.

adopt for a subject either a single textbook, for use in all schools in the state, or a multiple listing of books. In the latter case, each unified school district selects from the multiple adoption list the book to be used.

A state program for the special education of exceptional children was established in Kansas in 1949.[17] The Department of Public Instruction formulates standards for special programs, and staff members supervise the participating schools. State financial assistance is used to encourage schools to undertake these programs. Schools approved by the Department receive state reimbursements for special classes for mentally retarded children, and for special instruction for home-bound and hospitalized children. Under a more restricted reimbursement plan, the Department has also assisted in the organization of special programs for such groups as children with speech and hearing handicaps, the exceptionally gifted, the emotionally disturbed, and the physically handicapped.

The Department administers state aid for elementary and high schools. Largely clerical, this work requires the collection and tabulation of statistical information and the computation and distribution of the aid. The Department also performs most administrative duties related to the state Perpetual School Fund and the state Annual School Fund. The Perpetual School Fund and a few other small trust funds are invested by the State School Fund Commission, composed of a member of the State Board of Education, the Attorney General, and the Secretary of State.[18] The Commission has first option on the purchase of all bonds issued by local units of government.

The Department provides several aids in school administration and performs some administrative regulation. Through the School Facilities Services Program, it advises school districts on long-range planning by advising on enrollment predictions, planning of facilities and construction, district reorganization, and financial problems. The Department offers legal services by the publication of the school laws and by advising schools on administrative matters related to legal questions. Administrative regulation includes the preparation and distribution of several forms which school officers must use.

17. *K.S.A.*, 72-5344 to 72-5367.
18. *1968 Session Laws of Kansas*, chap. 143.

Because of the small staff, the Department gave little attention to internal organization before 1945. Since then, a rapidly increasing staff and additional duties have required more formal organization. Current concepts of state educational administration emphasize the leadership role. The state agency is expected to stimulate local action for educational improvement by various advisory and promotional activities. Consequently, a large portion of the departmental efforts are devoted to working with educational commission committees and other groups, and to offering various advisory services. It is hoped that the new organizational arrangement between the elected State Board and the appointed Commissioner of Education will facilitate this leadership role.

Vocational Education

In 1917 the United States Congress established a national program for vocational education by authorizing grants-in-aid to the states, and in the same year the state Legislature authorized the state to participate in the national program and designated the State Board of Education as the State Board for Vocational Education.[19] Other programs were added to the duties of the Board in recent years.

The Department of Vocational Education was a separate administrative unit from the State Department of Public Instruction, although the same board acted both as the State Board of Education and the State Board for Vocational Education. The Board had full responsibility for the policy and administration of the Department of Vocational Education, in contrast to its more restricted role in relation to the Department of Public Instruction. The Board appointed the executive officers and director of the Department, who was in charge of departmental activities subject to the regulations and supervision of the board. In 1963 the Legislature authorized the creation of a new Vocational Education Advisory Board. And at the time of this writing (1968), federal legislation is pending which would require the continuation of this advisory board.

The State Superintendent of Public Instruction had recommended that vocational education be made a part of the Department of Public Instruction. The 1966 constitutional amendment made it clear that the

19. K.S.A., 72-4302.

new Board would be responsible for vocational education. The new elected Board of Education that takes office in 1969 will determine how the vocational education activities are related to the other educational activities of the state.

Vocational training is divided into six instructional fields—agriculture, occupational homemaking, trade and industrial, technical, business education (distributive and office), and health occupations. Day and evening classes for adults, as well as classes for high-school students, may be organized in all fields except agriculture. Under a reimbursement policy adopted by the State Board, participating high schools receive grants from state and national funds for a specified percentage of the salaries of the teacher (currently 50 per cent). Federal funds are also granted to pay a portion of the Department's administrative expenses.

The vocational-education program is governed by a series of policies and standards known as the "state plan." It was drawn up by the State Board for Vocational Education and approved by the United States Office of Education. The "state plan" establishes the policies not only for the Department but also for participating schools. Various standards regarding enrollment, equipment, curriculum, and teacher requirements must be maintained by the participating schools.

In accordance with the state plan, the State Board designates one or more of the state colleges for training vocational education teachers. These schools receive national and state reimbursements for the teacher-training program. The Department staff also supervises the teacher-training programs.

Since the Vietnam war the State Board of Vocational Education has participated in several training programs sponsored by the U.S. Veterans Administration. These programs have been in the distributive, computer, and radio and television fields.

Vocational education is offered under a number of different institutional arrangements. At the secondary level, regular high schools have such programs as part of their regular curriculum or as special classes. Area vocational schools have been established and help service these students as well as high school graduates. Junior colleges and four-year colleges also offer vocational education. For adults there are special programs using high schools, area vocational schools, and junior and four-year colleges.

In Kansas high schools in the 1967-68 school year there were approved vocational education programs allowing for 272 classes in agriculture, 405 in homemaking, 378 in trade and industrial education, 130 in business education, 104 in technical education, and 45 in health occupations.[20] During the 1968 fiscal year there were 57,736 enrollees. In 1968, $11,186,905 was spent for vocational education plus $612,436 under the Manpower Development and Training Act. Local units raised over half of the money spent and received $5,272,575 in assistance from the federal and state governments for these programs.

Despite the number of such programs there is genuine concern as to whether enough is being done in this type of education in the state. In comparison to other states there seems to be good foundation for this concern.

The State School Retirement Board

The State School Retirement Board was established in 1941 to administer a state-wide retirement plan for school employees. It is composed of the state Commissioner of Education as ex officio chairman, the state Treasurer, one school employee, and three other persons appointed by the Governor for four-year, overlapping terms. The Board is authorized to employ an executive secretary and other necessary staff.[21]

The state retirement plan covers most school-district employees, including administrators, teachers, clerks, and janitors. The Commissioner of Education and employees of the Education Department are allowed to continue under the retirement plan if they were included within the plan previously. Although the statutes permit school districts in cities with a population over 5,000 to adopt their own retirement plans instead of the state plan, Kansas City is now the only city outside the state plan.[22] However, some of the first-class cities have city retirement plans to supplement the state plan.[23]

20. Unpublished data from the state Board of Vocational Education.
21. *K.S.A.*, 72-5501 to 5531.
22. *K.S.A.*, 72-1726 to 1734, 72-1758, 72-1759, 72-1759a, 72-1780, 72-1788, 72-1799, 72-1839 to 1847.
23. *K.S.A.*, 72-17, 108 to 17, 123.

Retirement funds come from two sources: a "service fund" from state appropriations and a "savings fund" collected from 4 per cent deductions from the first $3,000 of each employee's annual salary. The amount one receives upon retirement is based on length of service, the recipient's contributions, and standard actuarial tables. Provisions are also made for "disability annuities" for persons incurring permanent physical or mental disabilities while in school employment. School employees in Kansas were in 1955 placed under the federal old age and survivors insurance program, but this fact did not alter the provisions or benefits of the state retirement plan.

The State Institutions of Higher Learning

Kansas maintains six institutions of higher learning—The University of Kansas, Lawrence; Kansas State University, Manhattan (a land-grant college); Kansas State Teachers College of Emporia; Kansas State College of Pittsburg; Ft. Hays Kansas State College; and Wichita State University. Legislation in 1863 and 1864 established the University of Kansas, Kansas State College, and the State Normal School, now Kansas State Teachers College of Emporia. The teachers colleges at Hays and Pittsburg were organized in 1901 and 1903 respectively. Wichita University, previously a municipal university, was admitted into the state system in 1963. There are also two other state educational institutions, the State School for the Deaf at Olathe and the State School for the Blind in Kansas City, Kansas. Both were organized in the 1860's.

The State Board of Administration, organized in 1913, was the first single board to govern these institutions. Previously, separate boards controlled the University of Kansas, Kansas State University, and the state teachers colleges. At the time of organization, there were individual boards of trustees for the School for the Blind and the School for the Deaf. From 1876 to 1913, they were under the jurisdiction of a single board for the state's eleemosynary institutions. In 1925, the Legislature transferred the institutions of higher learning to the control of a separate Board of Regents. The schools for the blind and the deaf were placed under the Regents in 1939.

The State Board of Regents is composed of nine members appointed by the Governor with the consent of the state senate for four-year, overlapping terms. There are no statutory qualifications for appointees except that they must belong to one of the two major political parties, and no more than five may belong to one party. The regents receive no remuneration except expenses. They are authorized to appoint a secretary and set his salary. The Board elects its own chairman, following a policy of rotating the position annually.

The Board of Regents appoints the executive head of each institution under its jurisdiction—the chancellor of the University, the presidents of the State Colleges and the State University, and the superintendents of the Schools for the Blind and Deaf. Rules adopted by the Board govern the organization, educational programs, and other policies and practices of each institution.[24]

The Board of Regents adopts the proposed budgets for each institution under its control. The largest share of revenue comes from state appropriations, but substantial amounts come from trust and endowment funds, student fees, and service charges. Kansas State University also receives an important part of its revenue from federal grants to land-grant colleges. An educational building fund and a school-dormitory fund, both derived from state-wide statutory property-tax levies, provide funds for building purposes at the institutions of higher learning.[25] The regents may also issue revenue bonds for constructing student union buildings and dormitories.[26]

At each of the institutions various deans, directors, and other officers head the administrative divisions, the academic programs, student services, specialized programs, and state services. The University of Kansas is divided into the College of Liberal Arts and Sciences, the Graduate School, and schools of Business, Education, Engineering, Architecture, Fine Arts, Journalism, Law, Medicine, and Pharmacy. Various specialized programs include University Extension, the State Geological Survey, the Center for Business Research, the Bureau of Child Research, and the Governmental Research Center.

The academic program of the Kansas State University of Agriculture and Applied Science is organized into schools of Agriculture, Arts and Sciences, Engineering and Architecture, Home Economics, Veter-

24. *K.S.A.*, 76-108b to 108c.
25. *K.S.A.*, 76-6b01 to 6b02a.
26. *K.S.A.*, 76-6a14 to 6a15.

inary Medicine, and a Graduate School. Kansas State University conducts agricultural and engineering experiment stations in various parts of the state. It is also in charge of the agricultural extension service which works with agricultural, home demonstration, and 4-H programs in every county. The colleges at Emporia, Hays, and Pittsburg originally emphasized teacher-training, but now the last two have moved more toward offering general liberal-arts curricula.

Wichita State University is organized into eight operating units: Fairmont College of Liberal Arts and Sciences, College of Business Administration and Industry, College of Education, School of Engineering, College of Fine Arts, Graduate School, University College, and Summer School. The act admitting Wichita State University into the state system provided for it to be an associate of the University of Kansas. Graduate programs instituted after the incorporation into the state system were to be coordinated with those of the University of Kansas.

Though more specialized in the clientele served, the State School for the Blind and the State School for the Deaf are also administered under jurisdiction of the Board of Regents. The schools for the blind and for the deaf are open to all residents of the state between the ages of five and twenty-one with partial or total impairments of sight or hearing which make normal classroom instruction unsuitable. The schools furnish the necessary educational materials, room and board, and normal medical care to the students without charge.

Both schools provide an elementary and secondary education program with academic, vocational, and special training. The School for the Blind also has a one-year postgraduate course. In addition, both schools conduct annual institutes for parents of preschool age children having sight and hearing impairments. The School for the Blind also offers a summer school for adults with sight impairments.

Other Institutions of Learning

In addition to the state institutions of higher learning, there are junior colleges, municipal universities, and private colleges in Kansas. There are eighteen four-year and six two-year private colleges, all of which have religious affiliations.[27]

27. U.S. Department of Health, Education and Welfare, Office of Education, *Education Directory, 1958-1959, Part 3, Higher Education*, pp. 60-63.

Legislation authorizing the organization of junior colleges was first enacted in 1917. The junior colleges offered curricula including college, vocational, and general courses. They were closely related to the public-school system, since they were under the control and supervision of the school-district governing board and the school superintendent. The same persons sometimes taught in both the high school and junior college. The State Superintendent of Public Instruction exercised much the same general supervision over junior colleges as he did over elementary and high schools.[28]

In 1965 the organization in the state was significantly changed. Community junior colleges were separated from the local boards of education and were required to have their own boards of trustees and separate administrators. They no longer were to be considered as extensions of high schools. The State Superintendent of Public Instruction was made the state authority for junior colleges. The establishment of new community junior colleges was restricted, requiring (1) a feasibility study, (2) review by the State Advisory Council for Community Junior Colleges, (3) review by the State Superintendent, and (4) approval by the voters in the area. It became possible for areas outside the county to be included in the taxing district, but beyond the county a majority of the voters in the additional area had to vote in favor of being included.

By 1935 there were fourteen community junior colleges. No new ones were established from 1935 to 1964, while five were added in the four years from 1964 to 1968. In 1968 the Legislature banned the establishment of new community colleges. The new State Board of Education will be involved in studying the rapid increase in the number of junior colleges, their relation to the area vocational schools, and in broader terms the contribution that community junior colleges can make to the education of the citizens of the state.

Community junior colleges are financed by property-tax levies, state aid, and tuition payments. The board of trustees for such junior colleges may levy an ad valorem property tax for maintenance and operation (up to 5 mills in districts with less than $75,000,000 valuation, 3 mills in districts with valuations of over $75,000,000, and 8 mills in districts with more than one community junior college in the county).

28. *K.S.A.*, 72-3303 to 72-3304.

The colleges currently receive state aid at the rate of $8 per credit hour. They charge tuition to the students who attend and also receive tuition payments from counties for out-of-county students.

The city of Topeka maintains Washburn University under statutory provisions authorizing municipal universities. The University is controlled by a board of regents composed of nine members serving for four-year, overlapping terms. The local board of education appoints four of the members; the city-governing body appoints four; and the mayor is an ex officio member. The regents have general control of university affairs. They appoint the president, control university property, establish tuition charges, levy the taxes for public support, issue bonds for construction purposes, and delegate to the president and faculty such matters of internal administration as they deem desirable.[29]

State Libraries

Kansas maintains two libraries, the State Library and the State Historical Library. The State Historical Library was established following action by the Legislature of 1879, designating the Kansas State Historical Society as a trustee of the state for collecting, securing, and taking custody of historical collections.[30] The Society is financed by state appropriations and small amounts derived from membership fees and bequests. The Society offices and the State Historical Library are housed in the State Memorial Hall. The Society elects its own board of directors and officers to manage its affairs.

The State Historical Library includes a museum, a library emphasizing Kansas and regional history and genealogical materials, divisions for pictures, archives of state papers, manuscripts, microfilm, newspapers, and census. The Society also sponsors special research projects and publications, including the *Kansas Historical Quarterly*, which are financed by state appropriations.[31]

The State Library, which was established in 1861, is a depository for the state laws, court reports, legislative journals, official reports, and

29. *K.S.A.*, 13-13a01 to 13-13a16; 13-13a18 and 13-13a23.
30. *K.S.A.*, 75-2701, 75-2702.
31. "The Annual Meeting," *Kansas Historical Quarterly*, XXI (Winter, 1954), 291-304.

other publications of Kansas and other states.[32] To provide a different type of library service, the Legislature in 1899 established the State Traveling Libraries Commission.[33] The Kansas Social Science Federation (now the State Federation of Women's Clubs) had urged this in a plan which they submitted for encouraging reading and making books available to the people of the state. The Commission, which continued to exist until 1963, maintained a library for loaning books to small public libraries, school libraries, community organizations, and individuals, in order to supplement local collections and to provide library facilities in communities having no library. The loans were usually limited to towns with a population under 2,500. The Commission assisted in organizing public libraries and in advising on administrative and other problems of small libraries.

There was a close relationship between the State Library and the five-man Traveling Library Commission, for the State Librarian was chairman of the Commission and the State Library assigned a person from its staff to act as secretary to the Commission. The other four members of the Commission were three members appointed for three-year, overlapping terms by the directors of the State Library (the State Supreme Court justices) and the President of the State Federation of Women's Clubs. During this period (1899-1963) the State Librarian was appointed by the Governor, who by terms of the statute was required to appoint the person recommended by the Supreme Court.

For the sixty-four years ending in 1963 only five persons served as State Librarian. One of these persons served for thirty-eight years, another for seventeen, one for six years, and two for shorter periods. Aside from the turnover in the one position on the Commission held by the member of the State Federation of Women's Clubs, there was relatively little turnover in the membership of the Commission. The Commission seemed to answer a real need by loaning books and recorded an impressive growth in this service. Gradually, however, as books became more available and more local libraries were established, different assistance was needed to further the public libraries activities

32. *K.S.A.*, 75-2510.
33. Much of the information in this and the next several paragraphs is condensed from *The Kansas Traveling Library Commission: An Administrative History* (Lawrence: Governmental Research Center, Univ. of Kansas, 1965).

of the state. Extension library assistance, including in-service training for librarians, became more necessary than the boxes of books. At the same time, Federal funds to stimulate various public-library activities became available. In 1963 the state library service was reorganized and the Governor was given the authority to appoint the State Librarian subject to approval by the Supreme Court. The State Traveling Libraries Commission was dissolved. In a limited sense it was replaced by the new Library Advisory Commission, with the Chief Justice of the Supreme Court acting as ex officio chairman. The Commission advises and consults with the State Librarian, and it may make suggestions or recommendations to the Governor.

In 1965 the Legislature authorized a regional system of cooperating libraries. The State Librarian and the state Advisory Commission have encouraged the development of regional library systems, and now there are five systems which encompass generally the whole state. Individual libraries are free to participate in the systems or not. The Advisory Commission authorizes the creation of such systems, which are then legally authorized to levy up to a one-half mill property tax on all of the property of the region except where property tax is now levied for libraries. Federal funds have become an important mechanism for stimulating this movement to have regional library service. One of the challenges in the public-library field in Kansas has been to maintain local interest, participation, and at least a measure of control of local library services and yet have adequate public-library facilities for all parts of the state. The State Librarian continues in his role of librarian for the state government and leader in promoting adequate public-library service for the communities of the state. The function of state government in this field has changed markedly in the last two decades, with the state being cast in more of a leadership role for the cities and local units performing library services.

Other Educational Agencies

The state participates in a few other activities of an educational character. It frequently makes annual appropriations to the Kansas Academy of Science to assist in the publication of the Academy's *Transactions*. The state maintains as historic sites the first territorial capitol, Frontier Historical Park, Funston Memorial Home, Highland

Presbyterian Mission, John Brown Memorial Park, Marais des Cygnes Massacre Park, Old Kaw Mission, Old Shawnee Mission, Pawnee Rock Historical Park, Pike's Pawnee Indian Village, and Washington County Pony Express Station. In 1963 the general pattern was devised whereby the State Historical Society is responsible for the management and control of these sites, and advisory committees counsel the Secretary of the Historical Society in the administration of these properties.

14 | Public Health

The active participation of state government in problems of public health did not materialize until around the turn of the century. Before that time, state health activities were confined to the quarantine and isolation of persons with contagious diseases. It was not until the development of Pasteur's germ theory in 1866 that much thought was given by state health officers to the prevention and control of illness through environmental sanitation and epidemiology. The new emphasis on preventive medicine set the pattern for contemporary public health programs in the United States.

Through the use of grants-in-aid on a matching basis, impetus to state activity came from the national government in the early twenties and, with renewed vigor, after World War II. The Chamberlin-Kahn Act of 1918 provided grants to states for the control of venereal disease. From 1921 to 1929 the Sheppard-Towner Act provided grants for maternal and child care. In 1936, provisions of the Social Security Act included grants for use by state health departments. During World War II the national government sponsored a grant program for families of servicemen which included emergency maternity and child-care facilities. In 1944 the United States Public Health Service Act established a program of federal grants to states for general-health work, venereal-disease control, and tuberculosis control. Since 1946, the national government has initiated grants-in-aid for state mental-health programs, hospital survey and construction, and water-pollution control.

Public-health programs at all levels of government are determined largely by prevailing health problems. Great progress has been made in the last sixty years in conquering contagious diseases, so that now the emphasis is on research and programming in connection with diseases of the aged, such as cancer and heart disease, and on the diseases of newborn babies and the young.

Early Development of the Kansas State Board of Health

The early history of the Kansas State Board of Health is tied closely to the regulation of the practice of medicine in the state.[1] The Kansas Medical Society, which had been incorporated in 1859, was the leading advocate of the creation of a state board of health. In 1870, largely because of agitation by Society members, the Legislature passed the Medical-Practice Act, designed to protect the legitimate medical profession from the malpractices of the prevalent "quack" doctors.

After passage of the Medical-Practice Act, the Kansas Medical Society worked for the creation of an agency which would have authority to deal with the problems of disease on a state-wide basis. The Medical Society believed that such an agency should be empowered to investigate and take necessary measures to prevent the causes of diseases, and also be responsible for the accurate recording of information on births and deaths, which could be used for statistical research and comparison.

Although bills had been introduced earlier, it was not until 1885 that a state board of health was established. While the Medical Society was responsible in part for the creation of the Board, some of the impetus came from the National Board of Health, which had warned the Governor of the danger of Asiatic cholera. In the act creating the State Board, county commissioners were designated local health boards. The State Board of Health was charged with the general supervision of health interests of the state, supervision of the construction of public

---

1. Harriet S. Pfister, *Kansas State Board of Health*, (Lawrence: Governmental Research Center, Univ. of Kansas, 1955), p. 15. Mrs. Pfister's work was used considerably in preparing this chapter.

sanitation systems, and the collection of vital statistics and morbidity statistics. It also was given the responsibility of making recommendations to the Governor for the better protection of life and health in Kansas. Local boards of health were required to appoint county health officers and to carry out rules and regulations of the State Board.

Operations of the State Board of Health during the early years were handicapped by a rather general hostility to its activities and by weaknesses in the law which conferred authority on the Board. Hostility came from newspapers, certain members of the medical profession itself, and from within the Legislature. The press, which frequently opposed actions of the State Board of Health in editorials, seemed to fear the loss of advertising revenue if the regulatory powers of the Board were strictly exercised. This is explained by the fact that many medical practitioners, such as herb doctors and others with patent medicines, used the newspapers heavily for advertising their wares and services.

Members of the medical profession who made a living by selling nostrums to the public were bitterly opposed to attempted regulations by the new State Board of Health. They worked to stir up public resentment against actions of the Board and to prevent any extension of state-wide public-health powers.

There was a group of legislators who opposed the Board because they believed the public was not ready for such an agency. Even if the Board had value, it could be of no use if the citizens were not willing to accept its authority. Consequently these legislators disapproved of any attempts to strengthen the role of the Board in preserving public health throughout the state. In their opinions the time was not ripe for experimentation with so personal a thing as the health of individuals. In fact, several efforts were made to repeal the law which created the Board. While these efforts did not succeed, the position of the State Board of Health was precarious.

In addition to varied opposition from outside the structure of the State Board of Health, there were also internal weaknesses which hampered its effectiveness. The few powers granted it were often rendered advisory because of adverse rulings of the Attorney General on its actions. Examples include unfavorable rulings on a Board resolution requiring school children to be vaccinated and on the Board's

power to compel county commissioners to select a county health officer
as prescribed by law.

After it survived repeated attacks, the position of the State Board
of Health began to improve. During the early 1900's several laws were
passed which added to its powers and strengthened those assigned
under the original law. In 1901 the Legislature passed a law which enabled the Board to quarantine contagious diseases such as smallpox,
cholera, scarlet fever, and diphtheria and also appropriated funds for
suppressing tuberculosis. One part of the law provided for the confidential reporting of all cases of tuberculosis. In 1917 the Legislature
authorized the Board to make rules and regulations for the control of
all communicable diseases which it declared dangerous to public health.

Passage of the vital statistics law in 1911 was a significant advance
for the State Board of Health. This law created a Division of Vital
Statistics which began to collect morbidity reports and conduct studies
on the prevalence of reportable diseases. City and township clerks were
designated as local registrars of vital statistics in order to make the
system of registration of vital information more accurate and complete.
The local registrars were authorized to issue burial permits and receive
birth certificates for their districts. County health officers retained the
responsibility of submitting morbidity reports to the State Registrar of
Vital Statistics.

Another important area where legislation improved the position of
the State Board of Health was in problems of controlling water pollution and water-borne disease. The Board received many complaints
concerning the pollution of water supplies, but was unable to act effectively until 1907, when the Legislature passed a law to preserve the
purity of state waters. Under this law the Board was given the power
to pass on the adequacy of all new water supplies and sewage systems.
In addition, it was authorized to make investigations of stream pollution
which resulted from the discharge of industrial wastes. The law was
further strengthened in 1909, when the Board was given jurisdiction
over all water plants and sewage systems, regardless of the date of
construction.

The early years of the State Board of Health were turbulent because
of the hostility which frequently accompanies a new idea or institution.
However, as the value of a health agency with state-wide powers

became more widely known to Kansans, the concept was gradually accepted by the general public and its legislative representatives. This recognition resulted in the broadening of State Board of Health's powers and in an increase of responsibilities for state health officials. Almost each year since the first three decades of its existence has seen legislative and organizational additions and changes strengthening its powers and position.

Current Organization of the State Board of Health

The Kansas State Board of Health was reconstituted and reorganized by the Legislature in 1951. A completely new Board was appointed by the Governor with the advice and consent of the Senate. This new Board, representing as far as possible different parts of the state, is composed of five medical doctors, one pharmacist, one dentist, one veterinary doctor, one hospital administrator, and one sanitary engineer.

The Board members serve three-year staggered terms and are limited to two consecutive terms. They receive $15 for each day of work, plus necessary traveling expenses. The Board selects its own president and holds quarterly meetings, as required by law. Its annual meeting is held during June in Topeka. Special meetings of the State Board of Health may be called by the secretary whenever necessary.

The State Board of Health is authorized to make such rules and regulations as may be necessary to carry out duties assigned to it by law. These rules and regulations become official and have the force of law when they are filed with the Revisor of Statutes. Regulations passed by the Board deal with the administration of specific health programs such as water-pollution control, mental hygiene, licensing of hospitals and children's homes, and environmental sanitation.

Secretary of the Board

The State Board of Health elects a secretary who acts as executive secretary. Although not a member of the Board, he is responsible for keeping records of all Board transactions and documents, communicating with other state boards, and maintaining contact with all local boards of health in the state. The state Board may assign other duties to the Secretary, and may remove him for "just cause." The Secretary is referred to in the statutes as Director of Health (formerly State Health Officer), and he works under the general direction of the Board in health matters.

The Secretary serves as a member of the Advisory Hospital Council, of the Kansas Safety Council, and of examining committees for sterilization of institutional inmates. He files complaints of water pollution in abandoned oil or gas wells and serves as chief food and drug inspector. The Secretary reports to appropriate state officials the findings of the Board of Health's inspections of state children's institutions. He approves forms upon which reports of tuberculosis cases are submitted by the local health officers to the State Board of Health. The Secretary may act for the Board when the latter is not in session, in regard to violations of water-supply and sewage-disposal requirements.

For the administration of the various programs, the State Board of Health is organized into several divisions. While only three of the divisions have been created by specific statutes, all exercise powers and duties assigned to the Board. Although each division is responsible for a particular group of public-health activities, most of the programs are tied together by common goals of health-betterment; consequently there is considerable cooperation and joint planning among the various divisions. For example, service divisions, such as health-education services, provide program aids for all of the operating divisions.

Advisory Bodies

Associated with the State Board of Health are two agencies which have the power to assist and direct the Board in the administration of legislation relating to hospitals and laboratories. The Advisory Laboratory Commission consists of five persons: two appointed by the Governor; two appointed by the Chancellor of the University of Kansas; and one appointed by the President of Kansas State University. The Director of the Division of Public-Health Laboratories of the State Board of Health serves as ex officio Secretary to the Advisory Laboratory Commission. This Commission is authorized to formulate and recommend to the State Board of Health standards for persons performing serological tests and procedures for registering laboratories which conduct serological examinations. While the State Board of Health is solely authorized to promulgate rules, the statutes provide that "such rules and regulations shall be in conformity with recommendations made by the Advisory Laboratory Commission."

The Advisory Hospital Council, appointed by the Governor, consists of nine members: three representatives of the Kansas Hospital Association; two members of the medical profession; one registered nurse; and three representatives of users of hospital services. The Secretary of the State Board of Health is ex officio Secretary of the Council. The members of the Council elect their own chairman. The Council is empowered to supervise the State Board of Health in matters of policy dealing with the licensing, inspection, and regulation of hospitals. The Advisory Hospital Council approves regulations which the State Board of Health may adopt and reviews on appeal any order of the State Board of Health which revokes, denies, or suspends a license. The Council consults with and advises the Board with respect to the administration of the Hospital Survey and Construction Act.

The Coordinating Council for Health Planning has been established to advise the Governor and the State Board of Health in the development of a state health plan. This is part of a federal plan which seeks to make good health a human right. The goals of the national program are the ready availability of comprehensive health services to all who need them and life in an environment which contributes to healthful individual and family life. The state Council has subcommittees for health manpower, health facilities, and health services. The Legislature has authorized a comprehensive study of health resources to develop a long-range plan for public health services on a state-wide basis. A private consulting firm made a study and then made recommendations to the Legislative Council in 1968.

Powers of the State Board of Health

By statute, the State Board of Health is given "general supervision of the health of the citizens of the state" and is charged with making "intelligent and profitable use of collected records of the causes of sickness and death among people." Based on this general grant of authority, the State Board of Health has expanded the activities into many different areas. In some cases the Legislature has specifically outlined programs for the Board to carry out.

In order to facilitate the carrying out of its assigned duties, the

State Board of Health has been granted by law several administrative powers. The Board may engage committees or qualified persons to make or supervise sanitary investigations into the causes of disease and death and the effect of food and water supply on public health.

Extensive rule-making powers have been granted the State Board of Health by legislative acts. The Board may adopt and amend rules and regulations which deal with the administration of specific public-health programs. In order to have the force of law, such rules and regulations must be printed in the official paper and filed with the state Revisor of Statutes. For example, the State Board of Health may prescribe regulations for the collection, compiling, and use of vital statistics; it may pass rules governing the discharge of industrial and domestic sewage into waters of the state.

Another important administrative power of the State Board of Health is the authority to issue appropriate orders to individuals, governments, or corporations. In the name of the Board, its various divisions may issue orders to stop polluting state waters, to forbid supplying unsafe waters to the public, to construct municipal and industrial sewage-treatment works, and to prohibit the sale of misbranded or adulterated food and drugs, or similar orders.

The State Board of Health also has the power to license certain establishments and issue permits for the operation of other enterprises and for certain types of construction. Licenses are required for maternity and children's homes, hospitals, nursing homes, adult boarding homes, and convalescent homes. Permits are also necessary for supplying water to the public, for the discharge of sewage into waters of the state, and for the operation of slaughterhouses, sausage plants, packing houses, and poultry-dressing and packing plants. These licenses and permits may be revoked for due cause after a hearing.

The laws of Kansas prescribe penalties for violation of the statutes or of rules and regulations of the State Board of Health. In general, the violations are misdemeanors. Any person who violates the Board's rules or regulations concerning the control of contagious diseases is guilty of a misdemeanor. Penalties, which range from $25 to $200 fines or ninety days in jail or both, are assessed only through action in the appropriate court. The Board may turn over the case to the county attorney for prosecution or, in some matters, will itself prosecute. Fines for the violation of laws and regulations dealing with water supply and sewage disposal are considerably higher. Other areas of public health where penalties are provided for violation of rules and regulations include the operation of hospitals and maternity and children's homes, the sale of food and drugs, the upkeep of private property which may affect public health, the sale of caustic or corrosive substances, and the licensing of meat and poultry plants and packing houses. Broadly, however, the Board is concerned with persuading those concerned to know and follow the law. One official of the Board estimated that less than 5 per cent of the known violations were prosecuted.

Service Areas of the Kansas State Health Department

Environmental Health Service

Though for many years located at the University of Kansas at Lawrence, the sanitation activities of the Department were moved in 1957 to Topeka. A faculty member of the School of Engineering of the University of Kansas or Kansas State University is designated by the State Board as engineer and acts as the director of this area of activities of the Department. Permits are issued for the operation of the municipal water supplies and sewerage systems. Plans and specifications for these structures are reviewed and periodic inspections are made of their operation.

The Department has been increasingly concerned with reducing the pollution of streams in Kansas. In a number of instances the Board has issued orders to various cities to install sewage-treatment plants. Substantial progress has been made in removing this type of stream pollution. For the purpose of preventing stream pollution detrimental to animal and fish life, the State Board of Health may make rules and regulations governing the disposal of domestic and industrial wastes.

Another type of pollution—that from oil and gas fields—has led to the creation of a section to give advice to industries and farmers on how to control pollution from this source. Air pollution and the control of health hazards in industry and radiation have necessitated programs in these areas and the employment of specialists in these areas.

The Department maintains a fee-supported engineering laboratory to support the operations of this part of its activities. The laboratory performs a wide variety of chemical and bacteriological tests designed to determine the adequacy of treatments of water and sewage. All water testing is done by this laboratory. Samples from water supplies are tested on request, and advisory service is given on well construction and sewage-disposal systems. The Department prepares standards for plumbing and renders advice and assistance in regard to municipal refuse disposal, swimming pools, and the control of rats and flies.

Medical Health Services

Much of the public-health function can and must be carried out locally. The policy followed by the entire State Board of Health organization is that public-health work is best done on the local level by local departments which have the understanding and support of the communities they serve.

All services offered to local health units by other sections of the Department are channeled through the Medical Health Service. Personnel of the Department provide consultation to community groups and governmental agencies on problems of public-health programming and administration.

In these activities the Department is best able to work with full-time local health departments. However, in most of the state there are only part-time local health departments. In order to provide more local health services, the Secretary has urged adding staff for local health work to the six district offices of the Board which already exist primarily for sanitation work.[2] State and federal grants are available to local public-health units. This grant program is administered primarily by the Medical Health Services section.

Personnel of the Division engage in many educational activities aimed at improving local health service. The Department sponsors training courses for sanitarians and other local health personnel. Advisory aid is rendered to communities on health-education workshops, records and office procedure, child-health conferences, and surveys of local health needs.

Established in 1907, the Division of Food and Drugs is one of the oldest and most important components of the State Board of Health. Its major responsibility is to enforce state food and drug laws which

2. Thomas R. Hood, "The Future of Public Health in Kansas," *Twenty-seventh Biennial Report of the Kansas State Board of Health*, p. 29.

prohibit the misbranding and adulteration of food and drugs. It also administers a state meat and poultry law, which requires inspection of all meat and poultry plants and the granting of permits for their operation. In 1947, this Division was assigned the additional duty of enforcing the law that requires the enrichment of bread and flour with certain vitamins and minerals usually lost in the milling process. It enforces the Uniform Narcotics Drug Act, the Hazardous Household Article Act, and the Dangerous Hypnotic, Somnifacient, or Stimulating Drug Law.

A major responsibility of the food and drug inspectors in the Division is the inspection of all food and drug establishments. This is done regularly to maintain high standards of sanitation in the production and selling of these items. Division personnel also aid in the enforcement of the Standard Milk Ordinance and the Standard Restaurant Ordinance of the U.S. Public Service. In 1968 there were eight full-time drug inspectors, two veterinarians, and one milk-survey sanitarian engaged in these activities. Most of the laboratory work for the Division is done in the departmental laboratories, though occasionally specimens of drugs are examined by chemists at the University of Kansas School of Pharmacy, and specimens of foods are examined by both the University of Kansas and Kansas State University.

The Division of Maternal and Child Health correlates all health programs conducted for children. It sets standards of health services for mothers and children and promotes improved service by educational means, demonstration projects, well-child clinics, and community organization. The Division also assists in the investigation of epidemics among newborn infants.

Perhaps the main function of the Division is to license maternity and children's homes, as established by a law of 1951. As the licensing agency, the Division of Maternal and Child Health is responsible for setting standards for such homes and enforcing them through inspections and the issuance of licenses. Children's homes, which comprise the bulk of the division's work, must be inspected by representatives of social-welfare and health agencies before qualifying for a license. Division personnel are also responsible for inspecting state children's institutions and reporting results to the Legislature and the Governor.

The Disease Prevention and Control Division is composed of sections of epidemiology, tuberculosis control, and venereal-disease control. The section of epidemiology is concerned with the morbidity and mortality statistics of disease, which can be utilized to aid all divisions of the State Board of Health in planning health programs.

The sections of tuberculosis control and venereal-disease control are engaged in discovering cases of these diseases and encouraging treatment. A mobile X-ray unit takes chest X-rays on a county-wide basis and reports suspicious findings to local doctors. A state register is kept of all active and former cases of tuberculosis. Field workers in the section of venereal-disease control work with local health officers, military officials, and public-health nurses to locate and interview venereal-disease cases and contacts. The section purchases and distributes drugs for venereal disease to physicians and clinics. It also carries on an educational program in schools and lay groups throughout the state.

The Division of Hospital Facilities was created in 1947, shortly after passage of the Federal-Hospital Survey and Construction Act. Its primary aim is to plan and provide for adequate hospital facilities in the state. The Division is responsible for allocating funds provided by the federal law and supervising the hospital-construction projects.

In cooperation with the Advisory Hospital Council, the State Board of Health, through the Division of Hospital Facilities, prepares minimum standards for hospitals and is responsible for licensing all hospitals in the state. Personnel of the Division provide consulting services for hospitals on engineering and administrative problems. Sanitary inspections of hospitals are made by field nurses in the Division and in the section of public-health nursing services. In related activities this service inspects and licenses adult-care homes, which are classified as adult boarding homes, personal-care homes, or skilled nursing homes according to the type of service provided. It inspects and certifies hospitals to the Social Security Administration to establish their eligibility under the Medicare program.

The work of the Dental-Hygiene Division emphasizes prevention, education, research, and dental care. An active campaign of education is carried on through the use of posters and other literature in schools and in homes. A state-wide school dental-health program is sponsored by the Division in the belief that good dental health must necessarily be established during the years of teeth-formation.

Personnel of the Division conduct special surveys and research projects and cooperate with other governmental agencies in studies of dental problems. Consultation service is offered to local health departments and to lay and professional groups. The Division distributes information on the values of fluoridation and encourages cities to fluoridate their water.

The Public-Health Nursing Division keeps in contact with public-health and school nurses throughout the state. Staff members from the section make field visits to the nurses and prepare manuals and guides for their use in nursing work. The section also helps place nurses in areas which need public-health nursing services.

Laboratory Services

The Public-Health Laboratory Services are available to all divisions of the State Department of Health as the fact-finding agency in the control of infectious disease. The various laboratory sections perform tests to aid physicians in diagnostic work and prepare biologics to distribute to physicians for control of diseases such as typhoid fever and infantile paralysis. Laboratory personnel assist the Disease-Prevention and Control Division in the investigation of epidemics.

Since 1947 the state public-health laboratories have had the responsibility of approving other laboratories and personnel which perform serological tests. Annual approval is required and is given by this section in conjunction with the Advisory Laboratory Commission. Premarital blood tests for syphilis are performed by this section of the Department.

Administrative and Central Services

The Division of Health Education is primarily organized to meet the publicity needs of all other divisions. It cooperates with other divisions in the selection and preparation of health-information materials. Films, posters, exhibits, radio scripts, and news releases are distributed throughout the state to interested individuals, groups, and health departments. The Division of Health Education is responsible for the publication of the *News Letter,* the monthly bulletin of the State Board of Health.

On request, personnel of the Division will aid local health departments, rural and school groups, and individuals with the planning of health-education programs. This service includes the supplying of educational material and consultation on how to use the materials to the best advantage in a community.

The recording of births and deaths with related medical information is an important phase of public-health work. From data of this kind it is possible to collect and tabulate information of considerable medical importance. With old-age assistance and retirement programs, citizens are anxious to be able to get birth certificates from a central point. In the number of employees, the Vital Statistics Division is one of the larger divisions of the Department.

In addition to the business office and the personnel office in this service there is a small section concerned with health mobilization programming. This office coordinates and encourages local training courses in medical self-help, particularly for times of natural disaster and nuclear attack.

Organizational Change

The 1968 Legislature directed that a broad administrative study be made of the organization and operations of the Department and appropriate structuring and functioning of local public-health authorities. With the many sparsely populated counties in the state, there has long been question of the practicability of Kansas ever having *full-time* local health officers throughout the state. The Board on occasion has recommended using the district offices, which they maintain for other purposes, as the basis for developing "district public health officers."

Over the years the Department has been involved in activities with implications for social welfare. At one time the Department had a mental-hygiene division and a separate section on aging. The functions of both of these sections have been transferred to the Board of Social Welfare. On the other hand the licensing of adult-care homes, which was previously shared by the Social Welfare Department and the Health Department, is now the responsibility of the latter. In some states the mental hospitals are operated as a part of the public-health department, giving rise to the question of whether their operation is more one of health or of public welfare.

Finances of the State Board of Health

The financing of the public-health program is complicated in Kansas by a number of factors. The expenditures of local health units, both full- and part-time, are controlled by the county and are reported to the state only along with other county expenditures. Moreover, expenditures made by the State Board of Health come from a number of separate sources. As shown in the table below, special funds have, over the years, become an important part of the available assets.

The Board receives and administers several fee funds. In the 1969 fiscal year the Legislature limited the amount of expenditures from these funds as follows: vital statistics fee fund, $300,000; meat and poultry inspection fee fund, $121,000; food and drug permit fees, $6,419; oil field fees, $166,647; water and sewage fees, $80,534; federal public-health funds, $1,995,961; and federal hospital construction fund, no limit.

The substantial growth of federal grants has had an important effect on the State Board's operation. These federal funds normally require

TABLE 32

Appropriations and Other Revenues Available to the Kansas State Board of Health: Selected Years

Fiscal Year	State Gen. Rev.	State Fees	Federal Hospital Constr.	All other Federal Grants	Gifts	Total
1885	$ 950					$ 950
1895	3,500					3,500
1905	3,067					3,067
1915	30,550	$ 8,149				38,699
1925	64,974	12,668		$ 418	$ 3,145	81,205
1935	60,500	19,303				79,803
1945	87,134	83,025		1,216,934		1,387,093
1955	665,350	150,045*	$1,008,424	369,429	52,500	2,245,748
1965	1,168,416	528,210	1,840,023	710,160	144,253	4,391,062
1968	1,648,005	635,702	2,052,874	1,364,047	2,809	5,703,437

* Includes meat and poultry inspection fee fund.
Source: Unpublished data in offices of the Kansas Board of Health.

matching on the basis of one state dollar for each two federal dollars, but states may count for such matching expenditures of local health departments and certain funds spent by private health organizations.

Cooperating Agencies

Local Health Departments

As has already been mentioned, much public-health work must be done locally. Cities and counties are authorized to perform public-health functions, but frequently not much attention is given to these activities by the smaller, less populous units of local government which are so common in Kansas.

The act creating the State Board of Health also provided for the county commissioners to act ex officio as the county board of health. Each local board is required to elect a physician, preferably one versed in sanitary science, to act as the county health officer. The county board of health may levy a special tax on all taxable property. The proceeds of such a tax are placed in the county health funds, and can be used to carry out the health laws and rules of the state, pay the county health officer, and employ additional personnel to assist the county health officer.

Two or more cities, or counties, or a city and a county, may establish a joint board of health possessing the same powers conferred on existing city or county boards of health. The participating units in such a joint board of health may determine the tax rate for each unit, and the joint board has exclusive control over the expenditure of the funds. The joint board of health is required to file an annual report of its activities with the governing body of each participating governmental unit.

Though the statutes permit and the State Board of Health has encouraged the formation of full-time local health units, in most of the counties of the state there are only part-time public-health officials.

National and state authorities point to the difficulties of having the public-health work performed by a medical practitioner on a part-time basis. Frequently such doctors have not been trained in public health, are busy with their own practice, and accept the job out of a sense of duty rather than of interest. The American Public Health Association considers that at least 50,000 people are needed to provide efficient use of a full complement of professionally trained public-health workers. Since only five counties in the state have more than 50,000 people, obviously there are many problems in affording full-time public-health service to most parts of the state. In addition, there has been such a shortage of trained public-health doctors that even units which were organized and financially able to pay them were not able to obtain such doctors.

In 1968 there were twenty full-time local health departments of which eleven were city-county health units and one served two counties. These units are located in the most populous sections of the state; about 60 per cent of the people of the state live in the counties served by these organizations. In thirty-six additional counties there are partially staffed health departments. These departments generally have a full-time public-health nurse with some arrangements for clerical services. The American Public Health Association recommends a minimum population of 5,000 for having a public-health nurse.

There are six basic functions of a local health department. They are the collection of vital statistics, environmental sanitation, prevention of communicable diseases, public-health laboratory services, health education, and maternal and child health services. The basic personnel for a health department includes a full-time health officer, sanitarian, public-health nurse, and clerk.

Special public-health problems exist in the two million acres in the forty-three counties around the twenty federal reservoirs and twenty-three state lakes in Kansas. In 1968 the Legislature authorized the State Board to set up sanitation zone boundaries with a local reservoir sanitation officer to enforce minimum standards for water supplies, sewage disposal, and refuse disposal. While they will be administered locally, the regulations governing such areas will be prepared by the State Board of Health.

Examining Boards

Closely related to the work of the State Board of Health are regulatory activities of eleven state examining boards. These boards, while almost completely independent of any other state agency, issue licenses for dentists, pharmacists, doctors, and a number of other groups engaged in work which affects public health. The laws of Kansas have created relationships between several of the boards and the State Board of Health, providing, in some cases, a more unified control of particular health problems.

As an example of joint control, both the State Board of Health and the State Board of Barber-Examiners have jurisdiction over barber shops and barber colleges. The State Board of Health has such jurisdiction "in the interest of the public health, and to prevent the spread of contagious and infectious diseases." The State Board of Barber-Examiners is concerned with persons practicing barbering or serving as barber apprentices, and with barber schools and colleges. The State Board of Barber-Examiners may prescribe sanitary rules and regulations for the operation of barber shops and schools, but such rules and regulations for the operation of barber shops and schools must be approved by the State Board of Health. In addition, none of the powers granted to the State Board of Barber-Examiners "shall be construed to abrogate, affect the status, force or operation of any provision of the general laws of this state relating to public health or any lawful rule, regulation or order promulgated thereunder."

Examining boards which have special relationships with the State Board of Health include the State Board of Embalming and the Board of Registration for Cosmetologists. Other examining boards which deal with matters affecting public health are the Healing-Arts Board, the Board of Nurse Registration and Nursing Education, the State Dental Board, the State Board of Examiners in Optometry, the Board of Pharmacy, and the State Podiatry Board of Examiners.

Food Service and Lodging

The Food Service and Lodging Board operates separately from the State Board of Health, but is directed by law to assist in the enforcement of any orders issued by the State Board of Health relating to restaurants, hotels, rooming houses, and apartment houses. It is empowered to establish a uniform code of sanitary rules governing the preparation and sale of food in hotels and restaurants, but the code must be formulated by and with the advice of the State Board of Health.

Department of Social Welfare

The State Department of Health and the Department of Social Welfare work cooperatively on the program for licensing and inspecting maternity and child-care homes. The State Department of Health is the licensing agency with the approval of the Department of Social Welfare. Representatives of both agencies make inspections of such homes with regard to the sanitary and social environment. The two agencies work together to provide regulations and rules for the proper conduct of such homes.

Forestry, Fish and Game Commission

As the state water-pollution control agency, the State Board of Health is authorized and empowered to adopt regulations for the protection of soil and surface and subsurface water from pollution detrimental to public health and to plant, animal, and aquatic life. It cooperates with the Forestry, Fish and Game Commission in the investigation of fish kills caused by pollution of lakes and streams. Engineers employed by the State Board of Health investigate alleged fish kills reported to them by game protectors, biologists, and others employed by the Foresty, Fish and Game Commission. The State Department of Health gives technical aid and assistance to the Forestry, Fish and Game Commission in matters relating to water supply and sewage-disposal facilities erected on land owned by the Commission; and representatives of the two agencies serve on several interagency councils concerned with water quality conservation and recreational area development.

State Corporation Commission

Although the State Board of Health has the major responsibility in controlling water pollution resulting from oil and gas production, the State Corporation Commission shares some responsibilities in such matters. The plans and specifications for subsurface brine-disposal systems must be approved by the two agencies. In approving the plans, the Corporation Commission considers primarily the conservation of oil and gas resources, while the State Board of Health is concerned solely with the conservation of state water resources. The Corporation Commission has authority over the plugging of abandoned holes and is responsible for protecting the fresh-water resources from pollution by such holes. Any complaints which the Board receives concerning pollution of water from abandoned oil or gas wells are forwarded to the Corporation Commission. The secretary of the Board may file such complaints with the Commission on his own motion.

The Dairy Commissioner

Regulatory power over matters of milk sanitation has been entrusted to both the State Board of Health and the Dairy Commissioner of the State Board of Agriculture. The State Board of Health has general powers over the sale of adulterated or misbranded foods; the

Dairy Commissioner has specific power to prohibit the sale of unclean or unwholesome milk and to prohibit the handling of milk in unsanitary places.[3]

Local Registrars

The State Registrar (the Director of the Division of Vital Statistics) appoints a local registrar in each of the 142 districts into which the state is divided. Normally the city clerk in the largest city in the district is appointed, though on occasion a local public-health officer may be designated. The local registrar is responsible for enforcing the local registration requirements. Notice of all births, deaths, and stillbirths must be filed with the local registrar on forms provided by the State Board of Health. In cases where no other person is available for information concerning a birth, the local registrar is required to secure the necessary information and prepare a certificate himself.

The local registrar is required to transmit to the State Registrar all certificates filed with him, in accordance with regulations set up by the State Board of Health. For each certificate, the local registrar is paid a fee, which varies according to the number of such certificates. When there are no certificates, the local registrar is expected to report the circumstances surrounding a birth or death. Upon notice from the State Registrar of Vital Statistics, the county treasurer pays the local registrar from county funds.

Problems of Public Health in Kansas

A review of the history of public-health functions in Kansas suggests two problems. There have been and are pressing shortages of qualified personnel.[4] This includes public-health doctors as well as nurses, sanitarians, and other public-health technicians. Apparently many of those qualified can obtain more remunerative employment in private-health practice. The shortage of such qualified personnel may cause the health board to rely more on the part-time health official despite its officially stated position preferring full-time health units.

3. For further information on the Dairy Commissioner in the State Board of Agriculture and his relations to the Board of Health, see pp. 306-7.
4. Harriet S. Pfister, *Kansas State Board of Health* (Lawrence: Governmental Research Center, Univ. of Kansas, 1955), pp. 196-99.

Other related problems center on the question of the proper division of responsibility for public-health work between the state and the local health units. The thin distribution of the population of the state raises special problems for the establishment of local full-time public-health agencies with adequate financial support. This fact, coupled with ambiguities of the statutes defining local and state responsibilities for public health and the difficulties of getting cooperation between numerous local governmental units and part-time health officials, has caused some people to believe that the only solution in some parts of the state may be district health officers in the employ of the state. The state Director has recommended experimenting with such district health organization, though not urging the full centralization of the public-health functions from the local public-health units.

15 Public Welfare

Since the earliest days of Kansas history, there has been an awareness of the obligation of society toward the less privileged persons who, for one reason or another, have been unable to provide adequately for their own maintenance and well-being.[1] This responsibility has been discharged through the establishment and maintenance of institutions to care for those in need and through public assistance grants to those in need. The relative emphasis in these two different ways of helping the needy has changed over the years, but each method has been used and has a long history in Kansas.

The 1859 Constitution authorized the state to foster and support "institutions for the benefit of the insane, blind, and deaf and dumb, and such other benevolent institutions as the public good may require."[2] In 1866 the first state mental institution was established at Osawatomie, and thirteen years later a second mental institution and the Industrial School for Boys were set up in Topeka. Four more institutions were authorized in the next decade. During the next eighty years four additional institutions were authorized. These institutions are now all

---

1. In the preparation of this chapter considerable use has been made of a study by Mrs. Barbara Gardner, *State-Local Relations in Kansas: The State Department of Social Welfare* (Lawrence: Governmental Research Center, Univ. of Kansas, 1955).

2. *Kansas Constitution*, Art. 7, sec. 1.

under the control of the State Board of Social Welfare, and are discussed later in this chapter.

Historical Background of Public Assistance

From the adoption of the Kansas Constitution in 1859 through the enactment of the Social Welfare Act of 1937, Kansas has followed a consistent policy of placing upon county governments the major responsibility for administering to those in need of public aid. The Constitution of Kansas requires counties to "provide, as may be prescribed by law, for those inhabitants who, by reason of age, infirmity, or other misfortune, may have claims upon the sympathy and aid of society." Over the years of statehood the welfare activities of Kansas government have changed greatly, partly because of the influence of federal grants on such activities.

The organization and administration of public aid in Kansas may be divided into three periods. In the first period, from 1862 to 1932, two of the principles of the original English Poor Law of 1601 were firmly established: legal residence and settlement in the local political subdivision must be established before relief is given, and relief is a local responsibility.

In 1862 the Kansas Legislature assigned administrative responsibility for relief to the county boards of commissioners and the overseers of the poor (township and city officials). A few counties, above a certain population, could appoint a commissioner of the poor to supervise the relief program and report periodically to the county commissioners.

Through the early years, legislation was directed toward special classes of persons rather than toward the establishment of a comprehensive system of public welfare. For example, limited provision was made in the 1862 laws for a monetary allowance to be paid by the commissioners to parents of idiot or otherwise dependent children.

Public aid in effect in Kansas in this earlier period was primarily in the form of indoor relief (county farm), instead of outdoor, or direct relief (cash, food, clothing, work projects). Indoor relief seemed a simpler solution to the county officials, who were inclined to regard relief measures as unpleasant and time-consuming.

Divided authority, lack of coordinated and consistent relief policies, and a prevalence of untrained, often indifferent officials in authority characterized the administration of welfare. No standards were set up by law for the care of the poor, nor were any professional or experience requirements established for those administering the program. The elected local officials generally dispensed such aid as was necessary.

While a few counties undertook limited programs of work-relief, it was not until the effects of the nation-wide depression and the more localized "agricultural depression" of the late 1920's and early 1930's became more evident, that work-relief projects were substantially increased.

Public concern over the mounting numbers of distressed and impoverished citizens in the state culminated in 1931 in the Governor's appointment of a welfare commission, to study all phases of relief and make recommendations to the Legislature. The Commission made its report to the 1933 Legislature in which it recommended the establishment of a state welfare board and local boards of welfare with trained staff and personnel standards. These recommendations were not adopted. In the meantime, the number of those needing assistance increased, and application was made for federal funds for work programs in the state.

In the second period, 1932 to 1937, the Kansas Emergency Relief Committee was appointed by the Governor. The committee established state-wide policies for the organization and administration of relief funds from the federal government. Federal funds were exclusively for work-relief. Unemployables continued to be cared for by the counties in which they lived. As a result, federal authority did not supercede county administration of relief.

The most significant state legislation in 1933 was the revision of the old poor law relating to the administration of relief. Township trustees and city officials were relieved of their authority in relief matters and were replaced in every county by "poor commissioners" who were required to have certain qualifications. This was a step toward resolving the problem of divided local authority which had hampered relief administration for many years.

Under the federal Social Security Act of 1935, additional funds were made available to the states for giving assistance grants to certain classes of unemployables—the needy aged, dependent children, and the needy blind. To qualify for such grants it was required that there be

(1) a state-wide welfare plan, (2) state financial participation, (3) a single state agency to administer or supervise the administration of the program, (4) opportunity for anyone to apply and to have his application acted upon with reasonable promptness, (5) opportunity for fair and prompt hearings for those persons whose claims for aid had been denied, (6) submissions of reports as required by the Social Security Administration, and (7) state authority or authorities designated as responsible for establishing and maintaining standards for all types of public and private institutions where those in need may receive assistance.[3]

The Kansas Emergency Relief Committee, which has been authorized by law to direct the relief program in Kansas, presented plans to the federal Social Security Board for the state's participation in this new program, but Kansas could not qualify for federal aid with the laws then in effect. The matter was sufficiently important for a special session of the Legislature to be called in July, 1936. At this session, resolutions were adopted to submit two constitutional proposals to the voters. The first of these sought to authorize the state to participate financially in the assistance of needy persons, and to supervise and control the administration of such assistance. The second proposal aimed to allow the state to provide for unemployment compensation and for contributory old-age benefits, and to tax employers and employees therefor. Both propositions carried by substantial majorities at the 1936 general election. Thus it became the task of the 1937 Legislature to enact appropriate legislation which would enable the state to take part in the federal program.

The third period began in 1937 when the Social Welfare Act was passed, and federal requirements for a welfare system were met. A state-supervised, county-administered plan was adopted. The boards of county commissioners were designated county boards of social welfare and the State Board of Social Welfare was established as the state supervising agency. A state sales tax was enacted, and a part of the revenues was to be used for state participation in the assistance pro-

---

3. In 1939, proper and efficient administration, including a merit system, restricting information about assistance applicants, and consideration of all resources in determining need were added to the list of federal requirements.

gram. The broad outlines of the assistance program as established in 1937 are still in effect, but the emphasis has changed.

The Present Public-Assistance Program

As the program was first conceived, the federal government contributed to the support of those needy persons in specific categories—the old, the blind, and dependent children. The state and local units were expected to support these assistance programs beyond the level of federal contributions and to finance the general-assistance program to aid all those who were eligible for aid but who did not fit into one of the "categorical" aid programs. In general, cases which could be, were transferred to one of the federally-aided categories, thereby decreasing the costs of assistance that were borne by the state and local units.

Over the years the precise definition of the groups has changed, but the broad outlines of the financing have remained the same. The state and local units support the general-assistance program, while the federal government shares in the cost of grants to recipients and in the costs of administering the assistance programs other than general assistance. Now, for some reporting purposes, recipients of aid to the aged, the blind, and the disabled are grouped together. While efforts are made to rehabilitate welfare clients in this category, the likelihood that they will become self-supporting is not high, and therefore maintenance of these recipients is more important. A second category—aid to dependent children (ADC)—includes aid to familes with dependent children and aid to dependent children in foster-care homes. The newest categorical assistance program, that of medical assistance, is discussed elsewhere. The proportion of the public-assistance dollar which is spent in the various programs is shown in the accompanying table.

There have been dramatic changes in the old-age-assistance program, with less of the total assistance money now being spent for this group of beneficiaries. The decline in the assistance for this group has occurred largely because of the expansion of the federal social-security program to more persons and the raising of the level of benefits and, more recently, because of medical assistance.

On the other hand, the percentage for dependent children has increased and has caused considerable concern at both the state and national levels. Slightly over one-half of the persons receiving assis-

TABLE 33

Percentages of Public Assistance Expenditures in Kansas for Selected Years by Program

	Per Cent of Total—Fiscal Year				
	1950	1955	1960	1965	1968
Program					
Old-Age Assistance	63	59	55	34	20
Aid to Dependent Children	14	13	20	27	24
Aid to the Blind	1	1	1	1	1
Aid to the Disabled	0	6	9	10	9
General Assistance	16	14	6	5	3
Medical Assistance	0	0	0	9	29
Special Activities*	1	1	2	3	3
Administration	5	6	7	11	11
Totals	100	100	100	100	100

* County special activities, such as county homes, commodity distribution, work projects, health clinics, etc.

Source: "Twenty-nine Years of Public Assistance: Kansas," Kansas State Depart-
of Social Welfare (mimeographed), December, 1966, p. 67; and unpublished
data, Kansas State Department of Social Welfare.

tance do so under the ADC program. The increase in the percentage of our population which is in younger age groups, the overall total increase in our population, and the number of years that those receiving support may continue to need support make this a particularly important group of welfare recipients with which to work. A high percentage of cases in this category need assistance because of the absence of a parent. ADC has been criticized because a number of the children being supported are illegitimate. Because of the fear (for which there is some evidence) that families were being broken up because it was easier to get assistance under ADC than under general assistance, it is now possible for the state and local units to receive federal assistance for the grants to families with dependent children and an unemployed parent.

In 1967 Congress enacted legislation which limited the number of cases of dependent children that it would help support in each state. The assumption was that somehow if federal assistance was not forthcoming, the state and local units administering the program would find ways of not adding more cases. If more cases were added, the state and local units would have to finance the costs themselves without federal aid. This legislation was much criticized and may be changed, but it shows some of the hostility and the frustration over the increase in this assistance program.

In an effort to attack the problem of ADC in another way, Kansas began on July 1, 1968, to allow certain income of such families to be exempted when calculating the benefits to be paid. As an incentive, the first thirty dollars earned each month is not included as a resource of the ADC recipient, and one-third of the remaining dollars earned is also exempt. The hope is that the exemption will encourage the recipient to get a job, develop skills, and attain a higher earning capacity which will make it possible to stop the assistance. Another related effort is the work-incentive program under which certain ADC welfare recipients (mostly mothers) may be referred to the Labor Department for training and job placement.

Under the aegis of the nationally conceived "war on poverty," the whole public-assistance program has come under heavy criticism. Some critics charge that though it has been operating for three decades, the program has fallen far short of its goal and has largely failed in its efforts to rehabilitate the aid recipients. On the national level there is discussion of a negative income tax or other methods of guaranteeing certain minimum income levels for all. These programs envision doing away with a detailed case-by-case analysis of the resources (and thus, indirectly, the needs) of the individual welfare applicant. Theoretically the time of the caseworker and the money saved through accepting the individual's declaration of his need, could be spent in working to re-motivate, educate, or otherwise rehabilitate the welfare recipient.

As a step in this direction there are new efforts to try to break the poverty cycle. The emphasis in public assistance is presently on service to the families concerned. Service to the family may take the form of efforts to rehabilitate the family or the wage earner and instruction and counsel in the management of money and family budgeting and such subjects. The administration of such service-oriented assistance programs is more costly, as is shown in the accompanying table. It is the hope and expectation, however, that in the long run such assistance programs will be cheaper and more effective in reducing the proportion of our citizens receiving assistance.

Present Organization of the Department

Kansas has experimented with several types of boards for supervising the welfare function. Since 1949 the Board of Social Welfare has consisted of three part-time lay members. The members serve for four-year, staggered terms. Appointments are made by the Governor by and with the consent of the Senate "without reference to political or religious affiliations."[4] The Board advises the Governor on welfare matters and is the policy-determining body. It appoints two directors— one who acts as secretary for the Board and as head of the Division of Social Welfare and one who has responsibility for supervising the operation of all welfare institutions.

Division of Social Welfare

Public-Assistance Division.[5] In addition to the categorical assistance programs supported in part by the federal government, the Division supervises the administration of the state and locally supported general-assistance program. All of these are county-operated programs of assistance, but for the state to receive federal aid in these programs, they must be operated in accordance with a single state plan. To accomplish this, the Public-Assistance Division has prepared a very extensive and comprehensive manual which sets forth policies and procedures in considerable detail. The counties must follow this manual to receive federal and state reimbursements for money granted to assistance applicants. Counties are required to file with the State Welfare Board their budgets of estimated welfare revenues and expenses. These budgets are reviewed by the Public-Assistance Division and a staff finance section in the Social-Welfare Division. The Board has legal authority to require the county to change its welfare budget.

Medical Services Division

In June, 1967, Kansas began operation of a medical-assistance plan inaugurated with federal assistance. The Division administers this program which pays for the medical assistance given to any of those receiving categorical public assistance and to certain medically needy

---

4. *K.S.A.*, 75-3302.

5. The terminology used in this chapter seeks to follow that used by the Department. It may be confusing, however, to have several "divisions" within a "division."

groups. The latter groups include some who are not generally in need of public assistance but who may, because of their limited means, be unable to pay for medical services. Different means tests are used for these persons to establish their eligibility. The federal government now makes medical-assistance payments for services provided to certain patients in *state* hospitals, just as payments are made to the suppliers of other medical services to those receiving categorical assistance. (The federal government does not currently share in the payments for medical services for those over twenty-one receiving general assistance.) Amendments to the federal Social Security Act have allowed the state to make the medicare premium payments for the welfare recipients over sixty-five. Thus the recipients have a substantial portion of their medical care costs paid under that federal program. Throughout, the program has allowed clients to choose whom they wanted to provide their medical services, with reimbursements being made on a basis of reasonable cost.

Child-Welfare Services Division. The care and protection of dependent, neglected, defective, illegitimate, and delinquent children and children in danger of becoming delinquent is assigned to the Child-Welfare Services Division. While this responsibility was previously implied, in 1953 the Legislature specifically directed county social-welfare boards to provide child-welfare services paralleling those performed by the Child-Welfare Services Division of the State Board. Under this law, the Child-Welfare Services Division became more of an advisory, consultative agency supervising the work of county departments in this field than an operating agency. The Division has also prepared a manual for the county-welfare departments. The Division must review and approve all adoption cases and the placement of children committed to the State Department of Social Welfare. In 1968 the Legislature authorized the direct relinquishment of children to the Department for placement. While the State Board of Health licenses children's boarding homes, this Division makes social studies of these homes and makes recommendations to the Board concerning these aspects of the homes.

Services to the Blind Division. This Division operates programs for the restoration of eyesight, prevention of blindness, and rehabilitation of blind persons. It operates the Kansas Rehabilitation Center for the

Adult Blind, encouraging their vocational rehabilitation. It helps prepare blind people for normal employment and also operates two workshops where in "sheltered employment" blind workers can make various products. Paralleling the developments in the child-welfare field, the county welfare departments have been directed to provide services for the blind, subject to the rules and regulations of the State Board. A manual governing such activities has been prepared and distributed to the counties.

Services for the Aging Division. Broadly, this Division offers services to older persons in their own homes and in other situations, assists in the extension of local community resources for the older persons, and has administrative responsibilities under the federal Older American Act of 1965. The clientele for this Division continues to increase both in its numbers and in its proportion of our total population. A number of counties have councils on aging. The Division encourages the formation and operation of such councils and other programs such as planning for retirement. A number of local projects have received grants for community plannings, reserved services, and training which contribute to the well-being of old citizens under Title 3 of the federal Older American Act.

Vocational Rehabilitation Service. Vocational rehabilitation is another joint federal-state program. It is designed to assist the physically handicapped in securing employment by providing physical restoration, vocational counseling, and education and training. A "state plan," which outlines the policies to be followed, has been drafted by the State Board of Social Welfare and has been approved by the Office of Rehabilitation of the U.S. Department of Health, Education, and Welfare.

The rehabilitation service is offered through nine districts into which the state is divided. A client is assigned to a counselor, who determines if the client is potentially employable, and if so, arranges for the necessary services and counsels the client. Rehabilitation service may include all or part of the following: medical examinations; surgical, psychiatric, and other medical and hospital services for reducing disabilities; artificial limbs or other aids; vocational and personal counseling and psychological testing; vocational training—schools, correspondence study, on-the-job training; tools or other equipment necessary for beginning employment; placement in a job commensurate with the client's interests and abilities; follow-up counseling to insure satisfactory placement. The rehabilitation program is voluntary and depends on the agency being able to reach the persons needing its services. It has been estimated that each year in Kansas there are 5,000 persons under sixty-five years of age who become restricted in their major activities. A number of programs have been designed in addition to the state-wide counseling program. All claims for disability under the federal Social Security Act are determined by this service. The records of physical examinations of all draft rejects are reviewed by appropriate officials, and a counselor calls on the rejectee to help him correct the physical conditions which led to his rejection. There is a counseling staff at Topeka, Osawatomie, Parsons, and Larned state hospitals and at the state penitentiary at Lansing. It is expected that these operations will be expanded to include other state hospitals and penal institutions. There are two units at the Kansas Neurological Institute at Topeka— one for regular vocational counseling and another to prepare persons so that they can profit from the regular vocational counseling.

A Kansas vocational-rehabilitation center was officially opened on October 13, 1966, at Salina on a part of the former Schilling Air Force Base. The center serves as a vocational-evaluation facility and offers its services to those with any handicap but mental retardation. There is a separate section in the agency charged with the development of a master plan for vocational rehabilitation to take care of all of those disabled by 1975.

Service in counseling and arranging for rehabilitation are free for all clients. State and national funds are used to pay for other services, such as medical attention and vocational training, and for necessary transportation and maintenance costs according to the client's financial needs. For most of the activities of the agency the federal government grants 75 per cent of the funds. In some programs the federal government contributes 90 per cent, and in others it bears the full costs. In the 1968 fiscal year a total of over $2,300,000 was expended. During this year, services were provided for 4,267 clients, and 1,262 cases were closed with the employment of the client. From 1920 until July 1, 1968, vocational-rehabilitation work in the state was organizationally a part of vocational education. With reorganization required by the 1966 constitutional amendment in the field of education, the Legislature in 1968 transferred the Vocational Rehabilitation Service to the Board of Social Welfare.

Other Divisions of the Social Welfare Division. The Field Services Division has the responsible task of working closely with the county welfare directors and exercising general administrative supervision over the county welfare agency. This division has staff consultants who help the local directors in handling problem cases. These consultants may help to correct misunderstandings and differences which may arise between the county welfare directors and the county boards. They may help the county boards find adequate staffs for the local welfare workers. For a number of years there were special consultants for each different type of assistance, and each county would have to deal with different state representatives, depending on the type of assistance involved. More recently, however, the one state representative assists the county as fully as possible, regardless of the type of assistance concerned. The state representative may contact persons in the state office for technical assistance but will generally serve the county in its various needs.

In addition to these operating sections of the Division of Social Welfare, there are staff sections devoted to financial audits and accounts, research and statistics, personnel management, legal affairs, and the distribution of commodities. This last section distributes surplus federal commodities to schools participating in the school-lunch program and to institutions operating on a nonprofit basis.

Division of Institutional Management

The second major organizational part of the State Department of Social Welfare is the Division of Institutional Management. Although the state eleemosynary institutions came under the jurisdiction of the State Board of Social Welfare in 1939, it was not until the reorganization of the State Department of Social Welfare in 1953 that this Division was established. This reorganization was aimed at strengthening the management of the Division over the state eleemosynary institutions. A professionally trained medical doctor was appointed director of the Division, and he supervises the administration of all eleven of the state eleemosynary institutions: three mental hospitals (Larned, Osawatomie, and Topeka which includes the Kansas Treatment Center for Children), four hospitals for the mentally retarded (the state hospitals and training centers at Parsons and Winfield, the Kansas Neurological Institute at Topeka, and the Norton State Hospital), one tuberculosis hospital (Chanute), and three institutions for children (Boys' Industrial School at Topeka, the Girls' Industrial School at Beloit, and Kansas Children's Receiving Home at Atchison).

The accompanying table, reporting the average daily population at the various institutions for the last two decades, gives indication of the size of the operations of this Division of Institutional Management. Much of the administration and control of the particular institution is the responsibility of the superintendent of that institution, but the Office of the Director of Institutions provides consultant services in dietetics, fire prevention, safety, sanitation, personnel, nursing services, and social services. There is an admissions officer who processes admission papers and coordinates requests for admission. The county of

TABLE 34

Average Daily Population at Kansas Institutions: Selected Years

	Fiscal Years			
Institution	1953	1958	1963	1968
Larned State Hospital	1,691	1,401	1,047	744
Osawatomie State Hospital	1,577	1,481	1,016	712
Topeka State Hospital (Adults)	1,437	1,333	932	694
Topeka State Hospital (under 16)	0	23	91	108
Winfield State Hospital and Training Center	1,362	1,418	1,124	1,006
Parsons State Hospital and Training Center	640	515	599	594
Kansas Neurological Institute*	0	0	342	394
Norton (Retarded) †	0	0	0	133
Norton (TB)	409	210	119	17
South East Kansas TB Hospital‡	0	50	66	49
Kansas Children's Receiving Home§	0	55	51	35
Boys' Industrial School	146	176	209	233
Girls' Industrial School	67	70	89	96

* Opened for patients in January, 1960.
† Began receiving mentally retarded patients in 1964.
‡ Opened for patients in March, 1957.
§ In 1953 the Kansas Children's Home operated with an average population of 202, as separate from the Receiving Home with its average population of 30. These institutions were consolidated in 1955 under the name of the Kansas Children's Receiving Home.
Source: Data from the Board of Social Welfare.

residence of a mental patient determines which of the three mental hospitals he will be admitted to, but the mentally retarded and other types of patients are admitted to institutions without reference to their "home" county. The fiscal-services section maintains records with regard to accounting, budgeting, and purchasing and coordinates these activities of the Division. The personnel section, the legal section, and the public-information section service both the Division of Institutional Management and the Division of Social Welfare.

Over the years there have been many problems with respect to the various institutions. Before the creation of the Division of Institutional Management, the superintendents had more direct dealings with the Legislature; and some superintendents had long tenure and developed close personal ties with the legislators. Occasionally legislative committees were appointed to investigate particular happenings or the efficiency of the operation of the institution. There has been a general problem of properly classifying patients and, on occasion, of reassigning patients and redirecting the programs of particular institutions according to the need for more specialized treatment.

Many of the changes made in the eleemosynary institutions have centered around efforts to make the state hospitals treatment centers instead of places of custodial care. The older ideas of the care of the mentally ill emphasized the need for isolating those who were mentally ill. The strength of this concept is illustrated by the fact that mental institutions were referred to as asylums, not as hospitals. In 1947 it was found in a Legislative Council survey that the mental hospitals were crowded with many older patients who could not respond to treatment and were not being treated. These persons needed care, but of a more custodial nature than special mental care. Yet given the limitations of space and staff, the very presence of these older patients at the hospitals meant that many of the younger persons who could profit from treatment had to be denied admittance. For various reasons, including the location of the nationally known Menninger Foundation and Clinic in Topeka, the Legislature consciously gave priority to improving Topeka's State Hospital. In cooperation with the Menningers, a training program for psychiatrists and psychiatric aides was established at the Topeka State Hospital. It was expected that this training center would train personnel for the other two mental hospitals. These efforts to improve and increase personnel were accompanied by creation, on the state level, of the Division of Institutions and by the staffing of the Division with professionally trained persons.

Also as a part of the program emphasizing treatment, psychologists, psychotherapists, psychiatric social workers, and others are employed at the three state hospitals. The psychiatric social workers help develop case histories of new patients to assist in the proper classification and diagnosis of patients. These same case histories can be helpful when it becomes possible to release the patient. County welfare departments are increasingly being asked to help patients adjust to their home communities. Thus local welfare workers are being called upon to assist more and more in the institutional program of the state Department. Patients are being admitted for shorter stays and then are treated as out-patients, so that increasingly the average daily populations of the three mental hospitals do not present a complete picture of their operation.

Most important in the last several years has been the development of community mental-health centers. In the period from 1948 to 1961 the Kansas State Board of Health was designated as the State Mental-Health Authority. By 1961, nine local mental-health clinics had been established. In 1961 the Legislature designated the State Board of Social Welfare as the State Mental-Health Authority, and in turn this responsibility was delegated to the Division of Institutional Management. Since that time more community mental-health centers have been established, so that by June, 1968, seventy-eight counties were included in the operation of twenty-five such centers. Ninety-three per cent of the population of the state lives in counties with such services. The accompanying map shows the areas in which the centers have been organized.

There is a wide variation in their organizational patterns and in the level of services which the centers perform. The centers are supported by county ad valorem property-tax levies, fees charged patients, and some federal grants. The state does not give direct financial support to the local centers, but it does provide advice and consultation to local groups in organizing and maintaining such mental-health centers. Some federal funds are available to staff and to help construct buildings for comprehensive community mental-health centers.

The philosophy behind community mental-health centers reflects a sharp break with older ideas of separating the mentally ill from society. Rather, the local centers are built upon the idea that by keeping the person in his environment and assisting him, many who would otherwise need hospitalization may avoid it. The centers become agencies which are available to assist those hospitalized when they are released and return to their home communities. The expectation is that the centers will reduce the load on the mental hospitals and will make it possible for them to treat more effectively the more severe cases. The mental hospitals all operate out-patient treatment facilities and seek to make it possible to treat more persons in the earlier stages of their sickness when often the chances of recovery are better. In this way the community mental-health centers are related to the work of the institutions of the state.

From 1949 to 1961 there was an eight-member Advisory Commission on Institutional Management which inspected the various state and charitable institutions and consulted with the Director of Institutions and the Governor on policies governing the management and operation of the institutions. In 1961 the scope of this Commission was enlarged to include community mental-health programs, and its membership was

Kansas Community Mental-Health Centers

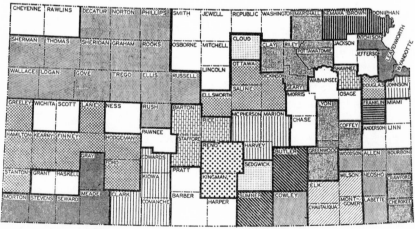

Shaded areas indicate the *areas* served by community mental-health centers. Groups of counties shaded similarly are served by a single center. Source: Unpublished data, Kansas Board of Social Welfare.

increased to twelve. This change reflects the close relation seen between the institutions and community mental-health centers.

Social Welfare at the County Level

The boards of county commissioners serve as the county board of social welfare. In accordance with rules and regulations of the State Board of Social Welfare, the county board provides aid, assistance, and service for those in need. The counties administer the welfare programs.

The county board appoints a county welfare director to carry out the welfare program on the local level. Typically the welfare director acts as a caseworker and interviews and investigates applications for assistance. The director makes recommendations to the county board on the amount of aid to be granted. These recommendations generally are accepted by the county commissioners. In counties with large social-welfare loads, there may be many caseworkers and casework supervisors who work under the welfare director. The county welfare staffs vary from one to over a hundred persons.

The number of cases assigned individual caseworkers varies according to the amount of travel involved, the amount of investigation needed, the amount of other welfare work handled, the capabilities of the individual worker, and the total case load.[6] It is important for the success of the whole program that the caseworkers have adequate time to investigate thoroughly and to counsel fully in each case. Too little investigation may result in granting assistance to some who are ineligible; too hasty work may result in the welfare worker's not being able to rehabilitate as many as would otherwise be possible. Present regulations require that each case be reviewed at least every six months to determine if the eligibility for assistance continues.

The functions of county welfare staffs are numerous and varied. Applications for assistance are processed, individual needs and budgets determined, cases recorded and developed and reviewed. Related activities include studies and reports on adult-boarding homes and foster-child-care homes, adoption studies for the child-welfare services divi-

6. There are wide differences between counties in the case loads of the social-welfare workers. For a report on these differences and some explanation of them, see the Legislative Committee on Economy and Efficiency, *Recommendations*, II, 74-75.

sion, and studies to facilitate treatment of the state institutions and to cooperate in the placement of persons discharged from the state institutions. Special cases are referred to other agencies, such as the U.S. Veterans Administration, the State Crippled Children's Commission, and private welfare agencies. The county welfare departments may get assistance in handling particular cases. Special consultants from the State Welfare Department are available to advise in cases involving aid to children and to the blind. These consultants are in addition to the field representatives of the Department who will visit and help local county departments.

The public-assistance manual prescribed by the Public-Assistance Division of the State Board contains interpretations of various statutory provisions, detailed instructions of procedures for establishing eligibility, and standards to be used in setting the amounts of aid in the several categories of assistance. There are five types of assistance given, but to qualify the applicant must establish his eligibility. To be eligible a person must:

(1) Need assistance. A needy person is defined as one who has not sufficient income or resources to provide a reasonable subsistence compatible with decency and health.[7]

(2) Not have transferred property within five years immediately preceding the application to establish his eligibility.

(3) Have resided in Kansas for five of the last nine years and continuously for the last year preceding the application.

(4) Generally, not be a resident of a mental or tuberculosis institution or in an unlicensed or unapproved public or private institution.

Reference has already been made to the general federal requirements which Kansas had to meet to qualify for federal assistance funds. The requirement of a state-wide plan administered or supervised by a single state agency and financed in part by state funds necessitated substantial changes from the way in which welfare had been handled in the past. To comply, the state has established manuals of detailed regulations and procedures concerning the assistance program. The public-assistance manual established the amounts which will be allowed for most items in the individual-assistance budgets. For example, the

7. *K.S.A.*, 39-709.

manual sets the amount which will be allowed for fuel in various parts of the state. In one study of a sample group of counties, county welfare boards reported that there were only a few areas in which they had any real discretion in the administration of the welfare program. Generally, counties have more discretion in determining "moderate home values" and rental policies, and in the maintenance and supervision of county homes.[8]

Financing Social Welfare

Financing the welfare program is a joint endeavor in which all three levels of government take part, as shown in the accompanying table.

TABLE 35

Sources of Public-Assistance Funds in Kansas by Percentage: Selected Years

Source	1950	1955	1960	1965	1968
Federal Government	42%	45%	51%	53%	50%
State Government	36	32	26	26	31
County Government	22	23	23	21	19
Totals	100%	100%	100%	100%	100%

Source: "Twenty-nine Years of Public Assistance: Kansas," Kansas State Department of social Welfare (mimeographed), December, 1966, p. 67; and unpublished data, Kansas State Department of Social Welfare.

For a number of years the part that the federal government paid of the recipients' assistance grants under the categorical-aid programs varied with the program and the grant. The formulas were established to encourage minimum payments, with the federal government paying a large percentage of the first part of the grant and a decreasing percentage of the larger grants. Now, however, the federal government pays a given percentage (57.9 per cent in 1968) of all categorical-assistance grants. The precise federal percentage is computed every second year and considers the per capita income in the state. The present sharing provides for a larger contribution in the higher grants than before. States and counties determine the level of benefit payments

8. Gardner, p. 95.

made, and there are significant differences in the average payments from state to state even under the same program. For example, the average old-age assistance grant in Kansas in December, 1967, was $86.80, while the national average was $70.15.

The state and the county pay the remainder of each grant under the categorical-assistance programs and all of the general-assistance grants. In both programs the county pays 48 per cent of the remainder (or total under general assistance) and the state 52 per cent. This means that currently under a hypothetical categorical-assistance grant of $100, the federal government would pay $57.90, the state $21.89, and the county $20.21. These amounts differ a little from those shown in the table on page 287 because of administrative costs and special projects.

Counties raise their share of the welfare costs primarily from the property tax. However, the different amounts of property in the various counties, the varying levels at which property is assessed, and the deviation in the number of welfare cases result in a wide variety of property tax rates for welfare. Since 1949 the state has made up any deficit incurred by a county in the welfare program if that county has levied a four-mill property tax for welfare. However, to prevent counties from taking advantage of low assessment rates, the county has to levy a tax for an amount equal to the amount which would be raised by a four-mill tax on the property if the county assessed at the state average assessment level. These provisions for the state to take over a part of the counties' normal share of the welfare costs have been particularly important in the counties in the southeastern part of the state, where welfare loads have been quite heavy. The wide variations in county welfare levies are shown in the following table.

In each county a welfare budget is prepared annually showing the expected expenses of the next year. The county indicates in the budget the amount it expects to raise from the property tax and other sources. This budget is submitted to the state Department, where legally it may be changed. Present policy of the State Board is, however, only to recommend changes. If necessary, the Department will make advances to pay current expenses, but counties are expected to adopt realistic budgets to arrange for the repayment of such state advances as are made.

From what has been described it must be realized that the share of

TABLE 36
County Ad Valorem Property-Tax Levy for Social Welfare: 1968

Rate of Levy Mills	Number of Counties
over 5.00	2*
4.76 – 5.00	11
4.51 – 4.75	3
4.26 – 4.50	5
4.01 – 4.25	4
3.76 – 4.00	4
3.51 – 3.75	3
3.26 – 3.50	2
3.01 – 3.25	5
2.76 – 3.00	3
2.51 – 2.75	4
2.26 – 2.50	2
2.01 – 2.25	5
1.76 – 2.00	9
1.51 – 1.75	6
1.26 – 1.50	10
1.01 – 1.25	7
.76 – 1.00	8
.51 – .75	5
.26 – .50	6
.01 – .25	1
	105

* Cherokee at 5.17 mills and Wyandotte at 7.3671 mills.

Source: "1967 County Tax Rates for 1968," *Kansas Government Journal*, January, 1968, p. 40.

the various units of government differ from county to county depending upon the type of assistance granted, and thus the extent of federal participation also differs. For example, counties with many general-assistance cases will pay a larger share of welfare costs than counties with most of the cases being ones under the federally subsidized categorical-assistance programs.

The accompanying map shows the number of public-assistance cases per thousand population in June, 1968. The highest number was in Cherokee county with 105 persons per thousand receiving assistance, with three counties (Johnson, Lane, and Stanton) having seven persons per thousand (the lowest). On a state-wide basis, thirty-seven persons per thousand received public assistance. In terms of the number of cash and nonmedical vendor payments, 46.4 per cent were for old-age assistance; 16.0 per cent for the permanently and totally disabled; 1.1 per cent for aid to the blind; 28.5 per cent for dependent children; and 8.0 per cent for general assistance. The average amount paid per person (including medical-vendor payments) was $105.10 for old-age assistance, $126.54 for aid to the blind, $162.58 for aid to the disabled, $61.49 for aid to dependent children, $141.53 for medical assistance only, and $74.67 for general assistance.

The primary source of revenue for the operation and maintenance of the social-welfare institutions is state appropriations from the general fund. Before the sales tax revenues were merged with the general fund, much of the moneys needed for the institutions came from this source. There is a state-wide ad valorem property tax levy for buildings at the charitable institutions and mental hospitals. Of the total of more than $30,000,000 for operating all the eleemosynary institutions, about 10

Persons Per Thousand Population Dependent upon Public Assistance: Kansas, June, 1968

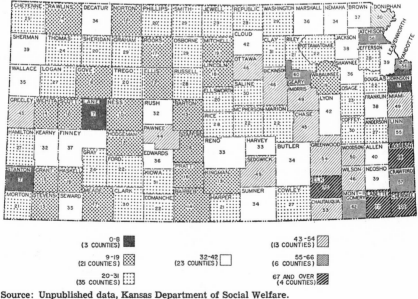

Source: Unpublished data, Kansas Department of Social Welfare.

TABLE 37
*Amounts Expended for Public Assistance in Kansas by Major Activity
and Source of Funds: Fiscal Year 1968*

Activity	Federal	State	County	Total
Assistance Payments	$39,766,767	$20,852,836	$13,638,093	$74,257,697
County Special Activities: County Home, Commodity, etc.		253,402	2,205,184	2,458,586
State Special Welfare Activities: Services for the Blind, Child Welfare Services, Institutional Supervision, Commodity Distribution, etc.	1,650,976	3,573,023		5,224,000
County Administration	3,842,566	1,726,703	2,633,754	8,203,022
State Administrative Expense	748,796	908,731		1,657,527
Totals	$46,009,104*	$27,314,696*	$18,477,031	$91,800,832

* Since amounts were rounded off to the nearest dollar, the columns do not add
exactly to the totals shown.
Source: Unpublished data from the State Department of Social Welfare.

per cent comes from reimbursements from patients or relatives and
other "third parties," such as insurance companies. As the community
health centers handle more cases and as county social-welfare workers
assist in "working up" cases for the hospitals, the financial participation
at the various levels of government becomes more intertwined and
difficult to identify with precision.

Related State Welfare Agencies

Crippled Children's Commission

In 1931 the Legislature authorized the establishment of a five-man,
gubernatorially appointed commission to help care for the special needs
of crippled children. The Commission approves at its discretion hospitals, convalescent homes, and boarding houses which provide medical
and surgical care for such children. It also passes on the charges made
for treatment, operations, braces, and other equipment to help crippled
children. The Commission keeps a list of persons and corporations
authorized to sell the equipment such children may need.

The Commission maintains an office in Wichita, employs a secretary, a senior medical-social consultant and four field nurses, and has eight district offices where public-health nurses help children who apply. The Commission, in the 1968 fiscal year, spent a total of $496,085, of which $184,627 came from the federal government as grants. The program is aimed to help "needy" children, but need is more liberally interpreted than in the social-welfare program.

Kansas Veterans' Commission

After experimenting with several types of organizations, the Legislature, in 1953, established the Kansas Veterans' Commission as a separate organization. The Commission, which consists of three members appointed by the Governor, employs a director in the unclassified civil service. The Director and his staff help veterans and their immediate family to receive various federal and state benefits and services which are offered to them. They seek to coordinate with respect to veterans the various state agencies having programs which might help veterans.

The Commission also operates the Kansas Soldiers' Home at Dodge City and Mother Bickerdyke Annex. Residents of the home are selected by the Veterans' Commission on the basis of need.

Trends and Future Developments

Encouraged by requirements from Washington and stimulated by the willingness of the counties to have other governments pay for welfare costs, the trend established in the last twenty years in Kansas has been one of increased state control and supervision of the welfare assistance programs. Many counties could not begin to finance present welfare programs with foreseeable revenues. A return to more local responsibility with more local financing does not seem likely. Instead, as suggested by the increasing participation of the state in the welfare programs, greater state aid and control seem probable.

It may be argued that control over the program need not be changed merely because of increased financial participation. However, when one examines the size and the detail of the assistance manual and other manuals, one finds ample evidence that the centralization has come not only in the financial field. The areas of discretion left to the county social-welfare boards are not large.

Centralization has been stimulated indirectly in another way. The professional county welfare worker has much in common with the state Department personnel. Professional meetings and the general professionalization in the field further these common interests and approaches. To some extent state Department personnel are considered as leaders in the profession and thus extend informal influence over the local welfare operations.

This is not to say that county commissioners are without powers and ways of exerting influence in the welfare field. Efforts have been made by the State Welfare Board to get the views of county commissioners, both through the welfare department field representatives and through committees of commissioners. The county commissioners can and do take active stands through their association for legislation, including measures in the welfare field. Illustrations of such laws would include the 1953 law authorizing the recovery of welfare assistance from the estates of deceased recipients of such assistance.

At the state level of operation there are increasing efforts to improve the organization of the Department. The integration of the field staff has been one of the important developments in the welfare department. Previously, the state was divided into a number of districts. For each district there was a public-assistance field representative; for perhaps a slightly different group of counties, there would also be field representatives for child welfare; and for still a third group, a field representative for aid to the blind. Under the integrated field-representative plan there is but one field representative of the department for any county. Technical problems arise from this reorganization, but the integration is simpler for the county welfare departments. The integration of the field service hopefully encourages a more balanced welfare program.

Associated with the integrated field-service program are the greater demands which are now made on the county departments to take part in the institutional programs. Increasingly the psychiatric social workers at the state institutions are turning to the county social-welfare workers to obtain information for case histories, for diagnosis and treatment, and for assistance in releasing the patients. The emphasis on treatment rather than custodial care at the institutions has served to bring the institutional aspects of the welfare program much closer to the assistance aspects of the program.

The future of the public-assistance program is uncertain. The assistance programs for the old, the blind, and the disabled have been somewhat stabilized. The general-assistance program fluctuates with the general employment situation, but there are clear indications of the intentions of the national government to adopt public-work programs and credit controls and other devices to try to insure a high level of employment. The aid to dependent children, for reasons and in ways discussed, presents a grave challenge to the social worker and to the social-welfare field. Located as most of these assistance cases are in our larger cities, the problem became immediately enmeshed in the larger problem of the urban ghetto—a problem which extends beyond the confines of what we normally think of as social welfare and includes education, housing, and employment.

16 | *Agriculture*

Despite the rapid growth of industry in Kansas, the state is still widely regarded as primarily agricultural. So it is natural enough that the farmers and farm interests should be represented in Kansas government. Besides the very substantial representation of farmers and rural areas in the Legislature, farmers also have an agency in the executive branch devoted to their interests. This agency, the State Board of Agriculture, performs a wide variety of promotional and regulatory functions. Members of the Board are elected by delegates from various farm organizations in the state rather than being appointed by the Governor as are the members of most other boards. Thus a unique situation exists, with a farmer-controlled agency empowered by the Legislature to regulate various activities in which farmers are interested or involved. The Board of Agriculture may be considered as an association recognized by law, financed by the state, and authorized to administer certain state laws, but responsible in a theoretic sense to the delegates elected from private farm associations. Yet for all practical purposes the Board operates much as any other public administrative agency. A knowledge of the history of the Board is necessary for an understanding of the reasons for this unique type of organization and its significance in light of the functions the Board performs.

Development of the Board

In the latter part of the eighteenth century, private agricultural societies were founded in many states to stimulate interest in the improvement of agriculture.[1] These societies were sponsored primarily by businessmen rather than farmers, because businessmen saw earlier than farmers themselves the importance of agriculture to the whole national life. These societies sought to educate the farmer in the latest scientific discoveries and agricultural techniques in hopes of improving his efficiency and the quality of his produce.

Such a society was formed in Kansas in 1857 and held two meetings before it ceased functioning in 1860. Two years later the group was re-established and was incorporated by the Kansas Legislature. The association was given the usual powers of a nonprofit corporation. Membership was open to any citizen of the state upon payment of an annual membership fee of one dollar. As it turned out, those who chose to join the society were primarily legislators, public officials, military officers, businessmen and professional men in the Topeka vicinity where the meetings were held. Very few farmers were represented in the society in the early days. Activities of the Kansas State Agricultural Society consisted of holding state fairs and annual meetings and publishing statistical information for the betterment of agriculture in the state.

As interest in activities of the society increased, the problem of obtaining adequate financial support developed. The desirability of receiving state appropriations soon led to a movement to give the society governmental status. This was accomplished in 1872, when the Legislature provided that the executive committee of the society should be known as the Kansas State Board of Agriculture. Board members were to be elected by delegates from county-fair societies, and the Board was to have offices in the State Capitol. An appropriation of $35,000 was made to help pay awards at the state fair. Expenses of Board members and the salary of the Executive Secretary were expected to be financed by membership dues and fair receipts. In effect, the Board remained a private organization with power to determine its own programs and policies and with no governmental duties except the preparation of an annual report.

1. For an account of the history and development of the Board, see *Kansas State Board of Agriculture* by Professor E. O. Stene. This study, which is published as No. 5 of the Governmental Research Series of University of Kansas Publications (1948), was used extensively in preparing this section of the chapter.

The two main activities of the Board in its infancy were the promotion of immigration to Kansas and the education of farmers in the improvement of agricultural techniques. Soon the collection and interpretation of agricultural statistics became a major concern of the Board and led again to the need for getting more funds. The Legislature had made an initial appropriation to help finance the state fair. After that, fair receipts and membership dues were expected to cover costs of the operation of the Board. This was not the case, however, and the Board went into debt. Therefore, in 1874 the Legislature began its policy of making annual appropriations to the Board. With annual appropriations, the Board had a new basis to claim status as a regular governmental agency.

Soon after the turn of the century, the need for certain regulatory services in the field of agriculture began to arise. For example, many types of commercial fertilizers were being placed on the market, and some regulation was needed to protect the farmer and indirectly the public from the sale of undesirable or fraudulent fertilizers. In 1903 the Legislature authorized the Board to inspect commercial fertilizers. The same type of regulation was needed to inspect feed, livestock remedies, and other such commodities used by the farmers.

There were some, including the Secretary of the State Board of Agriculture, who questioned the desirability of assigning regulatory duties to the Board. The Board had neither the laboratories nor the staff necessary to analyze products. Because the experiment station had these facilities, the Legislature in 1907 transferred these regulatory duties to the experiment station. However, other regulatory duties continued to be assigned both to the experiment station and to the Board.

The National Association of Commissioners of Agriculture in their fourth annual meeting in 1919 showed concern over the duplication of work between the state departments of agriculture and the experiment stations and agricultural colleges. The Association drafted a plan to eliminate the duplication of work existing between the agricultural colleges and the state departments of agriculture. According to the plan, the colleges should handle educational extension work, and the departments of agriculture should perform regulatory functions. The plan was generally accepted, and four years later several regulatory functions were transferred from Kansas State University[2] to the Kansas State Board of Agriculture in accordance with the Association policy. Since then the growth of regulatory functions of the Board has been rapid.

Organization

The State Board of Agriculture consists of two members elected for three-year terms from each of six districts into which the state is divided. Terms are staggered so that only four members are elected each year. The election takes place at an annual meeting in Topeka on the second Wednesday of January. Members of the Board meet at this time with delegates from the following state and local agricultural associations: each county or district agricultural fair; each state fair or statewide fair; each county farmers' institute; each county farmers' union with a paid-up membership of at least 200; each county grange and farm bureau with the same minimum membership; each livestock association of state-wide character; and each state-wide association for promotion of a crop or crops. Each of these associations sends one delegate and each delegate has one vote.

Certain requirements are imposed by law on the associations which want to be represented at an annual meeting. To be recognized, an association must file a copy of its constitution, bylaws, and list of officers with the Secretary of the Board. It must submit such reports on agricultural conditions in its locality as the Secretary may require. Delegates must be duly elected by the members of the organizations they represent and the Board must be notified. All delegates, except those representing local fair societies, must be bona fide farmers or breeders of livestock. The Board may take representation away from any fair association or society which does not comply with adequate standards for its fairs. Then the Board may assign representation to a fair society which does comply. Normally only one fair association is recognized in a county. An association which fails to hold a fair for two consecutive years usually loses its representation.

Annual meetings are usually well attended; the state pays part of the travel and hotel expenses of delegates. These expenses, plus all

2. The name of Kansas State College was changed to Kansas State University in 1959.

other actual expenses in holding the meeting, may not exceed $10,000. Meetings are open to the public and are primarily educational. Programs include speeches, films, panel discussions, and get-acquainted dinners. Staff members of Kansas State University frequently are on the programs. The educational phase of the annual meeting has become so important that it tends to overshadow the election of board members. After the selection of board members, the Board elects from its numbers a president, a vice-president, and a treasurer for one-year terms. The secretary is appointed as chief administrative officer for two-year terms.

Management within the Board conforms generally to the board-director type of organization. The Board meets quarterly to discuss and to formulate policy and to adopt rules and regulations necessary to carry out its functions. The twelve men comprising the board proper have final authority over the entire operation of the Department. The secretary's function is to formulate administrative policies within the Board's policies and decisions and to see that their actions are implemented.

Board members are divided into eight committees corresponding with the eight functional divisions of the agency. Each committee is composed of three Board members. These committees meet on call with

TABLE 38

Delegates to Kansas Agricultural Conventions by Agency Represented: Selected Years

Year	State-wide Fairs	State-wide Crop & Livestock Assn.	County Fairs	County Farm Bureaus	County Granges	County Farmers' Union	County Farmers' Institutes	Total
1941	2	17	48	103	18	6	3	197
1946	2	11	31	86	15	2	2	149
1950	1	16	44	94	18	3	2	178
1955	1	18	56	93	17	14	1	200
1960	1	17	49	87	22	8	1	185
1965	1	17	46	85	20	7	2	178
1968	1	12	35	82	15	1	1	147

Sources: Marcene Grimes, *State-Local Relations in Kansas: Activities of the State Board of Agriculture* (Lawrence: Governmental Research Center, Univ. of Kansas, 1954), p. 3; unpublished records, Kansas State Board of Agriculture.

the respective division heads to make policy decisions, and they meet collectively at the quarterly meetings. In addition to the functional committees, three Board members meet and serve with the Board president and secretary as the policy committee. This committee covers such items as budgeting and legislative policy. With only twelve Board members and eight committees, most of the members serve on more than one committee.

Technically, the Secretary is responsible for the day-to-day functioning of the agency. While most activities and actions of the Board require the Secretary's attention, his most time-consuming activity probably is serving as spokesmen for the agency in dealings with other state agencies, legislators, and the public. He is an ex officio member of the state Soil Conservation Committee, the state Safety Council, the Kansas Wheat Commission, the Board of State Fair Managers, and the Air Quality Conservation Commission. The Secretary appoints an assistant to relieve him of managing many of the day-to-day affairs of the Department. The assistant secretary serves as the general business manager of the agency and takes over duties of division heads in their absence. He is in charge of the central office of the Board. The general role of the central office is to supervise, plan, and coordinate the work of the various divisions. Central office personnel prepare the budget, handle finances, personnel records, and assignments, issue publications and reports, supervise the rules and regulations prepared for adoption by the Board, and manage the business of the department. The legal counsel and the publication editor are situated in the central office.

Four of the eight divisions of the Board (dairy, water resources, marketing, and weights and measures) have been specifically created by statute. The duties of the other four divisions (control, noxious weeds, statistical, and entomological) are assigned to the Board and its Secretary. The functional committees meet with the division chiefs, but all accept the fact that they are responsible administratively to the Secretary. At one time by statute the Board participated directly in the appointment of the division chiefs. Now all division heads[3] are under civil service, and the Secretary in concert with the Board makes the final selection from the appropriate civil service register. Clerical

3. Except for the head of the Statistical Division, who is appointed by the United State Department of Agriculture.

employees, field men, laboratory assistants, and others are under civil service and are appointed by the Secretary or the division chiefs.

Functions of the State Board

The Annual Census and the Collection and Interpretation of Agricultural Statistics

The collection, interpretation, and distribution of agricultural statistics, such as crop and livestock production data, was one of the first services undertaken by the Board of Agriculture. Pressure for this service came largely from farmers who wanted reliable information about agricultural production to help them plan their future production. The results of the agricultural reporting service now also benefit other groups, such as processors and distributors of agricultural products, manufacture of farm machinery and other goods used by farmers, lending agencies, consumers, and the United States Department of Agriculture in setting production goals and price supports.

Local agricultural organizations and local assessors supply much of the information used in the agricultural reports. The annual agricultural and population census is a local activity supervised by the Board of Agriculture. The deputy assessors collect much information about the farm and its operations when they visit the farms to assess the personal property. Since 1924 the Board and the U.S. Department of Agriculture have jointly maintained the Statistical Division to act as the agricultural fact-finding agency of the state.

Under this arrangement, a federal-state statistician is placed in charge of the Statistical Division[4] of the State Board of Agriculture. Some of the employees of the Division are under U.S. civil service and others are under state civil service. Despite these special circumstances, both the Division and the Board of Agriculture seem to consider the Division a part of the state Department. Expenses of the Division are shared by the United States Department of Agriculture and the state. The Statistical Division also conducts mail surveys. Questionnaires go to special groups such as mills, elevators, hatcheries, alfalfa-dehydrating plants, and dairy-processing plants. Rural mail-carriers are also used to

4. This Division uses a voluntary method of collecting information, known as the crop-reporting service. In Kansas in 1968 there were 2,984 regular monthly crop reporters operating in some nine districts.

distribute unaddressed questionnaire cards to farmers along their routes. County extension agents perform a valuable service by submitting weekly crop reports and supplying special agricultural information when requested.

Information collected from these various sources, including the assessors, is compiled and analyzed in the state office. It is distributed via daily newspapers, radio news releases, farm and trade publications, as well as direct reports from the Statistical Division to the public and to the Federal Crop Reporting Board in Washington, where the data is analyzed for its national significance.

In addition to the continuous informational program on agricultural statistics, the Statistical Division conducts an extensive program of data collecting. Some projects are financed by Federal Agricultural Marketing Service grants which must be matched by the state. Typical of the work conducted with the agricultural marketing funds are surveys to determine wheat, poultry, egg, and beef prices, wheat quality estimates, and the amount of commercial-grain storage-space available.

Control of Farm-Used Products

The growth of the regulatory functions of the Board has already been mentioned. The Control Division enforces the laws regulating the sale of commercial fertilizers, livestock remedies, commercial feeding stuffs, pesticides, and agricultural seeds. Basically, the object of these laws is to protect the users by assuring that the products meet the state requirements for truthful labeling. These laws are enforced largely through requirements for state registration and inspection.

Commercial fertilizers, pesticides, and livestock remedies must be registered annually with the Control Division. Registration is required before the product may be offered for sale. Before registering these products, the Control Division inspects labels submitted by the applicants to determine that they are correct as to contents and that they are not misleading. The law authorizes the Division to collect and analyze samples of the products prior to registration. In practice this is not done because it is felt that such samples would not be as representative as those taken from the market after registration.

The Control Division collects samples of fertilizers, feeding stuffs, livestock remedies, and agricultural chemicals, and sends them to the laboratory for analysis. The inspectors take samples of products of all firms and recheck as necessary. While all inspectors may work on pesticides, one inspector specializes in them. The Division maintains a laboratory in Topeka to analyze these products.

When field inspectors find incorrectly labeled products, the Control Division may initiate criminal proceedings and stop the sale of the product pending court action. However, before criminal proceedings are initiated, the Secretary of the Board holds a hearing. If he determines that there has been a violation, the registration may be canceled and, at the Secretary's discretion, the facts may be reported to the proper county attorney for prosecution.

With respect to pesticides, livestock remedies, and other products there is much cooperation between the state and the national government. Many of the products are sold nationally and are registered with the U.S. Department of Agriculture. In general, the industries regulated seem willing to be regulated and do, in fact, largely pay for such regulation. The industries benefit by having inferior products eliminated from the market.

Control of Insects and Plant Disease

The State Entomological Commission was established by the Legislature in 1907 as an independent agency. Under a general reshuffling of agricultural activities, it was placed under the supervision of the Board of Agriculture in 1919. In practice, however, the only real tie between the Commission and the Board was through the Secretary who acted as chairman of the Commission. For most purposes the Commission operated independently of the Board of Agriculture until 1963 when the Commission was abolished and its duties were transferred to the Board of Agriculture and the Secretary of the Board.

There are three entomologists who inspect annually all plant nurseries in the state and, on the basis of their findings, certify plants to be free from disease and insects and thus eligible for shipment in interstate commerce. The Division employs an apiarist who inspects honeybees and regulates their shipment into the state. It also licenses pest-control operators under the Kansas Pest Control Act. In cooperation with Kansas State University and the U.S. Department of Agriculture the Division is striving to eradicate all common barberry bushes which can act as hosts for black stem rust—a disease of wheat plants.

Marketing Activities

As a result of the increasing interest in the marketing of agricultural products, the 1947 Legislature created[5] a marketing division within the Board of Agriculture and authorized state cooperation with the United States Department of Agriculture. The Board of Agriculture has adopted the uniform federal grades for fresh fruits and vegetables. The Division may provide its grading service only on request to persons, partnerships, firms, companies, corporations, or associations engaged in the production, marketing, or processing of farm products.[6]

All poultry and egg grading is strictly voluntary, and fees are charged for the service. The program at present covers only fresh fruits and vegetables, although it is expected that the program may be extended to other farm products. All grades used in Kansas conform with the standard United States grades adopted by the United States Department of Agriculture. The program enhances the marketability of Kansas fruits and vegetables in distant markets. Obviously, such a program tends to increase the farmer's income inasmuch as it increases the salability of his product. All of these objectives ultimately benefit the consumer, since it is to his advantage to have products of recognizable quality in the market.

In one way or another all activities of the Division are aimed at increasing the quality of Kansas farm commodities and giving assurance as to their quality and improving their position in the market. More specifically the Kansas marketing law authorizes the Marketing Division to: (1) investigate the subject of marketing farm products; (2) promote their sales distribution and merchandising; (3) furnish information and assistance to the public; (4) study and recommend efficient and economical methods of marketing; (5) provide for such studies and research as may be deemed necessary and proper; and (6) gather and disseminate timely and useful information concerning the supply, demand, prevailing prices, and commercial movement of farm products. The last activity is a part of the market news service of the United States Department of Agriculture and of the Statistical Division of the State Board of Agriculture.

5. *K.S.A.*, 74-530 to 539.
6. *K.S.A.*, 74-532.

Regulation of the State's Water Resources

The Division of Water Resources of the State Board of Agriculture administers the law which provides for the control by the state of the construction of levees, dams, channel improvements, and other structures located on or near streams in the state.

Plans for the construction of such improvements by units of local government or by individual property owners must be submitted to the chief engineer of the Division for approval. The Division has the responsibility of administering the 1945 Water Appropriation Law. Under this law, Kansas is recognized as having a relatively scarce water supply and having adopted the doctrine of prior appropriation common in western states.

This doctrine is designed to permit the state to regulate and allot a given water supply. The law establishes a priority of uses for that supply. Domestic use of water for household purposes, watering of livestock, and irrigation of gardens and lawns are not affected by the water appropriation law. Next to domestic use, preference is given to these uses: municipal, irrigation, industrial, recreational, and water power. All appropriations of water are subject to the principle of beneficial use as specified by the Water Appropriation Law.

Responsibility falls on the Chief Engineer to approve permits for the appropriation of water. The majority of applications filed for such permits come from individual irrigators; a few come from irrigation companies and irrigation districts. Although an individual is not required to secure a permit to dig a well or to appropriate water, it is to his advantage to do so in order to protect his rights when and if the supply becomes limited and other persons with established rights compete for the supply.

Until water rights have been adjudicated, the Division of Water Resources is legally powerless to police each water supply. After the courts allocate contested water rights, the Division enforces the allocation. Although the Division has broad powers to regulate and allocate water supplies, it lacks the power to enforce the regulations and allotments it makes until these matters are defined by court decree.

Regulating the Dairy Industry

The supervision of milk supplies to protect the public health has been a concern of the state government since 1907, when the Office of

Dairy Commissioner was created by the Legislature. This became a function of the Board of Agriculture when the Dairy Commissioner's office was transferred to the Board in 1925. The dairy law[7] was revised considerably in 1927, and the licensing of all dairy manufacturers was provided for at that time.

The dairy law gives the state Dairy Commissioner supervision over the production, transportation, manufacture, and distribution of milk and dairy products. The object of state regulation is to protect the public from unwholesome milk and dairy products. At the same time, the Dairy Division is concerned with promoting the dairy industry in the state by seeing that the milk producer is paid a fair price for his butterfat and by urging the improvement of the quality of milk and dairy products produced and sold in Kansas. The Dairy Division licenses and inspects dairy manufacturing plants and all places where milk and dairy products are handled. Ideally, the Division seeks to supervise the milk supply "from the cow to the consumer."

The fees collected from the licensing are deposited with the state Treasurer in a special fee fund and are appropriated to the Dairy Division for financing the dairy inspections. Dairymen have generally agreed to pay for the inspection program through the fees, because they realize that higher quality of dairy products and the improved operating conditions which are expected to result from state inspection are to the industry's advantage.[8] Until 1947 the fees collected had proved generally adequate to finance the inspections. However, owing to the substantial decline in the number of licenses, state appropriations have been requested and received to supplement the fees collected.

The dairy law fixes extensive and detailed requirements for the handling of dairy products, seeking to insure cleanliness of premises and utensils. The Dairy Division has supplemented the statutory requirements with additional rules and regulations, covering such things as duties and responsibilities of field superintendents and penalties for violations, provision for temporary permits for station operators, methods of testing, and additional sanitary requirements in the production, handling and transportation of dairy products, and standards for Grade

---

7. *K.S.A.*, 65-701 to 721.

8. *The Kansas Dairy Industry Report of State Board of Agriculture* (Topeka: State Board of Agriculture), Vol. LXV, No. 275 (October, 1946), p. 15.

A milk. Requirements for cleanliness begin in the dairy barn and extend to all establishments handling the product on its way to the consumer.

The dairy law requires that all milk sold in the state must meet a minimum standard. Cities, at their own discretion, may adopt ordinances regulating their local milk supplies and may require higher standards than the minimum state requirements. Most of the cities in Kansas are not large enough to provide their own inspectional service. In 1928 the State Board of Agriculture devised a plan for the state to enter into cooperative agreements with the cities, whereby the Dairy Division would inspect for the cities. The Board believes that Kansas was the first state to set up such a cooperative inspection service for small cities. The city pays the state on a per diem basis for the services of the state dairy inspectors. These state officers inspect in the cities and also on the farms from which the city gets its milk supplies. Over eighty-two cities used this state service in 1968.

The problem and hazards of unsanitary milk raise questions of the proper relationship of the Board of Health and the State Board of Agriculture in milk sanitation and regulation. The Board of Health has a clear and natural interest in assuring a sanitary milk supply because of its responsibility for protecting the health of the public. At one time it was quite active in inspecting and regulating city milk supplies. On the other hand the Board of Agriculture has been given the responsibility for administering the dairy laws. The Dairy Division's interest encompasses a concern for public health as well as the promotion and development of the dairy industry.

The conflict of jurisdiction between the two agencies was taken to the State Supreme Court, which held that the Dairy Division had superior jurisdiction in the field. However, the Court conceded that the Board of Health had jurisdiction over the adulteration or misbranding of dairy products. In recent years the two boards have cooperated in an inspection program. The Board of Agriculture is the regulating agency in areas of the state where city inspectors do not operate. The Board of Health employs a sanitarian who inspects the quality of the local inspection (whether performed by the Dairy Division or by local inspectors). The matter is further complicated by the certification system devised and promoted by the U.S. Public Health Service for interstate shipments of milk. Only inspections by the state health authorities are accepted for this certification.

Regulating Weights and Measures

Since 1868 Kansas has had a weights and measures law, providing for the testing of scales used in commerce. For much of the time until 1947, major responsibility for inspecting weights and measures rested with the county clerks, who were subject to supervision by the Chancellor of the University of Kansas. For a number of reasons the enforcement of the law was sporadic and generally lax. In 1947 a new weights and measure law was passed, creating a Division of Weights and Measures in the Board of Agriculture.

The Kansas weights and measures law makes it illegal to sell, expose, offer for sale or use any weighing or measuring device that is inaccurate or to sell any commodity represented at a false weight or measure. The law establishes and defines official standards for measures of extension, weight, dry measure, liquid measure, and electrical measure. These standards, of course, conform to United States and international standards. The Weights and Measures Division acts as an impartial third party to see that equity prevails in all commercial transactions involving weight and measure.

The United States Constitution authorizes Congress to fix the standards of weights and measures applicable throughout the United States. The standards were furnished to Kansas in 1869. These "primary reference standards" are maintained in the Board of Agriculture laboratory and are used to test standards used in the field. Every ten years these standards are sent to Washington, D.C., for verification (calibration) by the U.S. Bureau of Standards. Here the Kansas standards are tested and sealed to an accuracy of 1/350,000 or better by comparison with standards maintained in Washington. These standards are copies of the international ones, which are preserved at Sèvres, France, by the International Bureau of Weights and Measures.

The state Sealer, who is Director of the Weights and Measures Division, and his deputies inspect the scales used in the state. There are programs directed at inspecting large-capacity scales, small-capacity scales, and "liquefied-petroleum gas meters." As more and more items are being sold prepackaged, inspection of the weights of such items has become an important part of the work of the Division.

Scales found to be relatively accurate are marked after inspection with a tag. Those which are above or below the tolerance limit are marked with a condemnation tag and cannot be legally used. The state Sealer or his deputy or a state-registered scale-service man may remove a condemnation tag. The importance of this program is suggested by the fact that when testing began, 38.5 per cent of the scales were condemned. Now less than 10 per cent are condemned.

As prepackaged foods have become more common, the prepackaged testing program has become even more important. In early testing, over 40 per cent of the packages were found to be underweight and slightly under 20 per cent had the correct weight. Currently over 70 per cent have the correct weight. In this program the packer is notified if his packages are consistently short or overweight. The Division also tests binder twine for tensile strength, length per pound, and net weight.

Other state agencies do some testing of weighing and measuring devices. The Motor-Fuel Tax Division of the Department of Revenue tests gasoline pumps at filling stations two to four times a year. Food and drug inspectors of the State Board of Health check scales used in making prescriptions. The Grain-Inspection Department and the Mine-Inspection Division of the Labor Department test scales in their regular inspections. A few cities (two in 1968) have their own weights and measures inspectors. Aside from annual reports to the state Sealer, the city inspectors work largely on their own. The Division has recently been assigned the task of enforcing a new safety law concerning anhydrous ammonia containers.

Suppression of Noxious Weeds

In an agricultural state such as Kansas the control of weeds is important. The weed law[9] makes it the duty of every property-owner to control the spread of and to eradicate the weeds declared noxious by the Legislature. There are ten plants which the Legislature has declared to be noxious; and county commissioners are authorized to assist in eradicating others. In eradicating noxious weeds, property-owners must use the methods adopted as official by the State Board of Agriculture. They must also undertake eradication "at such times" as are approved by the Board. The law also authorizes the Board to promul-

9. K.S.A., 2-1314 to 1330.

gate rules and regulations to carry the law into effect and authorizes the Secretary of Agriculture to enforce these rules and regulations as well as the law itself. Within the State Board of Agriculture a Noxious Weed Division has been created, and a state weed supervisor and several assistants have been appointed to administer the program.

To supervise weed eradication at the county level, the weed law directs the county commissioners of each county to employ a competent person as county weed supervisor. In addition, the governing body of any incorporated city or any group of counties or cities may employ a city or district weed supervisor. Appointments of weed supervisors are subject to the approval of the Secretary of Agriculture. The Board of Agriculture is authorized to contribute not more than one-fourth of each county weed supervisor's salary, but in recent years funds have not been appropriated to allow the Board to support this local activity. The State Board of Agriculture has general supervision of the program. The role of the state Weed Control Director is to advise the county supervisors about methods of weed eradication. The emphasis on the part of the state personnel seems to be on informal supervision through consultation and reports.[10]

Financing the Board of Agriculture

The Board of Agriculture is financed from regular appropriations from the general revenue fund of the state and from revenues derived from the Board's several fee funds. Most of the regulatory functions performed by the Department involve the collection of fees such as license, registration, and inspection fees. These fees are deposited in special fee funds in the state treasury and, provided the Legislature appropriates them, become available to the Division within the Board responsible for collecting the fee. The Secretary is responsible for management of finances subject to the general supervision of the Board. In fiscal 1968 appropriations from the general fund amounted to about 63 per cent of the total expenditures, with fee funds supplying most of the remainder.

Agricultural marketing-service funds are the only federal grants

10. Marcene Grimes, *State-Local Relations in Kansas: Activities of the State Board of Agriculture* (Lawrence: Governmental Research Center, Univ. of Kansas, 1954), pp. 113, 129.

TABLE 39

Expenditures of State Board of Agriculture by Activity: 1968

Division	Amount Spent	Percentage of Total
Central Office	$ 103,792	6.8%
Control Division	252,286	16.5
Dairy Division	201,148	13.2
Marketing Division	173,375	11.3
Noxious Weed Division	80,863	5.3
Seed Laboratory	65,194	4.3
Statistical Division	75,730	5.0
Water Resources Division	371,018	24.3
Weights and Measures Division	112,819	7.4
Entomological Division	92,874	6.1
TOTALS	$1,529,099	100.2%

Source: Data from State Board of Agriculture.

made to the State Board of Agriculture. Budgeting of agricultural marketing-service money is kept separate from the regular state budget, as these requests are sent to Washington. Since the state must match these federal funds, the state contribution shows up in the legislative appropriations to the various divisions using the federal money. A few employees of the Board are paid either jointly by the national and state governments or else entirely by the national government. In such cases, only the state's share shows up on the Board's budget.

Significance of the Board's Organization

The operations of the Kansas Board of Agriculture parallel those of agricultural agencies in other states, but its organization is now almost unique. The Board and its appointed officials are responsible in the first instance to the delegates from private farm associations rather than to the Governor, the Legislature, or the electorate. This is not to say that the Board or its officials are not responsive to the Governor, the Legislature, or the electorate, for they consider themselves a governmental agency and are largely dependent upon the Legislature for appropriations and authority to act. The Board follows normal channels for appropriations, purchasing, and personnel actions. Organizations similar to the Kansas Board of Agriculture were common among the states when the agencies functioned primarily as promotional agencies. As these agencies were assigned regulatory duties, they were reorganized and integrated more into the state government. Today New Jersey and Kansas are the only states with this type of organization. In Kansas no attempt has been made to change the organization in the last four decades.

The retention of the Kansas Board and its form of organization suggests the Board's effectiveness in representing the interests of the farmers as seen by the farmers and by the Legislature. It may also be a tribute to efficiency of both the Board and its operations. The secretaries of the Board and the division heads have had long tenure, which has contributed to the efficiency of the Department. It is claimed that the existing organization gives an excellent opportunity for farmers to make their feelings known to the state agricultural officials and to the Legislature.

The fundamental problem raised by this type of organization is one that allows no simple answer: Can the Board be expected to act in the interest of the general public should there be a conflict between these interests and those of the farmers? It seems probable that should such a conflict arise, it would find its way to the Legislature for resolution.

The Board of State Fair Managers

The concept of holding annual fairs in order to pool the ideas of farm communities has been carried to the state level in many of the states. Management of the Kansas State Fair was one of the original activities of the Board of Agriculture and its predecessor, the State Agricultural Society. Today there is an effort to separate the state fair from other activities of the Board of Agriculture. While a separate legal entity, the Board of State Fair Managers consists of the twelve members of the Board of Agriculture and its secretary ex officio. The fair managers have a permanent administrative office at Hutchinson, where the fairgrounds are located. The original fairgrounds, ceded to the state by Reno County, were enlarged in 1951 by purchase of additional land.

Members of the Board, in their capacity as fair managers, take an active interest in management of the state fair. Activities are handled through the permanent staff in the Hutchinson offices. Biennial reports of fair activities are submitted to the Legislature separately from the

Board of Agriculture reports. From a practical standpoint, management of the state fair and its finances are entirely independent of the State Board of Agriculture and many Kansans may not realize that the Board members and the Secretary are the fair managers.

The state fair is financed by fair receipts supplemented by legislative appropriations. In 1949, the Legislature provided for a special emergency fund in which the fair manager deposits money to build up a reserve to help defray costs of the fair in years when the revolving fund, because of poor attendance, is inadequate.

The Kansas Livestock Commission

In many parts of the state raising livestock and ranching are important aspects of agriculture. While there were various antecedent organizations, the Kansas Livestock Commission and the Livestock Sanitary Commissioner are now charged with the enforcement of various laws concerning livestock. The members of the Livestock Commission are appointed for three-year terms by the Governor, but he is limited in that the president of the Kansas Livestock Association is one of the seven members of the Commission, and the other six members must be recommended by the Executive Committee of the Livestock Association. One member is appointed from each Congressional district and one from the state at large. The Commission is a part-time advisory board for assisting the Livestock Sanitary Commissioner in determining policies and plans. The Commissioner is appointed by the Governor for two-year terms and must have the approval of the executive committee of the Kansas Livestock Association.

The Commissioner is responsible for enforcing laws protecting domestic animals from various diseases. He may inspect and quarantine animals suspected of having contagious diseases and condemn certain diseased animals for slaughter. The Commissioner also administers the community sales law which regulates sales of livestock made at livestock auctions and exchanges. Dealers are bonded and registered. All livestock sold through such sales must be inspected by an authorized veterinarian. The Commissioner licenses persons who dispose of dead animals and promulgates rules for the feeding of garbage to hogs.

The Brand Commissioner

In order to protect the owners of livestock there are arrangements for filing of individual brands with the state Brand Commissioner.[11] From 1939 to 1943 the state Brand Board adjudicated claims for various brands. Since 1943, the board of directors of the Kansas Livestock Association has been designated a state agency to award ownership of disputed brands and to advise with and approve rules prepared by the state Brand Commissioner, who is appointed for two-year terms by the Governor, from three persons nominated by the board of directors of the Kansas Livestock Association. The Brand Commissioner publishes a brand book showing the brands filed with his office. The latest book, with 21,819 brands, was published in 1965, and supplements with over 672 additional brands have been issued. It is estimated that about 22,500 brands are being used at this time.

Agricultural Extension

Agricultural extension is the biggest adult-education program in the state. It is aimed at improving agriculture and farm life. The groundwork was laid for future extension services when, in 1863, the Legislature accepted a federal land and money grant and a gift of the Bluemont Central College Association for the founding of Kansas State College of Agriculture and Applied Science. Early faculty members of the college were asked to lecture on agricultural topics throughout the state and thus to take part in the then-popular farmers' institutes, which were really short schools held at various points in the state. Shortly after 1900, attention turned from farmers' institutes to a new way of spreading information and ideas to farmers.[12] This plan called for taking the new ideas directly to the farmer through employing county agricultural agents who would be practical, itinerant teachers going from farm to farm. Leavenworth County began, in 1912, to employ such an agent, and now all the counties in the state have at least one agent. The Extension Service in the U.S. Department of Agriculture was established in 1914, and arrangements were made for the

11. *K.S.A.*, 47-414 to 431.

12. Edmund D. Brunner and E. Hsin Pao Yang, *Rural America and the Extension Service* (New York: Teachers College, Columbia Univ., 1949), p. 8.

national government to pay not less than $1,200 (raised later to $1,500) toward the salary of county agents.

As early as 1905 there were traces of the beginning of the program at Kansas State University, and in 1912 extension was made a division of that institution. The Legislature in 1915 authorized the levying of property tax to raise money to be used in extension activities.

Local farm organizations were recognized as necessary if full advantage was to be made of the work of the county agents. "Farm bureau" came to refer to all associations cooperating in extension work, and soon farm-bureau work became synonymous with extension. In 1920 a federation of the local farm bureaus was organized under the name of the Kansas Farm Bureau. The state-wide organization became interested in legislation, taxation, transportation, marketing, and subjects other than extension. The Kansas Farm Bureau grew to have 51,000 members and to join the American Federation of Farm Bureaus. Thus on a county, state, and national level the Farm Bureaus came to be interested in more than extension, though in Kansas and some other states the county farm bureaus remained the agencies through which the county extension agent was expected to reach all of the farmers.

Various difficulties arose over the farm bureaus acting as both private organizations and also as agencies collecting funds and directing the activities of the local extension workers. Non-farm-bureau members objected to the county agents being called upon to handle membership drives, collect dues, and handle other activities which pertained more to the Farm Bureau. This resulted, in 1951, in the Kansas Legislature providing for the distinct separation of the county farm bureaus and the agricultural extension work. Three extension representatives are now elected at annual meetings from each township and each city not a part of a township. One of these elected from each township or city is elected to represent agriculture, one to represent home economics, and one to represent 4-H club work. Those elected to represent agriculture form the Agricultural Advisory Committee. Similarly, there are home economics advisory committees and 4-H club advisory committees. Together all members elected form the Extension Council, which determines general extension policy and selects annually a chairman, a secretary, a treasurer, and six other members of the executive board. The executive board prepares the extension budget in cooperation with the county commissioners and the director of extension of Kansas State University. In most counties a property-tax levy of up to three-quarters of a mill is authorized for extension work.

Extension work was first conceived as spreading to farmers information and new methods and techniques for improving agriculture. Now the work has been broadened and expanded. Early extension work was directed to the farmer himself. The farm wives came to want similar services pertaining to their activities. Thus, to materials on planting and harvesting crops and raising improved livestock were added instructions on sewing, cooking, preparing food, homemaking, and the like. This new emphasis made it necessary to hire specialists in these other subjects, and so home-demonstration agents were hired. A third expansion of the program has led to the employment of club agents to work with the young people on the farms. More recently, a fourth type of specialist has developed. As a recognition of the extent to which farms are really business enterprises, several farm-management associations have been formed in the state. These associations employ special agriculture extension agents who are farm-management specialists. All counties have agriculture agents, most employ home-demonstration agents, about one third have club agents, and there are only a few farm-management specialists generally serving areas bigger than a county.

The Director of Extension at Kansas State University is appointed by the President of the University with the approval of the Secretary of the U.S. Department of Agriculture. The Director prepares and submits proposed programs for extension activities to the U.S. Department of Agriculture which, when approved, become the basis of federal grants. In the Extension Division at the university there are a number of specialists in various aspects of agriculture. Staff assistance is available to the county agent both for special programs and for technical questions. The state is divided into several districts, with district agents to visit and work directly with the county agents.

Local agents are selected finally by the executive board of the Agricultural Extension Council from among those nominated by the district agent. They are required to be graduates of accredited colleges. Persons who desire such employment file applications with the Extension Division of Kansas State University, where their applications are reviewed by a committee of resident college members. Only those approved are considered for training and employment. Such persons are given intensive instruction at Kansas State University and are the ones nominated by the district agent when vacancies occur.

17 Conservation of Natural Resources

When our forefathers moved westward, the abundance which they saw about them led them to be little concerned with conservation. As these resources were used, there came to be more concern about the supply of certain of them for the future. However, there are differing views of what constitutes the wise and proper use of our resources and of how important it is to try to save them. The diverse nature of the resources contributes to the fact that in Kansas there is not one but several agencies which are concerned with conservation.

Conservation means different things to different people. To the manufacturer it may mean keeping his supply of raw materials flowing. To the sportsman it will probably mean keeping streams stocked with fish and animals for him to hunt. To the farmer it will mean saving and restoring his soil for future crops. Conservation of natural resources involves many agencies and can appropriately be studied on the basis of the resource being conserved.

Conservation of the Soil

With its strong agricultural base, Kansas early became interested in soil conservation. In 1913 the Legislature enacted statutes to deal with the problem of wind erosion. With the advent of the federal Soil Conservation Act of 1935, federal funds became available to aid soil conservation. Two years later the Legislature passed enabling statutes allow-

318

ing for the establishment of community soil-conservation districts capable of carrying out local programs of conservation.

Under the requirements of the federal Soil Conservation Act, the Soil Conservation Service of the U.S. Department of Agriculture was directed to assign conservation technicians to any soil-conservation district organized under the laws of the individual state. "Memorandums of Agreement" are signed between the local conservation districts and the U.S. Department of Agriculture. While the Kansas statutes do not require such organization, all of the soil-conservation districts have been organized following county boundaries. A district has now been established in each county. The county soil-conservation districts are established under the laws of Kansas, and are not dependent upon or responsible to the U.S. Department of Agriculture.

Each district program is carried on with the cooperation, advice, and assistance of the County Soil-Conservation District Board of Supervisors, a five-member local board which serves without remuneration. Two of the supervisors are appointed by the State Soil-Conservation Committee, while the other three are elected at an annual election by the members of the county district. Both appointed and elected members of the Board serve three-year terms. The Kansas Legislature has given district boards general responsibility for encouraging conservation practices. They are forbidden to levy taxes, but may charge a membership or cooperator fee of $5 to the farmers of the district who desire to join, and may distribute conservation materials or conservation equipment. They may receive funds from any source and use them to further soil conservation in their district. Counties are authorized to raise from the ad valorem property tax an amount up to $3,000 for the district. The amount which the county raises is matched by the state and is used to maintain the local soil-conservation district office. All districts have a part-time or full-time clerk. Several of the Kansas districts have purchased trees to resell at cost, and some have purchased specialized conservation equipment. In practice, their primary activity is to act as an advisory group and to present local desires and needs to the Soil Conservation Service technicians within the county in accordance with the Memorandum of Agreement which each local district signs with the Secretary of Agriculture.

In most soil-conservation districts there is a conservationist who is an employee of the U.S. Department of Agriculture. These persons are paid by the federal government and are under federal civil service, yet their duties are to assist farmers and ranchers in planning, applying, and maintaining soil- and water-conservation practices. These technicians will prepare upon request a comprehensive conservation plan for any farm. The plan includes land usage, conservatory farming methods, and permanent conservation practices. Surveying, contouring, and the engineering layout of permanent conservation practices are performed free of charge to any farmer. The Soil Conservation Service is responsible for performing all lay-out work for conservation practices eligible for the incentive payments made by the Agricultural Stabilization and Conservation Service of the U.S. Department of Agriculture.

Farmers are encouraged by the U.S. Department of Agriculture to carry out certain soil-conservation practices by offering them incentive payments to defray part of the expenses incurred in making the improvement. The conservation practices which are approved for payment are those recommended by a committee of Kansas agricultural experts. They include such measures as the application of lime and phosphate materials to promote growth of soil-conserving crops; planting of green-cover crops; and construction of terraces, reservoirs, and dams. The complete list of approved projects is published in the state handbook of the Agricultural Stabilization and Conservation Service for Kansas.

If the farmer wants to participate in the program he must first receive the approval of the SCS technician for the practice which he desires. Then he applies to the Agricultural Stabilization and Conservation Service county committee, which is made up of farmers elected by the farmers within the county. If the practice is one of those approved and if his application is approved, the farmer is usually allowed about 50 per cent of the out-of-pocket cost as assistance in carrying out a recommended practice; but this varies from a maximum of near 80 per cent to a near-token payment, depending upon the nature of the proposed work. A national maximum-payment limit is established at $2,500 per farm per year, but state and county committees may set lower limits to spread available funds as far as possible. The work must be done satisfactorily and promptly in order for the farmer to obtain payment. Payments are usually made annually to each participating farmer.

As of July, 1968, over half of the farmers of the state—92,987[1] out of a total of 141,547—participate in the programs of the soil-conservation districts. Basic farm-conservation plans have been developed for 79,659 farms. A total of 3,291 farmers out of an eligible group of 60,729 participate in the special Great Plains Conservation Program. In this program the U.S. Soil Conservation Service shares in the cost of conservation practices in sixty-two of the western Kansas counties. The data in the accompanying table suggests that much progress has been made in soil conservation in Kansas, but much remains to be done.

To facilitate the work of these county soil-conservation districts

TABLE 40

Soil Conservation Progress in Kansas: June 30, 1968

	Unit*	Completed during FY 1968	Total Completed through June 30, 1968	Remaining to be done
Conservation Cropping System	Ac.	1,231,335	16,730,886	11,334,081
Contour Farming	Ac.	628,241	6,782,772	19,546,341
Stubble Mulching	Ac.	529,371	4,717,582	5,212,418
Pasture and Hay Land Planting	Ac.	36,033	1,004,069	596,181
Proper Range and Pasture Use	Ac.	1,430,615	10,865,672	7,108,328
Range Seeding	Ac.	35,856	1,690,683	991,362
Windbreaks	Ac.	547	56,634	58,085
Fish Ponds Stocked	No.	2,013	4,191	20,709
Wildlife Habitat Development	Ac.	626	69,502	1,130,598
Diversions Construction	Mi.	281	8,833	15,367
Grade Stabilization Structures	No.	834	30,659	54,447
Grass Waterways	Ac.	9,009	261,230	553,770
Farm Ponds	No.	2,263	82,443	66,557
Terracing	Mi.	9,735	238,360	510,140
Drainage Ditches	Mi.	184	6,015	8,635
Irrigation Water Management	Ac.	87,387	600,728	1,000,272
Irrigation Land Leveling	Ac.	39,362	417,034	453,966
Cropland to Other Uses	Ac.	63,596	1,157,183	670,000

* *Ac.* refers to acres, *No.* to number, and *Mi.* to square miles.

Source: Data supplied by the State Soil Conservation Committee.

1. Data supplied by the State Soil Conservation Committee.

there is a state Soil-Conservation Committee of nine members, of whom five are elected, two appointed, and the remaining two ex officio. The elected members are selected by the boards of supervisors of the district in each of the five areas into which Kansas has been divided. Each elected member of the state Committee serves for two years. Of the two appointed members, one is appointed by the Secretary of the U.S. Department of Agriculture (normally the Director of the U.S. Soil Conservation Service for Kansas) and the other by the Kansas Board of Agriculture. Both serve two-year terms concurrent with that of the Governor. The Director of Extension for the State of Kansas and the Director of the Kansas Experiment Stations are ex officio members of the State Soil-Conservation Committee.

The functions of the state Committee are to: (1) assist the supervisors of the soil-conservation districts; (2) keep the supervisors informed of the provisions of the soil-conservation district act; (3) coordinate activities of the various districts by advice and consultation; (4) secure the cooperation of the U.S. Department of Agriculture and state agencies in the work of the districts; and (5) disseminate soil-conservation information and encourage formation of districts. In practice the operation of the state Committee is limited, since the budget is large enough to pay the salaries and expenses of only an executive secretary, a field secretary, and an office secretary. The Office of the Executive Secretary facilitates the operation of soil-conservation districts throughout Kansas, approves election procedures of the various districts, and acts as a clearinghouse for information for the soil-conservation districts of the state.

In addition to its more traditional role of encouraging the operation of the local soil-conservation districts, the Committee, augmented by a representative from the Kansas Water Resources Board and the Division of Water Resources of the State Board of Agriculture, acts upon and makes recommendations on the application of watershed districts for federal assistance under the federal Water Protection and Flood Prevention Act.

In a more general way both the extension service and the agricultural experiment stations contribute to soil-conservation work. Normally, the county extension agent's activity with respect to soil conservation is of a general, advisory nature, while the soil conservationist assists in planning and executing conservation practices for a specific farm or locality. The state agricultural experiment stations are engaged in research on conservation as well as other aspects of agriculture.

Water Resources

The conservation of our soil resources is very closely related to the conservation of our water resources. From an agricultural point of view conservation of water resources has come to mean soil conservation, watershed management, and irrigation. Important as these aspects of water conservation are, other approaches are to be considered in any broad program directed toward the conservation of our water resources.

Perhaps flood control is the most obvious of these other approaches. The paths of the Kansas, Marais des Cygnes, Arkansas, and other large rivers have often been marked by a trail of destruction through the cities lining their banks and over the surrounding countryside. Major catastrophes like the great flood of July, 1951, and the flood in 1965 along the Arkansas River result in substantial destruction and cause renewed demands for workable preventive measures.

To the sportsman, water conservation means lakes where fish and wildlife may thrive. To him and others, water offers opportunities for recreation. To industry, water is often essential to some of the manufacturing processes. Increasingly cities are finding it difficult to keep pace with the demand for adequate supplies of water for domestic and commercial uses.

Unfortunately, the various purposes for which our water resources may be used cannot always be harmonized. For example, some of those interested in water for agriculture may oppose building big dams which will flood the rich bottom farm lands in the river valley just behind the dam. Others of those interested in agriculture may strongly favor big dams for irrigation. In the cities, however, the railroads and industries are generally located along the more level river plains, so that these areas are in special danger when the floods come. This clash of interests has been illustrated in Kansas by the opposition to the building, by the U.S. Corps of Engineers, of the Tuttle Creek Dam near Manhattan in order, it was claimed, to prevent further flood loss in the industrial areas of Kansas City.

The problem of harmonizing the possible approaches to water-resources development is complicated by the existence of various agencies at both the state and national level who are devoting their efforts to one or more of these approaches. Among these agencies and among the citizenry there are differences of opinion as to what relative emphasis ought to be given to these various aspects of the problem.

The complexity of the relationships between the various agencies concerned with water conservation has led to interagency rivalries and conflict. The control of water resources from a single major river such as the Missouri River and its tributaries is a problem which involves and concerns several states. To be most effective, each project, whether financed by the state or by the federal government, must fit into the total river-basin development. To provide a degree of coordination of federal projects and to get state participation and action in broad river-basin planning, regional committees have been established for the Missouri River Basin and for the Arkansas, White, and Red rivers.

More specifically, a number of local agencies are concerned with the conservation of water.[2] Regulation of the water resources of the state has been a major concern since the admission of Kansas to the union. Legislation near the turn of the century authorized the establishment of irrigation and drainage districts whereby residents of local areas could organize to prevent floods and establish irrigation systems. The constitutional provision which until 1958 prevented the state from engaging in "internal improvements" in water control did not apply to local agencies and thus made them the logical agencies to carry on these improvements. State action in the field was confined to general supervision rather than direct participation in such developments. The constitutional amendment which was approved by the voters in 1958 makes it possible for the state to "be a party to flood control works and works for the conservation or development of water resources.[3]

There are five irrigation districts operating in the state. Though there was an earlier law in 1891 to authorize such districts, all five of the existing districts were created under the procedures established in 1941. The chief engineer of the Division of Water Resources of the

2. The most complete inventory and description of such districts is contained in *A Presentation of Special Water Districts in Kansas,* prepared by the Kansas Water Resources Board in 1967. It was used in preparing this section of the chapter.

3. *Kansas Constitution,* Art. 11, sec. 9.

State Board of Agriculture is authorized to organize irrigation districts when petitioned under such restrictions or conditions as he imposes. The district is a corporate body and is governed by a board of directors. The districts are authorized to enter into agreements with appropriate federal agencies which, in the five districts in question, is the U.S. Bureau of Reclamation.

There are several laws authorizing the creation of drainage districts. One allows the board of county commissioners to incorporate drainage districts within their county when petitioned by at least 40 per cent of the taxpayers residing in the proposed district.[4] Three other laws envision districts which include more than one county and are incorporated under certain circumstances by the Governor or by the district court.[5] In 1968 there were ninety-three drainage districts of which sixty-two were active. All but five drainage districts operate within a single county. Eighteen drainage districts have been organized since 1950. In most instances they are formed to act as local sponsors for federally supported local-protection works. The chief engineer of the Water Resources Division approves all plans for projects and inspects the more important projects during their construction.

When interest was high after the 1951 flood, a new watershed district law was passed.[6] This law authorizes 20 per cent of the landowners owning 25 per cent of the acreage of a proposed watershed district to petition the Secretary of State and the chief engineer of the Water Resources Division to organize a district. Specifically, the chief engineer conducts an investigation of the need for the proposed district and either approves or disapproves the petition. Such watershed districts have broad powers to manage their affairs, although approval of their plans by the chief engineer is necessary for purposes of coordination. Watershed districts are authorized to cooperate with other local, state, and national governmental agencies, making it possible for a district to cooperate with such agencies as the State Highway Commission, the Board of Health, boards of county commissioners, city governments, Soil Conservation Service, Bureau of Reclamation, Corps of Engineers,

4. *K.S.A.*, 24-401 to 499.
5. *K.S.A.*, 24-501 to 529 and 24-601 to 655.
6. *K.S.A.*, 24-1201 to 1221.

and even with other states, both in the planning stage and in the division of payment of costs on a project.

The watershed law did not supersede, but merely supplemented, existing laws authorizing creation of irrigation and drainage districts. A watershed district may include land in existing drainage or irrigation districts. The general objective of the law is to provide means of creating districts to conform with natural watersheds. Although the State Division of Water Resources is designated as the coordinating agent, the intent of the law is to permit local control over financing and planning at all stages. As of July 1, 1968, sixty-eight watershed districts had been organized and twenty-two additional districts were in some stage of organizing. Most of these districts have been or are being organized across county lines.

The watershed district becomes a device for accomplishing improvements in water-resource control and development. The close relationship between some of these improvements and soil conservation is shown by the fact that the State Soil Conservation Committee functions as the Watershed Review Committee for applications for federal funds. Most watershed districts are created to be able to sponsor federal projects under the Federal Watershed Protection and Flood Prevention Act. A number of districts have sponsored construction, others have priority for funds for more detailed planning, and others are awaiting support for planning. The extent of federal participation depends on the type of project.

An additional state agency was created in 1955 for work in the water-conservation field. This is the State Water Resources Board which consists of several members appointed by the Governor with the advice and consent of the Senate. The Board employs an executive secretary and other personnel. It collects and compiles water-resource information and is charged with the responsibility of working out a state plan of water-resource development for each watershed in the state and coordinating water-resource development within the state.

In addition, all projects affecting stream flow are subject to the approval of the chief engineer whether they are undertaken by levee districts, counties, cities, townships, or individual citizens.

The boards of county commissioners were authorized in 1941 to establish rural water-supply districts, but it was not until 1957, when

Organizational Status of Kansas Watershed Districts: July 1, 1968

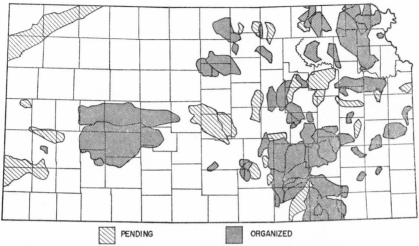

PENDING   ORGANIZED

Source: Map by Division of Water Resources, Kansas State Board of Agriculture.

a new law was enacted, that such districts were actually established.[7] Though organized by the county commissioners upon petition of landowners, the districts have their own boards of directors. They are legal corporations with the power to sue and be sued. They may exercise powers of eminent domain, own property and equipment, and cooperate with the federal government in specified programs. They do not have the power to levy property taxes. The appropriation of any water for other than domestic use is subject to state approval.

Much soil-conservation work is directly associated with the control of water. If the water is controlled on the land on which it falls, some of the problems just do not develop. The soil-conservation technicians within the soil-conservation districts are likely to encourage contour farming and the creation of farm ponds. In addition to the federal encouragement given to farmers to make farm ponds, the state requires the county commissioners to grant farmers certain tax reductions for building ponds. Under these programs, numerous farmers have built farm ponds to help in the control and conservation of water.

Another aspect of the conservation of our water resources is the prevention of pollution. This is primarily a problem of taking care of

7. K.S.A., 82a-601 to 629.

our human and industrial wastes in such a fashion that our streams and lakes are made wholesome for recreational uses and are safe sources of domestic water supply. The State Board of Health is concerned with this problem and has required many cities and others to modify their waste-disposal practices.

Wildlife Conservation

The first effort to conserve wildlife came in Kansas in 1861, when the hunting of deer and wild turkey was prohibited during certain times of the years.[8] During the next several years similar prohibitions were enacted against killing other animals, but little was done to enforce these laws and no regular enforcement machinery was established. Fish-conservation policies were undertaken, beginning in 1877. They consisted largely of small attempts to restock and distribute fish, to prevent the dynamiting of fish, and to limit the use of nets or seines. It was not until 1905 that a general wildlife-conservation program was undertaken in Kansas by the state Fish and Game Warden. Hunting licenses began to be required, with the fees going into a special fund for conservation. Somewhat later, fish hatcheries were constructed at Pratt, seasons were set up for the protection of wildlife, and county fish and game wardens were appointed to enforce the game laws. For various reasons, the state Fish and Game Warden was placed under the general supervision of the Board of Regents and later the Board of Administration. However, in 1927 the Forestry, Fish and Game Commission was established, and the state Fish and Game Warden was made responsible to it. This Commission was reconstituted in 1961 and now consists of a commissioner appointed by the Governor from each of four districts and one commissioner at large. The Commission selects its own chairman and an executive secretary who takes care of the day-to-day operations of the department.

The conservation program has become extensive with the Commission undertaking the development of parks and lakes to provide a

8. For a historical discussion of wildlife conservation in Kansas, see E. O. Stene, *Wildlife Conservation in Kansas* (Lawrence: Governmental Research Center, Univ. of Kansas, 1946). Information covering other activities in this field is presented in *Government and Natural Resources in Kansas: Wildlife and Recreation* (Lawrence: Governmental Research Center, Univ. of Kansas, 1958), by Joann Worcester.

system of refuges, preserves, and breeding places. State parks were constructed, and counties were authorized to establish parks. In 1934 the federal government gave aid to this movement through the Civilian Conservation Corps and other public-works projects. By July, 1968, there were forty-one state parks and lakes, three game preserves, and other properties.

The Game Division of the Commission seeks to provide Kansas sportsmen with the greatest quantity and highest quality of hunting possible while conserving the broad stock of wildlife. They do this through research and investigation of wildlife, wildlife propagation, and wildlife management. By June 30, 1968, the Commission had entered into agreement with the U.S. Corps of Engineers and the Bureau of Reclamation for the Commission to manage 98,093 acres of water and land in sixteen different locations. Further, the Commission has made arrangements with private owners for land under the U.S. Department of Agriculture Cropland Adjustment program to be opened for public hunting.

The Commission maintains a fish hatchery and rearing ponds to help increase the fishing opportunities and operates sixty-seven major installations at state lakes or park facilities. For purposes of enforcing the fish and game laws, the state is divided into six supervisory regions with a total in 1968 of some fifty-three game protectors.

Besides carrying on such programs, the Commission has worked both with the federal government and other states to expand the state's conservation efforts. For instance, agreements have been reached with Oklahoma to exchange animals and services in order to bring deer back into the state of Kansas. Another similar agreement has been reached with Minnesota, by which Kansas sends Minnesota small channel catfish in return for wall-eyed pike eggs. In such ways the state can exchange programs and enlarge each other's wildlife stocks. The federal government cooperates through the Pittman-Robertson Act and the Dingell-Johnson Act by granting up to 75 per cent of the costs of building approved conservation sites for the propagation and protection of both fish and game.

There are no appropriations from the state general funds for the operation of the Commission. The operating expenses of the Commission come from the sale of licenses and from federal funds. In the 1968

State Lakes and Parks in Kansas: January 1, 1969

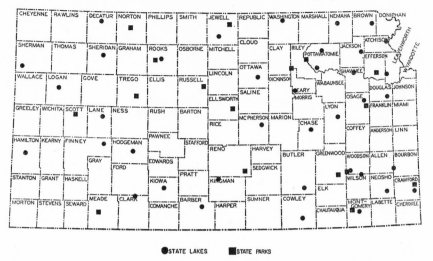

●STATE LAKES   ■STATE PARKS

fiscal year 716,571 licenses and permits of various kinds were issued, resulting in the collection of $2,168,681. Under the Dingell-Johnson Act providing financial aid to states for fish restoration and management, the federal government apportioned $156,847 to Kansas; and under the Pittman-Robertson Act for game conservation, $510,126 became available.

In general, then, the wildlife conservation program of the state, aided very materially by federal funds, is progressing toward a comprehensive plan of fish and game restoration, distribution, and protection. In this program, the state Commission has been helped by the formation of county fish and game clubs, which lend support and prestige to the conservation movement. This, together with an increasing number of people participating in hunting and fishing, has lent impetus to the program of wildlife conservation.

As part of a different but related program the Legislature established the State Park and Resources Authority to plan and develop park facilities. The facilities of the Forestry, Fish and Game Commission are designed to promote fishing, hunting, and related activities. The Park Authority, on the other hand, aims to develop its facilities for camping, picnicing, boating, and swimming. The latter type of use is likely to bring more people, which would be largely incompatible with the uses expected by the Forestry, Fish and Game facilities.

The managing board of the Authority consists of five members appointed by the Governor and four members serving ex officio and without vote—the Governor, the Director of the State Highway Commission, the Chairman of the Forestry, Fish and Game Commission, and the Director of the Kansas Economic Development Commission. The Authority has power to exercise exclusive control over state parks previously acquired and to charge admission fees. It also has the power to issue bonds secured by the revenues from admission fees and in this way to further the park system of the state; but to date this authority has not been used.

Early emphasis was on developing the facilities at Kanopolis. On June 30, 1968, there were seventeen state parks under the management of the Authority, as shown in the accompanying map. All but three of these state parks adjoin federal reservoirs. In fiscal year 1968, fees accounted for $215,849 of a total revenue of $1,447,691. Attendance in recent years has been approximately 4,000,000 persons annually.

State Geological Survey

The State Geological Survey was established in 1889 as a division of the University of Kansas. Supported by state appropriations, its responsibility is to "make as far as possible a complete geological survey of the state of Kansas, giving special attention to any and all natural products of economic importance, in order to determine the character, location, and amount of such products, and to prepare reports on the same."[9] The Geological Survey conducts a wide variety of investigations into all phases of Kansas mineral deposits as well as rocks, geology, and underground water resources. It prepares topographical maps and special reports of its various studies, and serves as a general-information service for the use of all persons interested in Kansas mineral resources.

While the Chancellor of the University is ex officio Director of the Survey, there is an Executive Director who administers the agency. There is also the Mineral Industries Council, appointed by the Chan-

9. *K.S.A.*, 76-322.

cellor under the guidance of the Board of Regents, which advises and consults with the Director in the work of the Survey. The Survey cooperates with such agencies as the U.S. Geological Survey, the Bureau of Mines, the State Mine Inspection Department, the State Division of Sanitation, and state conservation agencies. At present the work of the Survey is carried on by five departments.

The largest subdivision of the Geological Survey is the Department of Mineral Resources, which is concerned with investigations and reports on all rock and mineral materials in the state that have present or potential economic value. Studies are conducted to discover new processes and developments designed to foster new applications or uses for the mineral deposits of the state. Inventories are made of the amounts of various natural resources within the state, and cooperation is extended to federal agencies engaged in similar activities. The section of oil and gas maintains records on oil and gas drilling and production within the state, and conducts surveys of those industries. The ceramics section investigates the utilization of these products made from native Kansas materials. The petrography section studies and identifies specimens of rocks and minerals. The section of geochemistry makes analyses of Kansas rock and minerals, seeking such materials as salt, oil, and shale. A branch of the State Geological Survey is maintained on the campus of the Pittsburg State College.

The second largest subdivision of the Geological Survey, the Ground-Water Resources Department, is concerned with the quantity, quality, and distribution of ground-water resources in Kansas. Reports are made on the water supplies in the various districts, and water levels are measured periodically. Communities and individuals may apply to this division for information and advice concerning water problems. In addition there are departments of Basic Geology, Topographic Surveys, and Publications and Records.

While the Geological Survey is housed at the University of Kansas and comes under the control of the Chancellor of the University and the guidance of the Board of Regents, it is a service organization for the entire state. The Legislature traditionally appropriates funds for the Survey on a line-item basis within the appropriations for the University. In the fiscal year 1969 the Survey received an appropriation of $923,740 for its operation.

Conservation of Oil and Natural Gas

Much of the state action to conserve oil and natural gas has stemmed from the interest of the producers in receiving a "fair price" for their products. Action by individual states alone cannot be effective in these efforts to bring about conservation by regulating the exploitation of the oil resources. While the Federal Oil Conservation Board, which had been created in 1924, sought limited control over the petroleum industry, its efforts did not prevent serious conditions from developing in the industry during the Great Depression.[10]

By 1931, conditions in the industry were such that in Oklahoma and Texas the governors had called out the militia to enforce shutdown orders, which aimed to increase prices by reducing the amount of oil produced. Throughout the remainder of the oil-producing states there was a great deal of unrest and dissatisfaction. It was in this year that the Kansas Legislature passed its first statutes regulating the petroleum industry.[11] Four years later, a similar provision was enacted dealing with conservation of natural gas. The State Corporation Commission is authorized to "regulate the taking of crude oil from any pool within the state" in order to prevent waste[12] or the inequitable taking of such resources from the available supply. To accomplish these ends, the Corporation Commission is empowered to make and enforce rules for conserving and distributing equitably the natural oil resources. These rules include the prorating of allowable extractions among the individual oil companies of the state so as to prevent wasteful or excessive withdrawal of the resource. The total amount allowed to be extracted each month is based on several considerations, including the estimated consumer demand, offers to purchase, and the prevailing market prices. The prorating to each producer is made in relation to the productivity of each well, the efficient utilization of the reservoir energy in the pool, and such other factors as the Commission determines.

In 1935, in conjunction with its own conservation program, Kansas

---

10. For a well-documented discussion of the various approaches to control of petroleum, see Northcutt Ely, *Oil Conservation through Interstate Agreement* (Washington, D.C.: U.S. Government Printing Office, 1933).

11. *Session Laws,* 1931, chap. 226 (*K.S.A.,* 55-601).

12. Waste includes "economic waste, underground waste, surface waste, waste of reservoir energy, and the production of oil or petroleum in excess of transportation or marketing facilities, or reasonable market demands."

participated in the convention which drafted the Interstate Compact to Conserve Oil and Gas.[13] Along with five other states, Kansas ratified this Compact in 1935 and inaugurated a series of cooperative efforts to approach and solve common problems in this field. The Compact has grown to include twenty-two member states, four associate-member states, and five official observers from the federal government and foreign nations. The Compact Commission disseminates information on waste prevention, but does not make up any price extraction schedules or quotas. It depends for funds upon the voluntary contributions of the member states.

Thus, in the interest of conservation, prices are determined by the Corporation Commission. Of course, the immediate effect of such price-fixing is to limit the competition of the oil and gas producers. Problems develop, however, when the prices set by other states substantially differ from those set in Kansas. Particularly is this true when the same general producing field extends into other states.

Conservation of Human Resources

While the primary emphasis of conservation programs is generally considered to lie in the field of natural resources and mineral wealth, increasingly attention has been turned toward the conservation of our human resources. For a long time there has been legislation requiring safety precautions and safe working conditions, and restricting the employment of women and children—all designed to conserve human life and potential. The problem of vocational rehabilitation, the problem of aging, and concern over many facets of social welfare have come to be regarded as part of a program to conserve our human resources.

Several public programs exist in Kansas with responsibility for vocational rehabilitation of the disabled. The Vocational Rehabilitation Service and the divisions of Services for the Blind and Services for the Aging of the Board of Social Welfare attempt to revitalize the lives of individuals who have suffered disabling injuries or disease.

In 1962 the Kansas Citizen's Council on Aging was established at

13. For a history of the Interstate Oil Compact Commission see "A Summary of the Background, Organization, Purposes, and Functions of the Interstate Compact to Conserve Oil and Gas," a report distributed by the Interstate Oil Compact Commission, January, 1947.

the annual conference on aging. This private nonprofit corporation works with the Division of Services for the Aging of the Department of Social Welfare in concern for the aged within the state—a group which is particularly important in Kansas where there is an unusually high percentage of residents over sixty-five. In various programs there is an effort to work for the involvement of older persons in community activities and to encourage them to continue to make meaningful contribution to the life of the community.

In addition to these programs, agencies are set up to help dependent children, and those boys and girls of the state who come into conflict with law-enforcement officials. The Kansas Council for Children was organized in October, 1942, at a meeting of some fifty agencies. It grew out of the efforts of the National Citizens' Committee of the White House Conference on Children in a Democracy and the Kansas members of the 1940 White House Conference. Following the White House Conference of 1950 (known in some quarters as the Mid-Century Conference), where equal emphasis was placed on both *children* and *youth*, the title of the Council was changed to Kansas Council for Children and Youth. The Council acts as a central agency in the attempt to aid underprivileged children and youths who are in need of guidance. In this work, the juvenile (probate) courts, the Children's Division of the State Board of Social Welfare, county welfare workers, and a large number of state courts and agencies are joined by private groups and religious and fraternal organizations. The Council is currently cooperating with the Governor's Interagency Departmental Committee in planning for the 1970 White House Conference on Children and Youth.

The ramifications of the efforts to conserve human life and usefulness are too extensive to be covered in this section; they can be observed in the chapters on labor, social welfare, and education. Increasingly, conservation of human life has come to be recognized as an important part of the whole conservation program.

18 | Highways and the Regulation of Motor Vehicles

Beginning with the military roads built by the national government to connect the frontier forts in the Kansas Territory, one of the more important functions of government in Kansas has been to provide highways over which people may travel. In the 19th century, this was done almost exclusively by the local governments. The Kansas Constitution expressly prohibited the state government from "being a party to carrying out any works of internal improvement."[1] When the automobile came into common use in the present century, it became evident that a coordinated system of highways would be necessary. In 1928 the state Constitution was amended to permit the state to build highways, thus making possible the state highway system of the present day.

The topography and economy of Kansas seem to promote an extensive highway system. Containing primarily agricultural and small urban areas, Kansas needs a closely woven pattern of connecting routes to tie these many localities together. Fortunately the surface of the state lends itself to the establishment of these routes. It has great open plains without mountains, lakes, and other geographical barriers, and consequently lends itself to the construction of arteries of travel.

Kansas has slightly over 134,000 miles of highway, placing it third

---

1. *Kansas Constitution*, Art. 11, sec. 9.

among the states in total mileage; yet Kansas ranks thirteenth among the states in size. Within the state there are over 1,400,000 motor vehicles which make use of these highways, not to mention the great amount of tourist and interstate commercial traffic. As a governmental service, the building and maintaining of highways ranks as a major function of state governments, and is becoming even more important as the number of vehicles using them increases. In recent years over one-third of the total expenditures of state government have been for highways.

Road Systems

Within Kansas there is a variey of road or highway systems. While the classification of highways may seem complicated, it is used to assign the areas of responsibility for different governmental units. Roads and highways are classified according to the level of government responsible for their construction and maintenance. The state, the counties, the townships, and the cities are the major units which administer highway systems.

The state government is responsible for the state highway system. Kansas statutes provide that this system may not exceed 10,000 miles, that the mileage of state highways within each county may not be less than the sum of the east-west and north-south diameters of the county, and that the highways be routed so as to provide connecting routes between the county seats and the major market centers.[2] City streets may be designated as connecting links on the state highway system. The total mileage of the state highway system in August, 1968, was 9,806 miles.

All but a few miles of the state system were constructed with federal aid and are a part of one of the four classifications established by Congress—the interstate system, the primary system, the urban system, and the secondary system.

The interstate system is the major nation-wide highway system. Of the current (July, 1968) total of 41,000 miles in the United States, Kansas has been allocated 840 miles. In Kansas, it consists of the major highway from Kansas City through Topeka and westward toward Denver, Colorado, and a major highway from Kansas City south. The

2. *K.S.A.*, 68–406.

State Highway System: January 1, 1968

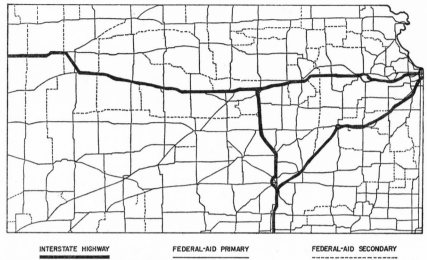

INTERSTATE HIGHWAY   FEDERAL-AID PRIMARY   FEDERAL-AID SECONDARY

Source: Kansas State Highway Department.

interstate system is considered to be of such importance that the national government will pay 90 per cent of the costs of construction. A portion of the turnpike has been designated as a part of the interstate system, though how much credit Kansas will receive in terms of future federal grants for those portions of the turnpike which are included has not yet been determined.

The federal-aid primary system consists exclusively of state highways, and is designated by the Kansas Highway Commission, subject to approval from the United States Bureau of Public Roads. The federal-aid primary system in Kansas contains slightly over 7,000 miles of highway, as shown on the map. The federal government contributes one-half of the costs of constructing highway projects in this and the two following systems.

The connecting links of the federal-aid primary system within cities of 5,000 or more population make up the urban system. For all practical purposes they form one continuous network with the primary system.

The secondary system consists of 2,000 miles of state highway and 20,000 miles of county highways, which have been so designated by the State Highway Commission and the county commissioners respectively.

Inclusions of parts of the state highway are subject to approval by the U.S. Bureau of Public Roads, while the inclusion of county highways is subject to approval by the State Highway Commission and the United States Bureau of Public Roads. Kansas statutes prescribe a complicated formula for apportioning federal-aid mileage among the counties.[3]

Local Road Systems

The classification of local roads is not necessarily related to the federal-aid classification. The fact that a highway is a part of the latter system does not assure that it has any particular local classification. There are two systems of classification prescribed by statute for local roads. Under the first, the county engineer and the county commissioners designate the major county highways as the county primary roads. The remainder of the rural roads are designated as township roads. On the other hand, if the county adopts the county-unit system of highway administration, the engineer and commissioners are required to use the second system of classification and divide all the rural roads into Class A and Class B, which are generally analogous to the county primary and townships roads respectively. Bridges and culverts generally follow the same classification as the roads, except that any structure on a township road with a clear span of more than five feet is the responsibility of the county.

Another major group of local highways is city streets. As was noted above, some city streets may be designated as being connecting links of the state highway system. In third-class cities below 500 population, the State Highway Commission may have exclusive responsibility for the state highways; while in the larger cities there is what amounts in practice to a joint responsibility on the part of both the state and the city. There are approximately 8,500 miles of city streets in Kansas.

3. The formula is: one-fourth on the basis of the ratio of county area to state area; one-fourth based on the ratio of the number of farms in the county to the total number of farms in the state; one-fourth based on the valuation of rural property in the county to the total valuation of rural property; and one-fourth based on the ratio of the average annual vehicle miles of travel on rural roads in the county to the state annual average on such roads in 1936 (excluding state highways). This formula determines the allotment of 92 per cent of the total permissible mileage of 25,000 miles, while the State Highway Commission has discretion in allotting the other 8 per cent (*K.S.A.*, 68-1703).

Local highways on military reservations and other property of the national government are the responsibility of the national government.

The Administration of Kansas Highways

State Highway Commission

All of the state highways except the Kansas Turnpike come under the jurisdiction of the State Highway Commission. This organization is headed by six part-time commissioners, appointed by the Governor for two-year terms. Three members are appointed each year. The commissioners are appointed on a geographical basis, one from each of the six state-highway divisions into which, by law, the state is divided.

The commissioners, upon the Governor's recommendation, appoint the Director of Highways, who serves at the pleasure of the Governor. All other employees of the Commission are civil-service employees except the state Highway Engineer, the Assistant Director of Highways, and the attorney. The latter is an assistant attorney general and is appointed by the Attorney General with the approval of the commissioners. The headquarters are located in Topeka, and there are six operating divisions, with division offices located at Norton, Garden City, Pratt, Chanute, Salina, and Topeka.

The organization, which has over 4,000 employees and is the largest employing state agency, is headed by the Director of Highways. There are staff sections for organization and method work, highway-safety coordination, public information, and legal matters. Other staff activities and operations have been grouped under the Assistant Director of Highway Administration. These include personnel, planning and development, highway safety, data processing, controlling (accounting, auditing, and purchasing), and the Motor Vehicle Department.

The Motor Vehicle Department is relatively separate and independent of other parts of the State Highway Commission, and is organizationally attached to the office of the Director. It was a separate agency until 1939, when the Legislature placed it under the jurisdiction of the State Highway Commission. This Department registers motor vehicles and keeps all the necessary records. Applications for motor-vehicle registration are received by the county treasurers, who collect the required fees. After deducting a small fee for this work, the county treasurers turn over the balance of the money to the state Treasurer and send a complete report to the Motor Vehicle Department concerning each license issued. Owners of motor vehicles are required to establish definite proof of ownership whenever a license is issued or transferred. This is done by requiring the registration of the title of motor vehicles. The purpose of this law is to protect the buyer of any automobile and to assure him that the seller has a clear title to the automobile.

The Motor Vehicle Department examines and issues drivers' licenses and administers the laws concerning drivers' licenses, especially the financial-responsibility law, which requires that persons who are involved in accidents must be financially responsible for the damages incurred, or their licenses may be suspended until they can submit proof that they will be able to pay for such damages in the future.

All courts in Kansas are required to report any case in which a person is found guilty of an offense which requires the suspension of a driver's license. The Motor Vehicle Department is responsible for keeping the necessary records on the suspension of the license. After the period of suspension, the Department restores the license upon application and the completion of any statutory requirements.

The operational work of the Highway Commission is performed under the supervision of the State Highway Engineer. There are sections devoted to the acquisition of rights of way and production control. An assistant state highway engineer is responsible for urban roads, secondary roads, design and location and design concepts.

The construction and maintenance of the state highways and materials are under the the general supervision of another assistant highway engineer. This responsibility is delegated to the Division Engineer in each of the six highway divisions. The Division Engineer has a dual responsibility, being responsible both to the Assistant State Highway Engineer and to the Commissioner from his district. Each division has an assistant division engineer for construction, one for maintenance, and one for materials. Maintenance operations, however, are conducted within defined geographic areas called maintenance districts. There are four or five in each division, with a total of twenty-seven in the state. Each maintenance district has its own headquarters and shops and is supervised by a district supervisor. The districts are further divided for maintenance purposes into sub-districts which have responsibility for about thirty miles of state road. Construction projects are supervised by resident engineers as their number and location demand, without particular reference to the maintenance districts.

The Kansas Turnpike Authority

The Kansas Turnpike Authority is headed by a seven-member board called the "Authority." Four of these members are appointed by the Governor for overlapping four-year terms, while the other three are ex officio members. The Chairman of the Committee on Highways of the Senate and the Chairman of the Committee on Roads and Highways of the House of Representatives are ex officio members. The seventh member of the Authority is the State Director of Highways, who serves as the coordinating agent between the Turnpike Authority and the State Highway Commission.

The board selects a general manager who is in charge of the day-to-day operations. Except when a turnpike project is under construction, the organization consists of an administrative staff at the headquarters located in Wichita and field staffs in charge of maintenance, patrolling the highway, and the collection of tolls. There are eight maintenance districts, with headquarters located at Bonner Springs, Burlingame, El Dorado, Emporia, Matfield Green, Topeka, Wellington, and Wichita. The board has entered into a contract with the State Highway Patrol for patrolling of the turnpike.

Local Highway Administration

County highways are under the jurisdiction of the county commissioners. The commissioners appoint a county engineer subject to the approval of the State Highway Commission. This approval is given except in very unusual circumstances. State law requires that a person appointed as county engineer be a licensed engineer. It is possible for the commissioners to appoint as acting county engineer one who is not licensed. In this case, however, the county must hire a consulting licensed engineer to prepare the plans for secondary roads and do any other technical engineering work which is required.

The county engineer usually supervises the county highway crews, although in some counties the county commissioners in effect act as crew supervisors for their district. More and more counties, however, are moving away from this practice and are turning the supervision of county highways over to their professionally trained county engineer.

The counties of the state may adopt the county-unit road system, under which the county commissioners are in charge of all roads in the county except state highways and city streets. The adoption of the county-unit highway system may be initiated either by the county commissioners or by the voters.[4] The first authorization of the county-unit system was made by the 1917 Legislature.[5] By 1930 the county-unit plan had been adopted by twenty counties. During the 1930's few counties adopted the plan, but beginning in 1944, a sizable number of counties adopted it. In 1968 there were sixty counties operating under the county-unit highway system.

Where the county-unit system is not in operation, the township roads are under the jurisdiction of the township officials. The township trustee usually supervises the road work, although he may ask for the help of the county engineer on technical questions. Most townships have a part-time equipment operator as their sole employee; his duties consist primarily of keeping the township roads graded and drained.

The administrative organization in charge of city streets depends primarily upon the size of the city. Very small third-class cities usually have a part-time equipment operator whose duties are about the same as those of the operator employed by the townships. In other small cities, these duties may be assigned to one of the other employees, such as the marshal or the water plant supervisor. In the larger cities, there is usually a city engineer or street supervisor who has charge of the work of the city street employees. The largest cities, such as Kansas City and Wichita, have large street departments which perform most of the engineering and maintenance functions performed by the State Highway Commission.

The construction and reconstruction of city streets which are connecting links of the state highway system is usually administered by the State Highway Commission under the terms of an agreement signed between the commission and the city for each proposed project. In general, the state bears the cost of constructing the kind of highway it wants through the city. If the city wants additional facilities, such as curb and gutter, which are not in the original state plans, the city will be asked to pay for their costs. In many cases this cost will be less than

4. K.S.A., 68-516.
5. *Session Laws*, 1917, chap. 264, sec. 25 (*K.S.A.*, 68-516).

if the city had to negotiate separately with a contractor for the same facilities. The cost of any right-of-way needed for the connecting link is shared by the state and the city. The share of each will vary, depending usually upon the size and financial resources of the city, but sometimes it also depends upon how anxious each of the two levels of government is to get the project started.

Highway Revenues

The money for highways in Kansas comes from a wide variety of tax sources. At the state level, the bulk of the money comes from taxes on the use of motor vehicles, such as the tax on motor fuels and the fees for annual licenses. The state also receives about 30 per cent of its highway revenues as federal grants-in-aid. This amount, however, is used for construction and is approximately two-thirds of the amount used for that purpose.

Taxes on Motor Fuels

The state taxes the fuels used by all motor vehicles on the highways in the state. The principal tax in this group is the five cents per gallon tax on gasoline and diesel fuel. Four-fifths of the receipts are placed in the state highway fund and the other fifth is placed in the special county road and city street fund. The motor-fuels taxes bring in about $62,000,000 annually.

In addition, in 1955, when the ton-mile tax on trucks was repealed, an additional special two-cent tax was placed on diesel fuel. This latter tax now yields about $5,000,000 a year. Also at this time, an importer-for-use gasoline-tax system was established for truckers. Truckers are required to report quarterly the total number of miles traveled and the number of miles traveled in Kansas, along with the amount of fuel consumed and also the amount purchased in Kansas. They must make a special fuel-tax payment on gasoline which has apparently been consumed in Kansas and upon which no Kansas fuel tax has been paid. Collection under this tax will never be large. Carriers doing interstate business will purchase their fuel in Kansas and pay the fuel taxes then.

Motor-Vehicle Registration and License Fees

The second major source of highway funds at the state level is registration and license fees. The license or registration fees for motor vehicles are based on the weight of the vehicle, so that owners of large trucks pay considerably more than owners of small passenger cars. The receipts from these fees average around $29,000,000 a year.

Federal Aid

The last major source of highway funds for the state is the grants-in-aid provided by the national government for use in constructing highways on the interstate, federal-aid primary, and federal-aid secondary systems. The total amount received by the state from this source varies from year to year, but in the fiscal year 1968 it was over $38,000,000. It consists of payments made for previously approved projects. Some of this is used to pay for the construction of county roads and city streets which are a part of one of the federal-aid systems.

Tolls

The funds of the Turnpike Authority come primarily from tolls collected from persons using the turnpike, although this is supplemented by royalties paid by the vendors of the various services provided on the turnpike, such as operators of filling stations and restaurants. The amount of the toll is set by the Turnpike Authority. The funds are used to pay for the maintenance and operation of the turnpike, and to pay off the bonds which were sold to finance its building. The original bond issue for the Kansas City-Oklahoma turnpike was $160,000,000. At some future session the Legislature might undertake to help pay off the bonds, particularly if Kansas receives a credit in federal grants for parts of the turnpike fully integrated into the interstate highway system. Strictly speaking, the bonds are not an obligation of the state government.

Local Highway Revenues

The primary sources of funds for local highway expenditures are the general-property tax, special assessments on property benefited by improving the highway, and funds returned to the local units by the state. Since property taxes and special assessments are discussed elsewhere in this text, no attempt will be made to give any details on them at this point.

Among the state funds returned to the local units of government is the distribution of $3,600,000 annually from the county and township road fund. The money is distributed to the counties as follows: 40 per cent is divided equally among the 105 counties, and 60 per cent is apportioned and distributed in proportion to the assessed valuation of the county, based upon the previous year's assessment. If the county has adopted the county-unit highway system, all of the money goes to the county. In non-county-unit counties, one-half of the money received by the county is divided among the townships in proportion to township road mileage and is spent by township officials.

A second type of payment made to local units is from what is popularly called the "fifth cent gasoline tax," and is paid into the county-road and city-street fund. The counties receive four million dollars a year from this fund, and the cities receive two and one-half million dollars per year. If there is any balance in the fund at the end of the fiscal year, it is divided equally between the counties and the cities. The county's share of these funds is required by law to be placed in a secondary roads fund, and is to be used to match federal aid for secondary roads under the jurisdiction of the county. Federal aid funds are not handled by any county officials, but are paid to the contractor by the State Highway Commission after the county commissioners have accepted the construction work on the highway.

Those cities which have streets that have been designated as state highway connecting links may, if they choose, receive an annual payment of $750 per lane mile of connecting link. In return for this payment, the city agrees to maintain that portion of the state highway within the city limits.

Reconciling Highway Needs and Revenues

Some idea of the importance of highways as a governmental function in Kansas may be obtained from a study of the amounts spent on highways. For the latest year (calendar year 1967) for which figures are available, the total expenditures on highways amounted to $142,500,000. Of this amount over $95,000,000 was spent on state highways; $9,400,000 on city streets; $31,400,000 on county roads; and $6,700,000 on township roads. The pattern of support for road construction and maintenance in the past may not be the proper or adequate way to finance the function in the future. Shifts of population and changes in the economy and society may reasonably be expected to generate needs for a different highway program and different financing.

There have been a number of surveys on highway needs. For example, in 1961-62 two surveys were made by two national consulting firms. One focused on the need for highways, and the other on the financing to meet the needs. Other studies and plans have been proposed including Governor Docking's highway program presented to the 1968 Legislature and what developed into a legislative counterplan. Charges and countercharges were made, and neither plan was adopted.

What should be the priority of projects in distributing highway revenues? What parts of the system are most in need of construction or reconstruction? In the final analysis there is the reconciliation of the need for an individual project with the need for another individual project somewhere else in the state or within the district. To what extent should the revenues be used on the highways where the traffic is heaviest?

Difficult as it is to get agreement on the general highway needs, it is probably easier to do this than to get agreement on how best to finance the improvements. Some point to the fact that no state has a lower gasoline tax than Kansas as evidence that gasoline taxes should be increased. (Kansas, Missouri, and Texas currently have five-cent-a-gallon taxes.) Since highways constitute a capital improvement whose benefits extend into the future, there is a case to be made for issuing bonds and thereby requiring those benefiting in the future to share in the costs of construction. To others the principle of the users paying for the highways seems particularly reasonable; and they see toll roads as the answer. Underlying the question of financing is that of *which* users should pay. Efforts to try to allocate the costs of highway construction and maintenance according to the costs occasioned by particular users have not developed agreement as to what is the fair share of each group of users. Moreover, there are probably some costs of highways which nonusers should help pay.

Increasingly there are indications of a consensus on needs and on the fact that present revenues are of doubtful adequacy to maintain our highway system at the present standards of sufficiency. With more people and more vehicles, the problems of highway construction and maintenance promise to demand even more attention.

19 The Regulation and Protection of Labor

Historically Kansas has been known as an agricultural state. In 1870, about 59 per cent of those employed in Kansas were engaged in agriculture. Changes of farm methods and transportation have gradually led to a reduction of the relative number of farmers and farm workers, until in 1960 only 13 per cent were so occupied.[1] Paralleling this development has been an increase in the percentage of those in other occupations. In 1960 approximately 33 per cent of those employed were in mining, construction, manufacturing, and transportation. Although state labor laws have some effect on persons in other occupations, they have especial significance for that large and growing portion of our population engaged in manufacturing and related industries.

Industrial Safety

As the Industrial Revolution developed in the western world, machines replaced the tools of handcrafts, and factories took the place of small shops. With the increase in the use of machinery came an increase in industrial accidents. Also, as more and more power was needed, coal mining with its many hazards became an important industry. As mining

1. For further, more detailed information see Table 2: Employed Persons by Industry Groups, Kansas, 1960, p. 10 above.

and industry spread to Kansas the worker experienced greater risks as he earned a living, and safety laws became a necessity.

Mines

The first industrial safety laws in Kansas were directed to the coal-mining industry. In 1875 mine owners were required to provide for escape shafts. Eight years later the Legislature enacted more detailed regulations for mine safety and established the Office of Mine Inspector to examine mines for compliance with the law. Factory inspection was first provided for by the Legislature in 1898, when it designated the Labor Commissioner as ex officio factory inspector and gave him power to order employers to make changes necessary for the safety and protection of employees. Then in 1903, more specific safety regulations were spelled out. Today the industrial safety legislation affects mainly mining and manufacturing and is enforced by the Factory, Mill, and Mine Division of the State Department of Labor.

State mining laws are concerned with both the health and safety of miners. Mines are required to have adequate ventilation in order that fresh air may be continuously supplied and that noxious gases may be removed. At least two openings must exist for all mines, and they must be equipped with means of signaling from the bottom and top of the shaft and within the mine. Sufficient prop timber must be provided, and the use of explosives is regulated. Also, miners in certain positions of responsibility must be examined by the Mine-Examining Board, which grants certificates to those considered qualified. Those positions include shot-firers, shot-inspectors, gas men, fire bosses, hoisting engineers, mine foremen, and assistant mine foremen. Although no detailed legislation has been enacted concerning safety regulations in lead and zinc mines, instructions have been drawn to guide the inspectors of such mines. These instructions are in general similar to the regulations concerning coal mines.

Manufacturing

Industrial safety laws relating to manufacturing establishments apply to all factories, mills, workshops, and mercantile establishments in the state. Safety regulations have been established concerning safeguards for vats, gearing, belting, and shafting of machinery; enclosures for elevators, hoisting-shafts, and well-holes; handrails on stairways;

and adequate fire escapes. In addition, factory inspectors investigate systems of sewage, location and condition of toilets and washrooms, and the lighting, ventilation, and heating systems in places where people are employed. When unsatisfactory conditions are discovered, the Department of Labor issues and enforces orders for correction and elimination of such conditions. There are reinspections to see that recommended changes are made. During the fiscal year ending June 30, 1968, there were 7,221 inspections of establishments which resulted in 6,950 recommendations.

Industrial Accidents

Should safety precautions fail and a worker be accidentally injured, he faces the problem of being unable to work at a time when he has extra medical expenses. In Kansas the worker is assured in almost every case that the state has provided some measure of redress for his injury by means of the Workmen's Compensation Law. This has not always been the case, for when Kansas became a state in 1861, the employer could escape responsibility for an accident if he could show that his injured employee had contributed to the accident by negligence or that another employee had been responsible; or he could argue that the workman assumed the risks of his occupation when he accepted employment. In the eighteen-seventies, the railroads were almost entirely deprived of these common-law defenses; in 1911 the Legislature completely took these defenses away from most other employers by enacting a workmen's compensation law. Claims arising under this law were first handled by the regular court system, but since 1927 these claims have been arbitrated by an administrative agency. At first the Commission of Labor and Industry administered the law, but in 1939 this function was transferred to the Workmen's Compensation Commissioner.

The Workmen's Compensation Law applies to all hazardous employment with three or more employees, including railway and motor transportation, factories, electric and engineering work, laundries, natural-gas plants, certain county and municipal work, and to all mines and building work without regard to the number of workmen employed.[2] In addition, any other employer, including any municipality,

2. For further information see Harry O. Lawson, "The Kansas Workmen's Compensation Act," *Your Government* (Lawrence: Governmental Research Center, Univ. of Kansas), IX (1954), 6, pp. 1-4.

may elect to come within the provisions of the law. Under the law each employer is required either to carry at his expense a workmen's compensation insurance policy from an authorized company, or to become a self-insurer. The former procedure is the more common, for very few businesses or cities are large enough to take the risk of being self-insured.

When a workman in an employment covered by the law is accidentally injured in his work, he reports the accident to the employer, who must in turn report it to the Workmen's Compensation Commissioner. The injured employee receives medical treatment by a physician selected by the employer. The insurance company pays the physician's fees according to a schedule established by law. The employee is notified by the Workmen's Compensation Commissioner of his rights under the act, which include temporary disability payments as well as awards for permanent disability. The maximum sum of the award varies with seriousness of the disability and is set by statute in the amounts shown in the accompanying table.

Payments are made to the injured workman by the insurance company or by the employer if he is self-insured. The workman or his representative and the insurance company representatives endeavor to settle the case, but all settlements are reviewed by the Workmen's Compensation Commissioner. Either the worker or the insurance company may appeal to the Commissioner to arbitrate the claim. Either party may appeal to the proper district court and, on some grounds, may appeal to the Kansas Supreme Court. In the year ending June 30, 1968, 3,750 claims were settled through the Director's office. During this year, 1,268 contested claims were settled and awards made. In about 4 per cent of the cases the awards were appealed to the district courts.

In 1945 Kansas established in the state treasury the Second-Injury Fund. This was done as an inducement for employers to hire persons who are physically handicapped. If such a person is injured, he is compensated just as those injured for the first time, but the insurance company concerned may bring a claim against the Second-Injury Fund to relieve the insurance company of liability.

If such a handicapped person has an accident, it is necessary to determine whether his handicap was responsible in whole or part for

TABLE 41
Maximum Benefits Under Workmen's Compensation: July 1, 1968

Medical and Hospital Allowances	$ 8,500
Death Payment to Dependents	16,500
Burial Allowance	750

Accidental Injury Disability	Number Weeks Payable	Total Compensation At $49 Weekly
General bodily	415	$20,335
Insanity or imbecility	415	20,335
Total paralysis	415	20,335
Loss both eyes	415	20,335
Loss both hands	415	20,335
Loss both feet	415	20,335
Loss both arms	415	20,335
Loss both legs	415	20,335
Arm	210	10,290
Forearm	200	9,800
Hand	150	7,350
Leg	200	9,800
Lower leg	190	9,310
Foot	125	6,125
Eye	120	5,880
Hearing, both ears	110	5,390
Hearing, one ear	30	1,470
* Thumb	60	2,940
* 1st (index finger)	37	1,813
* 2nd (middle) finger	30	1,470
* 3rd (ring) finger	20	980
* 4th (little) finger	15	735
Great toe	30	1,470
Great toe, end joint	15	735
Each other toe	10	490
Each other toe, end joint only	5	245

* Amputation through joint considered loss to next higher schedule. Partial loss of use of a member is compensable on a pro-rata basis. Amputation cases—Allow 10 per cent extra—not over 15 weeks for healing period.
Source: *1968 Session Laws of Kansas,* chap. 102.

the accident. Damages are assessed against the Second-Injury Fund in the proportion to which the handicap contributed to the accident. Employees can elect not to be subject to the Workmen's Compensation

Act, but such an election cannot be made a condition of employment. Employees can waive compensation from injuries arising from industrial diseases.

Conditions of Work for Women and Minors

The industrialization of Kansas took women and children from the home and placed them in the shop and factory. Some employers showed so little concern for the welfare of the women and children employed that legislative action became necessary. Before 1905 there was only piecemeal legislation to regulate child labor. An 1883 law prohibited the employment of children under twelve in mines, and allowed children from twelve to sixteen to work in them only with special permission; a law of 1889 forbade the hiring of children under fourteen as circus performers.

A more comprehensive child-labor law was enacted in 1905, and stricter provisions were added in 1909 and 1917. As this law now stands, employment of children under fourteen years of age in any factory, workshop, theater, mill, cannery, or packing house, or as elevator operators is prohibited. Children under sixteen may not be employed in hotels, restaurants, or mercantile establishments, or in the delivery of messages or merchandise before 7 A.M. or after 6 P.M., or for more than an eight-hour day or a forty-eight-hour week. No child under sixteen may be employed in any mine or quarry, or in any place dangerous or injurious to life, limb, health, or morals. Employers of children under sixteen, in occupations where such employment is permitted, must obtain work permits for each child hired.

Conditions of work for women were first given legislative attention by an act of 1901, which required employers to furnish seats for all women and girls employed as clerks. In 1915 the Industrial Welfare Commission was established to deal with the welfare of both women and minors. The Legislature instructed the Commission to conduct investigations and hold hearings so that it might establish standards of labor, hours, and conditions of work that would be reasonable and not detrimental to health and welfare. The legislative instructions were followed, and a series of industrial welfare orders issued. Although the Commission was abolished in 1921, its duties have been transferred through the various organizational changes to the Labor Department.

Occasionally new orders have been issued, and at any time the labor commissioners may hold new hearings and either change the old orders or add new ones.

At present, industrial-welfare orders apply to women and children in five areas of employment: laundry, manufacturing, mercantile, public housekeeping, and telephone. In laundries and manufacturing establishments a maximum of nine and one-half hours a day and forty-nine hours a week is permitted; in public-housekeeping establishments and in telephone companies the maximum is eight hours a day and forty-eight hours a week; and in mercantile establishments the maximum is nine hours a day, except for one day a week on which it may be ten, and fifty-four hours a week. With the exception of telephone operators, all workers under the orders are prohibited from night work. In manufacturing, laundry, and mercantile business, night work refers to employment after 9 P.M.; in public-housekeeping work it refers to work after midnight. Regulations relate to cleanliness, lighting, ventilation, drinking water, toilets, washrooms, and dressing rooms. Exceptions to the industrial-welfare orders may be granted temporarily by the Women's Division of the Labor Department, as was done in many cases during World War II, to permit women to work on night shifts in war plants.

The orders do not establish minimum wages. Early orders did, but these orders were declared contrary to the Fourteenth Amendment of the U.S. Constitution by the Kansas Supreme Court after similar laws in another state had been held unconstitutional by the U.S. Supreme Court.[3] The U.S. Supreme Court has since reversed itself, so that now it would be legal to fix such wages if the state wished to do so.

There are no general minimum-wage or maximum-hour regulations in Kansas except for those of the national government, which apply only to employment in interstate commerce. However, hours of work for women are regulated by the industrial-welfare orders as noted above; workers in lead and zinc mines and in public work may be employed only eight hours a day; and railroad workers must have at

---

3. The specific case in the Kansas Supreme Court was *Topeka Laundry Co.* v. *Court of Industrial Relations,* 119 Kan. 12 (1925). The Kansas Supreme Court was following the case of *Adkins* v. *Children's Hospital,* 261 U.S. 525 (1923), which was reversed by *West Coast Hotel Co.* v. *Parrish,* 300 U.S. 379 (1937).

least eight hours' rest after working sixteen consecutive hours. In no other occupations are there any regulations of hours of work.

Unemployment Insurance

Periodic booms and "busts" have been characteristic of the American economic system. In good times the worker usually has enjoyed steady employment; in bad times he has experienced unemployment. The evils of unemployment became particularly extreme in the Great Depression of the early thirties. In an attempt to overcome this recurring condition, Congress in 1935 established a joint federal-state employment-security program. After the adoption of an enabling constitutional amendment in the general election of 1936, the Kansas Legislature joined the federal plan by setting up an employment-security program for workers in the state. In its declaration of policy, the Legislature stated that periodic unemployment was a menace to the welfare of the people, and that the state would attempt to counteract this hazard of our economic life by the compulsory accumulation of funds to be used for the benefit of persons unemployed. Under the program an employment-security fund is maintained in the state treasury. To this fund employers pay contributions, and from it unemployed workers receive benefits. A separate account is kept for each employer and for each worker.

TABLE 42

Comparison of Unemployment Insurance Activities: Fiscal Year 1958 and Fiscal Year 1968

	Fiscal Year 1958	Fiscal Year 1968
Initial Claims		
Intrastate	95,324	49,818
Interstate, Kansas Agent	8,605	4,245
Interstate, Kansas Liable	15,436	6,224
Benefits		
Workers Covered by Unemployment Insurance	349,966	414,200
Rate of Insured Unemployment	3.1%	1.4%
Weeks of Unemployment Compensated	545,823	258,035
Amount of Benefit Payments	$15,281,315	$10,622,257

Source: Data from Kansas Employment Security Division.

In general, all employers of four or more workers are required to contribute to the fund. Governmental work, domestic service, agricultural labor, and certain types of employment are not covered by the law. Employers contribute a percentage of their payroll to federal and state funds. The employer's contribution to the federal fund is 0.4 per cent of the first $3,000 of the wages paid. The rate of contributions to the state fund depends upon the experience-rating of each employer. This experience-rating is based upon the amount of unemployment benefits paid to former employees (and thus charged against the employer's account) and upon the total annual payroll of the employer. These rates vary from nothing to 2.7 per cent of wages paid.

To receive benefits, an unemployed worker must file a claim and register for work with a state employment office. Also, he must have worked in the preceding year. Payments are deferred to any worker who is participating in a strike, who has been discharged for misconduct connected with his work, or who has failed to accept an offer for suitable work. Unemployment benefits may run for as long as twenty-six weeks and are never less than $10 a week. The weekly maximum payment in any calendar year is 50 per cent of the average weekly wage paid to all employees in insured work in the preceding year ending June 30. This amount was $53 in 1968. During the fiscal year ending June 30, 1968, an estimated average of 414,200 workers were covered by the employment-security law, and an average number of 4,962 were compensated each week with an average weekly payment of $41.17.

Employment Service

The state maintains a free employment service, with twenty-six area offices to help workers find jobs. These offices seek to aid employers to find suitable employees and workers to find suitable jobs. A worker registers at an office in his locality, is given an occupational classification, and is referred to employers who have job openings for which he is qualified. The worker may receive vocational counseling if he is having difficulty finding a job because of restricted opportunities in his regular line of work.

The service also administers, under contractual arrangements with the federal government, two programs for unemployment compensation for veterans and a program for unemployment compensation for federal

TABLE 43

Number of Placements by Industry: Fiscal Year 1958
and Fiscal Year 1968

| | Fiscal Year 1958 | | Fiscal Year 1968 | |
	Total	Per Cent	Total	Per Cent
All placements	130,257		83,721	
Agriculture	37,374	28.7	16,102	19.2
Nonagriculture				
Mining	1,280	1.0	532	.6
Contract Construction	19,196	14.7	8,438	10.1
Manufacturing	11,127	8.5	11,440	13.7
Transportation, Communication,				
and Other Public Utilities	7,193	5.5	6,403	7.6
Wholesale and Retail Trade	20,786	16.0	16,707	20.0
Finance, Insurance and				
Real Estate	2,008	1.5	1,380	1.6
Service Industries (Except				
Private Households)	11,220	8.6	10,191	12.2
Private Households	18,420	14.1	9,681	11.6
Government	1,638	1.3	2,805	3.4
Other	15	0	42	0
Total Nonagriculture	92,883	71.2	67,619	80.8

Source: Data from Kansas Employment Security Division.

employees. In the fiscal year ending June 30, 1968, the service placed 83,721 employees in the industries shown in the accompanying table.

Particular efforts are made during wheat-harvest time when there is great demand for added farm workers. Special attention is given to directing migrant workers and others to areas where they are most needed.

Appropriately, the local employment offices handle applications for unemployment compensation. In this way the office knows of the local employment situation and can determine whether there are appropriate job opportunities or whether an otherwise qualified application for unemployment compensation should be approved.

Labor Unions

In an effort to make themselves more effective in protecting their interests in higher wages and better working conditions, workers have sought to organize themselves into labor unions. According to available information, the first union in Kansas was the Leavenworth Typographical Union organized in 1859. Since that time organized labor has grown until there are now over 940 local unions with a total membership of over 125,000.

Although labor organizations in many places have had to struggle to obtain the right of collective bargaining, this right has never been questioned in Kansas. The closed shop, in which a person must be a member of a union before he may be employed, was permitted until 1955. The right of workers in certain industries to strike was limited by the industrial court law of 1920, discussed later.

Injunctions in labor-management disputes are permitted under a 1913 law only when previous notice has been given and when the parties to be enjoined have been heard, unless it appears to the satisfaction of the court that immediate and irreparable injury is likely to ensue.

The Legislature in 1943 enacted a comprehensive labor-relations law. Under this law workers are permitted to organize and to bargain collectively with employers on matters concerning hours of employment, rate of pay, working conditions, and other grievances. All labor organizations are required to file their constitution and bylaws with the Secretary of State and to report annually certain information about the union. An employer is forbidden to interfere with employees in their efforts to organize and bargain collectively, and is also forbidden to interfere in the administration of any labor organization. Workers are restricted from picketing beyond the area of the dispute, from picketing in a nonpeaceful manner, and from coercing other employees in the enjoyment of their legal rights. Penalties are provided for violation of the act.

Changes were made in the act in 1955[4]. Employers were not to deduct union dues without specific individual authorizations and were not to employ spies upon employees or their representatives. The closed shop was forbidden, and it was made unlawful to violate the terms of a collective-bargaining agreement. The Labor Commissioner issues rules and regulations for conducting and canvassing union elections,

4. Portions of the 1943 act had been held unconstitutional in the U.S. Circuit Court of Appeals in *Stapleton* v. *Mitchell,* 60 F. *Supp.* 51. These sections were omitted or amended in the 1955 law.

for selecting collective-bargaining units, and for approval of union agreements and strike votes. The Labor Commissioner was specifically authorized to appoint mediators in labor disputes. The 1955 Legislature also passed a "right to work" bill which sought to prohibit union- as well as closed-shop agreements. Much to the consternation of many of the rural legislators, the Governor vetoed this bill. The matter became an election issue and was submitted to the voters as a constitutional amendment in 1958. The amendment passed, so that now union shops are outlawed.

Labor-management disputes have seldom caused any great difficulty to the economy of Kansas. The Labor Commissioner often works informally to settle such disputes, and he continually cautions labor unions against the use of violence. In the 1967 calendar year 20,400 laborers in Kansas lost on strike 113,000 days of work. This was a percentage of 0.09 per cent of total working days lost by strike at a time when the national average was 0.30 per cent.

Administrative Organization

For its first twenty-two years of statehood Kansas had no administrative agency for protecting or regulating labor. Until then the few labor laws which existed were enforced by the regular law-enforcement agencies. In 1883 the Legislature enacted a mine-safety law and created the office of Mine Inspector to enforce its provisions. Two years later the Bureau of Labor and Industrial Statistics under the direction of a labor commissioner was established. The Bureau was instructed by the Legislature to collect statistical details relating to labor and industry in the state and to present these statistics in annual reports to the Governor, who was to submit them biennially to the Legislature.

From 1885 to 1899 the Labor Commissioner was appointed by the Governor, with the consent of the Senate; but in the latter year the State Society of Labor and Industry was set up, and the secretary of the society was designated as ex officio Labor Commissioner in charge of the State Bureau of Labor and Industry. At the same time the State Association of Miners was organized by statute, and its secretary was ex officio Mine Inspector. Both organizations were composed of representatives of local associations. Then in 1901 the state Legislature provided for the establishment, in all first- and second-class cities, of free employment agencies which were placed under the general supervision of a director, appointed by the Governor. In 1913 these three agencies were consolidated into the Department of Labor and Industry. Two years later the Commission of Industrial Welfare was created in conjunction with the Department, and was given the responsibility to establish standards of wages, hours, and conditions of labor for most women and children.

After World War I there were many labor-management disputes throughout the United States. These disagreements came dramatically to Kansas in the fall of 1919, when the miners of southeastern Kansas, a closely organized group, struck as a part of a nationwide coal strike. No decision was reached between the miners and the operators, and the state took over the mines for twelve days before an agreement was made. Following this episode the Governor called a special session of the Legislature, which established the Court of Industrial Relations.[5] The Court had powers of arbitration over wages, hours, working conditions, and rates of businesses associated with the public interest, with authority to make decisions in these matters in order that reasonable continuity and efficiency in the operations of industries might be maintained. The Court had a stormy five-year career, receiving—for the most part—opposition from organized labor in the state. In 1923 the U.S. Supreme Court declared part of the Industrial Court Law unconstitutional.[6] The Court was abolished in 1925, though some sections of the law were allowed to continue in effect.[7] When the Court was abolished, many of its functions were assigned to the Public Service Commission.

By 1927 it had become evident that the Workmen's Compensation Law of 1911 placed too great a burden on the regular judicial system of the state. The arbitration of claims arising under the law was made the responsibility of the Public Service Commission. This function and the administration of the labor laws were given to a newly created Commission of Labor and Industry when the Public Service Commission was reorganized in 1929. The Commission of Labor and Industry oper-

5. Domenico Gagliardo, *The Kansas Industrial Court: An Experiment in Compulsory Arbitration* (Lawrence: Social Science Studies, Univ. of Kansas, 1941).

6. *Wolff Packing Co.* v. *Court of Industrial Relations,* 262 U.S. 522.

7. *Session Laws,* 1925, chap. 258.

ated ten years and was then abolished and replaced by two chief agencies in the field today—the Department of Labor and the Workmen's Compensation Commissioner.

Department of Labor

The Department of Labor is headed by the Commissioner of Labor, appointed by the Governor with the consent of the Senate. He is adminstrator and coordinator of the Department and has final responsibility for all decisions pertaining to policy. He represents the state in national conferences and conventions and thus gains valuable information. By statute, the Commissioner is required to be a member in good standing of a labor organization. Ordinarily all division heads in the Department are likewise union members. The work of the Department is performed by six divisions, and the Apprenticeship Council associated with it.

Employment-Security Division. The Employment-Security Division administers the employment-security law, by which unemployment benefits are paid to eligible workers during periods of involuntary unemployment, and the unemployed are aided in finding suitable work. The unemployment-compensation section receives the required contributions from employers, makes benefit payments to unemployed workers, and keeps separate records for each employer and employee concerned. The employment-service section counsels employees and helps place employees in jobs for which they are qualified. The administrative cost of the Employment-Security Division is paid by the national government through a federal grant-in-aid.

Industrial-Safety Division. The Industrial-Safety Division has the responsibility of enforcing safety conditions for factories, boilers, and mines and for enforcing industrial welfare orders for women and minors. The factory and mill section has factory inspectors who make regular and systematic investigations in factories, mills, workshops, mercantile establishments, and other places of employment in order to check compliance with the safety laws of the state. Not only do they inspect, but they also assist in the development of programs of accident prevention. A separate section of the Division is charged with inspecting some 441 boilers and registering 1,904 boilers which are covered by insurance and are inspected by deputy inspectors.

The Board of Coal-Mine Examiners, which was created in 1955 in the Department of Labor to assume the powers and duties of the previous Mine-Examining Board, is associated in its activities with the Industrial-Safety Division. The Board examines shot-firers, shot inspectors, gas men, fire bosses, hoisting engineers, mine foremen, and assistant mine foremen. One of the Board must be a practical coal miner, one a coal-mine operator, and one a citizen of good standing. The members are appointed by the Labor Commissioner with the approval of the Governor. During the fiscal year ending June 30, 1968, inspectors made 681 inspections which resulted in forty recommendations.

A fourth section of the Division, the women's and children's section, carries no inspections for the purpose of obtaining compliance with industrial welfare orders for women and minors. These orders have been promulgated by the Department of Labor and have the effect of law. Inspectors examine working conditions relating to cleanliness, ventilation, lighting, drinking water, toilet facilities, and safety guards on machines. Investigations occur both regularly and whenever complaints are received. An attempt is made to secure compliance with the regulations by willing cooperation, using compulsion only when persuasion fails.

Research Division. The Research Division is the fact-finding unit of the Department. It gathers statistical data on labor and industry so that the formulation of related public policy may be based upon adequate information. The Division maintains close contact with the Bureau of Labor Statistics of the U.S. Department of Labor and compiles data in such a manner that it can be used directly by the national bureau. A monthly publication, *Kansas Labor and Industrial Bulletin,* is issued by the Division. This bulletin presents statistical tabulation showing trends in employment, hours of work, wages, retail prices of food, and building construction. In addition, it promotes industrial safety.

Wage-Hour Division. A Wage-Hour Division is provided by statute, but no separate division is in operation, for Kansas has no laws establishing either a floor to wages or a ceiling to hours for all industry in intrastate commerce. However, an eight-hour-day law is in effect for public work and for lead and zinc mines, and the Department administers this law. The wages and hours of the many workers engaged in interstate commerce are subject to the federal Fair Labor Standards Act and federal regulation.

Labor-Management Relations Division. The Division regulates administratively certain aspects of collective bargaining between unions and some Kansas employers. Within limits, workers are guaranteed the right to organize and bargain collectively. Jurisdiction by the state is limited to intrastate labor relations and to those areas which Congress has ceded to the states. The Commissioner of Labor is authorized to appoint mediators in labor disputes and seeks to promote sound labor-management relations.

Apprenticeship-Training Division. In conjunction with the Apprenticeship Council, this Division promotes voluntary apprenticeship training in an effort to provide an adequate skilled work force. The Council is composed of eight part-time members, four representing labor and four representing management. The Council encourages the establishment of voluntary apprenticeship agreements and joint apprenticeship committees, composed of equal representation of employers and employees, which draw up apprenticeship standards in particular trades within their communities. The Council approves and registers these standards and the agreements made under them and issues certificates of completion to apprentices who complete their training and show competency in their trade. On July 1, 1968, there were 1,263 apprentices working under active agreements.

Workmen's Compensation Director

The Workmen's Compensation Director, who is appointed by the Governor for a four-year term, administers the Kansas Workmen's Compensation Law. The Director and six regular and four special examiners arbitrate claims for compensation contested by injured workers, employers, or the insurance companies. About 15,000 accidents were reported during the year ending June 30, 1968. The Director issues necessary rules and regulations and receives reports concerning accidents, settlements reached, payment of compensation, and releases of liability.

Fair-Employment Practices

In 1949 after a concentrated effort for the passage of a fair-employment-practices act, the Legislature established a temporary commission to study and report on acts of employment discrimination in the state.

This temporary commission reported to the Governor in March, 1951, as follows:

"1. Employment discrimination exists in the State of Kansas against citizens of the United States, at least on the basis of race, color, and national origin.

"2. Such discrimination is practiced by employers and labor unions, and usually manifests itself in general confinement of work to areas of unskilled, semi-skilled, and service or maintenance occupations, or in not hiring people from certain groups in the community."[8]

While a bill to create a permanent antidiscrimination committee was allowed to die in a legislative committee in 1951, a much-amended compromise measure was passed in 1953. A five-member Kansas Anti-Discrimination Commission was established and given funds to employ a small staff. The Commission was given the responsibility to develop a broad-range educational program designed to prevent and eliminate discrimination in employment against persons because of race, color, religion, or national origin and to receive and investigate complaints alleging discrimination in employment against persons because of race, color, religion, or national origin.[9] As established, the Commission had no regulatory powers and was not allowed to publicize its findings on individual violations. Subsequent sessions of the Legislature have significantly enlarged the powers and duties as well as appropriations of the Commission. Federal legislation requiring federal agencies to turn over cases to state antidiscrimination agencies also contributed to the increase in the number of complaints filed with the Commission.

Despite the enlargement of its powers, the Commission has centered its activities on publicizing the general value of nondiscriminatory employment practices. The Commission seeks to persuade and encourage nondiscriminatory practices, and it uses with restraint its power to issue cease-and-desist orders and to see them enforced through the courts.

In addition to its concern in the area of employment practices, the Commission is charged with enforcing the state policy of preventing

8. Kansas Commission Against Discrimination in Employment, *Report of Survey Findings on the Existence of Employment Discrimination Aganst Kansas Citizens Because of Race, Religion, Color, or National Origin* (Topeka: 1951), p. 2.

9. *K.S.A.*, 44-1001 to 1008.

discrimination in hotels, motels, cabin camps, restaurants, trailer courts, bars, taverns, barbershops, beauty parlors, theaters, skating rinks, bowling alleys, billiard parlors, amusement parks, recreation parks, swimming pools, lakes, gymnasiums, mortuaries, and cemeteries which are open to the public.

20 | Regulation of Business

Various special considerations apply to particular segments of the business community and have occasioned special state action. The monopolistic and essential nature of the services offered by that broad category of businesses referred to as public utilities has resulted in special state laws and agencies to regulate these businesses in the public interest. To help protect the public in the safekeeping of their savings and in their efforts to insure against certain of the catastrophes of individual life, laws have been passed regulating banks, savings and loan companies, and insurance companies. The sale of alcohol and intoxicating beverages has posed so many problems that there are state laws closely regulating this type of business.

One of the most general state regulations of business grows out of the state's power to grant charters of incorporation. Increasingly business has found it desirable to use the corporate form in conducting its affairs. Except for those desiring to engage in a limited number of special types of business, any group wanting to incorporate must file an application with the State Charter Board, which is an ex officio group consisting of the Attorney General, the Bank Commissioner, and the Secretary of State. Corporations which are organized in other states and which do business within the state must make somewhat similar applications. Both Kansas and out-of-state corporations are required to file annual reports of their finances with the Secretary of State. Private businesses, cooperative societies, cooperative marketing associations, religious, charitable, and other nonprofit organizations may also be incorporated.

In addition to these regulations which the state sets as a condition for incorporation, businesses whether conducted individually, in partnership, or in the corporate form are subject to the normal exercise of the police powers of the state. Frequently the Legislature, in the exercise of these powers, establishes a special regulatory board or commission to carry out the details of the regulatory policy which it establishes. Such agencies are broadly referred to as independent regulatory commissions. They perform executive, quasi-legislative, and quasi-judicial functions. The goal of such regulatory agencies is to provide protection of the public interest and also the interest of special groups that may be involved. This chapter is devoted largely to discussion of each of the several major state agencies involved in this regulation.[1]

The Corporation Commission

The State Corporation Commission, the chief state agency regulating public utilities, is the result of a series of administrative reorganizations over the last eighty-five years. Its predecessors include two public-service commissions, two public-utilities commissions, two boards of railroad commissioners, the Court of Industrial Relations, and one body with the rather singular title of the Court of Visitations.[2] The function of the Corporation Commission is to supervise generally all public utilities and common carriers doing business within the state, as well as to regulate other matters concerned with the public interest.

The State Corporation Commission is composed of three members who are appointed by the Governor with the advice and consent of the Senate and who serve full-time.[3] No more than two members may be

1. Various aspects of regulation of particular types of industry are discussed in other chapters—as, for example, the regulation of the sale of certain products used on farms, discussed in the chapter on agriculture.

2. For a history and discussion of the Kansas State Corporation Commission from the first Railroad Commission in 1883 to the Corporation Commission in 1945, see E. O. Stene, *Railroad Commission to Corporation Commission* (Lawrence: Bureau of Government Research, Univ. of Kansas, 1945).

3. *K.S.A.*, 74-601.

of the same political party. Appointments are for terms of four years, with the members electing one of their number to be the chairman. No person owning any stocks or property of any utility or common carrier is eligible for appointment. Perhaps unique is the "antinepotism" clause, which forbids the appointment or employment by the Commission of any individual related by blood or marriage to any member of the Commission. Salaries are $15,000 annually for the chairman, and $14,500 for the other two Commissioners.

According to the statutes, all provisions pertaining to the powers of the Corporation Commission are to be "liberally construed," and the statutes further point out that "all incidental powers necessary" are expressly granted and conferred upon the Commissioners.[4] Such a policy stems from a recognition of the difficulties attendant upon control of such complex business enterprises. In operation, the Corporation Commission sets forth the rules and regulations to be followed by the utilities. Failure to comply with these rules, or complaint regarding just and reasonable service, is followed by a hearing in which the Commissioners, singly or otherwise, hear the arguments on the case. This is followed by a conference of the Commissioners in which a decision is reached and a ruling is made. Although only one Commissioner may hear the case, the signature of at least two members is required to initiate an order. Hearings are conducted in a manner similar to legal-court procedure, but with more informality and discussion. In general, the more routine cases are heard by a single Commissioner.

Financing the State Corporation Commission is done largely through fees and assessments made on those engaged in the activity being regulated. In the utility field, this means an assessment on the gross revenue of the privately owned public utility. Motor carriers are charged fees for registration of their equipment. Security brokers and agents are likewise charged registration fees. Special fees are charged for inspecting new issues of securities. In general, revenues of the various sections of the Commission are related to the cost of their operation. The Securities Division and the Motor-Carrier Division, however, generally have revenues substantially in excess of the cost of operation. Normally there is a balance of about $540,000 in the latter Division, which goes to the counties for secondary roads.

4. K.S.A., 66-141 to 148.

Regulating Public Utilities

Public utilities are defined as "every corporation, company, individual, association of persons, . . . that now or hereafter may own, control, operate, or manage, except for private use, any equipment, plant . . . for the transmission of telephone messages, or for the transmission of telegraph messages in or through any part of the state, or the conveyance of oil and gas through pipe lines . . . except pipe lines less than 15 miles in length . . . or for the operation of any trolley lines, street, electrical or motor railway doing business in any county in the state, also all dining car companies, and all companies for the production, transmission, delivery, or furnishing of heat, light, water, or power."[5] Municipally owned utilities are specifically excluded from regulation by the Commission.

Within the Commission there are two divisions charged with the administration of this public-utility law—one for regulating common carriers and another for certain other utilities. Every public utility is required to furnish reasonably efficient and sufficient service and to establish just and reasonable rates for service, as well as just and reasonable rules and regulations.[6] Unjust, discriminatory, or unduly preferential regulations or rates are declared to be unlawful and void. All public utilities must file with the Corporation Commission copies of all schedules, rates, and regulations pertaining to any and all services rendered by the company. The Commission, either on its own initiative or upon the complaint of others, may investigate any utility company. If, after full hearing and investigation, the Commission decides that the submitted rules or rates are unjust, it may substitute such rates and regulations as it considers to be just and reasonable. Moreover, if, upon complaint, any service is discovered to be inefficient, insufficient, or unduly preferential, the Commission may order such service or acts as shall be acceptable.

Upon receiving a complaint in writing against any public utility made by any corporation, society, body politic, municipality, or taxpayer, the Commission is required by statute to make an investigation with or without notice to the organization named in the complaint. Following this investigation, it may order a hearing if the Commis-

5. *K.S.A.*, 66-104.
6. *K.S.A.*, 66-107.

sioners feel that the complaint is substantiated. Having held a formal, public hearing, preceded by due notice to the interested parties, the Commission may order such changes in rates, regulations, and service as it feels proper. All interested parties have the right to be heard at these hearings and to enforce the presence of witnesses and the submission of records involved in the subject matter of the hearing.

Various provisions limit the power of the Commission in ordering or denying rates, regulations, service, or changes. Any party dissatisfied with a decision may apply for a rehearing. In the event that this is denied or adversely decided, appeal may be had to the district court. Any public utility desiring to alter its rules, rates, or services must file a petition with the Commission, receive its approval for the changes, publish notice of the changes to the public, and wait thirty days before applying the changes.

In addition to the investigative processes and the system of hearings, the Corporation Commission exercises its supervision by requiring annual, regular, and special reports from all public utilities. The issuance of securities and declaration of dividends must receive prior approval from the Commission, and illegal or speculative dealings are forbidden. Before a utility may transact business within the state it must receive a certificate of public convenience and necessity. The Commission has access to all company records, and, in addition, requires a report on each accident involving human life or serious injury occurring upon the premises of the public utility.

Municipalities may contract with and grant franchises to public utilities in terms and conditions not inconsistent with the state utilities statutes. In the event of municipal action granting a franchise, citizens of the municipality may complain to the Commission on the grounds that such action is unreasonable, detrimental to the best interests of the city, or against public policy. The Corporation Commission holds a hearing on the charges, and if the complaint is upheld, the Commission recommends such changes in the ordinance or contract as may be required to make the franchise acceptable. If, after twenty days, the governing body of the municipality has not acted, the Commission may begin proceedings in a district court against the municipal governing body and the public utility, in the name of the state of Kansas, to have the ordinance or resolution set aside in whole or in part.

In the regulation of common carriers and of motor carriers which is discussed in the next section, there is the complicating problem of the interstate operation of most of the railroads and many of the motor carriers. All rates and rate changes must be filed with the Commission before they become effective. Moreover, the Commission must approve the rates and rate changes of common carriers before they become effective. In respect to through freight rates which the Commission finds unreasonable, it can ask the carrier to reduce them and appeal to the U.S. Interstate Commerce Commission if the carrier refuses. In addition to the general regulation of railroads by the Commission there are many specific statutory provisions concerning service and operation. The distribution, movement, and unloading of railroad cars, headlights on locomotives, announcements of passenger train arrivals, maintenance of signals, and issuance of passes are illustrative of some of the details of statutory regulations. Still in effect is an 1893 law that any railroad operating through a county seat must stop at least one passenger train daily going in each direction.[7]

Regulating Motor Carriers

A separate division of the Commission is charged with the regulation of motor carriers. Motor carriers are classified and are subject to regulation by the Commission in three different groups. Public motor carriers are those which offer their services to any who may choose to employ them. Contract motor carriers are those which transport for hire but are not classified as public motor carriers. Private motor carriers are those operated in the transportation of the owner's products or commodities, farm vehicles, and hearses. Private motor carriers which operate within a radius of twenty-five miles of their home city, school buses, and carriers used when no commercial service is available are excepted from regulation.

In general, contract carriers are not as closely regulated as public carriers, but in the course of effective regulation of the public carriers it has been found necessary to regulate the contract carriers. Both public and contract carriers must obtain approval of the Commission before they may operate. If contract carriers compete with public carriers, the Commission fixes minimum rates and charges for contract

7. *K.S.A.*, 66-2, 100.

carriers. Before any carrier, including those operating in interstate commerce, may operate in Kansas, certain information must be supplied to the Commission. All motor carriers subject to the supervision of the Commission must furnish proof of coverage by liability insurance before they will be allowed to operate within the state. Public carriers, railroads and motor alike, must obtain prior approval of the Commission to discontinue service.

In order to control the flow of commercial highway traffic into and out of the state, a system of ports-of-entry has been established. These ports are located on highways designated as entrance routes into the state for commercial use and are not more than fifteen miles from the state border. The operation of these ports is controlled by a three-member ex officio board composed of the Director of Revenue, the Director of Highways, and the Chairman of the State Corporation Commission. The ports-of-entry regulate the transportation of liquid fuel into and out of the state, help to prevent the improper use of the highways, and facilitate the collection of motor-carrier fees.

Control of Securities

In order to protect its citizens from fraud, the state of Kansas, as early as 1911, passed the famous "blue sky" law to prevent the sale of fraudulent securities. Today, the Securities Division of the State Corporation Commission is charged with the task of controlling the issuance and sale of securities in the public interest. To control securities the Legislature established three categories of such instruments: The first category is the "exempt" securities which do not fall under the supervision of the Division; the second is the securities which may be registered by notification; the third is the securities which require approval before registration. In the first category, the exempt class, are securities issued by the United States, states, or other political subdivisions including local units of governments which have the powers of taxation or assessment. Other securities in this class include those representing an interest, or obligation of, a national bank or federal agency and securities of private companies which are specifically regulated by state or federal agencies, such as railroad, insurance, banking, or savings and loan companies. The second category of securities includes those issued by a company which has been in operation for at least five years and which meets certain requirements as to net earnings, dividends, and stock, and those secured by first mortgages on agricultural land or improved city property subject to restriction as to the amount of money to be secured. Such securities are entitled to registration by the Commission upon notification. The third category includes all those securities which do not come within the first two classes of securities.

When registering a security by notification, the company, corporation, or trust which has qualified under the provisions of the statutes must submit to the Corporation Commission a statement of the income and financial standing of the issuer; the amount, price, and sales commission of the securities to be issued; a copy of the security and of the circular to be used in offering the security for sale; and information concerning the business, its incorporation, and location. To sell securities which fall into the third category, a business must submit a detailed statement to the Corporation Commission and must receive its approval prior to sale. This statement includes all the facts needed for simple notification plus more detailed information on the income and assets of the company, the character, value, and details of the plan for marketing the securities, and "any additional information that the Corporation Commission may deem necessary," all of which must be verified by oath. The Corporation Commission examines the proposed security issue and if it is deemed advisable, makes such detailed examinations, investigations, or audits as it considers necessary. This may include the appointment of appraisers to study the property of the applicant.

In addition to the registration of securities, the Corporation Commission also regulates the brokers and agents who sell securities within the state. All brokers and agents, including those selling securities in the exempt class, must register with the Commission. An applicant for broker's registration must file a form with the Corporation Commission which gives his business affiliations, general plan of business, and other information. In addition, he must be bonded in the amount of $5,000. This application for registration may be refused, or once granted, may be revoked after notice and hearing if the Corporation Commission determines that his actions or character of financial solvency indicates his inability to transact the business of a broker in line with statutory requirements. The application of an agent for registration must be accompanied by the signature of some person authorized to sell securities. This application may be denied or revoked after a hearing for misrepresentation, conviction of fraud, or any one of several other factors bearing on his general reliability as an agent selling securities.

In addition to the powers of registration and investigation which have been previously mentioned, the Corporation Commission has a general power of inspection and investigation of any phase of the problem of securities regulation which it considers necessary. Likewise, the Commission has control of advertising relating to this field, and general supervision of the accounting methods of the firms registered, as well as the right to seek injunctions against any company or individual to prevent fraud or other abuse.

Conservation Activities

The operations of the Commission in conserving oil and natural gas have been referred to earlier in chapter 17. The effect of these activities is essentially regulatory as viewed by the businesses concerned. In addition to controlling the amount of oil and gas allowed to be extracted, the Conservation Division of the Commission supervises the plugging of oil wells.

Commissioner of Insurance

Kansas adopted its first insurance laws in 1871. The original statutes were amended at various times over the following years, and in 1925 the Legislature appointed a special commission to investigate and to recommend changes in the laws pertaining to insurance.[8] The Commission formulated a code which was adopted by the Legislature in 1927. The new compilation contained many of the old statutory sections, combined others, and introduced some new provisions. Additions to the code have been made since 1927, but the general outlines of the regulative system are essentially the same as those of the original code. If there is any tendency in later legislation, it is to strengthen the code and to add power to the office of Commissioner. All types of insurance come under the supervision of the Department of Insurance.

The personnel of the Department of Insurance, as created by the code of 1927, consists of the Commissioner, an assistant commissioner, actuaries, two special attorneys, an executive secretary, policy exam-

---

8. *Session Laws*, 1925, chap. 188.

iners, two field representatives, and a secretary of the Commissioner. In addition to these employees, the Commissioner is authorized to appoint under civil service such other employees as are necessary.[9]

The office of the Commissioner is an elective post, filled every two years at the general election.[10] The occupant must be an elector, a person well versed in insurance, and without any interest in an insurance company except as a policyholder.[11] He must execute a bond in the amount of $20,000 prior to entering the office.[12] In the event that the office is vacated during a term, the Governor is empowered to fill the office by appointment, with consideration given to the required qualifications.[13] The Assistant Commissioner is empowered to perform all acts for the Commissioner in his absence; and the Commissioner is specifically made responsible for the acts of any of his assistants or employees.[14] The Commissioner's salary was increased to $12,650 in 1969.

The duties of the Commissioner include "the administration of all laws relating to insurance, insurance companies, and fraternal benefit societies doing business in the state, and all other duties which are or may be imposed upon him by law."[15] In order to accomplish these broad ends the Legislature gave the Commissioner "general supervision, control and regulation of corporations, companies, associations, societies, exchanges, partnerships, or persons authorized to transact the business of insurance, indemnity or suretyship in this state" and stipulated that he "shall have the power to make all reasonable rules and regulations necessary to enforce the laws of this state relating thereto."[16]

The statutory powers of the Commissioner are both broad and strong, and the state courts have consistently been reluctant to interfere in the application of those powers. Chief Justice Dawson summed

9. *K.S.A.*, 40-110.
10. *K.S.A.*, 40-106. Since 1927 only three persons have served as Commissioner of Insurance.
11. *K.S.A.*, 40-109.
12. *K.S.A.*, 40-107.
13. *K.S.A.*, 40-106.
14. *K.S.A.*, 40-110.
15. *K.S.A.*, 40-102.
16. *K.S.A.*, 40-103.

up the State Supreme Court's position when he stated, "The statutory powers conferred on the commissioner of insurance are necessarily broad and comprehensive. It is a well-known historical fact that in bygone years the people of this state suffered many evils at the hands of unsound and ill-managed companies; and the pertinent legislation dealing with that evil has been a progressive and continuous expansion of the state's supervisory authority over insurance companies which eventually culminated in the enactment of the insurance code of 1927."[17]

The provisions of the insurance code are extensive, and their general effect is to provide close scrutiny over insurance-company practices and policies. In order to engage in the insurance business, a company, either domestic or out-of-state, must receive a certificate of authority from the Commissioner.[18] To receive this certificate the company must file its charter, bylaws, forms of contract, and statement of financial position. The Commissioner's office then investigates the company, either through its own investigators, through recognized investigative agencies, or, in the case of an out-of-state company, through the facilities of another state's commissioner.

If satisfied with a company's integrity and financial condition, the Commissioner issues a certificate of authority which is valid until the next May, when all such certificates expire annually and must be renewed. The act of granting a certificate has been held by the courts to be a discretionary act and not subject to a writ of mandamus.[19]

Supervision of the certified companies by the Commissioner includes passing approval on their plans of operation, and prescribing their methods of bookkeeping and accounting. The investment of capital, surplus reserves, and other funds is likewise closely regulated, and the valuation of securities, real estate, and goods is prescribed.

Perhaps the greatest power held by the office of the Commissioner is that of rate-fixing. Each company, individually or through the offices of a rate-filling company, files its rates with the Commissioner, who then approves or disapproves them.[20] Hearings are allowed if the company feels the approved rates are too low. The rates which the Commis-

17. *National Mutual Casualty Co.* v. *Hobbs,* 149 *Kan.* 633.
18. *K.S.A.,* 40-214.
19. *Insurance Co.* v. *Wilder,* 40 *Kan.* 569.
20. *K.S.A.,* 40-925 to 943; 1111; 1112 to 1123.

sioner's office prescribes are maximum rates, based on statewide and national loss experience as determined by private rating agencies and insurance regulatory agencies in other states, the findings of the inspection service of the Commissioner's office, and a "judgment" factor which is computed to allow for expected economic trends. Fire-insurance rates further vary from city to city, according to the class to which the city has been assigned by the Western Actuarial Bureau. This agency groups cities according to their fire protective services on a scale prepared by the American Insurance Association. Rates for particular buildings are further determined by the type of structure and kinds of materials used in construction. Rates for automobile casualty insurance vary from county to county, based upon the number of vehicles registered and local loss experience.

Collections during the fiscal year ending June 30, 1968, were $9,912,888.[21] Ninety-one per cent ($9,048,836) was received by the Office and credited to the General Fund. By far the largest part of this ($8,412,858) came from the 2 per cent tax levied on insurance premiums. Other sources of revenue for the General Fund were retaliatory taxes[22] and agents' license fees. The Commissioner's Office collected $864,052, which was credited to special funds. Over half of these collections ($500,884) were for the firemen's relief fund which is largely distributed to cities. Another special fund is the Fire Marshal Tax Fund, for which the Insurance Commissioner's Office acts as a receiver, transferring 20 per cent of the collections to the General Fund and 80 per cent ($182,187) to the Fire Marshal. Other receipts were for examinations conducted by the Office and charged to the companies. The Office collects a fee which is assessed annually on each insurance company authorized to do business in Kansas and is credited to the School Fund. Appropriations for the operation of the Commissioner's Office amounted to $582,324 for the 1968 fiscal year.

As of September 25, 1968, 343 life-insurance companies, associations, and societies, and 465 fire- and casualty-insurance companies or exchanges had been admitted to do business in Kansas. Insurance companies operating within the state fall into a dichotomous grouping—

21. Unpublished data from the office of the Insurance Commissioner.

22. Retaliatory taxes are those applied on out-of-state companies in accordance with the other state's taxation of Kansas companies.

those incorporated in Kansas and those organized in other states. The Commissioner's Office has had control of the former companies from its inception. The latter companies, which are much more numerous, are normally certified for operation in Kansas by their meeting of operational requirements in their home states. However, the insurance code does specify certain minimums of surplus, reserves, etc., which they must observe. The Commissioner's Office is required to conduct an investigation into the soundness and the policies of each certified company at least once every three years, or in lieu of such an investigation, it may accept an investigation made by other recognized authorities. Only thirty-seven of the 465 fire and casualty companies are Kansas firms, while thirty-three of the 343 associations and companies issuing life insurance are domestic firms.

Several ties exist between the office of the Insurance Commissioner and that of the Fire Marshal. The Fire Marshal makes an annual levy on the gross cash receipts of all fire-insurance companies operating within the state for the purpose of defraying the expense of his office. The office of Insurance Commissioner collects this tax. In addition, the two offices work together when an insurance company appeals a claim on the grounds of arson. In such cases the Insurance Commissioner may give permission to defer payment, while the Fire Marshal conducts an investigation to ascertain the causes of the fire.

State Banking Board

In 1947 the Legislature passed a new code for the regulation of all state banks.[23] At the time the new code was adopted, the Legislature redefined the duties of the office of the State Bank Commissioner and the State Banking Board.[24] These statutory changes grew out of a dissatisfaction on the part of the bankers and the state authorities with the previous state laws. Between 1943 and 1947 the Kansas Bankers Association had a committee of thirty to forty bankers who worked with the State Banking Board and Commissioners in drawing up a new code. The association and the Commissioner's office describe the legislation as being more workable and more acceptable than previous laws.

The State Banking Board resembles the Federal Reserve Board,

23. K.S.A., 9–701 to 2018.
24. K.S.A., 75–1304 to 1308 and 74–3004 to 3006.

after which it was modeled. It consists of nine members, six of whom must be bankers, with one being appointed from each Congressional district and one from the state at large. One of these men must be from a bank in a first-class city; two from banks in second-class cities; the remaining three from third-class cities or unincorporated towns. The three nonbanking members may not have any interest in banks or trust companies except as depositors. One of these three public representatives must be actively engaged in the retail sale of goods, one in agriculture, and one in manufacturing. All members of the Board are appointed by the Governor for terms of three years, with no member serving more than two terms. Meetings occur monthly or oftener at the discretion of the Board and its Chairman, who is a member of the Board and is chosen annually by his fellow-members.

The State Banking Board receives applications from those who want to incorporate to conduct bank and trust businesses within the state. Upon receipt of such application, the Board directs a searching examination into the incorporator's financial status, character, the need for such a business in the community chosen, and other relevant considerations. If, as a result of such investigation, the Board approves the incorporation, the matter is turned over to the Commissioner. The latter ascertains that the incorporators have paid the required amounts of capital sums, surplus, and undivided profits into the corporation. He then issues a certificate of authority to the corporation to undertake banking or trust operations. The expense of the Board's investigation is borne by the bank or trust company in an amount not to exceed $400. The State Banking Board also has jurisdiction over changes in the place of business of a bank. The Board may specify data to be shown on books and records of bank and trust companies, the factors to be used in making real-property appraisals, the minimum amount of insurance to be carried on property owned by the bank, and the maximum amount of interest to be paid on deposits. Perhaps the Board's most sweeping power is its power to remove after a hearing any officer or director of a bank or trust company whom it adjudges guilty of "dishonest, reckless, or incompetent" conduct. Those involved may appeal to the district court for a review of the board's action.

The State Bank Commissioner, who acts as secretary to the Board, is appointed by the Governor with the consent of the Senate for a term of four years. He must have five years' experience in banking in a state bank, and, like the Assistant Commissioner and examiners, he must be bonded.

The duties of the Commissioner as defined in the banking code consist of examining each state bank and trust company at least twice yearly, with the provision that once a year in lieu of a direct examination by his office he may accept the examination and report of an authorized federal agency—in practice, either the Federal Deposit Insurance Corporation or the Federal Reserve Bank. No person making such an investigation may have any financial interest in the bank being examined. In addition to these regular inspections, the Banking Board may authorize the Commissioner's office to investigate the fiduciary affairs of anyone serving in a fiduciary capacity in any bank or trust company, as well as to conduct an examination into the affairs of any investment or holding company which is in debt to any bank or trust company. The fees which are charged for the conduct of examinations range from a minimum of $100 to a charge not in excess of fifteen-thousandths of 1 per cent of the resources of the company. When a federal examination is accepted in lieu of direct examination, half of the regular fee is levied by the Commissioner's office. Money received for appraisals and examinations are credited to a special fund. However, the office receives its operating money by legislative appropriation.[25]

Various reports are required by the Commissioner's office, including at least three resource and liability statements each year which must also be printed in part in a newspaper of general circulation in the area in which the bank or trust company operates. An annual report of receipts and disbursements of the previous calendar year must be made in January. In addition, the Commissioner may call for special reports on a bank's condition at any time—all of these report procedures are so designed as to coincide closely with the requirements of federal banking laws. In turn, the Commissioner must submit a biennial report to the Governor on the number, condition, and officers of banks and trust companies throughout the state.

In order to promote sound banking, and to protect the public, the

25. The Board received an appropriation of $384,349 in fiscal year 1969 to finance its operations.

Commissioner is authorized to revoke the license of any bank or trust company. With the concurrence of the Attorney General, the Commissioner may institute court proceedings to have a receiver appointed should any bank officer refuse to submit books, records, and instruments of the bank for examination, or refuse to be examined under oath concerning the affairs of the bank or trust company, or should an officer interfere in any way with an examination. Any bank or trust company which fails to comply with a lawful order of the Commissioner within ninety days forfeits its right to do business. In such a case the Commissioner revokes its certificates of authority, and the Attorney General institutes court action to have a receiver appointed. For the past several years this power to revoke a certificate or to remove a bank official has not been employed. Most bankers comply closely with the provisions of the code and cooperate with the Board and the Commissioner. There have been instances of failure to comply, but these are generally handled by informal action, and compliance has been secured by means short of formal hearings before the Board.

The Commissioner has the right to post rewards for the apprehension and arrest of bank robbers and burglars, and in the event that the Commissioner detects a bank officer committing a felony or misdemeanor, he is directed to notify the county attorney of the county wherein the bank or trust company is located. Instances of theft and manipulation are not unknown, but frequent investigations tend to hold such occurrences to a minimum. All records of the Commissioner's office pertaining to examinations or investigations are legally confidential and are not matters of public information.

Through these defined channels of authority, the State Banking Board and the Commissioner exercise control over all state banks and trust companies, enforcing the statutes concerning banks and banking. These cover the supervision and approval of a bank's organization, its capital stock and structure, maintenance of reserves, banking and trust transactions, handling of deposited public funds, and dissolution and revocation of authority to do business. Through the system of reports, examinations, and investigations, the activities of all state bank and trust companies are supervised.

Kansas banking regulations vary but little from those of most other states, since most present banking regulations stem from federal legislation. The chief differences lie in the amount of capitalization and undivided profits which a bank must have to incorporate and to maintain its license. The relationship between national and state banks in Kansas is one that is characterized by cooperation. Despite the fact that the State Banking Board and Commissioner have no direct control over national banks, these banks generally accept state laws and regulations. Regulations and examinations largely coincide, and the State Commissioner readily accepts the findings of examinations of state banks by the Federal Deposit Insurance Corporation and the Federal Reserve Board. There are provisions in the statutes for the transfer of banks from national to state status, or vice versa, but such changes are infrequent.

In Kansas in June, 1968, there were 432 state banks and two trust companies, which were regulated by the Board, the Commissioner's office, and twenty full-time examiners. As noted above, from time to time discrepancies arise and are detected, but in the last eleven years there has been only one bank failure.[26]

Credit Union Council

In 1968 the Legislature created the Credit Union Council as a seven-member board with responsibility to appoint the Credit Union Administrator and to exercise general supervision over the establishment and operation of credit unions. Before, the Bank Commissioner had been given exclusive responsibility for regulating credit unions. Certificates of authority are issued to credit unions by the administrator. Credit unions must make semi-annual reports to the Administrator. At least one examination is made annually of the financial standing of each union, and additional examinations may be ordered. Maximum interest rates allowed credit unions, their procedures for voluntary and involuntary dissolution, and a number of similar operational matters are covered by statute. As of June 30, 1968, there were 243 credit unions in the state.

Consumer Loan Commissioner

Though numerous bills had been introduced earlier, it was not until 1955 that the Legislature passed a law regulating the making of small

26. Unpublished data from the office of the State Bank Commissioner.

or consumer-type loans.[27] In that year the Office of Consumer Loan Commissioner was established. The Commissioner is appointed by and holds office at the pleasure of the Governor.

All persons who engage in the business of making loans for $2,100[28] or less (except banks, trust companies, savings or building and loan associations, credit unions, or pawnbrokers) are required to get a license from the Commissioner. All those who had previously engaged in the small-loan business were specifically authorized to receive a license. The Commissioner issues a license to others only "if the character and general fitness of the applicant is such as to warrant belief that the business will be operated lawfully and fairly within the provisions" of the law. Licenses may be suspended or revoked by the Commissioner. Appeals from his decisions may be taken to the district court.

The licensing fee is $125 a year, and the licensee must pay the costs of required annual examination of the books, accounts, and records. All but 20 per cent of the money collected is credited to a special fund from which it is expected that the operations of the office will be financed.

The maximum rate of interest charge on such small loans is 3 per cent a month on the unpaid balance on loans up to $300 and 10 per cent a year on all amounts loaned in excess of $300 up to $2,100. A borrower is entitled to a refund on prepaid interest charges if he repays his loan before the due date.

Certain practices are required among the licensees. They must furnish copies of the contracts to the borrower. The borrower may be required to take out insurance. However, there are to be no charges other than interest and no splitting of fees. False or misleading advertising is prohibited.

These procedures apply to the small loans for which normally there is less collateral and there is more risk involved to the lender. Aside from loans made by those licensed for small loans, the legal maximum-contract interest is 10 per cent. For installment loans of less than $2,000 the maximum interest rate is 8 per cent. Legal penalties are imposed on those violating these provisions.

27. *K.S.A.*, 16-401 to 426.

28. Such loan agencies may make loans in amounts in excess of $2,100, but different rates of interest apply.

In 1959 the Commissioner was given responsibility to regulate persons engaged, in whole or in part, in the business of purchasing retail installment contracts from one or more sellers. Licenses are required of such sales finance companies. The Commissioner has power to investigate practices of such companies and to revoke licenses. Maximum interest charges are established.

As of June 30, 1968, there were 379 consumer loan companies and 111 sales finance companies being regulated in Kansas. For operations in fiscal year 1969 the Office has been appropriated $104,353 from the Consumer Credit Administration fund.

Savings and Loan Commissioner

In 1943 a new savings and loan code[29] was adopted and a new Savings and Loan Department was created to assume the powers, authority, and duties of the Supervisor of Building and Loan Associations. Like the state banking code, the savings and loan code had been. formulated by a committee of savings and loan company managers working with the state administration officials.

The five members of the part-time Savings and Loan Board and the Commissioner of the Department are appointed by the Governor for four-year terms.[30] They must possess at least three years' experience in the operation and management of savings and loan institutions. The Commissioner, who may be removed only for cause, appoints his assistants, deputies, examiners, and other employees in accordance with civil service provisions.

The purposes for establishment of savings and loan associations as noted in the code are "to promote thrift and home financing." Each such association must apply for a certificate of incorporation from the office of the Commissioner. To obtain this certificate, the enterprise must meet the minimum capital requirements, which vary from $5,000 to $20,000 depending on the size of the locality, secure the approval of its bylaws, and pass the scrutiny of the Commissioner's office regarding the character of the incorporators and the need for such an establishment in the proposed community. At this time there is no actual on-the-spot examination of the company assets, as the chief concern of the

29. *K.S.A.*, 17–5201 to 5812.
30. *K.S.A.*, 74–3104 to 3115.

Commissioner is to check the reliability of the incorporators. The Commissioner passes on requests for incorporation and sends them with his recommendation to the Savings and Loan Board. If the Board approves the application, the Commissioner forwards a certificate of incorporation to the applicants.

Once the company has begun operations, a number of its activities are prescribed by law and supervised by the Commissioner's office. Annual inspections of the books and records are made, and regular and special reports on the financial structure of the company are required. The finances of the company are regulated by statutory limitations on stock issues or transfers, on the declaration of dividends, and on other dealings. Bonus and reserve accounts are regulated by law in order to provide a general guarantee of the public interest.

Various details of the operation of a savings and loan company are also regulated by law. The requirements for membership in the association, the holding of annual meetings, the amendments of bylaws, the changing of the corporate name or location, and the distribution of financial statements are covered by statute.

Mergers and dissolutions of savings and loan associations may be made with the approval of the Commissioner, and interclass transfers may be made from state to federal or federal to state savings and loan status. The federal-state relationship in this field approximates that in banking, since there is no direct tie between the associations regulated by the state and those under federal supervision; but cooperation is maintained in the best interests of the common objectives.

The State Savings and Loan Department is financed by appropriations from the savings and loan fee fund. The Department is self-sustaining in that its collections from fees imposed on savings and loan associations for incorporation and inspection are larger than its appropriations. All fee and examination money collected by the Department are credited to the general fund and are then used to reimburse the savings and loan fund. Fees for incorporation and inspection services are based on a sliding scale according to the assets of the company.

In order to enforce the provisions of the savings and loan code the Commissioner may order any association to discontinue any practice or to perform any lawful action he considers necessary. If the association does not comply within twenty days, a hearing is held by the

Commissioner and a conservator may be named to manage the affairs of the association under the supervision of the Commissioner. Within twelve months the Commissioner must determine whether he shall restore the association to the management, or require that a reorganization be effected or that the association be dissolved. If the last course is determined upon, the Commissioner appoints a receiver. Appeal may be made to the Savings and Loan Board, and the Board may overrule the Commissioner. These severe penalties open to the Commissioner are a threat which are always present but seldom used. Suggestions made by the Commissioner to an association or one of its officers usually clear up any irregularity prior to the holding of a hearing. There are at present in the state approximately seventy-one associations incorporated under the savings and loan code. There are four full-time inspectors who make the annual examinations required by the statutes and other examinations that may be necessary.[31] Most of the associations are also federally insured, and they are jointly examined by a federal official and a representative of the Commissioner's office.

Food-Service and Lodging Board

The State Food-Service and Lodging Board was created in 1965 to take over the power, authority, and duties of the State Hotel and Restaurant Board. The Board makes regular and thorough inspections of all lodging and food-service establishments. Members of the Board are appointed for two-year terms, with membership being restricted so that two members are active in the hotel business, three in the food-service business, and one in the motel business. Members of the Board annually select one of their number to act as chairman of the Board. With the approval of the Governor they appoint a Director of the Board who serves as secretary.

The Board is organized to enforce the statutes for licensing, inspecting, and regulating hotels,[32] lodging houses,[33] and restaurants. In 1965

31. For fiscal year 1969 the Legislature appropriated $82,498 for the operation of the Savings and Loan Department.

32. A hotel is defined as a structure or group of structures offering four or more rooms to transient guests. For purposes of the statute, motels, cabin camps, and tourist camps were specifically included as "hotels."

33. A rooming house is a structure offering four or more rooms to transient or permanent guests, but has no dining or café facilities in the same building. An

"restaurant" was defined to include any food-service business, fixed or mobile—coffee shop, cafeteria, grill, bar, night club, roadside stand, industrial feeding business, food-vending machine or catering kitchen. Each such place of business must purchase an annual license, which expires on the thirty-first of December. The fees for the license are based on a sliding scale, with larger hotels and apartment houses paying slightly higher amounts. The money collected from such licensing is paid into the state treasury, with 80 per cent of it going into the Food Service and Lodging Board fee fund, and the remainder staying in the general fund. The fee fund provides money for inspection, regulation, and payment of salaries of the Board members, director, inspectors, and clerical employees.[34] No charge is made for the periodic inspection of the various establishments. No fees are collected except for the fee in connection with the annual licensing.

Inspections of restaurants and lodging houses are conducted to secure clean and sanitary conditions and adequate plumbing, lighting, and ventilation. In some cases the statutes spell out the requirement in considerable detail.[35] Inspections are made at least once a year, and sometimes run as often as ten or twelve a year for establishments on the border line, even though the law simply requires a single annual inspection. The Board is empowered to serve notice of unsatisfactory conditions upon any establishment, and if conformity is not obtained within thirty or sixty days, depending upon the nature of the irregularity,[36] to close the establishment.

---

apartment house contains four or more apartments and offers light-housekeeping facilities.

34. For the fiscal year ending June 30, 1969, the Legislature appropriated $138,061 for the operation of the Food Service and Lodging Board.

35. For example, "All hotels and restaurants in this state shall hereafter, in the main public washroom, in view and reach of guests, during the regular meal hours, and where no regular meal hours are maintained, then between the hours of 6:30 a.m. and 9:00 a.m., and 11:30 a.m. and 2:00 p.m., and 6:00 p.m. and 8:00 p.m., and in each bedroom furnish each guest with clean individual towels so that no two or more guests will be required to use the same towel unless it has been first washed. Since [such] individual towels shall be not less than ten inches wide and fifteen inches long, after being washed." *K.S.A.*, 36-119.

36. Thirty days are allowed for conforming to regulations covering fire extinguishers, towels, bedding, and linens. Sixty days are allowed for compliance with regulations on plumbing, lighting, toilets, washrooms, etc., where major structural changes may be involved.

In all cases where the law or regulations are not being complied with, the license may be revoked by the Board. Such revocations are subject to review upon application for a writ of mandamus in the district court in the county in which the establishment is located. In addition, the person, firm, or corporation failing to comply within the stated period is guilty of a misdemeanor and subject to a fine. Revocation of the license has the advantage of stopping the operation and thus immediately protecting the public.

Another but less-used way of bringing about corrective action is to have the county attorney prosecute violations of the acts that are enforced by the Board. Complaints on oath may be brought by the state Board or by other persons. This constitutes a last resort to secure conformance, and is rarely called into play. The threat of legal action usually is sufficient; but over the past year, there have been a half-dozen cases of prosecution under these statutes.

In addition to the statutory standards, the Board and the State Board of Health have established a code of sanitary rules and regulations for the preparation, sale, and serving of food. While these two boards combine to establish the rules, the majority of the inspections pursuant to those rules fall to the Food Service and Lodging Board. The Board of Health conducts examinations by request; and then it will often delegate the inspection to the other board or to the municipal health agencies.

Most frequent violations of the state code by hotel and lodging establishments are their failure to meet the requirements pertaining to fire escapes and safety devices. The Board, together with the state Fire Marshal, has conducted an intensive drive to secure proper escape mechanisms in all rooming places. Among restaurants, most sanitary violations stem from the large number of small establishments, the high turnover of owners, inexperienced operators, and ignorance of the law. The Board combats this by having its inspectors educate the owners as to the provisions of the code, and by allowing them wide latitude of action in disposing of specific cases. In the last analysis, it is largely the public through economic pressure which aids most in requiring proper sanitary facilities.

The Board cooperates with municipal health and inspection officials and with the State Board of Health in enforcing proper standards of lodging and eating establishments. Sometimes the various agencies notify each other of more extreme violations, and they operate together and perform joint inspections. The magnitude of the inspecting operation may be seen from the fact that there are at the present time over 342 licensed hotels, 814 motels, 514 rooming houses, 6,594 apartments, and 7,855 eating establishments, all of which, according to present policy, are inspected at least once a year.[37] In the fiscal year ending June 30, 1968, 19,671 inspections were made. The Board has nine full-time inspectors and from time to time hires additional examiners.

Alcoholic Beverage Control

The manufacture and sale of intoxicating liquors was prohibited by the Constitution from 1880 to 1948. In 1947 the Legislature proposed a repealing amendment which was ratified in 1948 and ended prohibition. The general effect of the amendment was to free the Legislature to enact further regulations on the subject. Specifically, the Legislature was authorized (and expected) to provide for the prohibition of intoxicating liquors in certain areas, and the "open saloon" was forever prohibited.

The Legislature met in 1949 and implemented the constitutional amendment. In areas in which a majority of those voting on the constitutional amendment had opposed the amendment, prohibition was continued. Arrangements were made, however, for these and all other areas to be able to decide on a local-option basis whether to have or not to have alcoholic beverages sold. Although other alternatives were discussed, the Legislature decided in favor of privately owned package-liquor stores.

The office of Director of Alcoholic Beverage Control was established, with the Director being appointed by and serving at the pleasure of the Governor. The Governor also appoints a three-member Alcoholic-Beverage Control Board of Review. The Director receives applications for, and issues and revokes licenses for, manufacturers, distributors, and retailers of alcoholic beverages and certain private clubs. He fixes standards for the manufacture of alcoholic liquor and inspects any premises where alcoholic liquors are manufactured, distributed, or

37. Data obtained from the office of the director of the State Food Service and Lodging Board, October, 1968.

sold. He is authorized to call upon other administrative departments of the state, county, and city governments, sheriffs, city police departments, city marshal, peace officers, and prosecuting officers for such information and assistance as he deems necessary. The Director proposes rules and regulations which must be approved by the Board of Review before they go into effect. The Board also hears appeals on the denial, suspension, or revocation of licenses. As of June, 1968, there were 1,071 licensees operating retail liquor stores in Kansas and there were 608 private clubs.

Various qualifications are required of those to whom licenses are issued. For example, those who have violated liquor laws and certain other laws may not receive licenses. In addition to state license fees, which vary for manufacturers, distributors, retailers, and private clubs, the city levies an occupation tax of not less than $100 or more than $300. A gallonage tax is levied on all manufacturers and wholesale distributors. In 1968 this tax resulted in net collections of $4,174,353. In addition to these fees and taxes, a 4 per cent gross-receipts tax is levied on the liquor sold. One-fifth of the enforcement tax is credited to the general revenue fund, and four-fifths is distributed to counties, 50 per cent on a basis of the equalized tangible assessed taxable valuation and 50 per cent on a basis of the last state enumeration of population. Within the county one-half goes to the county general fund, with the remainder being divided among cities on the basis of population. A number of special restrictions are imposed on the retail dealers. They are not permitted to advertise. They may not sell liquor on certain days and may not buy from other than licensed distributors. They may not sell to minors or on credit. Drinking in public and drunkenness are made misdemeanors.

Before the constitutional repeal of prohibition, there were laws for licensing cereal malt beverage (beer) dealers. In general these laws continued in effect. Cities may issue licenses to such dealers within city limits, while counties license those outside corporate limits.

21 | Professional Licensing

Any consideration of professional licensing must concern itself in part with the question as to just what is a profession. Increasingly various occupational groups are organizing and, in many instances, aiming to develop a set of professional ethics. One way of gaining social status is apparently to be a member of a profession as distinguished from a craft or a trade. These pressures in our society have resulted in increased requests and an increased number of boards to license various occupational groups who want to be considered professions. As a workable definition for our purposes, professional licensing will refer to the regulation of those vocations or professions whose practitioners desire control in order to maintain standards for entrance into and for the operation of their calling.

Growth of Licensing Boards

The first of the licensing boards in Kansas was created in 1885, and since that time the number has steadily increased.[1] In fact, the increase has been so even that it almost represents an arithmetic progression. In 1900 there were only two boards, in 1910 there were seven; there were

1. Much of this chapter is based on an unpublished M.A. thesis entitled "A Study of Professional License Boards in Kansas" by Raymond Deane Postlethwaite, University of Kansas, 1948.

TABLE 44
Licensing Boards and Date Established

Board	Year Established
Kansas Dental Board	1885
Kansas State Board of Pharmacy	1885
State Board of Law Examiners	1903
State Board of Barber Examiners	1903
State Board of Embalming of Kansas	1907
State Board of Veterinary Examiners	1907
Kansas State Board of Examiners in Optometry	1909
Kansas State Board of Examination and Registration of Nurses	1913
Board of Accountancy (certified public accountants)	1915
Mining Examining Board	1917
Kansas State Board of Registration for Cosmetologists	1927
Kansas State Board of Podiatry Examiners	1927
State Board of Engineering Examiners	1931
State Municipal Accounting Board	1935
State Board of Examiners of Court Reporters	1941
Abstractors' Board of Examiners	1941
Kansas Real Estate Commission	1947
State Registration and Examining Board for Architects	1949
Basic Science Examining Board	1957
State Board of Healing Arts	1957
State Board of Examiners of Psychologists	1967
State Board of Examiners in Fitting and Dispensing of Hearing Aids	1968
State Board for the Registration and Examination of Landscape Architects	1968

Source: *K.S.A.*

thirteen by 1920, fifteen by 1930, seventeen by 1940, twenty-one in 1950; in 1957, through consolidation, the number was reduced to twenty. Since 1949 three new groups have been licensed, and some changes have been made in already established licensing boards.

Table 44 lists the boards chronologically by their complete names. For purposes of brevity, the full names will not be used in the text in this chapter.

Control has not always been exclusively vested in such boards. Medical doctors, lawyers, optometrists, and osteopaths were regulated to some extent before the creation of licensing boards.[2] In only one case has a board ever been abolished. The Barber Board was dissolved in 1905, and its functions were largely transferred to the State Board of Health until 1913, when the Barber Board was re-established.[3]

The increase in the number of independent boards has been accompanied by a corresponding increase in the amount of control which the boards exert. Few of the older boards still operate under the original law which created them. Most of the statutes have been changed. In addition to the growth of function of these boards through legislative enactment, there has been a steadily widening control through the use of rules and regulations which the statutes have allowed the boards to promulgate.

The earliest licensing boards were merely registration boards, and exercised only a clerical function of enrolling and filing. There was little need for examination, for academic achievement was an adequate index to competency. Later, as the number of such boards was augmented and began to include professions where formal training was not so clearly an evidence of capability, the added function of examination became common. At first, however, examination was considered as alternative to academic or experience qualification. The final step has been to make entrance into the profession contingent upon both examination and experience or education. All of this has greatly restricted the number who many enter the professions.

Another tendency in the same direction is the steady increase in educational requirements. In some cases this has been accomplished by legislation, but in many instances it ensues from an exercise of the board's rule-making power. The board may choose to "accredit" only those schools which teach a course of desired length. Concomitant with the increasing restrictions upon entrance into the profession has been the widening of the power to revoke licenses. This also tends to limit the number who may practice a given profession.

The latest emphasis seems to be in the direction of more control over the profession itself. Many boards now have annual registration, and several have required educational programs. The registration of schools is practiced in barbering, nursing, and cosmetology; and places of busi-

2. Postlethwaite, p. 2.
3. *Session Laws*, 1905, chap. 70; *Session Laws*, 1913, chap. 292.

ness are registered in barbering, optometry, cosmetology, and pharmacy, with the boards holding consequent inspectional powers. Only the Barber Board has any price-fixing power.

This increase in powers has required constantly more involved financial procedures and augmented revenues to defray expenses. Annual registration fees, the increase in the number of instances in which fees are levied, and the raising of fees have all added to the income of the boards.

Organization of the Boards

These small independent licensing boards are generally similar in their organization and particularly so in regard to the selection of board personnel. It is now customary for the state association of the profession concerned to submit to the Governor a list of nominees from which the board appointments are made. The laws regarding embalming, nursing, pharmacy, and optometry require that the Governor nominate on the basis of this list. The engineering law requires the Governor to "consider" such a list; and many other professions follow a similar procedure. In all probability, political considerations force the Governor to consult with representatives of the profession even where there is no prescribed institutional arrangement for the nomination of board members.

The members of nineteen of the twenty-three boards are appointed directly by the Governor. In addition, the Podiatry Board is composed of one member appointed by the Governor, one member of the Healing Arts Board, and the secretary of the latter board; and the Board of Coal Mine Examiners is appointed by the State Labor Commission with the approval of the Governor. The two remaining boards—those pertaining to attorneys and court reporters—are appointed by the Kansas Supreme Court. Senatorial approval is necessary for appointment to the Healing Arts Board.

The tendency seems to be away from the more complicated procedures in favor of direct appointment by the Governor. In 1949 the procedure of the Nursing Board was simplified, and in 1951 the Accounting Board was similarly revised. In the case of the latter, an advisory council was established to consist of the heads of business schools or departments in state institutions of higher education. Even this council is appointed by the Governor.

The qualifications for board membership vary little. The statutes regarding fifteen of the boards require that the members be residents of the state, and, in practice, this has been strictly adhered to even where there is no such statutory restriction. Geographic distribution is required of the Real Estate Commission, which must have a member from each of the state's Congressional districts. The abstractors have a requirement which has a somewhat similar effect: one member must be a resident of a county of under 9,000 population, one of a county of from 9,000 to 17,000 population, and one of a county of over 17,000. In practice, the appointments to all boards seem to recognize a certain geographic distribution.

The greatest variety in the occupational requirements is in the Municipal Accounting Board, where one member must be a county clerk, one a member of the governing body of a first- or second-class city, one a member of a board of education, one a county officer, and one the State Auditor in an ex officio capacity. The Court Reporters' Board must be composed of two district court judges, two practicing attorneys, and one official reporter of a district court. The Real Estate Board has the negative requirement that two members not be real estate brokers.

Some of the licensing statutes require that persons outside the profession be appointed to the boards, but most of the licensing board statutes require that the appointees to the boards (or at least most of them) be members of the profession. Some of the statutes require that the board members be licensed practitioners. In other cases requirements of experience serve the same purpose. The statutes regulating seventeen of the boards have such experience requirements, ranging from three to ten years of experience. The most common requirement is five years of experience which applies to eleven boards. In practice, members usually have more than the requisite years of experience. The Mining Board statute requires that both miners and mine operators be represented, and the Barber Board has a somewhat similar requirement for barbers and barbershop operators.

Several boards have provisions excluding those who might have a commercial or educational bias which would threaten their professional integrity, and several statutes prevent the appointment of anyone with doubtful professional ethics.

The number of members on the boards reflects the traditional theory that an administrative board should be composed of an uneven number of members. Nine of the boards have three members, eleven of them have five members, two have seven members, and the Healing Arts Board has eleven members.

TABLE 45

Licensing Boards, Number of Members, Terms, Compensation, and Expenditures in 1968

Board	Number of Members	Terms in Years	Compensation*	Total Expenditures in Fiscal Year 1968
Abstractors	3	3	$ 5.00 per diem	$ 3,316
Architects	5	4	expenses only	10,180
Certified Public Accountants	5	3	10.00 per diem	18,461
Barbers	3	3	200.00 per month	36,040
Basic Science	5	4	15.00 per diem	9,900
Cosmetologists	3	3	210.00 per month	80,477
Court Reporters	5	3	10.00 per diem	279
Dentists	3	4	20.00 per diem	25,231
Embalmers	3	3	10.00 per diem	25,484
Engineers	5	4	10.00 per diem	34,766
Healing Arts	11	4	15.00 per diem	35,069
Hearing-Aid Fitters	5	3	#	Estab. 1968
Landscape Architects	3	3	expenses	Estab. 1968
Lawyers	5	..	10.00 per diem	5,937
Miners	3	4	5.00 per diem	†
Municipal Accountants	7	4	expenses only	†
Nurses	5	4	10.00 per diem	61,288
Optometrists	3	3	10.00 per diem	4,730
Pharmacists	5	3	15.00 per diem	49,992
Podiatrists	3	3	10.00 per diem	167
Psychologists	7	3	10.00 per diem	2,610
Real Estate Brokers	5	4	10.00 per diem	108,863
Veterinarians	5	3	15.00 per diem	3,740

* Generally all board members are allowed certain expenses in addition to the per diem payment. Where state officials are members of the boards, they are allowed expenses only.

† Not available

Set by the Finance Council

Sources: *K.S.A.;* Department of Administration, *Financial Report for Period July 1, 1967, to June 30, 1968.*

The terms of board members are arranged to overlap. Where the term does not correspond to the number of members, there are years when no appointments are made, or years when two appointments are made. Table 45 gives the number of members on the several boards and their terms.

The Nursing Board members are limited by statute to two consecutive terms, while members of the Pharmacy Board are limited to a total of two terms. Other boards which are not so restricted have generally followed the practice of limiting service to two terms.

The statutes of eight boards have provisions for removal of members by the Governor for incompetency, misconduct, or neglect of duty. In addition, the Governor may remove any member of the Optometry or Accounting Board whose certificate is revoked. In all other boards, presumably, removal could be effected only by judicial process. The ruling of the Supreme Court of Kansas in *Barrett* v. *Duff*[4] is unambiguous: where there is an appointive office with a specified term of tenure and no express provision for removal, neither the Governor nor his successor may revoke an appointment. The Governor's only recourse in such a case would be ouster proceedings instituted in the state court. On the other hand, in the two boards which are appointed by the State Supreme Court, although there is no express provision for removal, the court uses its broad statutory powers to effect removal.

Actually, the removal power has been invoked quite infrequently. The process of nomination insures fairly competent members, financial compensation is too poor to constitute an attractive "job," and board activity is so limited in scope that there is little conflict with the executive.

Except for the State Auditor, who is the ex officio secretary of the Municipal Accounting Board, all other officers of the boards are chosen by the boards themselves. With one exception new officers are chosen annually. The presiding officer is designated either president or chairman. There is often a vice-chairman or vice-president. Most of the boards choose a secretary or secretary-treasurer from their own number, but in a few cases an outside officer acts as the secretary. The Real Estate Board hires a director, the Nursing Board hires an executive director, the secretary of the Healing Arts Board serves as secretary of

4. 114 *Kan.* 220.

the Podiatry Board, and the State Auditor serves as secretary of the Municipal Accounting Board. Only in a few cases is there a separate office of treasurer.

Bonding is required in only a few cases. All members of the Barber and Cosmetology boards are required to post bonds, but only the secretary-treasurer of the Nurses Board, the Optometry Board, and the Dental Board, the secretary of the Engineering Board, the treasurers of the Pharmacy and Chiropractic boards, and the director of the Real Estate Board are required to post a bond. Only two of the few remaining boards handle amounts of money comparable to those handled by boards with bonded members.

With the exception of the Board of Coal Mine Examiners and the Municipal Accounting Board, the examining boards have as their chief source of income the fees which they collect. The fees collected are deposited with the State Treasurer, where 80 per cent of the money is placed in the appropriate special fund for the use of the individual board and the remainder is credited to the state general fund. The theory behind this division is that the amount credited to the general fund covers the expenses of other departments relative to boards' operations. Collections made by the Board of Coal-Mine Examiners and the Municipal Accounting Board are credited to the general fund, from which appropriations are made for the operation of these licensing activities. The Legislature appropriates money from the special funds or from the general funds as the case may be, and is thus able to control the level of operations of the boards.

The Podiatry Board has a special relationship with the Healing Arts Board. The secretary of the latter board is ex officio secretary of the Podiatry Board, and frequently draws on the Healing Arts Board fund for expenses of the Podiatry Board.

Types of Professional Control

The professional licensing boards have two different types of jurisdiction. One of these is the control over the use of certain specified titles—"certified public accountants," "licensed municipal accountants," and "certified shorthand reporters." Anyone may practice as an accountant, expert accountant, or public accountant, but he may not represent himself as a certified public accountant or as a licensed municipal accountant unless he actually holds these designations. Certification of shorthand reporters confers certain privileges. Only those holding this certificate may be appointed official reporters of district courts. The licensing of municipal accountants is in a sense similar, for only licensed municipal accountants may be hired to conduct the required annual examination and audit of the accounts of a Kansas county or of a first- or second-class city.

All other professions are regulated because of the nature of the occupation as a whole. In most cases the statutes define these professions. In some occupations, however, the lawmakers have apparently relied upon common opinion. In the professions of chiropractic, embalming, and law, this attitude has proved adequate, but there has been some controversy over the position of osteopaths. Osteopaths have maintained that they are entitled to use drugs and practice surgery, while the medical doctors have held the contrary.[5] The courts have sustained the doctors in their contention.

Formerly, nursing was a form of optional certification. Anyone might practice as a practical nurse, but only a registered nurse could practice as an "R.N." Today practical nurses are also licensed, and hold the designation "licensed practical nurse." Nursing today is licensed as a profession.

Examining and Licensing Procedures

The examining and licensing process is the typical means of profes-

5. For a number of years there have been differences of opinion between the osteopaths and medical doctors on this point and their proper method of licensure. These differences were reconciled in 1957, and two boards were established. All those who want to become chiropractors, osteopaths, and medical doctors are required now, first to pass an examination in anatomy, physiology, chemistry, bacteriology, and pathology, which are referred to as the basic sciences. The Basic Science Examining Board gives this examination. Those who pass this examination may later apply to the Healing Arts Board indicating the specialty (i.e., medicine and surgery, osteopathy, or chiropractic) in which they desire to be examined. A special arrangement was made for those osteopaths who were practicing their profession on July 1, 1957, to allow them a period in which they could take the examination to practice medicine and surgery. The law defined the activities which were considered as practicing medicine and surgery, osteopathy, and chiropractic. The three professional groups are represented on the Healing Arts Board, with the medical doctors having five representatives and the osteopaths and chiropractors three each.

sional control. The qualifications required for eligibility to take the examination vary from board to board. In cases where these qualifications are high, there are relatively few who fail the ensuing examination. In other cases it may be the examination itself which weeds out most of the "undesirables."

With the exception of the Veterinary Board, all of the statutes require that the applicant be "of good moral character." The real estate law also calls for affidavits by three property-owning citizens attesting the applicant's sound reputation; and the court reporters' law calls for affidavits by three citizens, two of whom must be attorneys. Actually, the boards seldom collect enough evidence to make a fully considered decision on such matters. The pharmacy and barbering laws are more specific in requiring "temperate habits." Similarly the shot firers, shot inspectors, and others licensed by the Board of Coal Mine Examiners must not be "users of intoxicating liquors."

The boards of barbering, dentistry, law, mining, municipal accounting, and certified public accounting require that the applicant be a citizen of the United States. The nursing and real estate laws require either citizenship or a declaration of intent. In addition, funeral directors, court reporters, and attorneys must be residents of the state of Kansas; certified public accountants must either be residents or have established a place of business in the state; and municipal accountants must have established an office in the state.

Only the Abstractors' Board requires a $5,000 bond of all applicants. The Board seems to rely mostly upon this device for maintaining professional standards. An applicant for being licensed as cosmetologist or barber must present a sworn statement by a physician stating that he is free from any contagious infections or communicable diseases. Educational requirements are varied.

In most cases the examination is a requirement over and above the other qualifications. In only the Engineering and Architecture boards is it an alternative to academic requirements. Statutes usually require annual or semiannual examinations, and the Board may give other examinations in so far as the number of applicants warrants such a procedure.

Similarly, the number admitted to examinations varies. The Nursing Board may examine classes containing hundreds of individuals, while several boards may examine only three or four people a year.

All boards collect examination fees, which are not returned in case of failure to pass the examination. The boards of court reporting, osteopathy, podiatry, engineering, pharmacy, law, and architecture, however, require no new fees upon reexamination, and the Optometry and Public Accounting boards require a smaller fee in such a case.

Examinations which are entirely written are usually given at some easily accessible center of population such as Topeka or Wichita, while practical or demonstration examinations, which are given in the cases of barbering, court reporting, cosmetology, pharmacy, dentistry, and veterinary practice, are given wherever the facilities are located.

In most cases the examinations are either prepared by the board or by board officers. The Municipal Accounting Board, however, appoints an examining committee which prepares the examination and grades it after it has been administered. Certified public accountants and nurses are given a standardized examination which is prepared and graded on a nationwide basis. This, of course, enhances reciprocal relations and, in addition, quite often provides a more comprehensive examination. Similarly, the dental profession has established a national examining board which gives tests on a regional basis. Many other boards seem to be in favor of similar developments.

The qualifications and examinations have meant little at the time a board was established, for all licensing statutes have had provisions which allow anybody practicing the profession at the time of enactment to procure a license without having to meet the statutory requirements.

Some boards license those who hold minor positions in connection with the work of those licensed. In addition, the Pharmacy, Optometry, Barbering, and Cosmetology boards inspect and license the place of business itself. Barbers, cosmetologists, embalmers, funeral directors, optometrists, doctors, real estate brokers, and dentists all have restrictions placed upon their advertising and solicitation practices. The Barber Board has the powers of mediation in labor disputes and the power of price-fixing.

Eighteen boards have reciprocity arrangements with boards in other states, whereby licenses granted elsewhere are recognized in Kansas. In these cases some type of reciprocity is at least legally provided for. Only the abstractors, court reporters, hearing-aid dispensers, miners, and municipal accountants do not receive reciprocal treatment. In the cases of barbering and embalming, out-of-state licensees still must take an examination, but they are released from the apprenticeship requirement by virtue of having practiced elsewhere.

Four boards will license anyone who has formerly been licensed by a state whose board standards are approved by the profession's national accrediting agency. The Public Accountancy Board thus recognizes the American Institute of Certified Public Accountants, the Pharmacy Board recognizes the National Association of Boards of Pharmacy, the Real Estate Board the Central States License Law Association, and the Engineering Board the National Council for Engineering Regulation. In these cases the applicant is admitted without examination. Dentistry and cosmetology are somewhat different, in that although they recognize the National Dental Board and the National Council of Boards of Beauty Culture, they still administer the oral and demonstration part of the examination. The Law Board gives only an oral examination to any out-of-state licensee.

Most other boards may admit, without examination and at their own discretion, out-of-state members. The Healing Arts and Veterinary boards have certain formal arrangements with boards of other states. In other cases, apparently, reciprocity is granted only upon an individual basis after an examination of the particular applicant's educational and other qualifications. The Optometry Board is extremely strict in regard to reciprocity and has followed a policy of granting no licenses to out-of-state applicants.

The qualifications for out-of-state licensees are the same as, or similar to, those required of native members. It is common, however, to require, not that the foreign board have the same qualifications as the Kansas board at the time the licensee changes his residence, but that the qualifications of the two boards were the same at the time the licensee entered the profession.

Control of Practices

Board control now extends far beyond the mere limitation of membership. Each board has attained a certain amount of control over professional practice. Annual registration is the most common technique for effecting this control. By using this device boards maintain a continuing control over the profession. In addition to the annual registration fee, the cosmetologists and barbers pay an annual shop-inspection fee. Those who operate pharmacies must have a permit which involves an inspection of the equipment and premise. In the case of optometry, annual registration enforces educational standards by requiring an annual participation in professional educational programs. Several boards exercise some control of labor-management relations. In such cases, the members of the profession are separated into categories of apprentice and master.

Penalties for illegal practice are connected with the control over entrance into the profession. In most cases, illegal practice is merely practicing the profession without a license. In the cases where optional certification is the form of board jurisdiction, illegal practice is using a certain title which the individual actually does not have.

All of the licensing statutes provide for penalties for illegal practice. There are no specified fines or penalties in the attorneys' law. In this case, however, illegal practice would presumably be punishable by the court, and the penalties would be established by the court. In most cases violations are classed as misdemeanors.

Revocation of Licenses

Revocation is different from penalizing for illegal practice. It concerns the "back door" of the profession and not the "front." Revocation is a device for continuing control over professional practice. It seems to be more important as a threat than as a reality. In many cases a board will go for years without revoking any licenses, and the number revoked annually by any board is never more than two or three.

In the case of the Law and Court Reporters boards, revocation is reserved for the court. Disbarment involves a formal procedure of investigation by the bar association, prosecution by the Board, and judgment by the court. In all other instances revocation and the attendant investigatory power are in the hands of the boards. Appeal may be had in all instances to a district court, and certain procedural safeguards are always prescribed, such as a stated time interval, formal notification, and a hearing.

There are large differences in the statutes defining grounds for revocation. In many cases the statutes are vague and general, sprinkled with glittering phrases such as "unprofessional conduct," "unethical conduct," "gross immorality," "dishonorable conduct," "willful negligence," "incompetency," "ignorance," or other terms equally difficult to define. In other cases the grounds may be exhaustively listed in detail. The optometry law lists thirteen bases for revocation, the real estate law lists nineteen, and the dental law has a list of twenty-seven.

The most common reason for revocation is fraud or deceit in obtaining a license. Twelve boards have such a provision. Nine boards may revoke a license for "conviction of a crime involving moral turpitude," eight may do so for habitual drunkenness, seven for drug addiction, and six for "immoral conduct." Barbers and optometrists may have their license revoked if they are found to have an infectious or communicable disease, and embalmers similarly suffer if they fail to guard against such a disease. Barbers and cosmetologists must display their certificates in a prominent place, and barbers must also display the sanitary rules of the Barber Board and the State Board of Health.

Problems in Professional Licensing

The loose organizational framework of the licensing boards in the state government is manifest from this chapter. Some problems arise from the changing of officers (and offices) of the boards and the maintenance of records. The present diffuse operation of these boards, as well as their present methods of financing, makes it appear frequently that the licensing boards are almost private groups, rather than state agencies regulating the professions in the interest of the public. To meet some of these objections some states have provided for central state agencies to handle the mechanics of the licensing, with professional groups retaining the rule-making authority.

Some people have become concerned over the increase of occupations which desire (and in many states have) licensing provisions. The results have been to close substantial occupational areas from the free choice of those who might want to enter. While restrictions which are necessary to insure that the applicant is able to perform in the field are accepted by most people, some licensing boards are alleged to have set requirements primarily to be certain there are not too many people in a given field. The enthusiasm which many groups have for state licensing leads some people to question whether the licensing is wanted primarily to protect the public or to help the profession.

Realistically, however, licensing boards serve purposes which most people accept. The challenge to state government in this area is to see that such licensing boards become true instruments to promote the general welfare instead of instruments to perpetuate the control of certain special groups.

22 | State Planning

Some people view governmental planning as an undesirable and unnecessary function, more to be associated with socialism and communism than with our own democratic way of government. Kansas had a brief experience with a limited effort in state planning. Today there is no single state agency devoting its efforts to comprehensive state planning. Much of the planning which is done, is done by the Kansas Economic Development Commission and is focused on economic development and promotion.

Historical Background

In the winter of 1934, faced by the stark conditions of the nationwide depression, Governor Alf M. Landon invited a group of representative citizens to serve as the Kansas State Planning Board. This invitation was prompted by a suggestion from the federal Public Works Administration which was sponsoring the National Planning Board (later named the National Resources Committee). The federal agency desired to have state and regional planning boards established throughout the nation to combat the immediate effects of the economic situation, and to provide a long-range plan for development.

While Kansas was among the earliest participants in the state planning program, it is significant that the Governor's action was never followed by legislation which would have made the Board a permanent agency. In 1935 a bill to provide a suitable basis for a permanent board was passed by the House of Representatives but failed by two votes in the Senate. Two factors combined to defeat the measure—misapprehension of the Board's functions and fear of requests for increased appropriation.[1]

The program on which the board undertook its work included:[2]

1. Collection, analysis, and graphic presentation of available physical, social, and economic facts pertinent to Kansas.

2. Detailed study of the several urgent physical-economic-social problems with particular emphasis on land use, transportation, and water conservation, and flood control.

3. Definition of long-range objectives which would transform the more conspicuous, present, social-economic liabilities into social-economic assets.

As ambitious as this program was, the first years of the Board must have been unusual and uncertain. No state funds were available to the Board. To meet the financial needs of the organization, the Kansas Emergency Relief Administration supplied a staff, the Kansas Chamber of Commerce provided work facilities and office equipment, and later, the Spelman Fund made several annual grants to meet salary and expense needs. The ever-precarious position of the Board would have made work impossible had it not been for the cooperation and technical assistance rendered by other state agencies. The first *Progress Report* of the Board[3] cites as reasons for its progress the support of Governor Landon and especially the assistance of the Highway Department, the Health Department, the Agricultural Department, the Forestry, Fish and Game Commission, the Corporation Commission, Kansas State University, the University of Kansas, and the Kansas office of the Public Works Administration.

Despite the lack of legislative support and appropriations, the State Planning Board pursued an ambitious course, aided by the agencies noted above, and backed by an "extremely encouraging" public opinion. By 1939 the Planning Board could point to over forty-five publications dealing with the resources, potential, and planning for the state. However, during the five years of the operation of the Board, there were signs of differences of views as to what planning is. To some, state

---

1. Kansas State Planning Board, *Second Progress Report* (Topeka: 1935), p. 3.
2. Kansas State Planning Board, *Progress Report* (Topeka: 1934), p. i.
3. Kansas State Planning Board, *Progress Report* (Topeka: 1934), p. 2.

planning was a long-range, long-term project, with emphasis on planning for the future and only an incidental emphasis on the present economic situation. To others, the State Planning Board was a temporary body whose main purpose was to bring a certain amount of relief during the period of the Great Depression. To this group, the long-range aspects of planning were largely misunderstood. The failure of the Legislature to make the Planning Board a permanent state agency indicated an inherent distrust of "planning," or a lack of realization of the purpose intended, or perhaps both.

By 1939 the worst of the depression was over, and those who saw planning as an emergency measure saw little need for continuing the Board. Indeed, in retrospect it may be said that the State Planning Board reached its peak of importance in 1935 and after that began to decline. This was a result of the continued lack of appropriations by the Legislature and the loss, after a time, of the Spelman Fund support. Many of the projects of the State Planning Board were taken over by the Legislative Council—in a sense itself a planning committee for the Legislature. As the Legislative Council and its research staff became better established, it became an agency for doing some of the things a state planning board might do. In 1939 the Legislature established another agency—the Industrial Development Commission—which could also be expected to perform some of the same kinds of work as a state planning board. For a time both the State Planning Board and the Industrial Development Commission continued to exist, and a few joint reports were issued. By 1941, however, the State Planning Board had ceased to exist, and its staff and files were absorbed by the Industrial Development Commission.

The Kansas Industrial Development Commission was inaugurated with the purpose of fostering and promoting the industrial development of the state. The Commission originated and conducted a three-part program to accomplish this objective.[4] It included activities to encourage the development of both existing and new state industries, to aid in securing new and enlarged markets for Kansas agricultural and industrial products, and to increase the tourist and recreational traffic of the state. The Industrial Development Commission reported immediate

4. Kansas Industrial Development Commission, *Report to the Legislature*, February 28, 1941, p. 1.

success in its promotional campaign to attract new industry to the state and to encourage the expansion of existing facilities.

In 1947 the state Legislature gave the Commission responsibility to promote and encourage the aeronautical resources of Kansas. This gave emphasis to the aircraft industry and paved the way for an extensive campaign by the Commission to encourage aviation, to educate the public to its potentialities, and to assist cities in planning air facilities. However, for a number of years after 1956 no appropriations were available for this activity.

The Legislature in 1961 provided for the creation of the Governor's Economic Development Committee to study and make recommendations for the creation of a department of commerce and for investigating the economic conditions of the state and methods of improving the economy of the state. This Committee sponsored special studies on ten different aspects of the economy and made a number of recommendations for fostering the economic development of the state.

The recommendations of the Committee for the organization of arrangements for encouraging economic development were accepted and largely became the basis of legislation in 1963. In addition to the organizational changes described in the next section, the Committee recommended the strengthening of vocational education as a way of encouraging more economic development. Recommendations calling for a Kansas Economic Authority to administer a state economic-development revolving-fund and for changes in property-tax laws were not adopted.

The Present Organization

The 1963 legislation called for the establishment of the Kansas Economic Development Commission with nine members appointed by the Governor and serving for four-year, staggered terms. The Governor designates each year the members to serve as chairman and vice-chairman. The Commission acts as the coordinating and directing body for the Department of Economic Development. It appoints the Director and holds him responsible for the operation of the Department.

In general the Department is charged with acting as the official state agency for the economic development of the state through the promotion of business, commerce, and industry. More specifically, it coordinates the activities of state agencies in research work and other activities furthering the economic development of the state, and it may sponsor scientific and industrial research. It keeps current all available information on industrial opportunities and possibilities in the state, including the advantages of particular locations. The Department publicizes the economic advantages of the state and promotes tourism in the state.

The Department has sponsored research for developing additional uses for the state resources and agricultural products. The Department has sponsored a research study analyzing the state and has developed the concept that Kansas is composed of eleven separate regions. The individual regions have been encouraged and in some cases have fostered activities aimed at the economic development of those areas.

The Department has been designated as the state agency for the administration of the federal planning-assistance grants under section 701 of the Federal Housing Act. In this general area of activity the Department has assisted a number of communities in beginning planning programs. This agency has been assigned the broad responsibility for developing a comprehensive plan for the development of the state, to be known as "Kansas 1975." To the extent possible, the local plans of individual communities will be merged into the regional plans and then will be consolidated into the state plan.

The availability of federal assistance in this area has led to a significant acceleration of interest in the area of planning. Much of the work done has been the basic collection of information and facts needed as a basis for developing plans.

There is some question as to where organizationally the planning function—as distinguished from the promotional aspects of the work—can best be handled. A consultant's report under the federal 701 funds was made in 1967 recommending that state comprehensive planning be assigned to the Department of Administration or to a separate division of the office of governor. The thought was that the function should be done in close association with the budgeting function and should be directly responsible to someone who is elected. Enlargements of the Governor's office frequently bring up questions of partisan considerations. This proposal has been given consideration but has not been adopted.

It is expected that short-range planning will continue to be done in and by the operating units or that it will be done by an agency that is reasonably close organizationally to such units. But in addition to this kind of planning there is need for long-range comprehensive planning. Those engaged in operations are "caught up" in the day-to-day operating problems and frequently do not have time to reflect and plan for the future. On the other hand, if the planning is done by agencies that are too far removed from the operational unit, it may be unrealistic and may propose objectives that are not obtainable.

Operationally, the Department is organized into a planning division, an industrial division, a commerce division, a travel division, and a newly constituted aviation division. The expenditures of the travel division are about one-half of the total appropriations. This division publishes a slick-cover quarterly—the picture-filled color magazine *Kansas*—and is engaged in a wide campaign to attract tourists to Kansas.

From this brief review of the program of the Kansas Economic Development Commission, it can be seen that the Commission furthers and enlarges certain aspects of the programs of the former State Planning Board and Kansas Industrial Development Commission. The emphases of the three agencies have been somewhat different. The Board was primarily a physical-economic-social planning agency, while the first Commission was promotional in nature, with a research program designed to increase the industrial and agricultural potential of the state. The present Commission is strongly oriented toward promotion of tourism and economic development, but it does in one of its divisions do some planning work not dissimilar to the work of the earlier State Planning Board.

As a part of the reorganization in 1963, the Office of Economic Analysis was established. The Chief Economist, who heads this office, is appointed by the Governor. He is essentially an advisor to the Governor and gathers essential information concerning the economic growth and development of the state. He is responsible for examining state programs to assist the Governor in devising an "internally self-consistent administrative structure for the development of the state's economy."

The creation of the Office in a sense seeks to give the Governor an arm parallel to that of the President's Council of Economic Advisors. In another perspective this Office is to keep the Governor informed on the state of the economy in Kansas—something that the agency charged with promotion of the economy might find difficult to do in an unbiased fashion. A faculty member in economics at the University of Kansas and one at Kansas State University have each served a term as the Chief Economist. To assist the Chief Economist, there is the Council of Economic Analysis, consisting of two qualified members of the state universities or colleges appointed by the Governor.

23 | *Municipal Government*

Kansas has often been thought of as primarily an agricultural state. However, the percentage of the urban population in Kansas has gradually been increasing until, in 1960, over 60 per cent of the people in Kansas lived in urban places. The movement of out-of-state people to expanding industrial areas, particularly during World War II, and the continued movement of the farm population to the city account for this change. New farming methods have made it possible for farmers to move to cities and still continue their farming.

Kansas has a large number of cities in relation to its population, but many of these cities are small. Only 95[1] of the 624 cities in Kansas have 2,500 or more people, the number which the U.S. Bureau of the Census has long used as the dividing line between rural and urban areas. However, the cities above 2,500 contain 83 per cent of the population of the state living in cities and 63 per cent of all the people of the state.

Most of the cities, then, have a population of less than 2,500. The median or middle-sized city in 1968 had between 460 and 464 people. In these smaller cities the government is likely to undertake few functions and to be relatively simple and informal.

---

1. The 1968 population census of the Kansas State Board of Agriculture was used for this and other 1968 population information on this page.

413

TABLE 46

Per Cent of Urban Population and Number of Incorporated Places in Kansas by Federal Decennial Census

Year	Number of Incorporated Places	Per Cent of State Population Urban
1968	624	63.3
1960	617	61.0
1950	599	52.1
1940	589	41.9
1930	589	38.8
1920	525	34.8
1910	470	29.2
1900	349	22.5
1890	323	11.6
1880	117	5.6

Sources: Kansas State Chamber of Commerce, *Kansas Yearbook* (Kansas State Chamber of Commerce, 1938); U.S. Bureau of the Census, *Population, 1910* (Washington, D.C.: U.S. Government Printing Office, 1913), II, 664-66; *idem, Population 1930 (ibid.,* 1931), I, 422-26; *idem, Population 1950 (ibid.,* 1952), I, 16-22 to 16-24; *idem, Statistical Abstract of the U.S., 1952 (ibid.,* 1952), pp. 29 and 30; *idem, Statistical Abstract of the U.S., 1920 (ibid.,* 1920), p. 49; *idem, Statistical Abstract of the U.S., 1966 (ibid.,* 1966), p. 16.

The Cities and the State

City-state relations are most important for cities. Cities are created by the state and have only such powers and duties as are given them by the state Legislature or by the state Constitution. While cities are for some matters thought of as instruments or agencies to carry out local functions, they are dependent upon the state, and particularly the state Legislature, for their incorporation, powers, and functions.

In Kansas as in other states many of the early cities were incorporated by acts which applied only to them. Many of the early laws concerning cities were special laws, in that they applied to an individual city or at best to several cities. It became common legislative practice to take care of the legislative needs of cities by such special laws, enacted sometimes at the request of the council or citizens of the city concerned and sometimes over the objections of the city, the citizens, and occasionally even over the objection of the legislators from the area concerned. There were such numbers of these latter instances that a national movement began to restrict the legislatures in their dealings with cities. The Ohio Constitution, after which the Kansas Constitution was modeled, contained such a restriction on state legislative action, so that such a restriction was incorporated into the Kansas Constitution.

In this connection, the Kansas Constitution originally provided that "all laws of a general nature shall have a uniform operation throughout the state; and in all cases where a general law can be made applicable, no special law shall be enacted."[2] Thus, the Constitution allowed some special laws to be enacted. In interpreting this provision the state Supreme Court was called upon to distinguish between a law of a general nature and a general law. A law of a general nature was held to be one in which the subject matter was one common to the people of the entire state, whereas a general law is one that operates uniformly through the state.[3] In 1906 the Constitution was amended,[4] and the courts were assigned the duty of determining whether or not a law was repugnant to this provision of the Constitution. Since this time the courts have taken a somewhat more strict interpretation, and occasionally acts have been declared unconstitutional. However, there are still many special laws for Kansas cities.[5]

Normally the Legislature passes special acts under the guise of laws which pertain to all cities of a given class. Three general classes of cities have been established according to population. First-class cities are those with population in excess of 15,000; second-class cities are those with population between 2,000 and 15,000; and third-class cities are those under 2,000. Until 1953 third-class cities reaching 2,000 population and second-class cities reaching 15,000 were to certify the fact to the Governor, who issued a proclamation advancing the city to the next

2. Article 2, sec. 17, of the Kansas Constitution. There are two constitutional provisions concerning special legislation: one forbids the passing of special acts conferring corporate powers (Art. 12, sec. 1), and the other requires that provision be made by general law for the organization of cities (Art. 12, sec. 5).

3. *Richardson* v. *Board of Education,* 72 Kan. 632.

4. The clause "and whether or not a law enacted is repugnant to this provision of the constitution shall be construed and determined by the courts," was added in 1906 to the above-quoted constitutional prohibition against special acts.

5. For example, one study has shown that of 439 acts affecting cities passed from 1937 through 1947, 192 concerned individual cities. The "big three" cities (Wichita, Kansas City, and Topeka) are the cities involved in many of the special acts. Such acts for small cities are rare.

class. However, on occasion cities have reached the required population without changing classes. Now this practice has been legitimatized. A city may choose to remain in its class after it has become eligible to go into the next class. Second-class cities may continue as second-class cities until they reach a population of 25,000, in which case they are required under the present law to become first-class cities. Similarly, third-class cities may continue in their class until they reach 5,000.

There are instances in which cities have had the required number of persons to be a city of one class and have had their population fall below the level required. Such cities frequently remain in the higher class. Thus the range in population in each class is greater than the legal requirements for such classes.

Much of the legislation concerning cities applies to all cities within a given class. There are chapters of the general statutes which apply to each class and one more general chapter which concerns all cities. In addition there are a number of other general laws which apply to all governing units including cities.

Even a cursory perusal of the general statutes pertaining to cities will reveal that many of the laws in the section do not apply to all cities within the class and in many instances are in fact special laws. An almost infinite number of special classes can be devised within any one of the three general classes by adding special requirements of population, assessed valuation, and geographic factors. The frequent pattern used in Kansas was to establish within a class of cities a special class with somewhat narrow population limits and then to differentiate the city intended from all others in the population grouping by making the act apply only in counties with certain populations and/or certain assessed valuations.

In determining the legality of such "general laws" the court is frequently called upon to determine whether a classification of cities established by an act is reasonable and germane to the purposes of the act. The mere fact that it applies now to only one city is generally not sufficient for it to be considered unconstitutional. Particularly is this true as long as the classification is not closed and other cities may enter the class.

There was some dissatisfaction with the legal relations between the cities and the state, but it should not be concluded from the earlier mention of legislative abuses of special legislation that all special acts were harmful and that they were instances of legislative interference with local control of local affairs. On the contrary, most by far of the special acts were passed by the Legislature at the request of the local citizens and in many cases at the request of the governing body of the city concerned. The special acts covered such a wide variety of subjects that many cities would find it almost impossible to carry on many essential operations without them.

Special acts make it possible for the Legislature to give special attention to the individual peculiarities and differences between cities, but many problems grow out of their use. Valuable legislative time is taken up with the passing of bills on essentially local matters. Some feel that legislative occupation with such matters takes legislative attention away from matters of statewide interest. According to one survey,[6] some legislators were frank to admit that the special acts gave them a way of getting credit among their constituents.

From the point of view of the city, special acts give flexibility, for normally a city can get a special act passed without too much difficulty. However, the city may frequently have to delay its plans until the Legislature meets and enacts the desired law. Most important, the system tends to divide responsibility for municipal affairs between the state Legislature and the city governing body.

City-state legislative relations have been a problem in many states. Other states have experimented with cities being given more control over their own affairs. This movement is referred to as home rule. The aim is to give cities control over all local matters, but not to disturb or lessen the power of the state over matters of statewide interest. As might be expected in these states, there have been numerous court cases to determine what is a matter of local concern and what is a matter of statewide interest. The cities may be granted home rule by either legislative or by constitutional action.

The home-rule movement has aroused some interest in Kansas. In 1949 the Legislative Council was asked to study the possibility of home rule for Kansas cities and counties. The council committee held hearings and reported that there was no strong sentiment for home rule. In

6. Francis L. Janes, "Special Legislation for Cities in Kansas" (unpublished M.A. thesis, Univ. of Kansas, 1949), p. 128.

1953 after the Supreme Court had declared in broad terms a special act designed for Kansas City, Kansas, unconstitutional, a senator from that area introduced, and the Legislature approved for submission to the voters, a constitutional amendment which was heralded by some as a home-rule amendment. The proposal, adopted in 1954, allowed the Legislature to designate areas in counties as "urban" and "to enact special laws giving to such counties or urban areas such powers of local government and consolidation of local government as the legislature may deem proper."[7] This provision can be used by the Legislature to authorize special acts for individual cities or to allow the Legislature to pass laws giving more powers to the governing body of such cities.

After study and endorsement by both the Legislative Council and the special governor's committee to study constitutional revision, the Legislature in 1959 approved for submission to the voters a much broader constitutional amendment for home rule. This plan was patterned after the Wisconsin plan of home rule. The voters approved the constitutional amendment for home rule in 1960, and it became effective in the next year.

The amendment empowers cities "to determine their local affairs and government including the levying of taxes, excises, fees, charges and other exactions." No effective guide, however, was established in the constitution as to what are "local affairs," and there have not been any court cases to spell out the boundaries of this authority. The intention of the Legislature and voters seems to have been clear, since the amendment provides that it "shall be liberally construed for the purpose of giving to cities the largest measure of self-government."

This broad grant of power was made to *all* cities of the state, but it had several restrictions. The Legislature may limit the revenue raising powers of cities as long as it treats all cities in a class uniformly and has no more than four classes of cities. Further, cities may exercise these powers of local determination and government subject only to (1) legislative enactments "of statewide concern applicable uniformly to all cities," (2) other enactments applicable uniformly to all cities, and (3) enactments prescribing limits of indebtedness. Cities exercise these powers normally by enacting ordinances through their regular procedures.

7. *Kansas Constitution*, Art. 2, sec. 17.

Additionally each city is given the power to enact *charter ordinances,* which exempt it from state laws that would otherwise apply to it. A city may pass such ordinances except to relieve itself from the operation of laws of statewide concern applicable uniformly to all cities, other laws applicable uniformly to all cities, and laws prescribing debt limits. The effect of this provision is to allow any city governing body to change any of the laws which the Legislature had enacted or might enact specially for it. Thus cities were given a new kind of protection against special laws which become outdated or are for some reason objectionable to it. With this broad grant to cities to determine their local affairs it was expected though that there would be less need for the Legislature to enact special laws.

During the first thirty months of the operation of the new amendment at least 128 cities passed either charter or ordinary ordinances based upon the amendment. Somewhat over one-third of the ordinary ordinances concerned the investment of funds and almost one-third of the charter ordinances dealt with the election and appointment of officials. Since that time the amendment has continued to be used, and there has been some discussion of extending it to counties.

Thus far, our discussion of city-state relations has been limited to relations between the Legislature and the cities. However, there are increasing instances of relations between state administrative agencies and cities and city officials. These relationships are described further in chapter 25.

Municipal Powers

Municipal governments are created by the state and are regarded as agents of the state in many of the functions they perform. It was a long-accepted rule of legal interpretation that a municipality had only: (1) those powers which were expressly delegated to it; (2) those powers which were necessarily or fairly to be implied in, or incident to, the power expressly granted; and (3) those powers which were essential to the accomplishment of the objectives of the incorporation. Whenever any doubt arose about whether a city had been granted a particular power, the doubt was resolved in favor of the grantor (the state) against the grantee (the city). The effect of following this long-accepted guide to the interpretation of municipal powers has been to make cities dependent upon the state. These were the interpretations and circumstances which helped stimulate interest in home rule. The home-rule amendment in Kansas has modified the legal status of cities, but precisely how much will have to await judicial decision.

Though cities have the constitutional grant of home rule, they still have the powers granted them by the Legislature. Such grants of authority are generally to be found in chapter 12 of the general statutes for all classes of cities, in chapter 13 for first-class cities, in chapter 14 for second-class cities, and in chapter 15 for third-class cities. There are other grants of powers and provisions affecting municipalities in other sections of the statutes.

Police Power

While they are related, there is a difference between "police power" and the power to police. In the American framework, the police power refers to the broad power of the state to make necessary regulations to promote the health, safety, and morals of its citizens. This is indeed considered by the courts as an extensive power of the state government. Many state laws are based on this power. The courts have been unwilling to define specifically this power, but have upheld such regulations enacted under this grant as they consider reasonable.

The state Legislature exercises the police power, but it can and has given to the cities in Kansas power to "enact, ordain, alter, modify or repeal any and all ordinances not repugnant to the constitution and laws of this state, and such as it shall deem expedient for the good government of the city, the preservation of the peace and good order, the suppression of vice and immorality, the benefit of trade and commerce, and the health of the inhabitants thereof, and such other ordinances, rules and regulations as may be necessary to carry such power into effect."[8]

The governing body of the city, that is, the city council or commission, exercises this power by passing ordinances. This broad grant of power is in addition to a substantial number of more specific grants which conceivably are included under the broad general grants, even

---

8. *K.S.A.*, 14-401. There is a substantially similar provision for third-class cities (15-401). The provision for first-class cities is not so broad and general, but does authorize cities "to make all needful police regulations necessary for the preservation of good order and the peace of the city, and to prevent injury to or destruction of or interference with public or private property" (13-423).

under the close interpretation of municipal powers which is typically given. For example, first-class cities are authorized to:

Regulate the construction and location of billboards, signs, and other appliances on public streets and property adjacent thereto.

Regulate the entrances to public halls, churches, and other public buildings.

Regulate and prescribe the construction of and compel the building and cleaning of smokestacks, chimneys and hot-air flues.

Regulate the distribution of handbills, posters, and other advertising matter.

Provide for the inspection and regulation of meat markets and shops.

Adopt all such measures as may be necessary for the protection of strangers and the travelling public in person and property.

Make regulations to prevent the introduction and spread of contagious diseases in the city.

Make quarantine laws.

Punish persons for carrying firearms.

Prohibit and suppress tippling shops, saloons, dramshops, clubrooms, opium dens; to restrain, prohibit and suppress houses of prostitution, disreputable houses, games and gambling houses, dance houses, keno rooms . . . and all kinds of indecency and other disorderly practices, disturbances of the peace, assault and battery.

The enforcement of ordinances after adoption by the governing body of the city is normally a matter for the marshal or police officers. Other sections of the statutes authorize the establishment of police departments and the appointment of police officers. City police are charged with apprehending those who violate state law, as well as those violating city ordinances.

Some standards of law enforcement suggest that, as a minimum, there should be one policeman for each thousand people in the city. Many Kansas (and other) cities do not meet this standard, but considering the need for 24-hour, seven-day-a-week coverage, even those communities that do meet it are likely to be able to have only a few men on duty at a given time. In the median Kansas city with a population of about 450, and indeed in all third-class cities, relatively little can be done in the way of an organized police effort. Some first-class cities in Kansas find it impossible to have police departments which have even the most elementary specialization of work. These conditions make the sheriff the primary law-enforcement officer in most of the state.

As in other states, more and more time of the law-enforcement officer is taken up with traffic problems and less with criminal investigation. The work of the Kansas Bureau of Investigation, the Highway Patrol, and other law-enforcement agencies that may be invited to assist local police departments has been discussed in an earlier chapter.

Licensing

Licensing may frequently be used for regulation and/or raising revenues. In regulation, licensing may be considered as a device for policing. It is an effective tool of control to require those to be regulated to apply for and be considered for a license before they can legally enter a business or calling. In 1961, following the adoption of the home-rule amendment, the Legislature passed a general law authorizing cities to establish license fees for the privilege of engaging in any business, trade, occupation, or profession.[9] However, the amount of such fee can not be based on the income or on the amount the licensee sells or services.

Zoning

An integral part of city planning, zoning is predicated on the police powers of cities. Under zoning, the right of the individual property holder to use his property as he sees fit is restricted. By setting aside part of the city for residences, part for retail businesses, and part for industrial uses it becomes easier for the city government to provide the necessary streets, sewage, fire, police, and sanitation services for each type of area, and property owners have the value of their property protected. Zoning guides the future development of the city and aims to make our cities more attractive, pleasant places in which to live.

The governing bodies of all cities in Kansas are authorized to appoint planning commissions who recommend to the governing body the establishment of and boundaries for various zoning districts within the cities.[10] After a hearing has been held, the council or commission may adopt the recommended regulations of the planning commission. Once such regulations are adopted, the zones may not be changed until proposed changes are submitted to the planning commission and have been publicized. If a protest petition is filed by 20 per cent or more of the

9. *K.S.A.*, 12–141.
10. *K.S.A.*, 12–701 to 12–715.

property owners in front or behind the land to be rezoned, the city governing body can approve the change only by a 4/5 vote.

Zoning looks to the future. All property which is being used for nonconforming uses when the zoning ordinance is adopted may continue to be used for that purpose. Only *new* nonconforming uses are forbidden, and alterations and modifications of existing structures employed in nonconforming uses are closely restricted. Boards of zoning appeals may be established in cities where zoning ordinances have been enacted. Such boards are allowed to make exceptions to the zoning ordinances. Approximately 134 cities have planning commissions.[11]

Fire Protection and Prevention

First-class cities are specifically authorized to maintain fire departments, and other cities are allowed to buy fire trucks and equipment and to make needful rules and regulation for the use of the equipment. All cities may make regulations on building materials and construction which might be dangerous in promoting fires.[12]

It is estimated that there are fewer than thirty cities in Kansas which maintain full-time paid fire departments. A number of others have some full-time employees but depend mostly on volunteers for the operations of their departments. City fire departments frequently have arrangements to provide fire-protection services to the surrounding rural areas. Some townships contribute to the support of the department. For a number of years the Legislature has made a specific item appropriation to the University of Kansas to support firemanship training. An annual fire school is held, and an instructor is employed by the university to help in firemanship training throughout the state.

Power to Acquire and Maintain Streets

Cities may acquire streets by dedication, prescription, purchase, or eminent domain. In some respects the basic provisions for the dedication of streets in second- and third-class cities are contained in an 1868 act, which was apparently designed for cities on initial incorporation. At the time of this act there was only one first-class city (Leavenworth). Additions to second- and third-class cities are also

11. Based on information reported in the *Directory of Public Officials in Kansas, 1966*, pp. 1–84.
12. *K.S.A.*, 13–442, 14–421, 15–427.

covered by this act. When a plat is filed, the land indicated for a public use is considered dedicated, and no specific acceptance (beyond the filing of the plat) is required.

A number of cities grew around township and county roads. When incorporated, the city took over the maintenance of these streets. Other streets are added as new areas are platted. All cities with planning commissions are able to exercise considerable control over plats of lands within the city and within three miles of the city limits. Where there are such commissions, plats must be submitted to the commission and must be approved by the city governing body before they are accepted.

Normally a road is improved at the expense of the adjoining property-holders. Once improved, however, the city is authorized to maintain the streets. There are a number of provisions which govern the circumstances in which the different classes of cities can repave a street, either wholly or partly at general expense.

While city streets form only 7 per cent of the road mileage in the state, they carry 42 per cent of its traffic.[13] A city may elect to have the State Highway Department maintain state highways within city limits or to receive a payment and maintain the highway itself. Counties make like arrangements with cities.

Ownership and Regulation of Public Utilities

All cities in Kansas are authorized to purchase or to construct and operate utilities to supply the city and its inhabitants with natural or artificial gas, water, electric light, heat, or street railway or telephone service.[14] Such action requires approval of the majority of the voters. Once so approved, the city may issue bonds up to 15 per cent of the valuation. Where there are such municipal plants, the city may sell to those within and outside the city at rates set by municipal ordinance. Municipally owned utilities are not subject to regulation by the State Corporation Commission.

Most municipal utilities are operated as departments or divisions of the city government, with the council or commission being directly responsible for the utility operation. Frequently there is a utility super-

13. *Kansas Highway Needs: An Engineering Appraisal* (Washington, D.C.: 1962), pp. 22 and 85.
14. *K.S.A.*, 12-801.

intendent appointed by the governing body. However, there is authority for the governing body of any city with a utility to appoint a board of commissioners to operate the utility. In several cases there is special legislation to allow for these boards to be elected and to be independent of the governing body.

In cities where utilities are privately owned, they are required to get a franchise from the city as a condition to entering upon streets, alleys, or public parks or grounds.[15] The city is given the power to contract with such utilities to further the interests of its citizens. It can require standards of service and set maximum rates for service not inconsistent with the rates determined by the Corporation Commission. The city can require additions and extensions of the plant. The Corporation Commission can hold a hearing upon complaints about a franchise or contract and can instruct a city to change a franchise or contract. Occasionally representatives of cities appear before the Corporation Commission at the hearing over rates and regulation of privately owned public utilities.

Cities are allowed to purchase a privately owned utility at expiration of its franchise. This may be done without the consent of the utility if approved by the voters. Under these conditions, special commissioners determine the value of the utility subject to appeal to the courts by either party.

Power to Undertake Public Improvement and Services

Cities are authorized to engage in a wide variety of public improvements and services. Cities may acquire and maintain public parks, squares, and markets both within and without the city.[16] Similarly, cities may establish and maintain tourist courts[17] and cemeteries.[18] Likewise cities may build docks and wharves, river terminals,[19] and drains, canals and other flood-protective improvements. These improvements are frequently financed from general tax levies.

In addition to these, cities may construct and maintain sewers and drainage systems. A city governing body may divide the city into the

15. *K.S.A.*, 12-2001 and 66-133.
16. *K.S.A.*, 12-1301.
17. *K.S.A.*, 12-1308.
18. *K.S.A.*, 12-1401 to 12-1439.
19. *K.S.A.*, 12-672.

number of sewage districts it deems necessary, and costs are borne by the benefited property. Lighting districts may also be established in first- and second-class cities. Streets and sidewalks are common and important types of public improvement, largely financed by special assessments against the benefited property.

All cities are authorized to provide or contract for the collection of trash and refuse.[20] First- and second-class cities are also allowed to acquire and operate off-street parking lots.[21]

Other Activities

Though in part removed from the city government proper, cities may establish special boards to supervise and manage municipal libraries, recreation boards, and municipal universities. These boards are appointed by the mayor and the governing body. They are responsible for managing the activity, and normally recommend the tax levy for their particular function to the city governing body.

To accomplish the functions outlined above and other functions assigned cities by the statutes, the city has certain incidental powers necessary to such accomplishment. For example, cities have the power to take private property by eminent domain, to enter into contracts, and to tax.

Municipal Finance

Municipal finances are divided among several funds, the number varying from city to city and class to class. The legislation authorizing the collection of revenues directs the particular fund to which the revenues must be credited. Similarly, expenditures may be made only from the funds for the purposes indicated. Therefore, money is normally collected with the expectation that it will be used for a particular purpose. Each fund must balance, and transfers between funds are generally restricted. The system of funds tends to create inflexibility. At the request of cities, the Legislature has allowed an increasing number of cities to make a single levy for a general operating fund instead of requiring them to have separate funds for the various separate functions. All second- and third-class cities and first-class city-manager cities are allowed to use a general operating fund. In addition, cities are author-

20. *K.S.A.*, 12-2101.
21. *K.S.A.*, 12-2201.

ized to have bond-and-interest funds for making public improvements and funds for operating public utilities, as well as certain other funds.

There are substantial variations within classes and between classes of cities in the amount and sources of revenues and the amount of expenditures for particular functions. In general, with respect to revenues, however, about one-half of the total revenue for municipal government comes from ad valorem taxes on real and personal property. The Legislature has authorized cities to levy property taxes for some of the funds. Within the mill-rate limits[22] established by the Legislature, the city governing body may levy as much property tax as it considers proper. In addition to the limits for individual funds, there are also aggregate limits setting the total that a city may levy. However, as pressures to raise revenues have increased, some levies have been taken out from under the aggregate, and thus these levies may be made without respect to the levies for other funds. Because of the differences which exist between various counties in the state in assessment levels, tax limits expressed in mill rates have limited effectiveness.

In Kansas, the counties act as the assessing agent and collecting agent for all property tax.[23] The city governing body certifies to the county the amount of tax, within the statutory limits, to be collected for it. This amount is then computed into the total property tax to be levied against each parcel of property. The county treasurer collects the tax for all the property-tax-levying units and distributes the money to the cities and other units.

Kansas cities receive a number of different types of aid or shared taxes from the state. One such aid is the sales-tax residue[24] which is distributed to the counties, 50 per cent on the basis of the county's assessed valuation and 50 per cent on the county's population. Within

22. A mill rate is merely a convenient way of expressing an ad valorem tax rate. It refers to the number of mills (tenths of a cent) that a property owner must pay for each dollar of assessed valuation of his property. A 16.2327 mill rate, for example, means that a property owner must pay 1.62 cents for each dollar of assessed valuation. Sometimes the rate is expressed in terms of the tax for each $100 or for each $1000 of assessed valuation. Thus, to continue the example, a 16.2327 mill rate means $1.62+ per hundred or $16.23+ per thousand dollars of assessed valuation.

23. For special assessments the city does make an assessment to determine the values of the properties benefited, but such special assessments are collected for the city by the county.

24. For further information on the sales-tax residue see p. 139.

the county the residue is distributed among all the property-tax-levying local subdivisions which comply with the budget law. Each unit shares with others in the proportion that the amount of property tax levied last year bears to the total amount levied by all the units within the county. Bond and interest funds are excepted from these computations and do not receive any part of the residue.

The liquor-control-enforcement tax is distributed among counties on the same basis as the sales-tax residue, but, within the county, the county keeps half of the enforcement tax and the other half is divided among all the cities of the county in proportion to population. The cigarette tax is divided among the counties on the basis of population. Within the county, the cigarette tax is distributed on the same basis as the liquor-control-enforcement tax.

Cities receive several payments for streets and highways. Annually they get $2,500,000 for a special county-road and city-street fund which includes part of the state gasoline tax. This money is distributed directly by the state Treasurer to the cities on the basis of population. Cities are paid additional money from this fund if any remains after certain payments are made to the counties. Cities may also receive grants to maintain state highways in cities at the rate of $750 per lane mile and grants to maintain county roads at $250 a mile. Upon special application, in certain cases cities can share in federal and state funds for highway construction.

Cities receive payments from the state for the Firemen's Relief Fund, and a few cities are given federal grants through the state to encourage certain public-health functions.

Cities collect charges for various services which they perform: for trash and refuse collection, sewage disposal, and in connection with municipal swimming pools, cemeteries, airports, and with sale of certain kinds of property. Municipal property may be rented. Of a somewhat similar nature are transfers from municipally owned utilities. Generally some payment is made by the utility to the city in lieu of taxes. However, some cities make much more substantial transfers from utility funds to other funds. Occasionally these transfers are so large that no property tax has to be levied, and such cities are popularly known as "tax-free" cities. In such cases, however, taxes are merely being collected under the guise of utility charges.

Amounts are also received from licenses and occupation taxes and fines and fees. Parking-meter collections are important parts of the amount raised from fines and fees. There are a limited number of other miscellaneous sources of revenue.

In addition to the revenues needed to finance the normal operating costs of city government, a city may borrow to make many municipal improvements. Normally when money is needed to finance a revenue-producing function of the city, bonds are issued against and secured by the future revenues of this particular city operation. Such revenue bonds are issued frequently for the construction or expansion of municipal waterworks, power plants, and sewage-disposal plants. Also cities may issue general-obligation bonds which are obligations against the general city revenues and credit. These bonds are to be distinguished from special-assessment bonds which are used to finance municipal improvements that so benefit the adjoining land that the owners are required to pay for the improvement. Streets, sidewalks, and sewers are frequently financed by special-assessment bonds, while a city hall might be financed by a general-obligation bond. In a measure, the city merely acts as a collecting agent for special-assessment bonds. In case of default, the bondholder's avenue of recourse is first against the benefited property and secondly against the city.

After the delays of public improvements caused by World War II when materials were not available, the debt of Kansas cities increased. A considerable share of the current revenues of cities is spent to retire debt and to pay interest on bonds. In some classes of cities over a third of the total revenues are spent for this purpose.

The Legislature has imposed restrictions on the procedure and amounts of each type of bond which cities can issue. For example, second- and third-class cities can issue general-obligation bonds up to 15 per cent of their total assessed valuation, but the total indebtedness may not exceed 25 per cent.[25]

Many cities are hard pressed to find enough revenue to carry on the services which seem to be necessary. The home-rule constitutional amendment in 1960 seemed to give to the cities some relief in the financial field, but the Legislature acted soon to restrict cities from raising revenues from some of the sources which cities had hoped to

25. *K.S.A.,* 10-303.

TABLE 47

Forms of City Government in Kansas: 1968

	1st Class	2nd Class	3rd Class	Total
Mayor-Council	1	46	512	559
Commission	4	18	2	24
Commission-Manager	10	19	4	33
Mayor-Council-Manager	1	7	0	8
Total	16	90	518	624

Source: League of Kansas Municipalities, *Kansas Government Journal* (Topeka), LIV (1968), 86.

use. The League of Kansas Municipalities has been active in pointing to the need of cities for more revenue.[26]

Forms of City Government

All classes of Kansas cities are allowed to operate under any of four basic forms of city government—the mayor-council, the commission, or two varieties of the city-manager plan. As shown by the table above, most of the cities in Kansas use the oldest of these forms of city government—the mayor-council plan.

Most authorities on municipal government differentiate between the strong and the weak mayor-council variations of city government. As is suggested by the names, this difference centers on the powers of the mayor and inversely, therefore, the powers of the council. Specifically, in the strong mayor-council plan the mayor has more appointive power, more power over finances, and in general more power to control the administration of the city's affairs and to take part in legislative matters than in the weak mayor-council plan.

In Kansas, the statutes give to the mayor some of the powers given to that office under the strong-mayor variation. He is elected at large in all classes of cities. He presides over the council and has a veto. He has the power of requiring reports from any municipal officer, and, while the wording differs from class to class, he is given general super-

26. "Financing the Public Services of Kansas Cities," *Kansas Government Journal* (Topeka: League of Kansas Municipalities), LII (1966), pp. 440-42, 460-62, 486-88, 522-23, 525, 532-34, 570-71.

vision over the affairs of the city. On the other hand, his appointments of other officers of the city must be confirmed by the council; by the general rule that removal power is a corollary of the appointive power, he must share this power, too, with the council. The mayor must also share his pardoning power with the council, in that he can pardon only with its consent. Perhaps most important in this connection is that the 90 per cent of the cities with the mayor-council form of city government are third-class cities in which, because of their size, government is likely to be informal and casual. Under such a circumstance it is likely that few mayors develop their positions as "strong" executives, so that probably more mayor-council cities in Kansas are of the weak-mayor variety. The accompanying table shows the municipal officials elected under the various forms of city government, their method of election, and terms of office.

The Kansas Legislature was quick to respond to the national reform movement which ushered in the commission form of city government in the early 1900's. In 1907, the same year that the Iowa Legislature approved the commission plan for Des Moines, the Kansas Legislature allowed first- and second-class cities to adopt the commission plan of city government. Six years later third-class cities were similarly allowed to operate under this plan.

In first-class commission cities there are typically[27] five commissioners—commissioners of finance and revenue; of streets and public improvements; of waterworks and street lighting; of parks and public property; and of police and fire, who is also mayor. Second- and third-class cities are organized along slightly different lines with a mayor and two commissioners.[28] In all classes the mayor is elected as mayor. In first-class cities each commissioner is elected commissioner of a given department, while in second- and third-class cities the commission assigns the commissioners to specific departments.

27. Kansas City, Kansas, the largest commission city in the state, operates under a special law with only three commissioners.

28. In second-class cities the mayor is commissioner of police, fire, public health, parks, and public property. One commissioner is in charge of finance and revenue, and the other commissioner supervises the streets, public utilities, and public improvement. There is much the same division of duties in third-class cities except that the commissioner of finance and revenue also supervises the waterworks and municipal utilities.

TABLE 48

Election of City Officials by Form of City Government, Class, Type of Election, and Term

Government Form, Class	Frequency	Partisan or Nonpartisan	Elected Officers	Term	Year Elected
MAYOR-COUNCIL					
1st Class	Annual	Part.	Mayor	2 years	Odd
			2 Councilmen, each ward	2 years	Odd
2nd Class	Annual	Part.	Mayor	2 years	Odd
			Police Judge	2 years	Odd
			Treasurer	2 years	Odd
			2 Councilmen, each ward	2 years	Odd
3rd Class	2 years	Part.	Mayor	2 years	Odd
			Police Judge	2 years	Odd
			5 Councilmen	2 years	Odd
COMMISSION					
1st Class					
Over 125,000	4 years	Nonpart.	Mayor	4 years	1967
			2 Commissioners	4 years	1967
			5 mem. Bd. Pub. Utilities	4 years	1967
60,000 to 150,000	2 years	Nonpart.	Mayor	2 years	Odd
			4 Commissioners	2 years	Odd
Other*	2 years	Nonpart.	Mayor	2 years	Odd
			4 Commissioners	2 years	Odd
Under 20,000†	2 years	Nonpart.	Mayor	2 years	Odd
			2 Commissioners	2 years	Odd
2nd Class	Annual	Nonpart.	Mayor	4 years	Odd
			2 Commissioners	4 years	Odd
3rd Class	Annual	Nonpart.	Mayor	4 years	Odd
			2 Commissioners	4 years	Odd
COMMISSION-MANAGER					
1st Class					
Over 125,000‡	2 years	Nonpart.	5 Commissioners	4 years	3 in 1967 2 in 1969
65,000 to 125,000	2 years	Nonpart.	5 Commissioners	4 years	3 in 1967 2 in 1969
18,000 to 65,000	2 years	Nonpart.	4 Commissioners	4 years	2 each elect.§
			1 Commissioner	2 years	1 each elect.§

TABLE 48 (concluded)

Government Form, Class	Frequency	Partisan or Nonpartisan	Elected Officers	Term	Year Elected
Under 18,000	2 years	Nonpart.	2 Commissioners¶	4 years	1 each elect.§
			1 Commissioner	2 years	1 each elect.§
2nd Class					
Over 8,000	2 years	Nonpart.	2 Commissioners¶	4 years	1 each elect.§
			1 Commissioner	2 years	1 each elect.§
Under 8,000	Annual	Nonpart.	3 Commissioners	2 years	Odd
3rd Class	Annual	Nonpart.	3 Commissioners	2 years	Odd

* Leavenworth elects a five-member Waterworks Board for four-year terms, three members at one election, two at the next.
† Cities in this group are generally included in the law pertaining to cities of less than 30,000 and may come under either law.
‡ Must also be in a county with an assessed valuation of over $250,000,000.
§ Elections in odd years.
¶ Cities over 8,000 may increase number of commissioners to five.
Source: *K.S.A.*

Under the commission plan of city government, the commissioners acting together form the governing body of the city. In this capacity they enact ordinances, appropriate money, and adopt revenue measures. As a group the commissioners superintend the general affairs of the city and make appointments, though on occasion this amounts to a ratification of choices made by an individual commissioner for his department. Individually, each commissioner acts as the administrative chief of the departments assigned him. While the mayor presides over the commission, he does not have a veto and is merely one of the commissioners in transacting the commission's business.

Two types of city-manager government are authorized for all classes of Kansas cities. The older variation is the commission-manager plan, first allowed in 1917. Under this plan, three or five commissioners are elected at large and form the governing body. In this capacity they pass ordinances, appropriate money, approve the budget, and select a city manager. As far as policy and administration can be separated, the commission makes decisions on policy, and the manager carries out the policy. Since the manager serves at the pleasure of the commission, he can be removed at any time with or without cause. The manager is responsible for the general day-to-day superintending of the city's business.

In 1935 the Legislature authorized another form of city government —the mayor-council-manager plan. Under this plan, mayor-council cities may continue under their general plan of operation except that after a referendum, the council selects a manager who assumes responsibility for superintending the affairs of the city's business. Under this plan the manager assumes some of the duties of the mayor under the older mayor-council variety. Under the law as first drafted, there was possibility for a difference of opinion between the mayor and the manager over each's responsibility. In at least one city this became a real problem, and in 1951 the Legislature acted to clarify the powers of the mayor and manager.

There remain three differences between the mayor-council-manager and the commission-manager plan in first- and second-class cities. With the former plan elections are partisan, while with the latter plan they are nonpartisan. The members of the governing body are elected at large under the commission-manager plan and by wards in first- and second-class cities with the mayor-council-manager plan. The number of members of the city's governing body is larger with the mayor-council-manager plan than with the commission-manager plan.

While most cities in Kansas use the mayor-council form of city government, over one-half of the urban population of the state lives in cities using the commission-manager plan. Wichita, Hutchinson, Salina, Lawrence, Parsons, and Atchison use this plan, along with about one-fifth of the second-class cities, including some of the larger ones. City-manager government has notably increased in the state since World War II. Twenty-five of the forty-one cities now using the manager plan have adopted it since that time. Most manager cities previously had commissions and now operate under the commission-manager plan. One city has abandoned the manager plan.

Problems

Any discussion of the problems of municipal government seems today to involve finances and more particularly revenues. With citizens asking for more and better services, cities are searching for new and easier ways of raising money. Increased state aid is looked upon with favor by many as not only a popular way of getting more city revenues, but as a way for cities to get more of the money which their citizens contribute to the state government. For others the increase of state aid appears less desirable, for it is feared that with state aid will come state control. In any event, greater city revenue will require in many cases state authorization of higher rates and the use of new sources of revenue.

The state is gradually becoming aware of the fact that there are now at least three areas of the state which are highly urbanized and have many of the problems of metropolitan government—Topeka, Wichita, and Kansas City, Kansas, with adjoining Johnson county. Here particularly there are pressing problems of intergovernmental relations involving water, sewage-disposal, law-enforcement, city-planning, and related areas.

The passing of the home-rule amendment and its subsequent use by cities may have eased somewhat the legal position of cities. Now there is concern for improving the financial capacity of cities by enlarging their power to raise revenue.

24 | *County and Township Government*

Kansas counties were organized in the period from 1855 to 1892. Since 1900 there have been 105 counties. The following table reports the formation of the counties and reflects the westward movement of people in the late nineteenth century. This was a period of expansion[1] and growth marked with rivalries between various cities for becoming the seats of the newly formed counties.

The county is created largely at the desire of the state to perform state functions locally. Most of these functions are assigned to the

TABLE 49
Organization of Kansas Counties

Year	Number of Counties
1855	35
1860	53
1870	81
1880	103
1890	106
1900	105
1960	105

1. Some of this expansion later proved to be unwarranted. An illustration would be the creation of Garfield County and its later dissolution and incorporation as Garfield Township in Finney County.

county in the nature of duties, the counties having limited choices as to whether they perform them. Secondarily, the county serves as a unit of local government and performs locally demanded services. Legally a county is a quasi-municipal corporation as distinguished from a city, a municipal corporation.

It is possible to overstate the extent to which the county exists as an instrumentality of the state. First, and perhaps most important in this connection, is the fact that most of the county officials are elected. While they can do only what the Legislature authorizes or directs them to do, there are many ways of accomplishing any particular function. These elected officials seek to enforce the laws, for example, and in other ways to conduct the affairs of county government as their constituents want. Topeka and the state officials are far away in comparison to the local voters whom the county official must please if he is to be re-elected. In this sense the county is a unit of local self-government.

Also the county is becoming more of a unit of local government, in that more of the functions given counties are permissive and voluntary —for instance, the recreation and hospital functions.

Helpful to an understanding of county government in Kansas will be an awareness of the wide differences which exist between counties in many of their essential characteristics. The table on page 438 shows differences in population from 343,231 to 2,069. Only nineteen counties (18 per cent) have more than 25,000 people, and the median county has about 10,000. About one-fifth of the counties have fewer than 5,000 people. Wide differences in population are accompanied by variations in the amount of real and personal property, from $456,146,160 in Sedgwick County to $6,762,195 in Chautauqua County. Since counties rely substantially on the ad valorem property tax, this wide difference in valuations presents numerous problems for uniform county revenue legislation.

Organization of County Government

Most of the chief county officials are elected and thus responsible directly to the voters. This results in considerable diffusion of responsibility for the work of the county. In a measure, each county official works independently of the others.

TABLE 50
Basic Data for Kansas Counties

County	County Seat	Population (1968)	Per Cent Urban (1960 Census)	Total Assessed Valuation Rural-Urban (1967)
*Allen	Iola	16,369	42.1	$ 21,290,115
*Anderson	Garnett	9,035	33.6	17,090,202
Atchison	Atchison	20,898	60.0	22,935,740
Barber	Medicine Lodge	8,713	35.3	14,827,645
Barton	Great Bend	32,368	73.1	60,009,182
*Bourbon	Fort Scott	16,090	58.5	21,203,677
Brown	Hiawatha	13,229	25.6	24,224,345
Butler	El Dorado	38,395	49.4	43,490,695
*Chase	Cottonwood Falls	3,921	0	12,927,990
*Chautauqua	Sedan	5,956	0	6,762,195
*Cherokee	Columbus	22,279	52.6	17,443,090
*Cheyenne	St. Francis	4,708	0	13,552,599
*Clark	Ashland	3,396	0	8,096,902
Clay	Clay Center	10,675	43.2	19,860,215
*Cloud	Concordia	14,407	48.7	25,500,995
Coffey	Burlington	8,403	0	13,503,905
*Comanche	Coldwater	3,271	0	11,040,310
Cowley	Winfield	37,861	67.0	50,829,815
*Crawford	Girard	37,032	50.4	26,763,915
Decatur	Oberlin	5,778	0	14,665,905
Dickinson	Abilene	21,572	48.4	35,709,368
*Doniphan	Troy	9,574	12.4	12,687,675
Douglas	Lawrence	43,720	75.2	64,699,130
Edwards	Kinsley	5,118	0	10,836,229
*Elk	Howard	5,048	0	8,652,345
*Ellis	Hays	21,270	56.2	23,129,105
Ellsworth	Ellsworth	7,677	0	21,436,960
*Finney	Garden City	16,093	73.4	32,510,450
Ford	Dodge City	20,938	64.6	43,193,355
*Franklin	Ottawa	19,548	54.6	26,609,450
*Geary	Junction City	28,779	65.0	20,479,035
*Gove	Gove	4,707	0	14,121,338
*Graham	Hill City	5,586	0	11,256,160
*Grant	Ulysses	5,269	59.9	17,023,185
*Gray	Cimarron	4,380	0	11,199,100
*Greeley	Tribune	2,087	0	15,321,475
Greenwood	Eureka	11,253	36.0	17,100,975

TABLE 50 (continued)

County	County Seat	Population (1968)	Per Cent Urban (1960 Census) Rural-Urban	Total Assessed Valuation (1967)
*Hamilton	Syracuse	3,144	0	11,720,741
*Harper	Anthony	9,541	28.8	20,471,340
Harvey	Newton	25,865	57.5	42,119,810
*Haskell	Sublette	2,990	0	8,439,170
*Hodgeman	Jetmore	3,115	0	16,543,545
*Jackson	Holton	10,309	29.4	14,135,665
*Jefferson	Oskaloosa	11,252	0	14,601,245
*Jewell	Mankato	7,217	0	16,866,150
Johnson	Olathe	143,792	84.9	156,121,770
Kearny	Lakin	3,108	0	14,090,795
Kingman	Kingman	9,958	36.0	19,639,534
*Kiowa	Greensburg	4,626	0	7,313,025
*Labette	Oswego	26,805	52.0	22,191,295
*Lane	Dighton	3,060	0	12,412,260
Leavenworth	Leavenworth	48,524	45.4	35,051,430
*Lincoln	Lincoln	5,556	0	14,237,885
*Linn	Mound City	8,274	0	11,898,620
Logan	Russell Springs	4,036	0	9,144,910
*Lyon	Emporia	26,928	67.6	40,206,850
McPherson	McPherson	24,285	51.9	28,492,445
*Marion	Marion	15,143	0	28,545,430
Marshall	Marysville	15,598	26.6	43,353,865
Meade	Meade	5,505	0	9,685,340
*Miami	Paola	19,884	47.3	25,901,010
Mitchell	Beloit	8,866	43.3	21,714,875
Montgomery	Independence	45,007	75.7	42,472,215
*Morris	Council Grove	7,392	36.0	13,561,080
*Morton	Richfield	3,354	0	11,646,320
Nemaha	Seneca	12,897	0	23,838,005
*Neosho	Erie	19,455	55.8	19,155,420
*Ness	Ness City	5,470	0	20,984,840
*Norton	Norton	8,035	41.6	11,885,725
Osage	Lyndon	12,886	0	16,517,355
Osborne	Osborne	7,506	0	16,227,168
*Ottawa	Minneapolis	6,779	0	17,161,460
Pawnee	Larned	10,254	48.8	30,012,040
Phillips	Phillipsburg	8,709	37.1	18,070,710
Pottawatomie	Westmoreland	11,957	0	22,567,935
*Pratt	Pratt	12,122	67.3	22,236,335

TABLE 50 (concluded)

County	County Seat	Population (1968)	Per Cent Urban (1960 Census)	Total Assessed Valuation Rural-Urban (1967)
*Rawlins	Atwood	5,279	0	9,007,750
Reno	Hutchinson	59,055	63.6	84,464,575
*Republic	Belleville	9,768	30.1	21,014,170
Rice	Lyons	13,909	33.0	25,935,190
Riley	Manhattan	41,914	54.9	41,805,115
*Rooks	Stockton	9,734	31.9	14,822,720
*Rush	LaCrosse	6,160	0	19,391,130
Russell	Russell	11,348	53.9	18,903,065
*Saline	Salina	54,715	79.0	65,773,850
*Scott	Scott City	5,228	68.0	10,072,920
Sedgwick	Wichita	343,231	90.7	456,146,160
*Seward	Liberal	15,930	86.7	21,255,345
Shawnee	Topeka	141,286	84.6	134,140,600
*Sheridan	Hoxie	4,267	0	11,864,974
Sherman	Goodland	6,682	66.7	20,020,772
*Smith	Smith Center	7,776	0	18,758,130
Stafford	St. John	7,451	0	18,027,225
*Stanton	Johnson	2,108	0	13,946,415
*Stevens	Hugoton	4,400	66.2	7,853,845
Sumner	Wellington	25,316	39.6	38,512,995
Thomas	Colby	7,358	57.2	23,768,082
Trego	WaKeeney	5,473	51.3	8,822,685
Wabaunsee	Alma	6,648	0	14,416,205
*Wallace	Sharon Springs	2,069	0	11,311,910
Washington	Washington	10,739	0	24,752,015
*Wichita	Leoti	2,765	0	18,094,230
*Wilson	Fredonia	13,077	52.2	19,899,435
*Woodson	Yates Center	5,423	0	11,334,625
Wyandotte	Kansas City	185,495	88.5	107,480,430

* Has county-unit road system.

Sources: U.S. Bureau of the Census, *U.S. Census of Population: 1960, Number of Inhabitants, Kansas* (Washington, D.C.: U.S. Government Printing Office, 1961), pp. 18-14, 18-15; Kansas State Board of Agriculture, *Population of Kansas, January 1, 1968* (Topeka: mimeographed, 1968), p. 1; Property Valuation Department, Kansas, *Report of Real Estate Assessment Ratio Study: 1967* (Topeka: 1968), pp. 17, 18; League of Kansas Municipalities, *Directory of Kansas Public Officials: 1967* (Topeka: 1967), *passim*.

Board of County Commissioners

As far as there is a central governing body for the county, it is the board of county commissioners. It approves the county budget which determines the amounts available to the elected county officers for supplies, equipment, and salaries for hiring deputies and other personnel needed for the operation of the county offices. The officers themselves generally have their salaries set by statute, and the fact that they are elected gives them a measure of independence from the county commissioners.

The duties of the board are reflected in the fact that it serves ex officio as the board of health,[2] the board of social welfare,[3] and the board of highway supervisors. In addition, the board is given a miscellany of powers and duties, including the power to maintain a public library; create special benefit districts for sewers, fire protection, and public lighting; establish and maintain public parks; and maintain abandoned cemeteries. Many special acts allow certain counties to engage in still other functions.

Each county is divided into three districts for the purpose of electing a commissioner from each district. The commissioners are elected for four-year terms which are staggered, so that no more than two new commissioners are elected at any one election. The commissioners elect one of their own number to be chairman of the board.

County Clerk

The county clerk acts as secretary of the Board of County Commissioners and maintains the records of the board. Probably for most citizens the most important duty of the clerk, and certainly the most time-consuming, is the assessment of real and personal property. In all but nine of the most populous counties, the clerk serves as the assessor for most property in the county. The State Department of Property Valuation assesses the property of railroads, motor carriers, and telegraph, telephone, pipe-line and electric-power companies, and divides the assessment among the several counties in which the utility owns property.

While the county clerk is responsible for assessing most property

2. *K.S.A.*, 65-201.
3. *K.S.A.*, 39-711.

within the county, he does not do the assessing himself in many of the counties. The clerk appoints deputy assessors who view the property and assign the value to the parcels of real and personal property in the county. The clerk receives the completed assessment forms and checks them. He is instructed by law to revise as needed the values assigned by his deputies, to make them conform to those prescribed in manuals, and to make other values uniform. Though the board of county commissioners has powers similar to those of the clerk for changing the assigned values, in most cases the values assessed will be those which have been set by deputy assessors.

Part of the problem of assessment of property stems from the number of part-time assessors who actually assign values to property. Having different scales of values, they assign different values to like property. The extent of the difference of assessment levels has long been known, because the Department of Property Valuation publishes annually the results of the assessment ratio study. All sales of real estate are reported to the Department, and the ratio of the assessed valuation of the property to its sale price is computed. For example, if a property which is assessed at $2,300 sells for $10,000, the assessment ratio is 23 per cent. The ratios of the properties sold are presented in frequency distribution charts county by county, so that it is possible to see how evenly the properties which changed ownership in the year are assessed. The closer the concentration of ratios, the more equitable the assessment. The median ratio for each type of property for each county and the state as a whole is reported in the study. In 1967 the median sale in counties ranged from 29 per cent of sale value to 8 per cent of sale value. The state average was 18 per cent.

Thus a property holder in the county (Washington) with a 29 per cent ratio paid on a *state* property tax levy over three times as much theoretically as the property holder of similarly valued property in a county with an assessment ratio of 8 per cent (Haskell or Meade). It should also be mentioned, however, that the county with a high ratio receives proportionately more state-shared funds than the county with a low ratio.

Most of the property tax is levied by local units of government within the county. To this extent uniformity of assessment levels within a county is more important than uniformity or equality of assessment

Governmental Structure of Kansas Counties: 1968

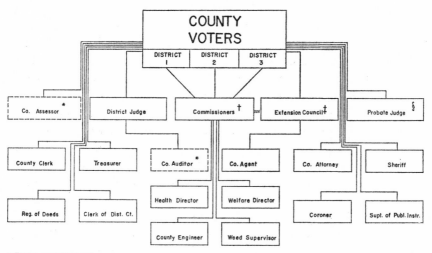

* Some counties only.
† Also County Welfare Board, Board of Road Supervisors, and, with the Health Officer, County Board of Health.
‡ Elected by farm voters; sits with Commissioners on extension budget matters only.
§ In most counties, also County Judge.

between counties. Substantial differences exist within counties and are revealed in the annual assessment ratio studies. Dissatisfaction with present assessment methods was sufficient for the Legislature in 1953 to authorize the appointment of a state citizens' committee and local county citizens' committees to study assessment procedures and to make recommendations. Local study groups were organized in all but one of the counties, and the state committee held meetings and issued a report summarizing the local reports.[4] The state committee made a number of recommendations to the 1955 Legislature, some of which were adopted. The procedures were simplified for the adoption, on a local-option basis, of a system of an appointive assessor. The county was clearly made the assessment district, and the law now provides for the continuous appraisal of property. The assessor is now legally instructed to install and maintain such records and data on property as may be required by the State Department of Property Valuation. In

4. Kansas Citizens' Commission on Assessment Equalization, *County Committee Assessment Equalization Reports* (Topeka: 1954), *passim*.

general the responsibility and authority of the State Department of Property Valuation has been increased.[5]

In the assessing process, the clerk has the further responsibility of checking the returns of the deputy assessor to see that no property escapes taxation. He prepares the assessment rolls and serves as clerk to the county commissioners when they meet as the board of equalization to hear complaints about the assessments and to equalize the assessments in the whole county. The county board may make such changes as it considers proper, but the assessments do not become final until they are equalized by the board of tax appeals. The State Board of Tax Appeals hears the appeals of those who are dissatisfied with their assessment even though they have appeared before the county commissioners; it also hears the appeals of those whose property had been assessed by the Department of Property Valuation.

The county clerk is then informed by the State Board of Tax Appeals of the equalized valuation of all the property in the county. Basing it on the budgets which the various taxing units have filed with the county clerk, the clerk computes the tax against the holder of each parcel of property. These computations then are turned over to the county treasurer for collection.

In addition to these duties, the clerk is in most counties the chief official for election administration. He receives nomination petitions for county office and is responsible for having the ballots printed and distributed. He administers the absentee voter laws.

Thus the clerk's duties in elections and in assessing make him an important official for all units of local government. In many parts of the state the clerk helps township, school district, and city officials prepare and, in some cases, administer their budgets.

While the relationship between the clerk and the county commissioners varies considerably from county to county and depends largely upon personal factors, the clerk in some instances is given other administrative duties.

County Treasurer

The county treasurer is the custodian of county funds. He receives

---

5. For more information on the activities of the State Department of Property Valuation, please see page 150 and following.

such money as is due the county from the state. He collects the ad valorem property tax of tax-levying jurisdictions in the county and then distributes it according to the levies made by the various local units. He pays out county funds upon proper authorization of the board of county commissioners. The county treasurer also collects automobile registration fees and sends the money to the state government. He issues other licenses. The original Kansas Constitution included a provision that county treasurers could serve no more than two consecutive terms. In 1968 the voters deleted this prohibition from the Constitution, so that now there is no restriction on the number of terms a person can serve as county treasurer.

County Sheriff

The sheriff is the chief law-enforcement officer of the county. He is charged with the duties of maintaining law and order and of enforcing state law. Also the sheriff acts as a servant to the court. He and his deputies serve subpoenas and processes and execute orders of all courts of record in their county. He maintains the county jail and is responsible for the safekeeping of those persons committed to jail.

The sheriff is elected for a two-year term and now is not restricted as to how many terms he may serve. From 1861 until 1964 the Constitution forbade persons from serving more than two consecutive terms. The salary of the sheriff depends on the population of the county. The county commissioners allow other expenses, including the hiring of deputies. The sheriff is entitled to retain some of the fees which he collects.

County Attorney

Another important official in the law-enforcement process is the county attorney, who acts as prosecuting attorney. In this capacity he represents the county (and the state) in both criminal and civil cases. As public prosecutor, the county attorney conducts criminal investigations and determines whether there is enough evidence in a given case to prosecute. In some instances he may have to decide whether to prosecute for a more serious crime or for a lesser one which can be more easily proved.

The county attorney gives legal advice to county officers as requested and represents the county in civil cases. He may investigate, and file ouster proceedings against, public officials.

County Coroner

In 1963 the Legislature provided for the judge of the district court to appoint a district coroner from the two or more licensed practitioners of medicine nominated by the local medical society or societies. This system replaced a system of elected county coroners. Under the elected system many of the coroners were not physicians or surgeons, and there was concern about the need for persons trained in medicine or criminal investigation—hopefully in both. There is a district coroner appointed for each judicial district, and the district coroner may with the approval of the district judge appoint deputy coroners.

The district coroner holds inquests regarding persons supposed to have died by unlawful means or the cause of whose death is unknown. In these cases a group of six citizens of the county is impaneled to form a coroner's jury. The coroner may subpoena witnesses. The jury renders a verdict indicating the "means, weapon, or accident" which resulted in death and whether it was feloniously caused. The coroner then issues a warrant to the sheriff for the guilty person. In some instances the coroner may perform an autopsy.

Register of Deeds

The register of deeds is primarily concerned with the routine important service of recording permanently the ownership of real property. He registers liens, conditional sales contracts for real and personal property, mortgages, and other documents affecting real estate. In this manner the individual citizen is more secure in his ownership of property and does not need to retain the document itself.

Probate Judge

Each county of the state elects a probate judge. This official probates wills and settles estates, handles guardianship proceedings and control of infants' property, and considers the commitment of the insane. He also presides over the juvenile court for his county.

The probate judge is elected every two years. There are no requirements of legal training, and some probate judges have not had any. In ninety-three counties of the state the probate judge is also judge of the county court, whose jurisdiction has been described in chapter 11.

Clerk of the District Court

Each county elects a clerk of the district court, who receives papers filed in that court and maintains its records.

Other Officers

In addition to these elected county officials there are a number of appointive officials. Two of the most important are the county engineer[6] and the social-welfare director, whose duties have been discussed in earlier chapters.

County Reorganization

This listing of county officials and brief enumeration of their duties suggests the extent to which authority and administrative power are diffused. No single official, or even small group of officials, is responsible for county affairs. (Though cities have experienced two major structural reform movements in the twentieth century, county government in Kansas continues to be structurally much what it was a hundred years ago.)

A few counties throughout the United States have adopted the county-manager form of government patterned after the city-manager plan. Though the Legislature in Kansas presumably could centralize some responsibilities in a governing board and allow them to appoint a manager, it would take a constitutional amendment to abolish the offices of sheriff and treasurer, mentioned in the Constitution. The Legislature has considered giving counties the option of centralizing the administration of county affairs under a manager or administrator, but it has not authorized this change.[7] Despite the widespread use of the manager plan by Kansas cities, the county-manager plan is not authorized and is not used.

County Functions and Finances

Welfare and roads are the biggest functions of the county in terms

6. In most counties the county engineer acts as county surveyor in determining the boundaries of property and road rights of way. In counties with more than 60,000 population but less than 190,000 and having a city over 40,000, the county surveyor is elected.

7. For more information on these proposals see William H. Cape, *The Emerging Patterns of County Executives* (Lawrence: Governmental Research Center, Univ. of Kansas, 1967), pp. 99-107.

of dollars expended. These two functions have been discussed elsewhere. Of these two, most county commissioners are likely to consider roads more important, because they have wider discretion in spending the highway money and because the counties performed this function first. While of limited financial significance, noxious-weed eradication, county fairs, parks, libraries, public health, and agricultural extension are service activities performed by the county.

The counties raise money for local schools, but the money is turned over to the school districts for spending. Particularly since the 1966 constitutional amendment eliminating the office of county superintendent, it can hardly be said that the county is deeply involved in the education function.

Any figures on expenditures are somewhat misleading because of the differences among counties in expenditures for particular functions and in total expenditures. The wide difference in number of welfare cases per thousand population, already reported in chapter 15, is of course reflected in the county expenditures. Counties which have adopted the county-unit road plan, as described in chapter 18, generally spend more for roads than those counties in which there are township

TABLE 51

Number of Counties Making Property-Tax Levies by Mill Rates: 1968

Rate of Levy (By Mills)	Number of Counties
39.00–40.99	4
37.00–38.99	3
35.00–36.99	3
33.00–34.99	4
31.00–32.99	11
29.00–30.99	14
27.00–28.99	13
25.00–26.99	16
23.00–24.99	16
21.00–22.99	10
19:00–20.99	7
17.00–18.99	1
15.00–16.99	3
	105

Source: *Kansas Government Journal*, January, 1968, pp. 40–41.

roads. Counties generally get more than half of their revenues from the property tax.

Many problems are presented by this heavy reliance of the counties on the property tax. The general sentiment that the property tax is raising as much of the total costs of government as it can reasonably be expected to, has resulted in strong pressures to keep the property-tax rate down. Moreover, the county must share the property tax with other units of local government.

Counties, along with those other units depending largely on the property tax, have experienced financial problems in the postwar inflationary period. While the total valuation of property has increased, it has not kept pace with the increased demand for more tax dollars. The counties have found it necessary to ask the Legislature for relief, which has taken various forms. In some instances the Legislature has raised the amount of levy which the county could make for particular functions. It also has increased the total or aggregate levy that the county could make and placed outside this aggregate some of the levies or parts of the levies authorized for particular functions. In some cases this was done by special act, and in others by general acts.

Because of the wide difference in assessment levels, as well as in the amount of property, counties raise different amounts from the same mill-rate levies. The mill rate which may raise adequate funds for one county may be wholly inadequate for another. The distribution of the 1967 mill-rate levies for 1968 by counties is shown in Table 51.

Another important source of county revenue is returned state funds or what in some states might be called state aid. The formulas and the methods which determine the amount of returned state funds a county receives for welfare and highway purposes have been described in earlier chapters. Like other property-tax–levying units of local government, the county receives a share of the sales-tax residue.[8] The liquor-control–enforcement tax is distributed by the state to counties on the same basis as the sales-tax residue, but within the county 50 per cent goes to the county government. The state distributes 50 per cent of the cigarette tax to counties, each county's share being determined by its population. Within the county, half of the amount received is

8. For more information on the distribution of the sales-tax residue, see p. 139.

credited to the county general fund and the remainder is divided among the cities of the county.

Amid requests for additional state assistance there is every indication that state aid to counties will be continued, if not increased. In general, counties have not been allowed to use service charges or utility "profits" to finance their operation.

The Future of County Government

Despite the growth of the cities of the state, the county is an important unit of government in Kansas and promises to continue as such. Besides being central to the operation of the other units of local government, it is important in the functions which it handles for the state. With the increasing use of nonpartisan elections in cities, political partisanship at the county level becomes more conspicuous. The political parties are quite naturally organized along county lines, and in a sense the state political party organization is a loose organization of the local county political leaders. The county was for decades essentially the unit of representation in the House of Representatives and is still used in many instances to form House and Senate districts.

In addition to the problem of need for structural reform within the county, there is the further problem of revision of county lines or the consolidation of counties. One study of the characteristics of effective local units of government concludes that "reasonable efficiency is probably unobtainable with units of fewer than 25,000 inhabitants, while maximum effectiveness probably requires a population of 50,000."[9] By this standard, 85 per cent of Kansas counties are of a size which makes reasonable efficiency impossible. There have been a few instances where a single person, such as an engineer, a social welfare director, or a health officer, has served for more than one county, but these are exceptional. Despite the great changes in transportation and communication since the time when the counties were established, county boundaries have remained unchanged for decades. It may be that as we become more accustomed to multi-county House and Senate districts, the consolidation of counties will become more politically feasible.

9. Council of State Governments, *State-Local Relations* (Chicago: Council of State Governments, 1946), p. 202.

Township Government

Like Kansas counties, townships were organized substantially in their present pattern before 1900.[10] The number of townships per county ranges from thirty-two in Reno County to three in Grant, Greeley, Haskell, and Stanton counties. Townships vary in size from 1.5 square miles in Oberlin City Township, Decatur County, to 430.5 square miles in Garfield Township, Finney County. The median or "average" township has 35.6 square miles.

Township offices include a trustee, a clerk, a treasurer, two justices of the peace, and two constables, all of whom are elected. The trustee, the clerk, and the treasurer form the township auditing board, which has the general responsibility for supervising township finances. In counties which have not adopted the county-unit road system, the board also acts as the township board of highway supervisors.

Frequently meetings of the township auditing board and the township board of highway commissioners are held at the same time. Decisions concerning the construction and maintenance of township roads are made at these meetings. In general the road work is to be done in accordance with plans and specifications and general regulations prepared by the county engineer. One study indicated that frequently this statutory requirement was not followed.

To a limited extent the township trustee is the general supervisor of township government. He divides the township into convenient road districts and appoints road overseers. In addition to his general management responsibilities he is a judge of elections. In some townships the trustee may himself be road overseer. In some counties he is appointed deputy assessor and assigns the value of property for tax purposes—a function which he formerly had as an ex officio duty. In some townships the trustee has duties in connection with prairie-dog eradication, the cemetery, and water and sewer systems. The duties of the clerk and the treasurer are described by their titles.

The justice of the peace was established as the judicial officer for the township. The jurisdiction of this court was never large, but in recent

10. The materials for this section have been drawn largely from *Township Government in Kansas,* by James W. Drury (Lawrence: Governmental Research Center, Univ. of Kansas, 1954).

years it has been further restricted.[11] First- and second-class cities constitute separate townships for the election of justices of the peace. With each of the 1,551 other townships in the state allowed two justices, over 3,200 offices of justice of the peace are authorized. Only a small percentage of this possible total number of offices is filled. Where the court does exist, it is often concerned with violations of highway weight laws and game and traffic laws.

The township law-enforcement officer is the constable, who is directed by the statutes "to apprehend on view or warrant, and bring to justice, all felon disturbers and violators of the criminal laws of the state . . . and generally to keep the peace of his proper county." The constables are also ministerial officers of the justice-of-the-peace courts. Like the office of justice of the peace, only a small percentage of the offices of constable are filled.

Generally there is relatively little interest in the township offices. In one study of elections, in almost half of the townships no candidates had filed in the primary, and in a large number of cases only one candidate had filed. Thus in almost 90 per cent of the township offices there was no contest in the primary, and frequently people are elected by a few write-in votes. The practice seems to be for the incumbent to be re-elected. The average tenure of a sample number of trustees was almost seven years, although each term is but two years.

The adjoining table shows the number of townships in different regions of the state performing various functions authorized for townships. The construction and maintenance of roads is by far the most common and most expensive function of township government in the state. When the county assumes the responsibility for their care and construction, the total township expenditures are so reduced that the amounts spent for general overhead costs become proportionately very large.

The property tax is the main source of revenue for townships. As property-tax-levying units of local government, they share in distribution of the sales-tax residue. Townships also receive state aid from the state gasoline tax.

In those parts of the state where the counties have assumed the management of the roads, township government has almost died of

11. For further information see page 198.

TABLE 52

Number of Townships Performing Selected Functions by Region:
1951, 1952, 1953*

Function	North-east	South-east	North-central	South-central	North-west	South-west	Total
Roads	191	12	166	335	69	21	794
Cemetery	63	43	48	140	22	20	336
Prairie Dogs	0	0	86	33	89	11	219
Weeds	71	0	51	45	28	8	203
Fire	48	15	2	55	0	7	127
Library	1	0	0	8	0	3	12
Light	4	1	5	1	1	0	12
Water Hydrants	4	0	0	0	0	0	4
Band	2	0	0	1	0	0	3
Park	0	0	0	1	1	0	2
Township Patrol	1	0	0	0	0	0	1
Trash Collection	1	0	0	0	0	0	1
Judgment	1	0	0	0	0	0	1
Hospital	0	0	0	1	0	0	1

* This table was adjusted to include the most current information on number of counties with the county-unit road system. The rest of the table is included despite its age because no more recent information is available.

Source: James W. Drury, *Township Government in Kansas* (Lawrence: Governmental Research Center, Univ. of Kansas, 1954), p. 35.

atrophy. As is true of other units of government, once established, township government is difficult to abolish. The townships function as election areas and as districts for assessing property. These are functions which must be continued, and the statutes make no provision for them to be performed by any other agency than the township. There is no provision for any territory outside of a township or incorporated area to be recognized. Township government has materially changed where the county-unit plan for roads has been adopted, but township government continues throughout the state. Its future importance will largely depend upon extent of adoptions and use of the county-unit road plan.

25 | *Intergovernmental Relations*

In a narrow sense "intergovernmental relations" refers to the relationships of one unit of government with another, but since governments can act only through their officers and agents, such relations also consist of the contacts and dealings of the officials of one governmental unit with the officials of another. These relations in some instances are highly formal, as would be illustrated by the amending of the United States Constitution, or they may be quite informal as, for example, when a city governing body might agree with the county officials to improve jointly a street which is a common boundary. Today these relationships exist in practically all areas of governmental activities and take many forms.

While dramatic instances of intergovernmental cooperation in sponsoring some important improvements or in apprehending a criminal may come to our attention in the newspaper, the bulk of these intergovernmental relationships are carried on through routine correspondence and contacts between administrative officials. In Kansas the city clerk, as the local registrar of vital statistics, receives and forwards reports to the State Board of Health; the deputy county assessor establishes assessment of real property which is used as a base for city and township taxes, as well as for county taxes; and in many other ways local officials without any particular notice or ado cooperate in getting the work of government done. Without these and numerous other instances of intergovernmental relations, many of the services which we expect from our government could not be performed. For most purposes intergovernmental relations are classified according to the units of government involved.

National-State Relationships

The general framework for national-state relations is established by the U.S. Constitution. Though there have been relatively few formal changes in the Constitution, the whole pattern of federal-state relations has changed greatly in the 180 years of governmental operation. Wars and depressions have caused Congress to search more closely the provisions of the Constitution, and power has been found for the expanded operation of the national government. Though sometimes with hesitation, the recent pattern has been for the U.S. Supreme Court to acquiesce in the exercise of the powers. For example, from the power to regulate commerce Congress has found that it has the power to regulate labor-management relations in companies engaged in interstate commerce. Expansions in this and many other areas have led some to fear that federation is gone.

There can be no doubt that the tremendous expansion of the national government's power has meant many changes in our long-established pattern of federal-state relations. However, expansions at the federal level have occasioned expansions at the state level. The welfare and highway programs illustrate this point. More and more the federal and state governments have found ways to cooperate in providing services for their citizens. More recently the new term "creative federalism" has come into popular usage. The new term is used with different emphases, but in general it encompasses the concept of cooperative federalism, and for many it includes the idea of greater freedom for the state in joint federal-state ventures and broad, new, innovative programs for jointly attacking the contemporary problems of our society.

Despite these many changes, the basic framework of federalism remains. The national government and the state governments are legally coequal units, each with its own power to pass laws and enforce them, and each with its own power to collect taxes and spend money for governmental purposes. The national government has only those powers which are given it by the Constitution. Other spheres of governmental activity are reserved to the state governments or to the people, but these spheres are not listed. There are also a great many fields of governmental activity in which both national and state governments may participate, with the precise limits of their activity being determined from time to time by Congress and by decisions of the United States Supreme Court.

In the early years of Kansas' statehood, almost all of the national-state relations consisted of state and national officers' requesting help from each other in cases where domestic peace and law and order were threatened by Indians, outlaws, or guerrilla forces fighting for or against slavery before and during the Civil War. While cooperation between national and state officers in law enforcement is still an important activity, most present-day national-state relationships occur in other activities in which both governments are interested. The most important of these activities are in the fields of agriculture, welfare, health, education, and highways. In each of these fields, cooperation between the national government and the state takes the form of grants-in-aid programs.

The amount of money received by the state from federal grants-in-aid at ten-year intervals over the past half-century is shown by

TABLE 53

Total Federal Grants-in-Aid Received by the State of Kansas:
Selected Years

Year	Amount
1905	$ 25,000
1915	116,348
1925	303,617
1935	8,030,792
1945	7,789,419
1955	43,219,546
1965	116,115,801
1968	155,307,478

Source: *Federal Grants-in-aid in Kansas* (Lawrence: Governmental Research Center, Univ. of Kansas, 1953), p. 17; Department of Administration, State of Kansas, *Financial Report for Period July 1, 1954, to June 30, 1955* (Topeka: 1955), p. 15; *Financial Report for Period July 1, 1964, to June 30, 1965* (Topeka: 1965), p. 23; *Financial Report for Period July 1, 1967, to June 30, 1968* (Topeka: 1968), p. 21.

Table 53. In 1905 Kansas received one grant, for the College of Agricultural and Mechanic Arts. By 1925 there were additional grants for highways and public health, and in the mid-1930's sizable grants were added for emergency relief and welfare purposes. Shortly after 1945 there were sizable increases in grants for all purposes.

Since 1950, the amount of money provided annually to the state of Kansas by grants from the national government has ranged from $30,000,000 to $155,000,000 in the 1968 fiscal year. This constitutes a significant portion of state revenue. Table 54 shows the amounts and kinds of grants paid to state and local units in fiscal year 1967 by the federal government.

TABLE 54

Federal Aid Payments to State and Local Units: Kansas,
Fiscal Year 1967

Kind of Grant	Amount
Department of Agriculture	
Basic scientific research grants	$ 35,126
Cooperative agricultural extension work	1,454,700
Cooperative projects in marketing	119,921
Cooperative state research service	959,529
Food stamp program	175,194
Forest protection, utilization and restoration	150,673
National grasslands shared revenues	22,073
Removal of surplus agricultural commodities, value of commodities distributed	1,037,179
School lunch program	2,440,107
Special milk program	1,160,802
Watershed protection, flood prevention and resource conservation and development	3,920,696
Commodity Credit Corporation	
Price support donations	1,200,865
Rural water and waste disposal grants	279,950
Department of Commerce	
State technical services	45,924
Development facilities grants	35,772
Department of Defense—Army	
Civil Defense	266,740
Flood control lands—shared revenues	262,490
Funds Appropriated to the President	
Accelerated public works program	12,762

TABLE 54 (continued)

Kind of Grant	Amount
Disaster relief and state and local preparedness	2,941,734
Office of Economic Opportunity	
Adult basic education	138,266
Community Action Programs	3,592,065
Neighborhood Youth Corps	1,720,356
Adult work training and development	184,000
Work experience and training programs	49,730
Department of Health, Education, and Welfare	
Administration on Aging	52,018
American Printing House for the Blind	17,812
Vocational Rehabilitation Administration	1,402,999
Office of Education	
Arts and humanities educational activities	5,329
Colleges of agricultural and the mechanical arts	251,783
Assistance to public schools, construction	181,376
Higher education facilities, construction	1,610,609
Cooperative vocational education	2,884,933
Defense educational activities	1,382,823
Educational improvement for the handicapped	353,000
Elementary and secondary educational activities	11,893,399
Library services	725,393
Maintenance and operation of schools	9,671,613
Higher educational activities	413,719
Public Health Service	
Chronic diseases and health of aged	207,137
Communicable diseases activities	175,546
Community health practice and research	160,191
Hospital and health research facilities, construction	3,753,353
Waste treatment works construction	1,561,634
Control of tuberculosis	111,480
Control of venereal disease	29,223
Dental services and resources	9,928
National Institute of Mental Health	64,740
Radiological health	16,803
Water supply and pollution control	160,823
Medical care services	15,685
Welfare Administration	
Bureau of family services, public assistance	36,372,702
Children's Bureau, maternal and child health and welfare services	1,709,373
Department of Housing and Urban Development	
Low rent public housing program	364,072

TABLE 54 (concluded)

Kind of Grant	Amount
Open space land grants	177,382
Urban planning grants	526,213
Urban renewal	4,828,417
Urban mass transportation	160,000
Department of the Interior	
Bureau of Indian Affairs	12,000
Commercial fisheries research and development	11,954
Certain special funds, shared revenues	44
Fish and wildlife restoration and management	565,947
Mineral leasing act payments, shared revenues	135,107
National wildlife refuge fund	17,496
Water resources research	138,285
Land and water conservation fund	1,013,054
Department of Labor	
Manpower development and training activities	265,729
Unemployment compensation and employment service administration (trust fund)	3,938,783
Department of Justice	
Law enforcement assistance	25,205
National Foundation of the Arts and the Humanities	18,323
Department of Transportation	
Bureau of Public Roads, highway trust fund	38,566,276
FAA—airport program	361,107
Federal Highway Administration	
Beautification and control of outdoor advertising	192,261
Landscaping and scenic enhancement	537,527
Veteran's Administration	
Veteran's Administration	87,741
Water Resources Council	39,200
TOTAL GRANTS TO STATE AND LOCAL UNITS	$149,384,201

Source: U.S. Treasury Department, *Annual Report of the Secretary of the Treasury on the State of the Finances, 1967* (Washington, D.C.: U.S. Government Printing Office, 1968), pp. 696-711.

The grants-in-aid programs have not been adopted without opposition. People opposed to federal grants of the states often argue that it is unnecessarily complicated to pay taxes to the national government, only to have the latter turn around and return the money to the state.

They point out that national officials must be paid to collect the taxes and to keep account of what is received and what is paid to the states, and that the salaries paid to these national officials could be saved if the taxes were paid directly to the states. The opponents also will frequently object to their state's not receiving as much of the grant proportionately as another state. States, it is said, are sometimes so anxious to get federal grants that they match federal funds only to realize later that there is an imbalance in the use of state resources to solve the problems confronting the state. Probably some opposition to federal grants comes consciously or unconsciously from an opposition to the government program or activity in the area covered by the grant.

Much of the argument over federal grants is related to the degree of federal control that has come with the federal grants. Undeniably national grants have been accompanied with some degree of federal supervision. However, the type of supervision has varied greatly from grant to grant. The state agency receiving the grant may be required to submit a plan indicating how the money will be spent. The plan may be a simple affair, or it may be a complicated document, depending upon the program. Usually the national agency supervising the administration of the grant also requires periodic reports from the state agency and frequently sends out inspectors or auditors to check the work being done by the state agencies, in order to insure that national funds are being used in accordance with national requirements. Most differences of opinion about the program are settled by conferences between national and state officials, but if the state agency persists in doing something which the national agency considers illegal or improper, the national agency may stop the grants. While the national government seldom takes this drastic action, the threat of doing so is always in the background and influences state agencies to do things the way the national agency suggests.

National requirements accompanying grants may extend to requiring states to maintain certain standards with respect to the state personnel employed in programs covered by grants. For example, the U.S. Social Security Act requires that a merit system be used for all employees connected with the state and welfare agencies which administer the program partially supported by national funds. As a result, employees of county welfare departments in Kansas are selected under the merit system and are under all the usual civil-service requirements for appointment, promotion, salary increases, and retirement.

The supporters of federal grants will generally look to the "bright" side of the various aspects of supervision. They may consider, for example, the requirement of merit-system coverage and the interchange of ideas and information, stimulated by the national supervising officials, not really "interference" and federal control but merely desirable aspects of the program which may contribute to its efficiency. Such persons are not likely to be disturbed by the shift of power to Washington, for they remember that they elect their Senators and Congressmen and sometimes actually feel that they are more adequately represented in the national legislative chambers than in state legislatures.

The supporters of federal-grant programs point to the "national" nature of many of the areas customarily handled by state government. Public health, for example, they suggest, is a nationwide problem. Disease germs do not stop at state lines, and therefore attempts to prevent the spread of disease must be carried on all over the country. Many of the people of the United States move around, so that what is a health problem for one state today may become a health problem for another state next year.

Argument about federal grants-in-aid may persist, but it seems likely that Kansas will continue to accept federal aid. Indeed, it is impossible to see how Kansas could continue its operations today without federal aid, unless there should be a major revision of revenue sources. The tax resources of the federal government are so much broader than those of the state that by comparison the state's powers seem restricted. Certain types of taxes which the federal government collects cannot effectively be collected by states. Today our state tax structure is predicated upon a continuation of the federal-grant programs.

If we accept, as apparently we must, the likely continuation of such programs, attention must be called to one further fundamental problem. Most national grants are offered on a matching basis—i.e., the state government receives federal funds in amounts based upon what it contributes. Caution must continually be exercised to see that grants programs do not result in unbalanced state operations.

Generally in the chapters on each of the subjects concerned—public welfare, health, highways and law enforcement—attention has been given to the operating relationships which exist between the national government and the states.

Interstate Relations

Interstate Compacts

Article I, section 10, of the United States Constitution provides a formal method for states to set up governmental machinery for dealing with problems which affect two or more states. The states may, with the approval of Congress, enter into compacts or agreements with one another. Congress has given its approval in advance to some types of compacts. For some types of agreements, contracts, and compactlike agreements it has ruled that Congressional approval is not necessary. The precise number of compacts or agreements which Kansas has entered into depends upon how closely the terms are defined and how amendments are counted. Moreover, one of the compacts is dormant and another was probably void from the beginning.

By January, 1969, Kansas had formally consented to the following compacts or agreements:[1]

1. Concerning water boundaries, water resources, and bridges:
    Missouri River Toll Bridge Compact of 1933 (*K.S.A.*, 68-1601),
    Republican River Compact of 1943 (*K.S.A.*, 82a-518),
    Arkansas River Compact of 1949 (*K.S.A.*, 82a-520),
    Kansas and Missouri Boundary Compact of 1949 (*K.S.A.*, 82a-521), and
    Arkansas River Basin Compact of 1966 (*K.S.A.*, 82a-528);
2. concerning crime, correction, and law enforcement:
    Compact on Crime Prevention (1934: Kansas 1936) (*K.S.A.*, 62-2501),[2]
    Interstate Compact for the Supervision of Parolees and Probationers (1935: Kansas 1947) (*K.S.A.*, 62-2701),

1. The list provided by James T. Havel in "Interstate Compacts," *Your Government*, Vol. XXVI, No. 8 (1967), was used and brought up to date. When the date is a part of the title, Kansas joined in the year of the compact. When the compact was started and Kansas joined later, two dates are given in parentheses. Instances with one date indicate the year the compact was officially started and the year Kansas joined.

2. Dormant, largely incorporated into the Interstate Compact for the Supervision of Parolees and Probationers.

Interstate Compact on Juveniles of 1965 (*K.S.A.,* 38-1001);

3. concerning conservation, safety, civil defense, mental health, and taxation:
    Uniform Motor Vehicle Registration Probation and Reciprocity
        Agreement (1929) (*K.S.A.,* 8-126),
    Interstate Compact to Conserve Oil and Gas of 1935 (*K.S.A.,* 55-801),
    Model Interstate Civil Defense Compact of 1949 (1951) (48-910),[3]
    Vehicle Equipment Safety Compact of 1963 (*K.S.A.,* 8-1201),
    Driver License Compact of 1965 (*K.S.A.,* 8-1212),
    Interstate Compact on Mental Health (1967) (*K.S.A.,* 65-3101),
    Multi State Tax Compact (1967) (*K.S.A.,* 79-4301),
    National Guard Mutual Assistance Compact (1968) (1968 *Session
        Laws of Kansas,* Ch. 68);
4. concerning the Kansas City, Kansas, and Kansas City, Missouri, area:
    Kansas and Missouri Water Works Compact of 1921 (*K.S.A.,* 79-205),
    Greater Kansas City Port Authority Compact of 1951 (*K.S.A.,*
        12-2501),[4]
    Mo-Kan Metropolitan Development District and Agency Compact of
        1957 (1965) (*K.S.A.,* 12-2514),
    Kansas City Area Transportation Compact of 1965 (*K.S.A.,* 12-2524),
    Kansas City Area Transportation Compact Amendment (1967)
        (*K.S.A.,* 12-2534)

One of the earlier compacts was that on crime prevention in 1936. In 1947 the Legislature authorized the Governor to execute the Interstate Compact for the Supervision of Parolees and Probationers. Today all fifty states are members of this compact, which provides for the supervision of parolees and probationers of one state by the authorities of another state. In this way it is easier for a person convicted of a crime to move about and get a new start in life.

In 1939 Kansas became a member of the Interstate Oil Compact, in which twenty-one oil-producing states now participate. The purpose of this compact is to prevent the waste of oil and gas resources. The governing agency, the Interstate Oil Compact Commission, encourages research, helps to acquaint member states with technical information, and proposes state legislation which it feels will be helpful.

Kansas entered the Republican River Compact in 1943. The other

3. Inoperative, despite general legislative authorization. The Kansas Attorney General has ruled that specific legislative approval is necessary for such compacts to become effective.

4. As of January 1, 1969, the Missouri Legislature had not ratified this compact.

members of this compact are Colorado and Nebraska. The purpose of the compact is to provide for efficient utilization of the waters of the Republican River. Kansas, as the state farthest downstream, is vitally concerned with the ways in which the states further upstream make use of these waters. Colorado and Kansas joined forces in the Arkansas River Compact of 1949. Its purpose is similar to that of the Republican River Compact.

In 1949 Kansas and Missouri established the Missouri River Boundary Line Agreement. The purpose of this agreement was to solve the problems raised by the shifting of the Missouri River, which had the effect of putting certain areas of land first in one state and then in the other. This compact was ratified by Congress in the following year, but since it was concerned with relatively minor problems it may be that the courts would have regarded this agreement as one for which Congressional approval was not necessary.

Of considerable financial importance to the state is the Uniform Motor Vehicle Registration Proration and Reciprocity Agreement. Under this agreement, interstate carriers pay a fee to Kansas based on the percentage of miles traveled in Kansas to the total miles traveled in all states.

Law Enforcement and Extradition of Persons Accused of Crimes

When a person who commits an offense against state law flees across a state line, national police officers, such as the Federal Bureau of Investigation, have no authority to apprehend and to try him. Officers of the state in which he committed the crime normally request help from the offices of the state to which the criminal has fled, and the officers of the second state arrest the criminal and hold him for the proper authorities of the first state. The chief exception to this procedure arises in cases of "hot pursuit," when the police from the state in which the crime has been committed closely chase a suspect but do not catch him until he has crossed the state line. In this instance, officers may arrest the suspect but must then turn him over to the proper authorities of the second state, who hold the suspect in custody until he can be legally turned over to the officers of the state in which the crime was committed.

Once the suspect is in the custody of the officers of the second state, the state in which the crime was committed must make a formal request that the suspect be returned to it. This request and the subsequent legal proceedings are called extradition. In Kansas the county attorney forwards the request for extradition to the Governor, who in turn makes a formal request to the Governor of the state in which the suspect is being held. Generally the Governor of the second state grants the request and directs the officers having custody of the suspect to turn him over to the first state for trial.

Reciprocity between States in Licensing

A third type of intergovernmental relation is found in the activities of the various licensing boards described in chapter 21. As is noted there, legal provisions for reciprocity exist in the case of eighteen of the twenty-three boards. The amount of recognition which will be given to licenses from other states varies from board to board, but the general rule seems to be that where the requirements for the license were about the same as they are in Kansas, a Kansas license will be granted.

Administrative Relations with Other States

In the day-to-day activities of a great many state agencies there are a considerable number of instances in which an agency deals with a similar agency in another state. For example, the materials department of the State Highway Commission has the duty of inspecting all materials used in state highways to insure that they are of the quality needed. The easiest and best way of inspecting most of these materials is at the plant which produces them. The department keeps inspectors at all plants within the state which are producing materials for highways. Since several of the oil-producing companies in Kansas sell their products to highway departments in other states, the other states are also interested in having those products inspected.

Moreover, the Kansas Highway Commission buys materials produced primarily in other states. The highway departments of those states usually maintain inspectors at the plants producing these materials. It would be more expensive for Kansas to send an inspector to the other state and pay his living expenses while there than to have the other state's inspector make the inspections in Kansas. The other states charge Kansas for the cost of doing such extra inspection work. Similarly, Kansas Highway Commission employees inspect oil products going to highway departments of other states, and bill the other states for the cost of making these inspections. In this way all of the states concerned are assured of getting adequate inspection of the materials they are buying, at the same time keeping the costs of inspection as low as possible.

Commission on Interstate Cooperation and Associations of State Officials

The Kansas Commission on Interstate Cooperation was established in 1941 and has fifteen members. Five of these are the members of the Committee on Interstate Relations of the state Senate, five are the members of the Committee on Interstate Relations of the state House of Representatives, and five are the members of the Governor's Committee on Interstate Relations. The Governor's Committee is composed of the Governor, the Attorney General, the Executive Director of the Department of Administration, the Chief of Staff of the State Planning Board (or the equivalent Kansas official), and one other administrative official appointed by the Governor.

Each of the fifty states has a Commission on Interstate Cooperation, and all of them are affiliated with the Council of State Governments. The Council is a voluntary organization which maintains offices in Chicago. Each state pays membership dues to the Council. The Council is run by a board of managers chosen by the state commissions on interstate cooperation.

Also affiliated with the Council are eight more-specialized associations of state government officials. These are (1) the Governors' Conference, (2) the National Association of State Budget Officers, (3) the National Association of Attorneys General, (4) the National Association of State Purchasing Officials, (5) the Conference of Chief Justices, (6) the National Legislative Conference, (7) the Parole and Probation Compact Administrators' Association, and (8) the National Conference of Commissioners of Uniform State Laws.

The Council and these various associations hold national and regional conferences, set up committees to study problems of interest to state officials, do research on interstate problems, and publish information of interest to the states. They also recommend uniform legislation on interstate problems for consideration by the state legislatures. Kansas has adopted twenty uniform and model acts and has passed four others in an amended form.[5]

Among the recommended legislation in recent years have been (1) improvement of voting laws to permit absentee voting by members of the armed forces, (2) reciprocal legislation to enforce support of dependents by persons legally liable who abscond across state lines, (3) a civil defense and disaster compact, (4) an interstate highway use tax law to eliminate the present confusion and duplication of taxes on out-of-state trucks, (5) a model antigambling act, and other similar legislation.

The Council and its related voluntary associations are among the more effective means of getting cooperation between the states. These groups also serve as spokesmen in giving the national government the states' opinions on various problems confronting both national and state governments. For example, they have recommended that the national government stop taxing the sale of gasoline as soon as it can conveniently do so, in order that this tax source can be used exclusively by the states.

State-Local Relations

The state has much tighter control over local units than the national government has over the states. The powers and the duties of local officials are set forth in state statutes as modified by home rule. Whenever any of the local governments want to do something not authorized by these statutes, they must go to the Legislature and ask for a new law permitting them to undertake the new activity. Many of the activities of local officials, particularly county officials, are concerned with state business rather than county business. The activities of the sheriff and the county attorney are good examples, since most of the laws which they enforce are state laws. The district courts in which county attorneys prosecute cases are state courts, and laws under which they act are also usually state laws. The state itself is often dependent upon county officials for enforcement of state laws, since the state has only a limited number of law-enforcement agencies.

State-local relations are frequently somewhat arbitrarily classified

5. Council of State Governments, *Book of the States, 1968-1969* (Chicago: Council of State Governments, 1968), pp. 89-93.

as legislative or administrative.[6] In general, the nature of the state legislative relations has been described in the earlier chapters on city and county government. In this section supervision by state administrative officials will be emphasized.

The range and the amount of such administrative supervision over local government officials by state officials in Kansas have increased steadily. In the past two or three decades this increase has been especially noticeable in the administrative supervision exercised over some local government functions such as agriculture, public health, highways, and social welfare. While the county is the local unit most concerned in the state supervisory activities to be considered, some state officials are charged with supervising city officials.

Many of these local units in Kansas have a predominantly rural character. State supervision is here faced with much the same conditions found in other rural areas of the United States. One competent observer[7] has described these conditions, emphasizing their flexible, human, neighborly nature and the efforts to construe the laws generously in order to arrive at an interpretation which helps the local persons affected. While many of the local units of government in Kansas are becoming more urban in character, the informal rural and small-town atmosphere still persists.

The supervision exercised by a state official over a local official is not comparable in many ways to the supervision exercised by one state official over a subordinate state official. It may sometimes happen that the state officials and the local officials have different, and not necessarily compatible, goals in mind. For example, the goal of state administrators in a public-welfare program may be to provide a decent standard of living based on the needs of the recipients. On the other hand, the objective of some of the local officers in the same program may be to spend as little money as possible in order to keep taxes down. In this case the state officials will attempt to persuade the local officers to work toward the state goal.

The increase in the amount of supervision that state administrative

6. For more information on state administrative supervision see *State Administrative Supervision of Local Government Functions in Kansas,* by Clarence J. Hein (Lawrence: Governmental Research Center, Univ. of Kansas, 1955).

7. Lane W. Lancaster, *Government in Rural America* (New York: D Van Nostrand Company, 1952), pp. 155-56.

officials exercise over local officials in Kansas has not been accompanied by any noticeable decrease in the amount of legislative supervision over local officers. While there has been a general trend toward turning some of the supervision over to state administrative officials, the legislators are still burdened with a substantial amount of local government business at every session. Administrative supervision has the advantage of being a continuous, year-round process, while legislative supervision can usually be exercised only when the Legislature is in session. Where the supervision needed is of a specialized and technical nature, administrative supervision seems to be more effective.

Another factor of considerable importance in the increase of administrative supervision has been the inducement offered by the national government in the form of grants-in-aid. If local units of government were to participate in a program, one condition frequently attached to a grant of money from the national government has been the requirement that a single state agency supervise the local officials in administering the program. An example of this is the public-assistance program set up by the national Social Security Act. To comply with this condition, the Legislature established the State Board of Social Welfare in 1937. Twenty years earlier, a similar requirement had caused the Legislature to establish the State Highway Commission.

The administrative supervision exercised by state officials over local government officials in Kansas takes many forms and varies considerably from function to function. Local officials are required to file annually a budget for their local unit. Some local units are also required to file an annual audit. Local bond issues must be submitted to designated state officials for a review of their legality. This state supervision applies rather generally to all of the financial aspects of the operation of a local unit of government. State supervisory activities are usually exercised by a general fiscal agency such as the Department of Post-Audits of the state auditor's office, or the Department of Property Valuation.

The problem of the most efficient and economical area for administering government services in which both the state of Kansas and the local units are interested has been attacked in a number of different ways. Most state-local programs are now based on the county as the local unit of administration. Kansas has 105 counties, and while they vary in area, the average area is somewhat smaller than that of the average county in the United States. On occasion both county and state officials question whether many of the counties are large enough in area and in population to be efficient units of administration. However, unless the counties are willing to join voluntarily and make more use of jointly provided services, the prospects for most programs being more efficiently administered by the local units of government are very dim. The probability is that over the next half-century more and more of the responsibilities for these services will be transferred to the state government. The state programs would then probably be administered on the basis of large districts set up to meet the administrative requirements of the particular service.

While citizens with local loyalties to their county may not like the fact that services formerly performed by local units are gradually being transferred to the state government, they have thus far not indicated much interest in taking action to stop or reverse the trend. The hard fact is that most local units, including the county, do not, as presently constituted, have the financial resources to carry out the programs. Instead of attempting to obtain the redistribution of taxing powers necessary so that the revenue can be raised, the present local attitude is to allow services to be transferred to the state.

In Kansas, the general trend has been toward a more cooperative approach to problems raised by joint state and local interest in the administration of a particular function. The basic purpose of most state supervision has been to stimulate local officials to take certain actions or to prevent local officials from taking unwise action. Experience has taught the supervisory officials that these purposes can be accomplished more readily in an atmosphere of mutual respect and confidence.

This general trend toward a cooperative program has not, however, eliminated the regulatory aspects of state supervision. Officials of both levels of government are aware, without a specific threat being made, of the prospect of cutting off state grants-in-aid if certain requirements are not met. Many local officials have come to accept this supervisory process as a proper one when the state provides a substantial part of the funds for a program. Some local officials are aware of the finer nuances of this relationship, in that they are quite certain that the state would not withdraw funds for a welfare program or a public-health program unless local officials were seriously delinquent. This fact gives these local officials considerable leeway in their response even to the regulatory aspects of state supervision. As a final resort, local officials who are disturbed about a particular aspect of state supervision often can exert considerable political pressure upon the Legislature. This possibility tends to mitigate the regulatory aspect of state supervision.

National-Local Relations

Most of the programs of the national government in which local units of government participate are channeled through a state agency, so that they are really national-state-local programs. There are some programs in which the local government deals directly with an agency of the national government. One of these is the federal-aid airport program, in which cities may apply for federal aid in building or improving municipal airports. Applications go directly to a regional office of the Federal Aviation Agency, and all subsequent dealings are between the city and the national agency. Another program in which there are direct relations between the municipality and the national government is the slum clearance and urban development program, administered by the Department of Housing and Urban Development.

Aid may be given to the local schools by the Office of Education of the Department of Health, Education, and Welfare in a number of different circumstances when (1) the revenue available to the school from local sources has been reduced by the acquisition of real property by the national government; (2) the local school system provides education for children residing on property of the national government; (3) the local school provides education for children whose parents are employed by the national government; and (4) there has been a substantial and sudden increase in school attendance because of some activity of the national government. Any school district faced with one of these problems may apply directly to the Department of Health, Education, and Welfare for a grant. A similar program administered by the Housing and Home Finance Agency gives assistance to any community which has a difficult housing problem as a result of national defense activity.

Direct contacts between the cities and the national government have expanded through programs sponsored by the Office of Economic Opportunity and the Department of Housing and Urban Development. Several cities in Kansas have local agencies for urban renewal and/or public housing. While authorized by state law, such agencies deal directly with the federal government. In recent years there seems to have been increased sympathy for programs like the one for more open space for cities and for model cities. However, the war in Vietnam and other national problems have resulted in lower federal appropriations for these federal-city programs than the proponents would like.

Relations among Local Units

Like many other states, Kansas has numerous units of local government, as shown in the accompanying table. It is not surprising, therefore, that there are many contacts between local officials. Particularly is this true when one considers that local boundaries have little relation to many local services and problems.

Some local intergovernmental relations have been discussed in the previous chapters. There are many financial ties between the local units. Fiscal relations among local units of government in Kansas center around assessment and taxation, and the redistribution of state grants and shared taxes. Local taxes are collected by the county treasurer, who then distributes them to the local units which levied them. State grants-in-aid and shared taxes usually go to the county treasurer, who then gives the cities or townships their share. Less frequently, a tax levied by one local unit is given to and spent by another unit.

TABLE 55

Number of Governmental Units in Kansas: 1968

Kind	Number
State	1
County	105
Township	1,543
Cities	623
Special Districts	1,037
School Districts	360

Source: U.S. Bureau of Census, *1967 Census of Governments: Governmental Organization* (Washington, D.C.: U.S. Bureau of Census, 1968), I, 26, 27, 36, and 38.

The budgets of townships and rural school districts are often made out with the help of the county clerk, who usually cooperates with the clerks of these smaller units in any way he can.

While local units of government generally will carry out their functions independently of the local units around them, there are some instances of informal cooperation and even a few instances of formal cooperation. An example of the more formal type of cooperation is a city-county health unit. An example of the more informal type of cooperation is the services provided for other units by the city street or county highway departments. The mayor of a small city may talk to the county engineer about getting the city's main street resurfaced when the county road connecting the city with neighboring cities is resurfaced. The city agrees to pay the county for the costs, and the county then goes ahead and resurfaces the city street at the same time it resurfaces the county road. A bill is sent to the city, which then reimburses the county for the amount spent by the county on the city street.

Intergovernmental relationships in the state cover a wide range of activities and vary greatly in their formality. At the one end is a simple oral agreement between officials of two units to cooperate on some small project. At the other end is a complex written agreement involving the spending of several millions of dollars by several governmental agencies, whose officers know each other chiefly through correspondence. As technological progress changes the day-to-day living habits of the people of the state, it seems probable that the intergovernmental relationships will increase and become more complicated.

26 Reflections on Kansas State Government

The preceding twenty-five chapters have been devoted primarily to describing the activities and agencies of Kansas state government. To gain a better perspective of the government of the state today, one must consider the developments of the last several decades within our own state and in other states. Such a historical and comparative approach leads to the formulation of some tentative conclusions about trends which seem to be manifesting themselves within the government of Kansas.

Expansion of State Activities

The last several decades have witnessed a large expansion of state activities. A review of the present activities of Kansas government shows that the most costly of the present-day government services were simply not undertaken even thirty years ago or, if they were performed, were performed at a level much lower than what is now expected. An example of a new state activity would be that of highways, for only forty years ago the state Constitution was changed so that the state was authorized to engage in highway construction. Before that time intercity automobile travel was negligible and what road travel there was, was in vehicles that did not require the smooth surface demanded by our present-day motor cars.

The mental-health program in Kansas well illustrates those services which have long been performed but which are now performed in a quite different and more expensive manner. Kansas has long had mental hospitals, but until recently the institutions aimed largely at providing primarily custodial care for those unfortunate persons who were legally committed. Today the emphasis is on treatment and rehabilitation, so that the patients may become again self-sufficient members of the community. Outpatient treatment is provided, and efforts are made to assist those who have had mental illness to adjust to their home communities.

The expansion of state services and activities is further borne out by the charts in chapter 7, showing the substantial increase in the number of departments and agencies. The increase in the number of employees and in total state government expenditures also indicates this trend.

Tendencies Towards Centralization

Coupled with this expansion of state services and activities has been the transfer of functions from local units of government to the state. An analysis of the present functions of Kansas state government reveals a greater centralization of government in Topeka. Many functions formerly thought of as belonging to local units of government are now largely directed by the state. The growing interdependence of our people, the specialization of our workers, the migration of persons from farms to cities, changes in our family and social life, the changing composition of our population, improved transportation and communications, and other technological changes are among the causes of this tendency.

Three of the most important functions of state government—welfare, highways, and health—illustrate the extent to which Kansas state government has followed this trend. Within a thirty-year period the old concept of local responsibility for those in need has yielded to a much broader conception of social welfare in which all three levels of government have a part. Previously, responsibility for helping the needy was discharged by nongovernmental agencies and by limited local-government programs of assistance. Now there is a multi-million dollar program with social-welfare workers in every county of the state dispensing state, federal, and county funds to persons in need. While it is true that the county remains the administrative unit for discharging the governments' responsibility for welfare, the county operation is guided by policy manuals prescribed by the State Department of Social Welfare. Indeed, that department may require counties to make tax levies for financing what the state considers an adequate welfare program.

The coming of the automobile and the mass ownership and use of this vehicle have raised many problems which currently may best be solved by an extensive state program in this field; counties and townships can no longer be concerned with the intercity movement of persons. The concept of local responsibilities for our highways has changed in recent years so that their construction and maintenance has become one of the most important functions of Kansas state government.

The need for, and more attention to, public-health facilities has been accompanied by efforts to try to find a satisfactory way of administering public health in a sparsely populated state. While many of the public-health activities of government must necessarily be essentially local activities, the sparsity of the population in many parts of the state has made it difficult to have a fully operated public-health program. State public-health authorities have experimented with various types of state organization which have aimed to coordinate effectively local health activities.

These new and expanded activities of government have considerably altered the traditional pattern of Kansas state government. Many cooperative relationships between state and local units of government, which have also served to enhance the importance of the latter, have developed. Each of the programs illustrated above has required local governments to expand their activities. Thus, while the total effect has been for a substantial centralization of power and authority in Kansas state government in these areas, it has been accompanied by expanded local activities. These programs have demonstrated that Kansas state government can work cooperatively in many areas with the units of local government.

Search for Larger Administrative Areas

Related to the centralization described above, the search to find a satisfactory area for administering many of our governmental programs has continued. It is essential that such areas conform to the economic and social needs of the time. Areas satisfactory even thirty years ago can no longer be considered so. The counties in the western part of the state have shown some willingness to experiment with various cooperative relationships. For example, a few counties have joined together to make in effect a joint appointment of an engineer, an extension agent, or a social-welfare worker. This does not in itself change the area for administering the function, but it is a step in the direction of trying to consolidate various county activities. Centralization of functions is more likely to occur in Kansas than the changing of county boundaries. Local custom and tradition are such that changes of areas are difficult to make.

However, the atrophy which has taken place in many of the townships in Kansas illustrates this search for larger areas of administration. About one-half of the counties in the state have taken over the maintenance of what were formerly township roads. Where the township loses the road function, the general pattern has been for a township to lose still others.

With changed methods of agriculture it appears also that there will be even fewer persons on the farm, so that it will become even more difficult for rural sections to find satisfactory areas of administration.

Another type of change is taking place with respect to administrative areas. Kansas continues to have a large number of very small cities, but is also getting an increasing number of cities which have demonstrated a marked growth pattern. These cities have expanded their boundaries and often are called upon to perform many of the services which people in metropolitan areas are now demanding. There are three such metropolitan areas in the state. While it does not appear likely that there will be a large increase in the number of such areas, several cities strategically located in parts of the state will probably continue to grow. Thus many local units are becoming "larger" in the sense of having to serve more people.

Concentration of Authority

Various competent observers of state government have noted the general weakness of the chief executive as the administrative leader in state government. This has been accompanied with considerable autonomy of various state agencies. According to this view, state government is described as being merely a general collection of only broadly related autonomous or semiautonomous agencies. Some of the reasons for this have been discussed in earlier chapters. Here it is pertinent to observe that in Kansas the trend has been toward increased centralized control over state agencies.

This enhanced centralized control over state operations has been accomplished primarily through improved control over finances. The establishment of the Department of Administration and of machine accounting has made it possible for both the Governor and the Legislature to exercise more accurate and more detailed control over the activities of Kansas state governmental agencies. This development has been marked with some rivalry between the Legislature and the Governor as to who shall exercise this enhanced centralized control.

The Legislature has used its increased information to exercise closer supervision over the activities of state agencies by more detailed examination of budget requests. Through the Finance Council individual members of the Legislature, acting presumably in the name of the Legislature, have exercised additional powers over finances and certain aspects of state administration.

Now, however, the Governor, armed with an expanded budget staff, is able to require and examine more closely agency requests for funds and the justifications given for these requests. The power of the Governor in preparing the budget assumes added importance in view of the fact that, in the main, state agencies have accepted the Governor's recommendations as the maximum limit for which they may ask funds from the Legislature. The financial reorganization of several years ago has enhanced the Governor's power to control the operation of state government.

This legislative-executive rivalry must be viewed from a perspective of what is apparently happening to the political complexion of the state. In four of the last seven gubernatorial elections a Democratic candidate was elected. During this time the Legislature remained strongly Republican, even with the several reapportionments. While some explain the recent Democratic victory as due to factionalism within the Republican party, this explanation may not be complete. The growth of our cities and other considerations give the Democratic leaders hope for making Kansas more of a two-party state.

Responsive State Government

One of the necessities of any government is to adapt and readjust to the changes which are occurring in the economic and social milieu in which the government operates. Kansas state government is no exception. The ways in which it has adapted and adjusted itself to changed conditions have been described in the preceding pages.

An appropriate challenge and goal for Kansas government is to adjust and readjust, so that the government will be made more fully responsive and responsible to the needs and desires of the citizens. While the problem is not yet settled, the Legislature has made several efforts and did significantly change the legislative apportionment to adjust to the expectations of the one-man, one-vote rule. The matter of revising the Constitution has been revived and may be susceptible to new approaches now that the matter of legislative reapportionment has been largely removed as an obstacle to constitutional revision. These are but two aspects of making the government responsive. The recruitment and staffing of state government with competent, public-spirited employees is also a necessity. Vigorous political leadership in both the Legislature and the governorship is an objective to be desired. Such are some of the avenues to an improved, responsive and responsible state government.

Index

KANSAS POLITICAL

PERMANENT ORGANIZATION

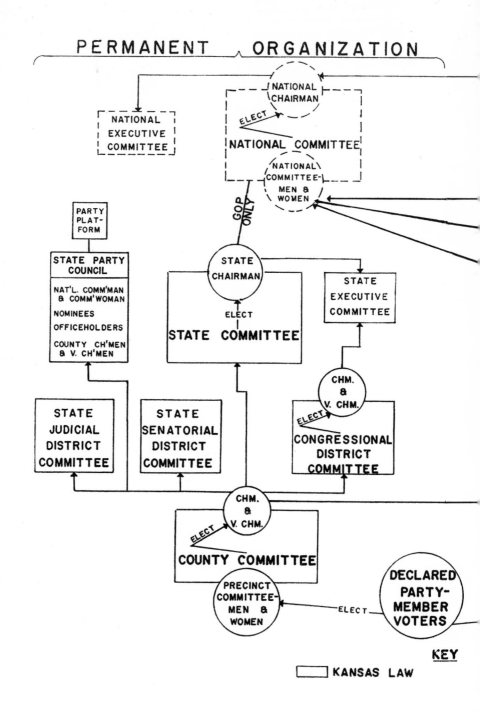

NATIONAL CHAIRMAN

NATIONAL EXECUTIVE COMMITTEE

ELECT

NATIONAL COMMITTEE

NATIONAL COMMITTEE-MEN & WOMEN

GOP ONLY

PARTY PLATFORM

STATE PARTY COUNCIL

NAT'L. COMM'MAN & COMM'WOMAN

NOMINEES

OFFICEHOLDERS

COUNTY CH'MEN & V. CH'MEN

STATE CHAIRMAN

STATE EXECUTIVE COMMITTEE

ELECT

STATE COMMITTEE

CHM. & V. CHM.

ELECT

STATE JUDICIAL DISTRICT COMMITTEE

STATE SENATORIAL DISTRICT COMMITTEE

CONGRESSIONAL DISTRICT COMMITTEE

CHM. & V. CHM.

ELECT

COUNTY COMMITTEE

PRECINCT COMMITTEE-MEN & WOMEN

ELECT

DECLARED PARTY-MEMBER VOTERS

KEY

KANSAS LAW